SECURITY CONCERNS OF ASIA

21st Century Discourses

SECURITY CONCERNS OF ASIA

21st Century Discourses

Edited by

Prof. Sarika Dubey

PENTAGON PRESS LLP

SECURITY CONCERNS OF ASIA: 21st Century Discourses
Edited by Prof. Sarika Dubey

ISBN 978-93-90095-48-3

First Published in 2022

Published by
PENTAGON PRESS LLP
206, Peacock Lane, Shahpur Jat
New Delhi-110049
Phones: 011-64706243, 26491568
Telefax: 011-26490600
email: rajan@pentagonpress.in
website: www.pentagonpress.in

Printed at Aegean Offset Printers, Greater Noida, U.P.

Dedicated to God

Contents

Foreword

As we enter a new decade of the 21st century, the world around us is evolving at such a rapid pace, with a scale and scope often difficult to comprehend. For scholars and pundits, older paradigms have ceased to be adequate in guiding their analyses about the national and global political environment. Policymakers, for their part, are being forced to respond in real time to the challenges from multiple dimensions. The year 2020 was a reminder that history can be made up of events—and their consequences—beyond anyone's control. The world was blindsided by the COVID-19 pandemic, which has not only taken lives and livelihoods but is accentuating the trends that were already visible in the last few years: changing the global balance of power, weakening multilateral institutions, growing disenchantment with the global economic order, and challenges to the extant normative consensus.

The key aspects of the global order will be sculpted by the legacy of the year 2020. And perhaps no other factor will have as much of an impact on international affairs as China's foreign policy trajectory under President Xi Jinping. Xi has already veered away from his predecessors in carving a more ambitious and aggressive approach to the external world. As the COVID-19 outbreak reached pandemic proportions, he used the crisis as an opportunity to expand China's geopolitical footprints across the world—from the South and East China seas to the Himalayas, from Europe to the Middle East. As Xi lays down a blueprint for a new world order hinged on the Chinese Communist Party's worldview, the rest of the world will be anxiously looking for a greater balance in the global matrix.

One area where there is emerging consensus not only in the USA but globally as well is the challenge that China poses to US interests and to the global order. The US-China contestation is shaping up as the epochal geopolitical contest of the coming years. Even if Biden decides to engage China after assuming the presidency later in January, it is unlikely to change the longer-term trajectory of this bilateral relationship. The sharpening of their tensions will be accentuated in the domains of trade and technology—the two areas that have been driving the global economic order in the last several decades.

Attempts by key global actors towards trade and technological decoupling are setting the stage for a conflict that is challenging the fundamentals of globalisation as we have known it since the early 1990s. An ongoing backlash against globalisation is likely to gain further momentum, especially as the costs of global integration are seemingly rising by the day. Already, there is a recalibration happening across the West where even mainstream political parties have been changing their long-held positions on issues such as trade and migration. It is unlikely, however, to be restricted to the West. As the world becomes more fragmented—from supply chains to connectivity initiatives—shoring up support for globalisation will only become more difficult.

This fragmentation will influence the future of global multilateralism. While most nations continue to profess their abiding faith in multilateralism, the institutional manifestations underpinning the extant order are being hobbled by their internal contradictions. Indeed, a global health pandemic should have been the high point of the search for a collective solution; instead, it has turned out to be its nadir. Not only is China challenging an order that it believes was created in its absence, but even the USA, which was its most important founder, seems dissatisfied with the status quo. The same liberal order that has arguably been central to maintaining peace and prosperity worldwide for more than seven decades is proving incapable of finding equitable and effective solutions to today's common challenges. This signals a remarkable retreat: a fragmented global order is emerging not only in traditional spheres of global governance but also in those areas where new norms are needed to be set—such as space, cyber, and emerging strategic technologies.

The most consequential theatre of this emerging geopolitical and geo-economic jostling will be the Indo-Pacific, which is already the centre of gravity of global opportunities and challenges–a process that will pick up speed in the near future. For all of China's attempts to discredit the idea of the Indo-Pacific, its unprecedented acceptance—from Western Europe to the far shores of the Pacific—merely shows that its time has come. The churn in this maritime geography will see a strengthening of "coalitions of the willing" in the absence of any formal institutional architecture and in the light of an intensified major power contestation.

As a consequence of this churn, national security challenges are being reconfigured almost in real time. National security remains a highly contested term. According to Arnold Wolfers, it is "an ambiguous symbol meaning different things to different people". Security is not an objective term that leads to an agreed set of issues and remedies. What is considered a security threat varies across time and cultures. There has been a vigorous debate in academic literature on the concept and its implications for policymaking.

The Indian security policy has largely been characterized as a reactionary, one that has attempted to address security threats sporadically as and when they arose. One of the major impediments in articulating an agreed national security strategy has been a lack of political consensus in not only understanding the nature of security threats but also in ways of addressing them. This lack of consensus has occasioned ad hoc responses to security challenges that are driven prominently by the nature and instincts of the top political leadership. The Indian security policy will have to respond to these meta-trends by crafting an approach that is more than just the sum of its bilateral and multilateral engagements. The China challenge is exacerbating by the day even as the world's expectations for India to play a larger global role are heightening. An aspirational India in the third decade of the 21st century will no longer be satisfied with sitting on the margin; it is eager to play in the big league. Like the rest of the world, India will have to deal with its health and economic crises in 2021. At the same time, however, it will also have opportunities to mould global discourse and outcomes, whether with its purported role as the "pharmacy of the world", or as a non-permanent member of the United Nations Security Council. The ability and willingness of Indian policymakers to make use of these opportunities will not only determine India's global footprints but will also outline the trajectory of global politics in the coming decade.

It is, therefore, commendable for the editor, Dr Sarika Dubey, to put together this very expansive volume on the security concerns of Asia in the evolving 21st century. This timely volume brings together scholars from India and the world to survey the security landscape in Asia. Touching upon key traditional and emerging threats to national security in the region, this volume should play an important role in enhancing our understanding of Asian security. It seeks to go beyond the traditional security framework and develop ideas around 'new' security challenges that confront India and the wider Asian region including countering violent extremism online, environment, and cyber and gender inclusivity.

Prof. Harsh V Pant
Professor of International Relations at King's College London and Director, Studies and Head of the Strategic Studies Programme, Observer Research Foundation, New Delhi

Preface

Security is a very basic need of individuals, society and nation as well as a supreme necessity for survival and development. It has been the prime objective of international politics and the heart of the study of international relations. Asia is the Earth's largest and the most populous continent that covers almost 60 percent of the global population. Therefore, security study of this region matters a lot. It has some important regions like the Asia-Pacific, South China Sea, the Indian Ocean region and the Himalayan region - which have been the important centers of global, economic and commercial activity. Any kind of disturbance in such areas and global change significantly affects the security environment of Asia. Politically, Asia is divided into many countries but culturally it appears like a single unit which has deep rooted shared cultures and values and the majority of the people are enjoying it. Despite this, Asia has faced many clashes and wars in its long history. All such things have drawn my attention to study on the security perspectives of Asia. This intension became even stronger when I had the opportunity to visit the Asian Institute of Technology, Bangkok, Thailand to deliver a lecture on Environmental security on 2-3 October 2017, where I met academicians and friends from different Asian countries. During and at the end of the conference we had long discussions on our common cultural legacy, socio-political concerns and major issues of human security in Asia from different perspectives. Then I came to realize two things first, that there are some common concerns and challenges for common people regarding their survival whether they belong to different countries and are of different origins. Second, the concept of security is relative to nation and each nation has its own security perspective having different approach from others but there are some interconnected issues affecting entire humanity that need to be addressed collectively. All this inspired me to work on the most important aspects of security from different perspectives, regions with the help of learned scholars.

One of the major thrust areas in recent times has been how the globalised world has added several new perspectives in this area. In the current global scenario many new dimensions of security from traditional to non- traditional have emerged that expanded its content and definition. Thus it becomes a necessity to deal security in a broader perspective. Asian security milieu has a great impact on the South Asian and the Asia-Pacific regions. Hence, a deeper understanding of Asia's security aspects is quite essential for economic progress, peace and stability of this entire region. There is an urgent need of preparedness and commitment on part of the big Asian powers including India to face the innumerable challenges that emerged due to global competence, hegemony, strategic interests and several other reasons. This book is an attempt to understand the various dimensions of security in the changing global environment in a broader perspective. It analyses the political economic and other aspects of Asian Security and finds ways to promote, peace, security and stability in the entire Asian region through collective efforts and cooperation.

In conceiving and executing the idea of writing this book, I received unstinted cooperation and constant encouragement from my friend, Dr. Ashima Ghosh, I express my sincere thanks to her. I am extremely thankful to Prof. C.C. Tan, Prof. Higuchi, Prof. K.P. Wiest, Prof. Pankaj Srivastava, Dr. Neelam Gupta for the thoughtful discussions that helped me to shape the idea. I would like to thank Prof. M.P. Dubey, Prof. Muchkund Dubey, Prof. Rumki Basu, Prof. Harsh V. Pant, and waterman Dr. Rajendra ji for their inspiration and good wishes. I am also grateful to Dr. A.K. Verma and Brig. Bhutani for their comments and thoughtfulness. I am very thankful to the Defence department, University of Allahabad, Prof. Prashant Agrawal and Prof. Bharti Das for sending me helpful research materials. I also express my heartfelt thanks to my friends Dr. Ajita Bhattacharya, Dr. Shaista Irshad and Dr. Pallavi Srivastava for helping in editing this volume. I also express my deep sense of gratitude to Prof. Beatriz Lucia, Ana Angelica and Mr. Abhinaw Mishra for their valuable support and advice. I am very much thankful to all the contributors of this volume for their chapters and unflagging encouragement and patience. I am grateful to all my family members for giving me constant support that helped me balance my several responsibilities. In the end, I must place on record my sincere thanks to Mr. Rajan Arya of Pentagon Press LLP for publishing this book in a short time. It has been my pleasure to work with him. Lastly, it would have not been possible for me to complete this work without divine instigations and blessings of God.

Prof. Sarika Dubey

Contributors

Abu Sayed Md. Nazmul Haider is Associate Professor in the Department of Public Administration, Rajshahi University, Rajshahi, Bangladesh

Akhilesh Mishra is Professor at C.S.A. University of Agriculture & Technology, Kanpur, U.P., India

Anurag Ratna is Associate Professor in the Department of Political Science, G.S.P.G. College, Sultanpur, U.P., India

Ashima Ghosh is Associate Professor in the Department of Political Science, Ewing Christian College, Prayagraj, U.P., India

Bhawana Pokharna is Associate Professor in the Department of Political Science, Meera Girls College, Udaipur, Rajasthan, India

Chai Ching Tan is Professor & Head in the School of Management, Mai Fah Luang University, Thailand

Chandra Mohan Upadhyay is Professor and Principal, Kalicharan P.G. College, Lucknow

David Sweeny is a social activist and former U.K. Chartered Accountant, Founder of AAOI, U.K.

Kenichiro Higuchi is Professor in the Department of Korea Studies and Comparative Culture Studies, Sugiyama JogaKuen University, Nagoya, Japan

Manisha Ashish Mehrotra is Associate Professor in the Department of Economics, Banaras Hindu University, Varanasi, U.P., India

Rahul Tripathi is Professor & Head in the Department of Political Science, Goa University, Goa, India

Richa Bhatt Ranade is Associate Professor in the Department of Political Science, Mount Abu College, Rajasthan, India

Rumki Basu is Professor of Political Science at Jamia Milia Islamia, New Delhi, India

Sandeep Kumar is Professor of Economics at D.D.U. University, Gorakhpur, U.P., India

Sandhya Pathaniya is Associate Professor in the Department of Geography, Meera Girls College, Udaipur, Rajasthan, India

Sarika Dubey is Professor in the Department of Political Science, P.M.V. Degree College, Prayagraj, U.P., India

Shalini Saxena is Associate Professor in the Department of Political Science, Amity University, New Delhi, India

Sudhanshu Tripathi is Professor in the Department of Political Science, Uttar Pradesh Rajarshi Tandon Open University, Prayagraj, U.P., India

Sumit Saurabh Srivastava is Assistant Professor at the Centre for Development Studies, University of Allahabad, Prayagraj, U.P., India

Vinod Kumar is Associate Fellow at Institute for Defence Studies and Analysis (IDSA), New Delhi, India

List of Abbreviations

A2/AD	Anti-Access/Area Denial
AAGC	Asia Africa Growth Corridor
AAoI	Abused Angels of India
ACIC	Australian Criminal Intelligence Commission
ACT	Affect Control Theory
ADIZ	Air Defence Identification Zone
AI	Artificial Intelligence
AIC	ASEAN India Centre
AIIB	Asian Infrastructure Investment Bank
AQI	Air Quality Index
ARF	ASEAN Regional Forum
ASEAN	Association of South East Asian Nations
ASG	Abu Sayyad Group
AWDO	Asian Water Development Outlook
BBIN	Bangladesh, Bhutan, India, Nepal Initiative
BGB	Border Guard Bangladesh
BGP	Border Gateway Protocol
BIMSTEC	Bay of Bengal Initiative for Multi-Sectoral Technical and Economic Cooperation
BOP	Balance of Payment
BRF	Belt and Road Forum
BRI	Belt and Road Initiative
BRICS	Brazil, Russia, India, China and South Africa
BSCCL	Bangladesh Submarine Cable Company Limited
BSF	Border Security Force

BSNL	Bharat Sanchar Nigam Limited
BTTC	BRICS Think Tank Council
CAD	Current Account Deficit
CBT	Community Based Tourism
CCIT	Comprehensive Connection on International Terrorism
CCP	Chinese Communist Party
CCPWC	Cyber Crime Presentation for Women and Children
CENTO	Central Treaty Organisation
CERT	Computer Emergency Response Team
CFI	Comparative Fit Index
CGD	City Gas Distribution
CHEC	Chinese Harbour Engineering Company
CHS	Commission on Human Security
CHT	Chittagong Hill Tracts
CII	Critical Information Infrastructure
CISA	Cybersecurity and Infrastructure Security Agency
CISO	Chief Information Security Officer
CO_2	Carbon Dioxide
COVID-19	Corona Virus Disease
CPEC	China Pakistan Economic Corridor
CPR	Common Property Resources
CRA	Contingent Reserve Agreement
CSO	Civil Society Organisation
CTBT	Comprehensive Test Ban Treaty
DDoS	Distributed Denial of Service
DMZ	De-Militarized Zone
DNA	Deoxyribo Nucleic Acid
DPRK	Democratic People's Republic of Korea
DSCI	Data Security Council of India
ECRL	East Coast Rail Link
EEZ	Exclusive Economic Zone
EIU	Economic Intelligence Unit
EM-DAT	Emergency Database
ESCAP	Economic and Social Commission for Asia and Pacific
EU	European Union

FAO	Food and Agriculture Organisation
FATF	Financial Action Task Force
FDI	Foreign Direct Investment
FGM	Female Genital Mutilation
GCA	Global Cybersecurity Agenda
GCI	Global Cybersecurity Index
GDP	Gross Domestic Product
GFSI	Global Food Security Index
GHG	Green House Gas
GMC	Greater Mekong Cooperation
GTD	Global Terrorism Database
HDI	Human Development Index
HDR	Human Development Report
HS	Human Security
HT	Hizb-ul-Tahrir
HUJI	Harkat-ul-Jehad-al-Islami
ICANN	Internet Corporation for Aligned Names and Numbers
ICBM	Inter Continental Ballistic Missile
ICT	Information and Communication Technology
IDS	Intrusion Detection System
IESS	India Energy Security Scenarios
IETF	Internet Engineering Task Force
IFPRI	International Food Policy Research Institute
IGF	Internet Governance Forum
IHME	Institute of Health Matrices and Evaluation
IIASA	International Institute for Applied Systems Analysis
ILO	International Labour Organization
IMF	International Monetary Fund
IMU	Islamic Movement of Uzbekistan
INDC	Intended Nationally Determined Contributions
IOR	Indian Ocean Region
IOR	Indian Ocean Rim
IORC	Indian Ocean Rim Countries
IOs	International Organisations
IPC	Indian Penal Code

IPCC	Intergovernmental Panel on Climate Change
IR	International Relations
IRA	Irish Republican Army
IS	Islamic State
ISI	Inter-Services Intelligence Agency
ISIS	Islamic State in Iraq and Syria
IS-K	IS-Khorasan
ITU	International Telecommunication Union
JAD	Jamaah Ansharut Daulah
JDL	Jewish Defence League
JeM	Jaish-e-Mohammad
JI	Jemaah Islamiyah
JICA	Japan International Cooperation Agency
JMB	Jamat-ul-Mujahideen Bangladesh
JMSDF	Japan Maritime Self Defence Force
JOCV	Japan Overseas Cooperation Volunteers
JPP	JICA Partnership Program
LAC	Line of Actual Control
LBA	Land Boundary Agreement
LeT	Lashkar-e-Toiba
LIC	Life Insurance Corporation
LIC	Low Intensity Conflict
LNG	Liquefied Natural Gas
LOC	Line Of Control
LPP	Language Planning and Policy
LSC	Liberal Security Community
LTTE	Liberation Tigers of Tamil Eelam
MACOCA	The Maharashtra Control of Organised Crime Act
MDGs	Millennium Development Goals
MNCs	Multi-National Companies
MNRE	Ministry of New and Renewable Energy
MP	Member of Parliament
MPI	Multiple Poverty Index
MSP	Minimum Support Price
MSR	Maritime Silk Road

MW	Mega Watt
NAFTA	North African Free Trade Agreement
NAM	Non–Alignment Movement
NASSCOM	National Association of Software and Services Companies
NATO	North Atlantic Treaty Organisation
NCIIPC	National Critical Information Infrastructure Protection Centre
NCS	National Cybersecurity Strategies
NCSC	National Cyber Security Cooperation
NDB	New Development Bank
NDSO	National Database on Sexual Offenders
NFHS	National Family Health Survey
NFI	Normed Fit Index
NMEEE	National Mission for Enhanced Energy Efficiency
NPR	Nuclear Posture Review
NPT	Non-Proliferation Treaty
NSCS	National Security Council Secretariat
NSG	Nuclear Suppliers Group
NTPC	National Thermal Power Cooperation
NWS	Nuclear Weapon States
OBOR	One Belt One Road
ODA	Official Development Assistance
OECD	Organization for Economic Cooperation and Development
OIC	Organisation of Islamic Countries
OIC	Organisation of Islamic Cooperation
OPEC	Organisation of Petroleum Exporting Countries
OTOP	One Village One Product
PAN	Permanent Account Number
PCA	Permanent Court of Arbitration
PDR	People's Democratic Republic
PLA	People's Republic Army
PLAAF	People's Liberation Army Air Force
PLAN	People's Liberation Army Navy
PLO	Palestine Liberation Organisation
PNE	Peaceful Nuclear Explosion

POA	Plan of Action
POCSO	Protection Of Children from Sexual Offences Act
POK	Pakistan Occupied Kashmir
POTA	Prevention of Terrorism Act
PPP	Purchasing Power Parity
PRC	People's Republic of China
PV	Photo Voltaic
QUAD	Quadrilateral Security Dialogue
RATS	Regional Anti-Terrorist Structure
REC	Renewable Energy Certificate
ReCACP	Regional Cooperation Agreement on Combating Piracy
RevCon	Review Conference
RFI	Relative Fit Index
RMSEA	Root Mean Square Error of Approximation
SAARC	South Asian Association of Regional Cooperation
SAGAR	Security and Growth for All in the Region
SARS-COV2	Severe Acute Respiratory Syndrome
SCO	Shanghai Cooperation Organisation
SCS	South China Sea
SDF	Syrian Democratic Forces
SDGs	Sustainable Development Goals
SEATO	South East Asia Treaty Organisation
SEM	Structural Equation Modelling
SLA	Sustainable Livelihood Approach
SLOCs	Sea Lines Of Communications
SLT	Social Learning Theory
SNW	States with Nuclear Weapons
SOE	State of India Environment
SOR	Stimulus Organism Response
SDOMD	SAARC Drug Offences Monitoring Desk
SREB	Silk Road Economic Belt
SROCC	Special Report on Ocean and Cryosphere in a Changing Climate
SSF	Strategic Support Force
STF	Special Task Force

STOMD	SAARC Terrorist Offences Monitoring Desk
SWS	Society of Wetland Scientists
TADA	Terrorist And Disruptive Activities Prevention Act
TAPI	Turkmenistan, Afghanistan, Pakistan and India
THAAD	Terminal High Altitude Area Defence
TLI	Tucker Lewis Index
TSGP	Trans Sabah Gas Pipeline
TVE	Total Variance Explained
UHDP	Ultra High Density
ULFA	The United Liberation Front of Assam
UN	United Nations
UNCLOS	United Nations Convention on the Law of the Sea
UNCRC	United Nations Convention on the Rights of the Child
UNDP	United Nations Development Program
UNESCAP	United Nations Economic and Social Commission for Asia and Pacific
UNESCO	United Nations Educational, Scientific and Cultural Organisation
UNFCCC	United Nations Framework Convention on Climate Change
UNHRC	United Nations Human Rights Council
UNICEF	United Nations International Children's Emergency Fund
UNMIK	United Nations Interim Administration Mission in Kosovo
UNO	United Nations Organisation
UNODC	United Nations Office on Drugs and Crime
UNSC	United Nations Security Council
UNTFHS	UN Trust Fund for Human Security
USA	United States of America
WCEFA	World Conference on Education For All
WHO	World Health Organisation
WIFJAJC	World Islamic Front for Jihad Against Jews and Crusaders
WMDs	Weapons of Mass Destruction
WOM	Word of Mouth
WTO	World Trade Organisation

Introduction

Asia is one of the most significant regions of the world and is well known for its multicultural character and its growing political and economic importance for the world. The continent is home to the world's largest population that constitutes almost 60 per cent of the global population and covers 30 per cent of the Earth's total land area. The region has become the engine that drives global economic growth. The road to global peace and stability in the 21st century passes through this region. It has become a new locus of international affairs and the centre of power politics where security is mostly influenced by geopolitical factors.

The emergence of a strong China has been a very significant strategic event of the 21st century, which is affecting the entire security framework of this region. China has threatened the global position of the USA as a superpower, which was enjoyed by the USA unilaterally after the end of the Cold War. China has strengthened its position as an economic superpower. This has been an important factor triggering a movement for unilateralism to multi-polarity. India is another important player in the geopolitics of Asia. It is playing a key role in shaping regional security structures and balancing Chinese dominance in the region. ASEAN is emerging as an important economic association. China, India, Japan, South Korea, and Indonesia are the top five economies that are now playing leading roles in Asia. Recently, three important events have exercised significant influence on the existing security arrangements in Asia and the Pacific. First, China's Belt and Road Initiative and policy of "deep pockets" for China's neighbours, led by President Xi Jinping; second, the abandonment of the Trans-Pacific Partnership (TPP) and policy of "America First " by the American Administration under the leadership of D. Trump; and third, China's post COVID aggression. The contemporary strategic context in Asia could be best defined by the interests of major powers and rising economies in the region. Besides these basic factors, recent developments in Afghanistan, the growing China–Pakistan nexus, China's assertion of sovereignty in the South China Sea, North Korea's nuclear posture, emerging trends in transnational terror networks, sectarian violence, the US-led global war on terror, China's aggressive posture on Hong Kong and India, are issues that have created deep security concerns in the entire region.

The 21st Century World

The political world order has been changing rapidly. After the disintegration of the USSR, the USA solely enjoyed the status of a superpower for some time. Capitalist ideology became the prevalent driving force in the world economy. Bipolarity was replaced by unipolarity under the domination of the USA. Many developing countries formed regional groupings with the direct support of the USA. Rapid technological development and the communications revolution changed the basic character of war and altered the concept of distance and mobility. The efforts of developing countries to create a new economic order to bridge the gap between the rich and the poor did not make much progress. This was largely because of the failure of the political leadership to fulfil the aspirations of the people due to resource scarcity and political instability. Moreover, most of the Asian countries remained engaged in border and other disputes with neighbours due to the arbitrary demarcation of boundaries by the erstwhile colonial administration. This created unnecessary border tensions and threats to security. These circumstances provided an opportunity for the arms market to flourish. It also increased the nuclear arms race among developing countries in Asia. Nuclear proliferation therefore remained a key political agenda of international politics. Amid a rapidly changing political order, a significant economic phenomenon was taking shape in the form of globalization. It was a process by which the world was transformed into a single arena. It was not merely an economic integration of the world but covered all the aspects of modern life—economic, cultural, political, humanitarian, social, etc. Mckinsey's Kenichi Ohame defines it as the 'end of geography' (Harris, Stuart, 2002). Globalization increased mutual interdependence among nations as never before in past history. It brought economic factors to the core in international relationships. As a result, many changes took place before the dawn of the 21st century. The world became more integrated and interdependent. It was generally recognized that states alone cannot handle global problems, which called for global cooperation and that of the people, to seek solutions. This is all the more so because problems like terrorism, environmental degradation, etc., are inter-connected.

There were several internecine wars in the Arab world, in which many governments were overthrown. Democracy remained the prevalent mode of governance. The European Union greatly expanded in the beginning of the 21st century and added more member-states. It had earlier introduced a common currency, the Euro, marking one of the biggest change-overs in history. The beginning of the 21st century saw a dramatic rise of the global economy and ascendency of the market system. The process of globalization became deeper, among others, through global value chains.

The emergence of China as a super economic and military power was an important outcome of globalization. China entered the WTO in 2001 and attained the maximum benefits from this platform by way of vastly expanding exports. China's growing military power and strong economy made it more assertive in matters of global affairs. The USA, which had been enjoying the status of the sole superpower, was challenged by China in all aspects of power. Apart from China, India, Russia, Brazil, and Japan were the other growing economies playing leading roles in global politics and determining the regional power balance. The collapse of the Berlin Wall in 1989 and the disintegration of the USSR in 1991 were critical events in world politics that transformed the international order. In the 21st century, the international system started moving from unipolarity to multipolarism. Some of the new power structures were now regional groupings like BRICS, Shanghai Cooperation Council, etc. Kocharyan (2005) pointed out, "the 21st century is gradually moving towards equilibrium of powers preventing a single nation to monopolise power and acting as the colossus is counter balanced by the acute efforts made by China". Regional associations remained significant in decision-making on development issues, and those of global peace human rights, and environment.

A significant trend in recent years has been a retreat from multilateralism, disarray of the world order and rise of narrow short-sighted nationalism. An important outcome of this trend is the rise of protectionism in the global arena that has turned the globalization clock back. In the context of the prolonged stagnancy and slow rate of growth, some Western countries imposed high tariffs to restrict imports in order to revive their economies. The USA imposed high tariffs on Chinese imports to protect its economy. Some of the protectionist policies include import tariffs, import quotas, domestic subsidies, exchange rate variations, and administrative barriers. It is quite obvious that protectionist policies have a major impact on international trade growth. It has weakened the global economy in the last few years. The USA under the Trump Administration considered protectionism and nationalism as their policy priorities. President Trump focused on his 'America First' policy and 'Buy American', 'Hire American' (World Focus, 2019). The US attitude towards the North America Free Trade Agreement (NAFTA) and denunciation of the Trans Pacific Commercial Agreement (TPCA) reversed the wheel of globalization. The USA–China trade war has also been part of this process, which has affected global economic growth in other Asian countries. Brexit and Euro scepticism have challenged the principles of freedom of movement and economic integration via globalization and affected the current international order.

The global pandemic of the corona virus that first emerged at the end of 2019, from the Chinese province of Wuhan, created a kind of suspicion against China all over the world. President Trump termed it 'Chinese Virus'. There are many who believe that the corona virus has come out of a lab in Wuhan. The delay by China in making the world aware of this phenomenon has reinforced the suspicion against it. While the whole world was struggling with the corona virus crisis, China was creating a new crisis by its aggressive behaviour in its neighbourhood. Most of the countries that depend on imports from China are now thinking to become self–reliant economies. This has been another factor putting globalization in reverse gear. It would not be wrong to say that today the world is socially and politically, globalised but economically, it has moved towards de–globalization.

Rise of Asia

Asia has emerged as the new locus of international politics in the 21st century. It has become the centre of power politics in terms of both politics and economics. After the Second World War, Asia faced a new dawn as political developments in Asia were in the form of newly-emerged independent nations and the establishment of democratic systems. Though religion played a dominant role in the region, yet secularism was established as a political principle in most of the countries in Asia. It has also experienced powerful socialist and communist movements in some countries like China, North Korea, Vietnam, and Russia where the Communist Party remained a major political force. Amid the process of development, Asian countries have faced many conflicts and wars after 1945. Despite tensions, a number of regional groupings have emerged in Asia to promote common interests and cooperation among its members. The Arab League, Association of South East Asian Nations (ASEAN), and Shanghai Cooperation Organisation (SCO), a Eurasian political, economic and security alliance, are such important regional associations that are playing important roles in constructing Asian political structures.

The evolution of Asia throughout the Cold War was quite different from Europe and the rest of the world. The region has never been part of the bipolar global system. The USA remained the dominant power in Asia. Multi-polar tendencies were observed as the emerging Asian powers—China and India—tried to maintain their strategic autonomy and commitment towards an independent foreign policy. Similar tendencies were visible in many other Asian countries like Indonesia, etc. (C. Raja Mohan, 2013). Throughout the Cold War, Asia faced many internal conflicts and contradictions among its nations but it has also enjoyed a prolonged period of peace since the 1980s but no one can claim that the trend will continue in the coming years. In fact, the current situation is definitely going to raise concerns. There are several hotspots in this region where a single incident can aggravate tensions and turn it into a war. These are: the South China Sea, the Northern Himalayan region, the Indian Ocean, the Indo–Pacific region, etc. It is quite obvious that Asian countries are facing deep security threats and challenges. The current security system in Asia is based on two primary assumptions—bilateral alliances and the quadrilateral security dialogue between the USA, Japan, Australia, and India (*Global Times*, 14 September 2020). The US-dominated bilateral security alliances can provide security but it maintains the US's security interests in the region while the Quadrilateral Security Dialogue works on the principle of balance of power which is much required in the context of Asia because China's rise and its aggressive behaviour towards other countries causes deep security threats in the region. In the above context, the USA which is a non-regional power in Asia can play a very significant role with regional powers to balance China. In the case of regional actors, the role of Russia is very important which cannot be under-estimated. Russia is a member of most of the regional organizations of Asia and is a technology leader in many areas. Under the leadership of President Putin, Russia has got back on its feet and is ready to play its role as a regional power.

So it is required to establish a more inclusive new security mechanism where realistic conventional and non-conventional challenges could be resolved under the framework of comprehensive security by encompassing all the regional powers.

Security Concerns of Asia

The concept of security has become predominant after the Cold War era. Several schools of thought have emerged in the field of security studies. There are two major schools of thought regarding the concept of security—Traditional and Non-Traditional. The Traditional school of security focuses mainly on military concerns and capabilities to protect national security, where the main referent object of security was the state. It includes issues that particularly denote the threats that are against the essential values of the state like territorial integrity and political sovereignty of the state. But after the Cold War era, lots of changes have been observed in the global scenario. Rapid technological advancement and developmental aspirations of globalization posed serious challenges towards the world community which could not be addressed at the level of the state alone. These global changes not only gave rise to a new dimension of security but also expanded its content and definition. Today, it covers a wide range of interconnected issues that affect human survival. It ranges from national security to human security that incorporates every problem that threatens human life. Thus, the Non-Traditional school defines security in the sense of human emancipation from all kind of challenges like epidemics, poverty, oppression, etc. This gives birth to the concept of Human Security where security manifests in a wider sense or in the sense of human dignity. These challenges matter a lot for the survival and well-being of people and states because they are interconnected and intertwined to each other having common roots in the globalised world. The current COVID-19 pandemic has proved how interdependent we are. Our security is inextricably linked to each other beyond the boundaries of state and geography. Therefore, regional actors are becoming increasingly relevant to meet the challenges by enhancing a comprehensive, non-partisan, and multi-lateral engagement and cooperation. Against the above backdrop, efforts have been made to focus on the myriad challenges, trouble spots, and their wide implications on the stability and security of the region, so as to enhance possibilities for cooperative preventive measures.

The concept of the book **"Security Concerns of Asia: 21st Century Discourses"** covers traditional as well as non-traditional security aspects in the Asian context. Asia, the largest continent, is divided into many parts like East Asia, West Asia, and South Asia, etc., and each part of Asia has some specific problems but there are some common security concerns affecting the whole of Asia. Our approach is to study Asia in general. Therefore, this book is an attempt to address some of the major security concerns confronting Asian countries which are most relevant these days. It is divided into three parts:

1. **Political Aspects of Security**
2. **Socio-Economic Aspects of Security**
3. **Environmental, Cultural, and other Aspects of Security.**

In the political aspect, most of the current issues that have been discussed include those directly linked with the security and stability of the region like nuclear issues, threats to national security, South China Sea dispute, geopolitical landscape of Asian security, changing paradigms of security in Asia, etc.

In the section dealing with the socio-economic aspects of security the issues discussed are security of women, food security, population and poverty, energy security, Belt and Road Initiative, trade imbalances, etc..

In the third part, cultural conflicts and extremism, environmental issues, sustainable livelihood security threats, terrorism, cyber security, and water security have been discussed which are the most relevant issues these days and are directly linked to the security of human life.

Major Themes of this Book

Considering the formidable task of appraising the global scenario and complex changes in the security perspective in the 21st century, in the present discourses of international relations, the set of papers here covers multiple dimensions of security including issues like cultural conflicts and extremism, nuclear issues, terrorism, environmental degradation, geopolitical, landscape of Asian security, cyber security, China's rise and the security challenges in the region; they form the heart of this volume. They recast international relations in the current phase of the 21st century through diverse perspectives by highlighting aspects related to conventional security and non-conventional security. Irrespective of such diverse perspectives, all the contributors have focused upon major security concerns existing in different parts of Asia. The book sets out new and innovative security principles that are highly pertinent today and creates a framework to ensure peace, cooperation, sustainable development, stability and the well-being of the Asian people. It offer a viable base to launch inquiries and deal with the multi-layer security order and relate effectively to the multi–actor universe comprising states, civil societies, and global and regional organizations. Similarly, the contributors have analysed the changing post-COVID scenario and its impact on regional security structures. The essays in this volume deal with wide–ranging issues from political or conventional to non-conventional or major aspects of human security and also present possible and viable solutions and suggestive measures to build a comprehensive security framework through a balance of security mechanisms. We shall proceed to capture the essence of the numerous themes that figure in this volume.

Sudhanshu Tripathi's paper offers a comprehensive analysis of national security in the era of globalization. His grand narrative eloquently traverses through a complex web net of security including conceptualization of security to national security. Sudhanshu discusses the ongoing debates as regards the mounting challenges before national security, including human security vis-à-vis the global corona pandemic against the backdrop of over-sweeping globalization. Sudhanshu accepts Friedman's perspective on the current phase of globalization 3.0 that the agent of globalization 3.0 is individual which is not hardware but software. He stresses that economic reasons are very important for all nations, whether big or small; thus, the overall interaction between and among nations are being shaped by these economic imperatives. Sudhanshu argues that the current global geo-politics has shifted towards the east; hence, he underscores that the prominent stakes are high for India to grab the opportunities offered by the ongoing globalization while not forgetting glocalisation and self-reliance so as to ensure the country's economic growth and progress. He also consolidates the ever-demanding necessities of national security.

Sarika Dubey has discussed the geopolitical landscape of Asian security and its strategic concerns in the 21st century. She argues that the concept of security has developed comprehensively in the post-Cold War era (1991) which is described as a paradigm shift from bipolarity to a unilateral world order. She argues that in the current scenario, geopolitical aspects are redefining the global power structure within the ambit of security and dominance. The emergence of a strong China as an economic superpower and the declining of the US's global position as a superpower has been the major event of this century that affected the security framework of Asia. Sarika highlights the geopolitical discourse of security and its importance in defining strategic issues in Asia. She also identifies hot spots in Asian security where geopolitics is playing a significant role. She has analysed the Asian political turbulence as the outcome of imbalance of power in favour of China and has also emphasized the role of regional organizations that can help in establishing peace and stability in the region.

Vinod Kumar has dealt with Asia's nuclear problematique and its security order in the 21st century. He examines the developments of the previous decade regarding global nuclear matters like nuclear proliferation, civilian nuclear programmes, the nuclear weapons ban treaty, etc., and has warned that the gains on nuclear matters were reversed in the second half through a series of events like Trump's decision to jettison the Iranian nuclear deal; the Korean peninsula being witness to nuclear sabre–rattling before a fragile truce was witnessed in Panmunjom in 2018, etc. He believes that India's decision to test the nuclear threshold while responding to cross-border terrorism and the pursuits of the great powers to augment their strategic arsenals had aggravated the competition in the Asia–Pacific. He views these developments in general and particular as well as in the context of Asian security. Vinod also examines the political dimensions of the Asian nuclear landscape and its impact on the region's security relationships and why the Asian nuclear enclaves, despite being the new nuclear epicentre, lack the influence to exercise leverage over the normative instruments of the global non-proliferation regime.

Chandra Mohan Upadhyay's paper offers a comprehensive analysis of the growing dominance of China and the security challenges before

India and the region. He views security as an important ingredient of international politics and the *summum bonum* of any foreign policy. Chandra Mohan believes that China's slogan of 'peaceful rise' is merely a charade and that the rise and domineering behaviour of China and its muscle-flexing in the region has created disequilibrium. He argues that China's civilizational aspiration to dominate the world reflects in its middle kingdom desire and Tinxia approach. He also underscores the importance of QUAD groupings to counter–balance the preponderance of power in the South China Sea. He believes that India can play a pivotal role in the restructuring of the global order and must stand for a multi-polar world with meaningful alliances.

Rahul Tripathi's paper focuses on India's quest for security in the region and in the world. He argues that India's security dilemma in recent years has focused on two broad parameters. At one level, it has been engaged in confronting the security threats that are shaped by domestic variables and outcomes while, on the other level, there are several external security threats posing severe challenges to national security. Rahul attempts to map this two-layered security discourse by looking at the complex interplay of the internal and external by looking at India's security threats within the neighbouring region and the world outside and explore whether there is a meeting point between the two. He argues that India's security coordinates are linked with local, regional and global aspects and therefore the policy options reflect this continuum much rather than seen in isolation.

Richa P. Ranade deals with the rise of extremism in South Asia. She views South Asia as a geopolitical region that plays an extremely significant role in world politics. It is a fertile ground to showcase the world powers' raised interests in areas as diverse as strategic, economic, diplomatic engagements, etc. Richa argues that the rapid economic growth of this region, especially India in the beginning of this century, as well as the marked rise of extremist Islamist militant groups in both Pakistan and Afghanistan and a growing rivalry between India and China make this region a hotspot and important one in the view of the strategic analyst. She reveals the fact that the poor literacy rate, rampant unemployment, growing economic disparity religious fundamentalism, weak industrialization, and uneven development pattern are predominant causes contributing to violence and extremism in the region and prepare the ground for terrorism. Thus, Richa attempts to explicate the possible measures to reduce regional tension by strengthening economies through structural reforms and robust trade regimes, and lays emphasis on diplomatic means, political dialogues, and negotiations at both bilateral and multilateral levels to settle inter-state disputes with global powers adopting a pro-active facilitative role.

Bhawana Pokharna analyses the challenges of the Chinese Belt and Road Initiative in the context of trade security. She argues that the Chinese Belt and Road Initiative is the most ambitious project of the 21st century that aims to enhance trade and cooperation by connecting three continents of the globe. China's visionary, President Xi Jinping, wishes to enhance Chinese assertiveness and power in the global arena. Bhawana explicates the hidden intention and unstated, underlying strategic objectives of the BRI through which China is attempting to expand its influence in the Bay of Bengal and the Arabian Sea by building ports in Sri Lanka, Pakistan, and Bangladesh. If the BRI leads to important neighbours like Bangladesh and Sri Lanka drifting into the Chinese orbit, it would represent a serious setback to India's traditional conception of the subcontinent as a privileged sphere. Bhawana views the entire project as a Chinese cobweb in which attempts have been made to trap small states and exploit geopolitical benefits that will also change the regional security structure of Asia. She focuses on the Chinese debt-trap diplomacy as a big threat that is undermining the liberty of small countries and putting them in compromising positions. Bhawana views China's entire BRI project as one to establish Chinese dominance and make China a superpower of the 21st century. It also reminds us of the revival of neo-colonialism and the dependency theory knitted around the Chinese ambition to become a power bloc. In fact, according to her, China is getting influence through the trade route and also flexing its muscles for making a China-centred new world order that will have deep security implications in the near future.

Anurag Ratna has discussed the changing practices of the foreign policy of India in the context of South East Asia and security concerns in the era of globalization. He argues that during the Cold War period, India pursued a non-alignment policy based on friendship with all countries, economic cooperation, stress on UN principles and world peace. But after the end of the Cold War, India focused on its national interests by developing economic cooperation and strengthened its relationships with ASEAN countries. Anurag observes India's search for economic security in terms of the 'Look East Policy' which has now matured into an action-oriented 'Act East Policy'. He advocates India's strong relationships with ASEAN countries not only from the economic perspectives but from security perspectives as well because India faces deep security challenges from its neighbouring countries like China and Pakistan. In this regard, the ASEAN region has its own strategic significance for India. He underscores the significance of the advanced cooperation among South East Asian countries and India due to security concerns in the Indian Ocean and in the Asia–Pacific region as the Chinese aggressive behaviour, dominance, and interference in the region has increased tensions manifold causing deep security threats to the entire region. Anurag also draws our attention towards other global threats like terrorism, environment, drug smuggling, and child and women trafficking which can be easily eliminated with multi-level engagements, commitment, and cooperation between India and the ASEAN countries.

Abu Sayed Md. Nazmul Haider has discussed Bangladesh–India relations in the context of South Asian security concerns. He argues that the relationship is rooted in a common civilizational heritage that encompasses political, economic, cultural, and strategic dimensions. Despite the proximity of their cultural traditions, a number of issues have clouded the Indo-Bangladesh relationship for years. He views the leadership of Modi in India and Sheikh Hasina in Bangladesh as positive that has led the two Asian neighbours to a new phase of bonhomie. Haider highlights the several issues that are a manifestation of sovereign reality and that are affecting relations such as the disputed boundary between the two countries, water issue, trade and transit, border management, border killings, etc., that have been in the limelight of settlement in the recent past. He focuses on the strategy and importance of geopolitical realities of both the countries for each other from the perspective of security. Haider holds that China is making deep in roads into India's backyard, it is imperative for India to renew its strategic ties with Bangladesh. It is also worthwhile to note that Bangladesh should maintain diplomatic relationship with India for its own security as it is surrounded by India from three sides. India in turn should have friendly relations with Bangladesh to avoid it becoming a playground of the India-China geopolitical game. Thus, the bilateral relationship is quite relevant and significant and has great strategic importance for both the nations from the perspectives of regional security. Haider offers a deep insight into the bilateral relationship and discusses political, economic, cultural, and strategic issues that affect the entire South Asian region.

Rumki Basu's paper offers a comprehensive analysis of the changing paradigm of security in Asia in the 21st century. She defines the security problem as traditional threats such as interstate war, intrastate war, and terrorism and as non-traditional threats such as economic recession, pandemic disease, and interstate migration in global politics today. She views the 21st century as a seminal shift in global power relations driven by the newly-emerging powers of the developing world situated mostly in Asia. Rumki has focused on the regional conflicts, unexpected alignments among states and cross-border migrations that involve not just the securitization of certain problems such as economic stability, public health, environmental protection, and migration but also internationalization of domestic problems like organized crime. She highlights the fact that a strong nation of state-centric security was provided in Asia for a long time but in the coming decades, a human security model is gradually coming to be accepted by the leaders in the region which is also relevant in the post-COVID-19 era. Her grand narrative explains Asia's potential of becoming the next economic colossus of the 21st century if the countries reduce their military expenditures and increase their human development outcomes by focused public policies and strong governmental actions.

Kenichiro Higuchi has discussed human security and linguistic views from the perspective of Japan's international cooperation. He defines human security as a concept that reinforces efforts to resolve various crises threatening human survival and dignity, including environmental destruction, violation of human rights, topics relating to refugees, poverty and other humanitarian issues. The Human Development Report focuses on seven areas of security and six of its threats. These areas of security are economic, food, health, environment, personal, community, and political security. The six threats are unchecked population growth, disparities in economic opportunities, excessive international migration, environmental degradation, drug production, and trafficking and international terrorism. Higuchi's emphasis on basic education which has an intrinsic value is thus: basic knowledge, skills, and values are needed to support human security. To boost education, improvements like building and running new schools, trained teachers, and improving female education should be made properly. He examines the relationship between human security and Language Planning and Policy (LPP) in the international perspective and lays emphasis on literacy because it gives freedom from poverty through prevention and restoration through economic empowerment. He highlights the Japan government's efforts towards these objectives. Higuchi raises two questions. First, how should literacy be defined? And second, which language should serve as the instrument to administer literacy?

Shalini Saxena has dealt with the COVID-19 outbreak and human security concerns amidst this global pandemic. She argues that the world scenario was changed after the Second World War which was a conventional threat to security but COVID-19 is a non-conventional threat that has posed an existential threat towards entire human civilization and shaken the world order including the leading powers. She explicates that the current pandemic has affected the process of globalization and reversed its gear towards self-reliant economy. She also takes into cognizance that human security is mainly connected to economic security, food security, health security, environment security, community security, livelihood security and personal security and that all the aspects of human security are severely challenged by the outbreak of COVID-19. Shalini has drawn attention towards all the emerging concerns regarding human security where every country becomes a stakeholder. She also highlights China's expansion policy and its aggression during the COVID-19 pandemic and how China exploits the pandemic situation in its favour. In the comprehensive analysis, attention has been paid towards political cooperation among nations at regional and global levels as well.

David Sweeny, in his paper, raised the issue of social security in the context of safeguarding the girl child and empowering women in South Asia. His paper reflects some of the work of the Abused Angels of India (AAoI), a voluntary, not-for-profit organization, which is symbiotic with many, if not all, of the other countries in South Asia. David believes that the main barrier can be identified as patriarchy, defined as "a system of society or government in which men hold the power and women are largely excluded from it". He argues that women who break through the 'glass ceiling' often themselves adopt a patriarchal attitude and mode of language. David observes that in South Asia, girls and women are marginalized more than anywhere else are in the world due largely to the percentage and number of the population suffering rural deprivation. According to him, the security of South Asia in terms of its citizens and its own economic security materially rests upon the region meeting the challenges set by the United Nations 2030 Agenda. David discusses the sociological aspects that are actually responsible for the subjugation of women in the entire region. Thus, empowerment of women cannot be achieved until girls and women firstly feel 'safe' and 'secure'. David in his analysis deeply focuses on the security threats to its very grassroots: the safety and security of its current and future generations through elimination of all kinds of violence against women, abolishing discrimination against girls and women, making societal change and development through education, and changing one's own mindset—only then social security in South Asia can be established.

Akhilesh Mishra has dealt with food security in Asia. He examines that increasing incomes, population growth, industrialization and urbanization continue as the driving forces behind the fundamental structural change in the global food production and market systems. Akhilesh argues while Asia's economic growth and ongoing structural transformation deepen the complexity in managing the limited natural resources required for food security, the biggest challenges are revitalizing agricultural productivity growth, preventing adverse impacts of climate change on agriculture, the participation of small farmers in modern food value chains, and tackling persistent malnutrition. Based on his comprehensive analysis, Akhilesh suggests that Asia's food security may be assured by strengthening agricultural production through better government policy, i.e., availability of funds, inputs and technologies to farmers along with biotic and abiotic challenges.

Sandeep Kumar's paper offers a detailed analysis of population, poverty, environment and its interrelated effect. He mainly focuses on three major problems of the Asian region—population and multinational poverty, increasing environmental degradation and their intermixing cumulative effect. In fact, according to him, interrelationships of these three elements have important socio-economic implications for developing countries. Sandeep highlights the asset-based poverty which is more prevalent in Asia and which is further pushed up due to population growth. He identifies poverty as a lack of income-generating assets. Assets may include natural capital, human capital, social capital, physical capital and financial capital. Sandeep makes an assessment on the basis of cumulative analysis which has been derived from past experiences that not only have past development policies failed but also the problems of population poverty and environmental degradation are interrelated which must be solved in the realistic conditions of Asian countries.

Manisha Ashish Mehrotra has dealt with BRICS, renewable energy and India's energy security. She discusses the global financial crisis and terms it as the 'greatest economic upheaval' after the Great Depression of 1929-30, which badly affected the global economy. This led to the emergence of a regional power confederacy, particularly within the developing world in the form of BRICS. The five member countries, Brazil, Russia, India, China and South Africa, started to cooperate and contribute in the global economy and offered alternative options to the IMF for other countries in respect of global energy sector finances. Manisha gives a deep insight towards the challenges facing BRICS countries in terms of implementing renewable energy solutions that has been the leveraging of finances and strengthening energy cooperation among the BRICS countries to ensure global energy security and reduce price volatility in the global energy markets. She focuses on India's energy sector, its potential, demand and challenges at the domestic level. Manisha tries to review the role played by BRICS nations in various areas of the energy sector within BRICS. She analyses the position of the BRICS countries in the global energy sector and energy security and explores new areas of renewable energy. According to her, India has an unlimited capability in the growth of renewable energy and, if explored and utilized properly, it can attain a dominant position not only in Asia but also in world energy sector.

C. C. Tan's paper offers a very comprehensive study on sustainable livelihood security which is based on community-based tourism initiatives. His grand narrative adopts some relevant socio–psychological theories to fill the gap between residents in highland communities and the experiences of tourists in his research which combines the underlying Sustainable Livelihood Approach (SLA) concept. In view of these theoretical bases, Tan advocates three sustainable livelihood determinants, namely, community development, community identity, and stakeholder support, which is based on a questionnaire-based survey and data collected from two communities that have coffee and tea as their dominant livelihood source that are shown capable to drive community–based tourism activities systematically in need for livelihood sustainability outcomes comprising economics and socio–cultural and environmental aspects. He provides a deep insight and his analytical observations support this statistical model by the qualitative in–depth interviews that provide the subtle dynamics of the roles and the significance of the constructs studied and their interrelationships. Tan's research provides significant and eloquent value to disciplines involving community–based tourism by centralizing on the concept of sustainable livelihood security and this equips the tourism participation of the communities for long–term sustainability.

Sarika Dubey discusses the issue of environmental security that is essential to combat global catastrophes. She argues that environmental degradation has severe impacts on human survival in the 21st century. Human activities are making an irreversible impact on nature. It is estimated that during the 21st century, the global surface temperature is likely to rise further by 0.3 to 1.7°C and is a moderate scenario or as much as 2.6 to 4.8°C in an extreme scenario. Sarika highlights the fact that the Earth is currently in the early stages of a human–caused mass extinction. It is believed in a survey that 20 per cent of all the living population could become extinct within 30 years. She focuses on the global catastrophic risks, which are a hypothetical future event which could damage human well-being on a global scale even crippling or destroying modern civilization. It includes both anthropogenic and non-anthropogenic risks. After a comprehensive analysis of environmental degradation, Sarika explains how environmental issues cross state borders and have become transnational issues. Thus, environment security has become an important dimension of global peace, national security and human rights. She explains that environmental security comprises the dynamics and interconnections among the nature resource base, the social fabric of the state, and the economic engine for local and regional stability. She examines the human impact on the environment during the COVID-19 pandemic and its impact on peace and sustainable development. Thus, the paper offers an urgent need for environmental security to sustain mankind.

Ashima Ghosh has dealt with terrorism in Asia which is a big challenge for national security and human rights. She explains the emergence of 'New Terrorism' in the form of 'global jihad' based on the view that there is oppression of Muslims world-wide as they believe that the West's military dominance and its economic strength is the main reason of oppression of Muslims; therefore, they reject Western cultural values. These terrorist groups use religion as a motivation to use violence to obtain political power so as to establish an order based on Sharia law. Ashima highlights the operation of some of the terror groups in Asia like the Ansar-ul-Sunn and Islamic State of Iraq and Syria (ISIS) that have caused immense damage to peace and stability in large parts of Asia. The activities of the LeT and JeM and similar militant outfits that have been provided tacit support by Pakistan their funding, recruiting and training activities and are nourished and provided a safe haven in Pakistan, e.g., Taliban and Haqqani Network, have posed severe security threats to India and South Asian regions. She focuses on state-sponsored terrorism as a severe security concern for the Asian region. Ashima provides a deep insight and reveals the fact how underdeveloped countries have been particularly susceptible to militant Islam's activities and to the rise of new terrorism. She has also analysed how globalization has allowed some terrorist groups to strengthen their networking, acquire sophisticated technology and procure weapons which can be used for grave destruction. Ashima especially highlights South Asia and Afghanistan and examines the effectiveness of counter-terrorism measures, efforts at the global level through the UNO and regional forums like ASEAN, SAARC, etc.

Sumit Saurabh Srivastava's paper offers a comprehensive analysis of cyber security in contemporary global times. He has structured his paper outlining multiple layers of cyber security and its features. He accepts Manual Castells' perspective of 'network society' and highlights the unfathomable vastness and bottomless expansion of cyber space that have affected today's geopolitics, economics, and social life. He not only discusses those digital footprints that have made our lives comfortable and advanced but also draws attention towards insecurities due to increase in cyber crimes and cyber attacks through computer virus and worms, identity thefts, online bank/financial frauds. Most importantly, being the nation-state's sovereignty, jurisdiction and control over itself are now being challenged and have became porous and superfluous in the wake of cyber activities and operations performed by the so-called activists or hackers. Saurabh analyses this issue broadly in terms of cyber sovereignty and cyber diplomacy. He presents an overview of cyber security measures as a protective mechanism from incidents of cyber crime legislation, i.e., national cyber security strategies (NCS) as practised by selected countries for their own cyber security. Sumit also focuses on the threats that emerged during the COVID-19 pandemic and the India–China Galwan face-off with deep insight and underscores the facts and reasons that became very important in the current geo–political scenario.

Sandhya Pathania has dealt with one of the most relevant issues of modern times—water security in Asia. She argues that sustainable development will not be achieved without a water-secure world. Water security can be achieved when there is enough consumable water for everyone in a region and the water supply is not at risk of disappearing. She analyses water security in Asia and highlights a number of factors that combine to threaten water security in Asia, i.e., natural climate, variability, human induced climate change, population increase and migration, settlement of hazard-prone land, poor service provision, uncontrolled discharge of pollutants into water, naturals hazards and politics. According to Sandhya, water resources cannot be easily accessed without pumps, pipes, taps, tanks and skilled people to manage them as part of service. Similarly, water supply services alone are of little use without water resources. She explains three things that are critical for water security in Asia—good quality, well managed water supply services and management of disaster risks. She also stresses that if services and water resources are unavailable or unreliable and disaster risk is not managed, then the people of Asia will not be water secure. Therefore, she advocates the adoption of new technological developmental interventions, understanding the implications of human influence on water and paving the way to manage and mitigate changes in the water system to make Asia a water secure continent.

Security is a wide concept that has multiple dimensions that pertains not only to national security but also becomes a glaring factor in human well-being and progress. In the true sense, it becomes important when life gets threatened directly or indirectly by any reasons. This book sets new and innovative security principles that are highly pertinent to our times. The chapters in the book not only highlight the major issues of current scenario but also present their possible and viable solutions by great academicians and experts from different fields, from India and abroad, which makes it quite effective. The primary objective of this study has been the security and stability of the region by presenting feasible solutions with a deep insight. I hope this volume will give readers the ability to navigate two different perspectives on security. On the one hand, security is clearly shaped by geopolitical events at the global scenario where political factors, regional and global power structures, economic scenario and national operation or nations' interests play vital roles and influences security. On the other hand, there are multiple interlinked factors in the form of non-conventional threats that directly affect human security beyond boundaries. It has been our effort to put all the important aspects of security and its comprehensive analysis at one place. I hope these essays will allow readers to come to their own judgment about security.

This volume brings together some of the finest minds from different disciplines from India and abroad. I would like to thank all the contributors for their whole-hearted cooperation and coordination with us.

REFERENCES

C. Raja Mohan, *Asian Geopolitics*, ADBI working paper series, no. 412, March 2013.

Kocharyan, A. (2005). Balancing between great powers in the 21st century, Hartwick College, Oneonta, New York.

Stuart Harris, Globalization in the Asia-Pacific context, Canberra: Dept. of the Parliamentary Library, 2002, http://www.aph.gov.au/library/pubs/rp/2001-02/02RP07.htm.

World Focus, June, 2019.

Wu Bing & Pan Xinyu, Why new Asian security structure is needed for emerging puzzle, *Global Times*, 14 September 2020.

PART I

Political Aspects of Security

1

Mounting Threats to National Security in the Era of Globalization

Sudhanshu Tripathi

Introduction

Indeed, the current process of globalization still occupies a predominant intellectual discourse among the entire global issues wherein COVID-19 has today become a threatening concern thereby describing the evolving national and international scenario in a holistic manner. Since the economic reasons are important today for all countries, the overall interactions among them are being shaped largely by these economic imperatives, sustained by expanding Information Technology. While the information revolution has led to an explosion of several innovative ideas in the field satellite-based communication systems, it has also put a severe strain on the national security, including cyber security, of several countries as rising cyber threats, particularly in the context of mounting terrorism and religious fundamentalism. In fact, rapid globalization has brought disparate cultures into contact with one another, and is, therefore, threatening the domination or disappearance of some groups while promoting others to consolidate. As required, India has also activated its foreign policy against the backdrop of China's mounting imperialist assertions across the Indo-Pacific. Again, with the evolving Sino-US Cold War tensions when global geo-politics is shifting over the South China

Sea, entire humanity is suffering today the worst trauma due to the corona virus supposed to be Beijing's latest clandestine bio-weapon to establish its global hegemony. Obviously, the stakes are high for India to grab the opportunities offered by the ongoing globalization while not ignoring glocalisation and self-reliance to ensure the country's economic progress through *swadeshi* and also consolidate the ever-demanding necessities of national security.

In fact, the continuing pace of globalization has become a part of everyday interaction throughout the world in the advancing twenty-first century, wherein COVID-19 has unfortunately become perhaps the most threatening global pandemic of this century. Despite the mounting threat of the epidemic, the ongoing globalization holds the promise of a brighter future for rich and powerful nations, but for others it represents various kinds of threats leading to their insecurity that need to be confronted and counteracted with full might. Today, in the age of fast-expanding internet facilities which is providing enough space to cyber-crimes wherein cyber hackers endeavour to peep into national secrets or even private personal documents or change or destroy important confidential information related to most of the vital services essential for critical sectors like defence, finance, and telecommunications. Since 'ongoing research and development' have become increasingly dependent on information technology and computer science, they have obviously become prone to various cyber threats. In fact, computer hackers target important government institutions and private mega-business enterprises and security-related secret establishments with the objective of stealing their intellectual property and sensitive information' (Sushma Devi, 2019) and thus earn billions of dollars by passing this vital information to enemy nations. Evidently, this means that deepening of knowledge of national security in contemporary circumstances is absolutely necessary because the term 'national security' is misused to connote different perspectives by both academics and policymakers so as to serve their own concerns and even vested interests. Some use it to refer to conventional statist threats whereas others employ it as a broad catch-all for anything that may create or imply threats against anyone in a particular polity. Still others use the term to justify a bunch of populist and politicized policy choices with apparently little to justify the link between the threat and the referent object that is 'state' in the context of international relations. Obviously, in such a confusing scenario, the state's capacity to identify, categorize and respond to different harms or threats have been stretched by the process of globalization and advancements in technology, besides mounting a host of threats from transnational actors to natural disasters (Matthew Sussex *et al.*, 2017), including possible bio-weapons like the corona virus, emerging as a human bomb, thereby adding a new threat to national security, particularly human security, all over the world.

Ongoing Globalization

Indeed, the current process of globalization is an entirely new paradigm of complex socio-economic, cultural and politico-military relations including most of the accompanying different kinds of relations, linking places and people to that extent which is qualitatively and quantitatively different from any other historical phase of global integration and increasing interactions. Unfortunately, the rising corona pandemic has today added perhaps the most frightening dimension in its onward course, which has, in fact, led to the collapse of many powerful European nations, particularly America. Obviously, this demands a fresh impetus to the ongoing interactions among nations to fight this global menace with renewed efforts, though the emerging global economic slump due to the pandemic is now a foregone conclusion. Notwithstanding these adverse economic consequences, the increasing political transformations due to globalization is simply the culmination of the growth of power of multinational corporations and the increasing role of global financial markets, wherein grave dangers for states have already emerged due to cyber invasions in almost all areas of state-interactions, particularly in the field of economics, security, counter-strategy, military-preparedness including socio-cultural and political stability, altogether getting adversely affected. The uniqueness of the process lies in the global spontaneity of transformations it produces with the help of amazing satellite-based information and communication technology and also the emerging cashless and quick money transfer facility in the world with a click of the mouse and that largely has resulted into "retreat of the state" or finally "end of the state", as Peter Newell argued, in the face of the unrelenting and powerful forces of over-sweeping globalization throughout the world such as global markets, global governance and such institutions (*World Development Report*, 1997). These process have led to emerge "a new dynamic between the local and the global", with a greater awareness of the importance of "glocalisation" or the "the interaction and merger between local cultures and global processes" (Bryan S. Turner, 2010). In the context of international relations what is perhaps the major challenge today, as globalists argue in favour of shedding international barriers and transforming the international community of nations into one global community under a world state, is that "political power or governance has been or is progressively being altered in the movement of politics from a primarily national scale towards an increasingly transnational global scale" (Chamsy el-Ojeili, et al., 2006). Although this does not mean that the state will become utterly powerless or definitely 'wither away', as Karl Marx argued, but most of the services essential for critical sectors, like defence, finance, and telecommunications have become increasingly dependent on information technology, which in turn leaves them open to different kinds of cyber threats. And they promote differences and compulsions between developed and under-developed or developing nations of the Third World. The most phenomenal trend is "towards a reconfiguration of power or governance, rather than simply the coming end of the state in the face of the expansion of capitalism" (Chamsy *et al.*, ibid.). Despite, all these factors adversely affecting the political community, the state still retains sovereign authority while facing grave threats to national security, particularly in the field of exercising independent foreign policy on grounds of merit-based judgment on each international issue, as India's policy of non-alignment sincerely has been adhering to ever since independence. It obviously enjoys good prospects and better opportunities brought by the current phase of the ongoing globalization, with implications on the dynamic nature of the nation-state as regards its external ventures, democracy, citizenship, economic progress and global peace and security. Indeed, the globalization has led to increased connectivity in all corners of the world, with faster and easier flow and open access to all information and communications. It has engendered free trade areas and regions to emerge with faster infrastructure build up, which has increased the volume of trade and traffic flowing across the entire world.

The present article discusses the ongoing debates as regards mounting challenges before national security, including human security *vis-à-vis* the global corona pandemic, against the backdrop of over-sweeping globalization. This has, inter-alia, compelled different cultures into contact with one another and is threatening domination or disappearance of some groups thereby considerably affecting the idea of the same and forcing them to explore still unknown threats to national security while historicizing and contextualizing contemporary discussions about globalization. It also provides an introduction to the ongoing discourses, practices, technologies and politics, all grouped together under these terms. It further discusses and analyses the challenges as well as prospects of the issues under discussion while analyzing India's rising assertiveness by revitalizing the foundational core of its foreign policy from the earlier doctrine of 'nonalignment' to the present 'Non Alignment 2.0'. Indeed India's rising peaceful assertions in the international arena will be an asset to the global system in the era of the eastward shifting global geo-politics and ongoing process of globalization as regards protection of the environment, human rights, energy security, food security, potable water security, nuclear disarmament, eliminating terrorism and global terrorism including Islamic radicalization. But the emerging bitter acrimony between China and the USA is likely to evolve as a new cold war between them as is visible on some recent issues like mutual trade imbalance and Huawei or AI besides already pending marked differences over North Korea, the South China Sea, Taiwan and also Tibet, may be the potential causes of serious concerns to the global peace and security which may gravely affect the national security of most nations and also disrupt the accruing benefits of the ongoing globalization in different ways and that underscores the perpetual relevance of glocalisation and self-reliance for all countries.

Thus, globalization is obviously an ongoing socio-economic and political phenomenon which has different connotations in different academic disciplines but today, all these are perhaps eclipsed by the ever-mounting fear of the COVID-19 epidemic throughout the world. While in the field of economics, it discusses challenges brought about by globalization ranging from a reduction of trade barriers to the unrestrained flight of capital and cut-throat competition, those in the area of politics are in the perpetual quest for minimizing mistrust among communities within nations and maximizing avenues for reciprocally beneficial cooperation among nations, besides sociologists weaving together all the contours of economics and politics, particularly in the context of the ongoing discourse on strong linkages between globalization and terrorism, including global terrorism. Against this backdrop, continuing globalization has led to increased interactions among disparate cultures and is therefore threatening the domination or disappearance of some groups at the cost of others, *i.e.*, a cultural version of "survival of the fittest", says a psychologist and terrorism-expert Fathali Moghaddam (Moghaddam, 2008). While terrorism continues to wreak havoc all around the world, the current discourse on terrorism including global terrorism has vociferously raised the issue of national security in internal and external affairs as well. In fact, the concept of national security in today's world has its focus on finding out ways to deal with these threats, the on-going process of globalization has resulted in serious dilution of the sovereignty and might of the state due to amazing technological advancements in the field of satellite-based and computer-assisted information technology and easy availability of small yet lethal firearms. As an obvious outcome, several non-state actors and organized cartels have mushroomed to challenge the peace, security and normal life of innocent people in the world, besides threatening the very existence and sovereign power of states. The macabre crimes committed by the ISIS, or earlier by the al-Qaeda in the recent past, are such horrible examples, whether humanity will be blown to smithereens or not. Though, globalization appears to have come out of political wrangles as there has been a qualitative difference in the way people are beginning to relate to one another, but this transition has occurred too slowly to comprehend in clear terms, as Friedman recounts: Globalization 1.0 began with Columbus' journey in 1492 and lasted till 1800, and the agent then was physical power. In Globalization 2.0 from 1800 to 2000, the driving force was Multinational Corporations (MNCs). In the current phase of Globalization 3.0, the defining force is the individual, "the lever that is enabling individuals and groups to go global so easily...is not hardware but software" (Friedman, 2005, ibid.). And here it is in the age of ever-developing technology of software designing and the rising computer power including the revolution in information technology that together has already complicated the security concerns of almost each nation. This obviously demands a thorough understanding and analysis of the concept of security, including human security vis-à-vis the mounting corona pandemic in the arena of international relations as well as in global affairs.

Concept of Security and National Security

In fact security, including human security, in the field of international relations is a broader concept encompassing all aspects of interactions between and among nations with respect to addressing potential threats from all directions to human beings as well as countries because they directly or indirectly affect their entire intercourse and interactions. Unfortunately, the concept remained a neglected one until the 1980s due to different factors; lack of interest among scholars or strategists, particularly among critics of Realism, or due to overlapping of the concept with 'power', or security experts remaining focused more in developing technology and strategies instead of investing in conceptual evolution and its enrichment; or sometimes even concerned policy-makers themselves deliberately letting the concept degenerate into confusion or ambiguity so that they may adjust it to suit their vested interests. However, consequent to several disturbing upheavals and resultant changes in the global scenario during the late 1980s and early 1990s and afterwards, the rising academic interest over the concept led to the emergence of various schools of security, namely, *realist*, neo-realist, critical theorist, liberals or Third World theorists to name a few, interpreting the concept in different ways in accordance with their own perceptions.

Prominent among the experts, namely, W.B. Gallie, Buzan Barry, Arnold Wolfers, Richard Smoke, K. N. Waltz, Ken Booth, Bernard Brodie, Knorr or Harold Brown, the US Secretary of Defence, besides many others. While Gallie considers security as an "essentially contested concept", it may be as one of appraisal for the neo-realists but Arnold Wolfers does not subscribe to it; or it is more appropriately described as confused or inadequately explicated so as to be defined as a clear policy objective. In the same way, Wolfers again distinguishes between subjective and objective dimensions of the security to add further to the dilemma. In fact, "the purpose of this discussion is not to settle the issue, but only to point out that this question is more difficult to answer than those who classify security as an essentially contested concept..." (David A. Baldwin, 1997), and that obviously requires considerable attention over alternative security policies with a view to lessen the degree of threat perception for a state as the degree of threat perception varies in the hierarchical order in the world. As aptly commented by experts "the threat matrix for virtually all the major powers has changed markedly alongside the securitisation of numerous challenges that are transnational, environmental and effectively 'inter-mestic' in nature" (Matthew Sussex *et al.*, 2017, ibid.). However, these may be divided between domestic and external forms of national security in the global community of nations given the global configuration of states on national parameters and may be considered as an integral and vital part of the domestic interests of the nations.

In fact, the term 'national security' is a very confusing term because being very much interpreted in a loose manner to discuss and define various situations to connote all possible meanings, expanding from all kinds of different forms of human security to all kinds of different forms of security of the nations as well. This broadly comprises the security of human beings, human rights, environment, energy, food, potable water, environmental and ecological balance, military and safety from nuclear and bio-weapons and many more such other aspects existing or likely to emerge, as that of corona virus today. Alongside the concept of security, the concept of national security has evolved over time due to a combination of domestic and external factors as per the requirement of the global economic, political, social and cultural conditions and their adjustment with national priorities as regards a nation state. It was known in terms of war or conflict until the onset of the current era of globalization, which has indeed, brought new dimensions to the concept of national security wherein corona virus assumes a significant position. In fact, national security is presently at the crucial juncture having a close nexus of the domestic and the international networks working hand and glove with terrorist organizations and separatists and fissiparous forces, as well as such constraints and compulsions, and that provides a conceptual approach for understanding and articulating emerging challenges in the interconnected world, such as in the cyber domain, where sovereignty is challenged by transnational factors causing various threats in the form of organized and macabre violence, heinous crimes, horrible civil wars and terrorism, human bombs, military interventions, biological and nuclear weapons, deliberate polluting of environment including potable water and food and other such unimaginable grave risks like the corona bomb. What is particularly worrisome as regards the evolution of the concept is the fact that it mostly revolves around the physical and material threats of an individual as well as the state as an independent and autonomous entity. However, these efforts are more concerned with redefining the different policy agendas of nation-states than with the concept of security itself, as a noted scholar (Baldwin, 1997) opines. Often, these agendas take the form of suitable proposals for giving high priority to such crucial issues like violation of human rights and suppression of democracy, global economic recession, environmental pollution, drug trafficking, epidemics and unknown infections, organized crime or civil war, or various socio-cultural injustices due to a still prevailing feudal-monarchic system particularly in the developing and poor countries of the Third World, besides other traditional concerns like security from external military aggressions and the current one being, perhaps, the severest threat of terrorism including global terrorism, religious fundamentalism and bio-terrorism. In fact, such proposals are usually upheld with the intermingling of normative and conventional arguments while ensuring the protection of the masses or diverse human groups, and empirical arguments as to the nature and magnitude of different threats to those values which should be thoroughly taken into account and analyzed with preventive measures.

In fact, relatively little attention is devoted to conceptual issues as such which may help in theorizing the concept as a meaningful tool of independent or autonomous research thereby leading to the emergence of new aspects or such interpretations which may enrich it as a theoretical concept undergoing independent and rigorous analysis to explore unfailing preventive measures. It is, therefore, extremely necessary 'to separate the concept of security from these surrounding normative and empirical connotations, despite manifesting reasonable as well as legitimate grounds of similarities causing considerable complications' (Baldwin, 1997, ibid.). While many scholars lay emphasis on conventional challenges or risks leading to physical injury or material losses or anything so defined, others use it on a broad fulcrum, including biological weapons, for those causes which may result in deprivation, dissociation, destruction or detrimental and traumatic or agonizing in any way possible against anyone in a polity or political society. In fact, information technology and the diffusion of internet facilities have evolved as marked features of the ongoing globalization with inherent opportunities for wrongdoers, computer hackers and cyber criminals to distort or even destroy or finally steal secret data to sell to enemies causing grave danger to the national security of a country. As it mostly happens, national security is supposed to include a particular set of meaningful and underlying decisions as regards the desired ways by which states may defend themselves against potential and destructive threats either inside or from the outer world. Evidently, 'national security is no more purely about domestic issues such as civil wars or counterterrorism as it is still largely confined to the old-fashioned considerations focusing on armed or para-military forces. In fact, in the current interdisciplinary study of national security, no nation or discipline can be totally isolated as an independent entity or an island having no interactions with the outside world' (Matthew Sussex, et al., ibid,). As obvious, the nation-state remains the referent object of security under so-devised defence mechanisms which may genuinely be characterized as the most reasonable and available and effective security measure and this is possible in connection with ensuring national security of the affected nations. However, it is mostly considered that the concept of national security stands for a particular kind of security ensuring fool-proof arrangements in all respects so that all stakeholders may relax in peace in their normal daily routine and may not remain in panic and anxiety due to being heavily preoccupied for a form of security of any kind whatsoever. As argued by an expert that it has now become a common place to refer to a 'traditional' national security paradigm, as though the state is somehow irrelevant or redundant or even incapable of adapting to the desired change (Sil and Katzenstein, 2010).

In fact, the concept acquires an operational dimension only when there is a real threat identified. In all discussions of security, opines Richard H. Ullman, from the personal to the international, there is an implicit or explicit element of threat. 'Security against recession, against illegal search and seizure, against military attack, against inflation, against erosion of security, etc., obviously assumes threat.' Hence, the debate really requires to be enlarged in scope but without losing the idea of core concerns of security because the excessively militarized character of national security portrays a profoundly wrong image of the concept as Ullman says, as it draws attention away from non-military threats that mostly include economic, social, cultural, environmental and also human issues as different kind of values. Instead, Wolfers' characterization of security as 'the absence of threats to acquired values' (Wolfers, 1952, ibid.) though seems to capture the basic intuitive notion underlying most uses of the term 'security' but remains unclear as it fails to rule out the ambiguity implied with the absence of threats. Hence, ignoring these issues could be more harmful and dangerous to the security of the nations (Ullman, 1981), as regards theorizing national security and that motivates one to incline towards neo-realism that "no theory of international politics emphasizes security more than neo-realism which posits it as the primary motive of states" (Baldwin, 1997). Another scholar discards it as foolish to depict national security as an old-fashioned (Newman, 2010) and an ambiguous and narrow concept. As evident, that it is wrong to reject it as the exclusive domain of real-politicking and outmoded conceptions of the national interests in the contemporary world. Obviously, in such a complex scenario, 'the observation held by Paul and Ripsman (T. V. Paul and Norrin Ripsman, 2010), comes out as quite reasonable and justified that states are indeed the basic security actors in international relations' (Matthew Sussex, et al., 2017, ibid.). And that essentially asks for a deeper exploration of knowledge about national security in the present contemporary situation of rising insecurities and mounting threats to the states in the world, especially due to the mounting threat of the global terror menace, or probably the elimination of humanity lest nuclear weapons or bio-weapons like the corona bomb clandestinely fall into the hands of terrorists who may destroy or eliminate humanity just with a push on a button. Similarly, Fisher emphasizes the non-military aspects of security because the insecurity of individuals and groups almost always leads to disorder and instability (Dietrich Fisher, 1993). Another expert, Brown, also criticized the extra-narrow focus of national security and advocated a wider perspective upon it than that covered by traditional focus on national military policy (Neville Brown, 1977). In fact, national security as a concept may be considered as 'a companion of power rather than the derivative of it and as a prior condition of peace rather than consequence of it, comments Buzan Barry (Buzan Barry, 1987). But, in the course of its evolution, the concept has been used in different contexts. According to Berkowitz and Bock, politicians have used it as 'a rhetorical phrase and military strategists have used it to describe a policy objective' (Mortan Berkowitz & P.G. Bock, 1968). Further, experts like Norman Padelford and Lincoln have described the concept as 'maintenance of status-quo' (Norman Padelford and George A. Lincoln, 1954), but Hoffman treated it as 'national interest' (Stanley R. Hoffman, 1981). Further, while Buchanan used it in terms of 'military strength' (Alistair Buchanan, 1966) Walsh found it close to 'survival' (J. Walsh, 1969). Despite these differing views, the essence of 'national security' is still political and military security but then, over and above, the substantial interdependence of political, economic, social and military dimensions too cannot be overlooked while formulating policy decisions. It is, therefore, both realistic and inevitable that socio-cultural, economic, political and environmental factors including military preparedness are integral to any kind of national security related decision-making process and consequent preparedness which are today under severe threat due to the fast spreading COVID-19 epidemic, thereby considerably affecting the ongoing social, cultural, economic and political interactions in India and the whole world.

COVID-19: Socio-Economic and Political Impacts

While the global pandemic due to the corona virus has vigorously shaken the entire world, most prominent global and major powers like the USA, Russia, England, France, Italy, Spain, India, etc., are today passing through perhaps the worst phase with consistently rising numbers of COVID-19 infected patients and resultant deaths every day. That may lead to possible realignment of global powers including regional and smaller powers so as to forge new arrangements as a new conducive international order along economic and politico-hegemonic lines, thereby affecting the ongoing course of globalization, wherein liberal-capitalist forces may unite under the global leadership of America with China being cornered due to its shady role in manufacturing the corona virus, and Russia making frantic efforts to regain its lost glory as a potential global counter-pole. Further, with Chinese influence gradually receding in global affairs due to the mounting pressure of US-led Western powers to isolate its economy facing severe economic sanctions and even limited military counter-offensives, particularly for liberating the South China Sea from Chinese presence, thereby ensuring uninterrupted passage through maritime channels, the emerging scenario may become difficult for both China and Pakistan to get the much-needed economic and military support from global financial institutions like World Bank and IMF and major arms traders like America, France, Israel, etc., respectively, to confront India's rising clout in the world. Fortunately, countries like India, Vietnam, etc., are becoming new destinations for many west European countries including prominent financial magnates like Japan, France, Germany, Britain and also the USA, which are on the way to wind up their investments in China. Notwithstanding all these concerns, COVID-19 will inevitably open new doors of social-cultural, economic, strategic and defence co-operation and also scientific and technical research between and among countries to overcome the post-corona national and global scenario. It has already engendered significant changes in the common styles of courteous behaviour where shaking of hands and other prevalent modes in different nations are increasingly being replaced by India's welcome gesture with folded hands. Followed by mandatory social distancing and declining social gatherings, the consequent scenario due to COVID-19 may witness considerably reduced social-interactions and community celebrations of mass festivals, marriages, etc., for a long time to come. Against this scenario, increasing digitalization is the need of the hour to preserve important data in the interest of national security and also that of human beings. This will also help accomplish the goal of *right to information* in the true spirit of democracy and fundamental freedoms, but there are grave challenges towards this goal of digitalization.

Challenges of Digitalization

In the present digital age, as the role of Information and Communication Technology (ICT) has already become an integral part of governance and business in India as well as in the world, the issue of cyber security has assumed considerable importance in the national security concerns of all nation-states. As greater and greater digitalization is very much required for ensuring accountability, responsibility and transparency in establishing good governance, there are grave inherent dangers too in implementing this process which leads to greater connectivity and reliance on the internet and computer industry through information technology to perform necessary tasks. But with such a wide and open platform available, the internet is no longer safe (Prabhakar Pillai, 2012). In fact, it is software that has enabled a tricky or wicked mind to cause any kind of unimaginable disruption or even destruction anywhere in the world in various forms, ranging from provoking communal violence, stealing confidential data, computer-hacking, secret monitoring of personal lives, economic crimes, leaking national secrets to enemies or terrorists and insurgents or anything beyond possible imagination or projecting horrifying pornography particularly to corrupt the new and young generations and ethical-moral traditional cultures in countries like India, based upon strong ancient cultural traditions and so-evolved moral value-based ethos. Indeed, the cyber-attacks in India, which are consistently rising "from 23 in 2004 to

62000 until mid-2014" (N. Manoharan, 2013) have the potential to adversely impact the nation's economy, social cohesion, political stability and public safety and national security as well. Obviously, the rising cyber-attacks on critical infrastructure may lead to heavy losses or disruptions that have made nations realize the significance of immediately protecting and securing their critical assets against such attacks. Thus the protection of cyber infrastructure has become a national priority and concern for cyber security has emerged as a critical and new component of national security (R. Kumar and N. Mukherjee, 2013). 'As the world increases its dependence on digital information devices for developing infrastructure and manufacturing sector and in the delivery of products and services securing critical information against the backdrop of the increasing number of cyber-attacks, all these cyber-criminal and nefarious activities are to increasingly come under the purview of threats to national security' (Sushma Devi, 2019). Obviously, for ensuring fool proof security of a country's vital national critical infrastructures from all kinds of cyber-attacks in the era of speedy globalization, an effective arrangement of a stable, reliable, secure, functioning yet indigenous and unfailing digitalization system must be evolved and pursued with regular monitoring of its successful operation so as to check emerging distortions in the ongoing globalization without undergoing any risk or threat.

Distortions in Globalization

In fact, the distorted system of globalization has, in fact, "often led to instability and also resulted in widening the inequality among nations. Empirical evidence shows that the income gap between developed and developing countries has widened. Even countries which seemed to have adapted well to globalization were seriously affected by the Asian financial crisis. Similarly, the structural-adjustment policies imposed by the World Bank on African and Latin American countries also led to disastrous consequences, as experienced in Argentina and Brazil" (Tripathi, 2014) and elsewhere in the Third World. As is quite clear, "there is no automatic process by which income levels of developing countries could converge with those of developed nations" (Tripathi, 2014, ibid.) in the Western Anglo-European world. The challenge before the international community is to ensure that globalization should take into account the development dimension with a human face along with equal sharing of its accrued benefits. In fact, "asymmetries and imbalances have intensified in international economic relations, particularly with regard to international cooperation, further widening the gap between the developing and the industrialized countries. As a result, the socio-economic conditions of these countries have deteriorated thereby turning them prone to different kinds of insecurities both internal as well as external. Further, the new technology from industrialized countries and their large-scale adoption have caused serious environmental risks of degradation and have virtually destroyed the traditional education and native skills commonly available among the common masses (Declaration of Group of 77 South Summit, Havana, Cuba, 10-14 April 2000). The lower and weaker sections of society are to become the worst sufferers due to being unable to find jobs or employment of any kind to sustain their family and house. "Consequently the income gap between the lower and upper levels of society has risen and this along with consumerism and its promotion through modern electronic means of communication has led to crimes, anarchy and destruction of social equilibrium and harmony. Hence, urgent and effective measures must be taken to address the needs of the large majority of the populace, in particular, women and children, who are forced to live in abject poverty" (Tripathi, 2014, ibid.). In fact, poor women and children are the worst sufferers as they have to suffer the worst kind of trauma and agony on their person as well psyche. Thus, such economic deprivation leads to their extreme wretchedness and that kills the spirit of brotherhood and social cohesion and equilibrium as well. All these factors hint at globalization causing damage to the national sovereignty and security of states because situations and perspectives of security differ from state to state. When a country is strong, its security may basically focus on protecting itself from external threats and when a nation is weak it will consolidate itself more against internally emerged threats than on those that emerged from across the border. In the present-day world, most of the threats facing nations are domestic ones, namely, economic recession, environmental pollution, large-scale corruption and lack of basic amenities and lack of popular participation in the national mainstream, violation of human rights, communal and organized violence, insurgency, terrorism, and religious fundamentalism including civil war. In a more global sense, a fear of cultural annihilation may help fuel terrorist sentiments, according to Fathali Moghaddam, as he argues that rapid globalization has forced diverse cultures to interact with one another and is threatening the domination or disappearance of some groups as against the flourishing of few others (Moghaddam, 2008). Indeed, it is rare to find a country facing only either internal or external threats. National security for most countries has both the aspects and both undermine the security of the nation as well as the security of its inhabitants. Ullman has aptly quoted Hobbes: "It did not matter much whether threats come from within or outside one's nation. A victim is just as dead if the bullet that kills him is fired by a neighbour attempting to seize his property or if it comes from an invading army. A citizen looks to the state, therefore, for protection against both types of threats." (Ullman, 1983, ibid.) But this does not spell the retreat of the state or the end of the modern nation-state system. Peter Newell argues that 'the economic changes associated with globalization, in many but not all cases, have been produced and continued to be produced by state actions and non-actions. Reaffirming state agency is important for understanding globalization historically and for engaging in debate about the future possibilities of state action for development (Newell, 2001, ibid.). While upholding this view, India too interacts with all countries, whether powerful or not, with the avowed purpose of establishing peace and security in the world by adhering to its eternal and moral values of peace, love, truth, non-violence, equity, justice, solidarity and brotherhood as enshrined and upheld in its ancient Indian classical heritage, altogether crystallized in its foreign policy.

Conclusion

Thus, the ongoing globalization is reasonably devoted to the protection and promotion of common interests of humanity particularly residing in Third World countries which, in fact, presupposes mutual cooperation among all states in the world, and that has become very pertinent today when global humanity is pathetically suffering the corona pandemic, thereby prominently raising the issue of human security. As each nation is committed for protecting its own security or national interest, it will be possible only when the social, economic, political, military and other associated aspects of them are equally protected on just parameters. But given the hierarchical structure of international relations, the process of globalization has become uneven and unpredictable and will remain so in times to come, but if it is properly harnessed while considering the broader view of security including the social, political, economic and military dimensions as that gives an enduring meaning to the idea of national security pursuing larger interests of humanity, can the foundation for equitable and sustainable growth at the national as well as international levels be laid? Obviously, national efforts need to be complemented by international cooperation in order to reverse the marginalization of developing countries and also to manage emerging challenges to seize the opportunities created by the ongoing globalization. As the amazing technological power and resultant financial integration have led the world to shrink at the click of a 'mouse', the ongoing globalization must remain in working order for the overall progress, security and welfare of the entire humanity, and here lies the core ideals of India's ancient cultural heritage and evolving moral traditions upholding eternal and universal values and such ideals in the true spirit of *vasudhaiv kutumbakam* (the entire world as a family) and also the *spirit of sharing and caring* and *mutual respect and benefit* for all. To accomplish these goals in the current scenario of ongoing globalization and rising level of multifarious insecurities putting severe strain on national security of the so-affected countries, India has to properly protect its national security and manage its entire affairs in a prudent manner. Thus, the stakes are high for India to avail the opportunities offered by the ongoing globalization while not ignoring glocalisation and self-reliance so as to ensure its economic growth and socio-political progress through *swadeshi*, or following an indigenous way, alongwith ever-demanding necessities of national security. This is possible as *nothing is beyond human endeavour.*

REFERENCES

Baldwin David A. (1997), 'The concept of security', *Review of International Studies*, British International Studies Association, Cambridge University Press, vol, 23, pp. 5-26.

Berkowitz, Mortan & P. G. Bock (1968), 'National Security,' *International Encyclopaedia of Social Sciences*, Macmillan, USA, vol. II, p. 40.

Brown, Neville (1977), *The Future Global Challenge: A Predictive Study of World Security*, London.

Bryan S. Turner (Ed). (2010), *Globalisation and World Society*, London: Polity Press, 1996, pp 1-6.

Buchanan, Alistair (1966), *War in Modern Society*, C. A. Watts and Company, p. 24.

Buzan, Barry (1987), *Problem in International Relations*, New Delhi: Trans Publishers, p. 18. Also see 'People, States and Fear: The National Security Problem in the Third World,' in Edward E. Azar and Chung-in-Moon (Eds.) *National Security in the Third World: The Management of Internal and External Threats*, Maryland: Centre for International Development and Conflict Management, University of Maryland, 1988, p. 40.

Dannreuther, Roland and John Peterson, (Eds.) (2006), *Security Strategy and Transatlantic Relations*. Abingdon: Routledge.

Declaration of Group of 77 South Summit, Havana, Cuba, 10-14 April 2000. www.g77/org/summit/Declaration_G77Summit.htm accessed on 24-7-1019.

Devi, Sushma (2019), 'Cyber Security In The National Security Discourse: A Study of India's

Critical Infrastructure and Smart Cities', *World Affairs,* New Delhi, vol. 23, no. 3, Summer (April-June) pp. 145-58.

El-Ojeili, Chamsy and Patric Hayden, *Critical Theories of Globalisation,* Basingstroke: Palgrave Macmillan, p. 97.

Fisher, Dietrich (1993), *Non-military Aspects of Security: A Systems Approach,* United Nations Institute for Disarmament Research, Geneva, Switzerland, p. 8.

Friedman, Thomas, L. (2005), *The World is Flat: A Brief History of the Globalized World in the 21st Century;* London, Allen Lane.

Gallie, W. B. (1956), 'Essentially Contested Concepts', *Proceedings of the Aristotelian Society,* N. S., 56, pp. 167-98.

Hoffman, Stanley R. (1981), 'Security in the Age of Turbulences: Means of Response in Third World Conflict and International Security', *Adelphi Papers,* International Institute for Strategic Studies, Taylor and Francis, London, England, no. 167, Summer, pp. 4-5.

Hughes, Christopher W. (2004), *Japan's Re-emergence as a Normal Military Power. Adelphi Papers* pp. 368–369. Oxford: Oxford University Press.

Ikenberry, G. John (2008), 'The Rise of China and the Future of the West.' *Foreign Affairs,* January–February, https://www.foreignaffairs.com/ articles/asia/2008-01-01/rise-china-and-future-west.

Ji, You (2015), 'China's National Security Commission: Theory, Evolution and Operations', *Journal of Contemporary China* 25 (98): 178–196.

Kumar, R. and N. Mukherjee (2013), *Cyber Security in India: A Skill Development Perspective,* New Delhi: Communication Multimedia and Infrastructure.

Lind, Jennifer (2016), 'Japan's Security Evolution'. *CATO Institute Policy Analysis* no. 788, February 25. http://www.cato.org/publications/policy-analysis/japans-security-evolution.

Manoharan, N. (2013), 'India's Internal Security Situation: Threats and Responses', *India Quarterly: A Journal of International Affairs,* vol. 69, no. 4, pp. 367-81.

Medcalf, Rory (2014), "In Defence of the Indo-Pacific: Australia's New Strategic Map." *Australian Journal of International Affairs,* 68 (4): 470–483.

Moghaddam, Fathali (2008), *'How Globalization Spurs Terrorism: The Lopsided Benefits of One World and Why That Fuels Violence/',* Praeger.

Mittelmann, James H. (2000), *The Globalization Syndrome: Transformation and Resistance,* New Jersey, Princeton University Press.

Newell, P. (2001), Global challenges to the future state, *Seminar,* no. 503, July, New Delhi.

Newman, Edward (2010), 'Critical Human Security Studies', *Review of International Studies* 36 (1):77–94.

Oros, Andrew (2008), *Normalising Japan: Politics, Identity and the Evolution of Security Practice,* Palo Alto, CA: Stanford University Press.

Paul, T. V. and Norrin Ripsman (2010), *Globalization and the National Security State,* Oxford: Oxford University Press.

Padelford, Norman & George A. Lincoln (1954), *International Politics,* New York: Macmillan, p. 289.

Pillai, Prabhakar (2012), "History of Internet Security", *Buzzle,* online at http:// www.buzzle.com.

Saltzman, Ilia Z. (2015), 'Growing Pains: Neoclassical Realism and Japan's Security Policy Emancipation'. *Contemporary Security Policy* 36 (3): 498–527.

Sil, Rudra, and Peter J. Katzenstein (2010), *Beyond Paradigms: Analytic Eclecticism in the Study of World Politics.* New York: Palgrave Macmillan.

Sussex, Matthew, Michael Clarke & Rory Medcalf (2017), 'National security: between theory and practice', *Australian Journal of International Affairs,* 71:5, 474-478, DOI:10.1080/

10357718.2017.1347139-332X (Online) Journal homepage: https:// www.tandfonline.com/ loi/caji20.

Tripathi, Sudhanshu (2014), 'Globalisation and National Security: Contemporary Views and the Ongoing Debate', *World Affairs*, New Delhi, vol. 18, no. 2, Summer (April-July), pp. 82-83.

Tripathi, Sudhanshu (2020), 'COVID-19: A pandemic must be overcome! *Times of India*, blog, New Delhi, April 5.

Ullman, Richard H. (1983), 'Redefining Security', *International Security*, vol. 8, no. 1, pp. 129-53.

Walsh, J. (1969), 'National Security', *Military Digest*, April, p. 40.

Webb Jennifer and Tony Schiratao, *Understanding Globalisation*, Sage International; 2004.

Webber, Mark, James Sperling, and Martin Smith (2013), *NATO's Post-Cold War Trajectory: Decline or Regeneration*. New York: Palgrave Macmillan.

Wirth, Christian (2015), "Power' and 'Stability' in the China–Japan–South Korea Regional Security Complex," *Pacific Review* 28 (4): 553–575.

Wolfers, Arnold (1952), "National Security" as an Ambiguous Symbol', *Political Science Quarterly*, 67, p. 483.

World Bank (1997), *World Development Report 1997: The State in a Changing World*, Oxford: Oxford University Press.

2

Geopolitical Landscape of Asian Security and its Strategic Concerns

Sarika Dubey

Introduction

In the twenty-first century, security has become a prime concern in the global perspective. It is a basic requirement of the individual as well as the state to grow and develop. The concept of security has become predominant after the Cold War era. The Cold War had a great impact on the political developments of Asia. After the Second World War, Britain had abandoned its security role and transferred its security responsibility to the USA. Japanese imperialism collapsed and European colonialism was shattered after the Second World War, whereas the USA remained the dominant power in Asia and enjoyed the status of a superpower for a long time. C. Raja Mohan (2013), a well-known Indian analyst of foreign affairs observed that "the inherent multi-polar tendencies in the region were underlined by the strategies adopted by two nations which had the potential to emerge as great powers – the PRC and India. Communist PRC demonstrated the capacity to align, de-align, and realign rather than accept the constraining bipolar logic of the Cold War". China always believed in pragmatic politics. In the early 1960s, China easily broke its close ties with Moscow and jumped on the lap of Washington in the 1970s and again in 2000 shook hands with Moscow. India after its independence tried to maintain its strategic autonomy and adopted a path of non-alignment and promote multi-polarity. Indian foreign policy later showed friendly gestures towards the USA and departed from its non-aligned policy to seek US military support when its northern border was facing threats from China. There is one common thing observed in the strategic behaviour of both the countries—that they believe in independent foreign policy and remained unwilling to leave their strategic autonomy during their close relations with a superpower. Similar behaviour can be seen in some other Asian countries like Indonesia, Thailand, Iran, etc., which somewhere ensures the multi-polarity of the region.

In the rapidly changing world order, we have entered a new phase of international affairs where the geopolitical scenario is ready to redefine global power structures in the ambit of security and dominance. The emergence of a strong China has changed the security dynamics of the region. China has strengthened its position as an economic superpower under the umbrella of globalization and threatened the USA's global superpower position. These changes have affected the security aspects of Asia where geopolitics and geo-economics play a complex role in the dominance game by two major powers. The issue of the South China Sea dispute or the US-China trade war or the nuclear issue of North Korea and Iran are all seriously affecting the entire security framework of the region. China's assertive behaviour in its neighbourhood and ambiguous and irresponsible role during the COVID-19 pandemic that originated from Wuhan, China, posed severe security challenges in the Asian region. Hong Kong aggression, Taiwan issue and China's border dispute with India in the Galwan valley of the Himalayan region and arms deployment in the South China Sea are issues that have badly affected the regional security structure and raised severe security concerns for Asia.

In the light of the above backdrop, this paper attempts to analyse the changing geopolitical landscape of Asia and its impact on Asian security. It not only discusses the concept of security and its theoretical foundations as a whole but also the efforts to understand and identify major security concerns that emerge due to the changing geopolitics of the region. It focuses on the major disputes that have been by-products of political rivalry and the game of dominance among big powers and provide viable solutions to ensure peace and stability in the region.

Concept of Security

Security has been the prime concern since human civilization came into being. It is the supreme necessity of the existence of individuals and survival of the nation-state. In the 21st century, the concept of security has emerged in wide perspectives. It is multidimensional in nature and has a complex connotation which reflects different meanings. There is no perpetual definition of security which could be equally acceptable to all. Generally, it is described as a psychological feature, a condition or status or a feeling which demands freedom from all kinds of fear. It can be defined as a measure or an act that requires protection or defence against threats. John E. Marz (1980) views it as a relative freedom from harmful threats, while Barry Buzan reiterated that it is not either power or peace but something in between. In his book, *People, State and Fear,* he identified three levels of security—individual level, national level or international level. He discussed various dimensions of security in this book like human security, environmental security, trans-cultural security, etc (Buzan, 1991).

The concept of security developed comprehensively in the post-Cold War era (1991) and it has been the much-hyped notion in the realm of modern international relations. Actually, the Cold War was a geopolitical tension between two superpowers—the Soviet Union and the USA and their allies. Ideology had been the core of this tension which raised deep security concerns and distrust from both sides. Thus, the political significance and importance of the study of security had increased tremendously. It provided a logical base to both the superpowers to pitch their sides against each other in the ambit of security and helped shape the way in which the Cold War was contested by the two superpowers. During the Cold War, the traditional conception of security shifted from national security to international security. National Security ensures the independence and sovereignty of a nation-state and protects its national interests and well-being of its citizens, and can be best achieved through a legal enforcement agency. Thus, national security can be measured in terms of military capability and it has been the prime object of the state to modernize and weaponise its army for national security. The Cold War had changed this perception. Now the new idea that emerged was that unilateral force improvement had no meaning until a nation became a member of any alliance as it ensured the security of every nation of alliance broadly based on the principle of collective security. NATO, Seato, Cento,

Warsaw Pact and many other alliances have emerged around this theory during the Cold War period. This gave birth to the concept of international security that is measured by the efforts of the state and regional or international organizations to ensure mutual survival and safety. Thus, international security can be best defined as national security in the global arena. After the Cold War period, the traditional realist conceptualization of security was challenged by academicians and many others as it was unsatisfactory in its own terms and not able to address several non-military concerns in general. During this period, a common consensus gradually emerged that a classical approach to security is inappropriate and there is an urgent requirement of a broader multi-sectoral approach to security which could address all the security concerns of civil society and the nation, state as well.

These changes reflected were widely at the academic and policy levels. International relations literature introduced chapters on non-traditional security threats like gender analysis, environmental security, etc., in the same way international organizations like the United Nations and NATO gave new dimensions to the definition of security and embraced the broader agenda beyond a military paradigm. Barry Buzan and the Copenhagen School identified several new domains and placed them under the ambit of security studies. During the 1980s and 1990s, the concept of security has emerged in a new flavour. Ken Booth, Richard Wyn Jones and many others played a vital role in extending the concept of security (Michael Sheehan, 2005). During this period, security studies had gained enormous popularity and importance in the field of international relations and politics. It has been pivotal to the debates over government policy agenda and remained significant in policy priorities. In fact, entire frameworks of international relations and its theories and practices are woven around the issue of security that makes its study worthwhile. The principle of war and peace, collective security the balance of power, arms control and disarmament are those aspects of security studies which have been at the core in the study of international relations. Der Derian (1995) describes its importance as "no other concept in international relations packs the metaphysical punch, nor commands the disciplinary power of security".

Geopolitical Landscape of Asian Security

It is quite obvious that the rapidly changing international political scenario leads to new changes in the global order. In the 19th century, ideology played an important role in the global system whereas the world had become economic centred in the 21st century. Globalisation played a major role in the economic integration of the world. Economic prosperity had become a new parameter of empowerment for nation-states. India and China were emerging as giant Asian economic powers. China's economic rise and military transformation has aggravated its desire for global dominance. Its strong temptation towards economic and natural resources created deep strategic concerns in the entire region. China's new geopolitical strategy is aimed at extending its sphere of influence and fostering new norms of international economic cooperation to promote a new world order. The BRI is the example of China's hidden geopolitical strategy to rule the world.

According to Dodds (2007), the term 'geopolitics' refers to great power rivalries and the geographical dimensions of global political power. Geopolitics has always been a matter of serious consideration in the field of power, in the study of foreign policy as well as in political debates, speeches that particularly focus on the geographical aspect to specify international political affairs. Traditionally, the term had been applied to matters of foreign policy making and used by politicians and elites in decision making (Dodds and Atkinsons, 2000). It continued to define global order but in the contemporary discussions of great powers, it was central towards geographical aspects and the grand strategies of such great powers (Grygiel, 2006).

The role of geopolitics has always been significant in the study of security analysis. During the Cold War period, the balance of power and geopolitical reasons remained dominant approaches that played an important role behind the construction of the NATO alliance in the 1940s. But the current scenario has increased its value manifold. Geopolitical discourse unveils the harsh reality of international political order which is woven behind the curtains. It draws attention towards the ways through which location, space, natural resources and distance influence the political powers to craft a specific strategy to restore and control geography to protect their strategic interests and security. Thus, it is quite obvious that geography plays a very important role in defining international policies and makes geopolitics an important approach in the study of global security order.

Geopolitics is closely linked with resource distribution and energy security. Therefore, it affects the policy structure of political powers. Whether it is the Gulf war in the 1990s, China's Belt and Road Initiative (BRI), the South China Sea dispute and the India-China Galwan face-off, geopolitical measures remained significant in all the cases. Sloam and Gray (1992:2) stressed that "Political predominance is a question not just for having power in the sense of human or material resources, but also of the geographical context within which that power is exercised". Geopolitics played vital role in shaping the security of any region. In the case of Asia, it becomes more important because it has many seas, strategic locations, the world's most important trade passes and corridors which attract political power for enrichment of their resources. Asian giant and economic superpower China is not only posing a challenge to the global superpower, America, but also adopting very aggressive behaviour in the region. China's expansionist policies towards its neighbours and temptation towards economic and natural resources have created deep strategic concerns in the region which can be viewed and understood in terms of geopolitical aspects. It has been said that the great powers become great because they control the seas and the skies. Therefore, geopolitical discourse of security has always been pivotal in understanding international politics.

Theorizing Security

The concept of security has always been significant in understanding international relations. There are numerous elements such as national character, nature of state, preferences and prejudices, resource capacity and citizens' approach that shape the overall understanding of the concept of security. Since the end of the Cold War, the main issue is the degree to which the concept of state is central to security. There are several other referent objects like the individual, civil society, social institutions, specific groups and the international community that play a major role in determining security. But after the 9/11 attack on USA, Weaver (2004 a: 56) observes that 'the state in extreme situations had a right to call on necessity and *raison d'état*'. Wolfers (1952) argues that there are numerous elements that shape an overall understanding of security but the most important is the lack of threat and fear against the values of a nation.

There are several schools of thought and approach regarding the concept of security like rationalism, reflectivism and constructivism. These approaches have crafted different kinds of security perceptions. There are two main rationalist theories—realism and liberalism. During the Cold War, realism had been the dominant approach in analyzing the security issues of the USA and the USSR. It emerged as a response to the liberal idealism of the 1920s and 1930s (Dunne and Schmidt, 2001). Realism can be further categorized into three parts—classical realism which was dominant until the first decades of the twentieth century; modern realism, which was dominant between 1939 and 1979 and neo-realism which began in 1979. Machiavelli and Carr were the main thinkers of historical realism while Thucydides, Morgenthau and Waltz belong to structural realism. According to realism, the world order is a system of competing self-interested state actors under anarchy (Baldwin, 1993:4; Buzan, 1996:60; Morgenthau, 1978). Therefore, it affects security directly as there is no one to govern independent states under the system of anarchy. Joseph Nye described such international politics as "anarchic in the sense that there is no higher government (Nye, 2009:4). Henry Kissinger, realist, academician and US Secretary of State, perceives national interests as a core security concern (Kissinger, 1976:182). Realists believe that no state will sacrifice its national interests to serve the larger community (Frankel, 1996: XV). Thus, security could be understood within the language of insecurity and threat to the nation. According to this approach, states cannot trust others in security issues. In fact, realists view the increase in security of a state leads to insecurity for others which is called the 'security dilemma' (Herz, 1951). Historical realist Carr in his book *Twenty Year's Crisis, 1936-1946*, explained that the main reason for World War II was moving away from a realist approach to liberal interpretations (Carr, 1946). Neo-realist founder Kenneth Waltz argues that 'a state will use force to attain its goals under anarchy (Waltz, 1959: 160); however, the ultimate concern for states is not for power but for security' (Waltz, 1988: 616).

The concept of Liberalism developed in Europe in the 18th century around the ideas initiated by the German philosopher Immanuel Kant, founder of Idealism who believes in the fundamental rights of men, right to live, freedom and poverty. Liberalism is a political doctrine which further nourishes and promotes such ideas like liberty and equality and its main components are constitutionalism, democracy, elections, human rights, free commerce, religious liberty, moral values, etc. Liberalists try to diminish the power that a state could practice on its citizens. They believe in democratic values and argue that a democratic country may be involved in conflicts but will never attack another democratic country. Actually, liberalists perceive the international community as a garden, which is essential to consolidate global security (Doyle, 1997: 19). Liberalists believe that world peace and security could be maintained only through the cooperation of the states by adopting democratic values and mutual understanding and promoting individual rights. Thus, only military interventions are not necessary steps to be taken. Liberalism focuses on two basic principles to maintain peace and security: (1) Collective security; and (2) Weapons control. Liberalists also follow liberal patterns of solutions to global problems based on four instruments: international law, international organizations, political integration and democratization (Badalan, 2009: 73).

Reflectivism, another international relations theory, is a broad umbrella under which there is a range of theoretical approaches that oppose the theory of rationalism on many grounds. Reflectivism focuses on the positivist conception of social science. It was popularized by Robert Kohane in his presidential address to the International Studies Association in 1988 (Kurki, Milija, 2008). It was entitled *'International Institutions: Two approaches*. One is Rationalism while the other is Reflectivism. Reflectivists claim that rationalists have ignored many important aspects of international politics. They believe that international relations should be reflexive. Reflectivist approaches include some Marxist theories like world-system theory, Gramscianism, critical theory and new Marxism. The concept of security is very significant for the Marxist theory of the state. Marxists believe that the dominant structures of the world, i.e., global capitalism, play a significant role in understanding world politics. They believe that the social world needs to be studied as a whole and that the security of the state is a dangerous illusion which is often used to divert attention from core issues like exploitation, alienation and material inequality and support police power. In place of such a kind of state security, Marxists favour food security and livelihood security for all human beings (Rigakos S. George, 2020).

Constructivism is another important school of thought of international relations. It is a social theory that is shaped by ideational factors, not material factors. Constructivists believe that identities and interests of actors are socially constructed and changeable, Nicholas Onuf has coined the term 'constructivism' to describe theories that focus on socially constructed character of international relations (Jackson, Robert Howard and Sorensen George, 2010). It gained popularity in International Relations during the late 1980s and early 1990s. Alexander Wendt, the most prominent advocate of constructivism, views it as a strong way for analyzing events occurring in the world (Wendt, 1999). According to constructivism, states express their identities in relation to other states. Constructivists view security, self-help and anarchy as unlikely to realists. They argue that the concepts of security, self-help, anarchy and threat are institutions that regain their meaning under the situation of anarchy which is an outcome of the actor's practices that define it and others (Wendt, 1992). Therefore, the perception of security and similar other concepts as institutions differ in different situations. These actors of the international system define them on the basis of situations based on their own assumptions and intentions relative to other.

All the above theories have different perceptions regarding an international system. Realism explains international relations as responses to the realities present in the real world which recognizes security as the first priority of the state. Liberalism emphasizes that material and ideas govern the behaviour of actors directly in international politics. Thus, it is believed that the security of the states can be provided through common interests among the sovereign states; Marxism explains security as the condition created by the capitalist system to protect its survival (Adler, September 1997), while Constructivism believes that both the ideal and real worlds matter. It is a way of re-describing the world by putting people and their activities at the core of the analysis (Kubalkova, Onuf et. al., 1998). According to prominent Constructivist scholar Alexander Wendt (1992), "Security gets meaning under conditions that states understand from their environment in which they act and form the meaning that they give to anarchy. Thus securities are merely matters of national power, nothing else" (Wendt, 1992). He described these cultures of anarchy, namely, Hobbesian, Lockeam and Kantian, in which states create specific kinds of security in every one. Constructivism views 'states' as agents that have specific goals to achieve in the international system. Therefore, these agents define and interpret concepts such as security and intensity as per their own interest based on the knowledge and information they have. If the behavioural patterns of agents are changed, the rules and norms will be changed accordingly. Therefore, agents can change the world by changing their perception about the world because all the norms and identities of any concepts are constructed by the agents or actors according to their perception (Wendt, 1992).

Major Issues and Strategic Concerns

Europe governed the 19th century, the USA dominated the 20th century and now it appears that the 21st century is the Asian century. Though it is a multicultural, diverse, politically fragmented region but it has immense potential of production and utilisation. The robust economic rise of Asian economies awakened the possibility of an Asian century. It holds the capacity to perform significantly on the world stage. During the 17th-18th centuries, Asia was the leading economic power. However, internal conflicts, fissures, lack of vision, strategic failures, military incompetency and a certain level of complacency led to deterioration. The revival of Asia began with the rise of Japan, South Korea and Taiwan with U.S. economic assistance. The rise of China and India played a major role in Asia's economic eclipse. India is now the world's third-largest economy in terms of PPP, while China exceeded the US economy in terms of PPP. Vietnam is one of Asia's fastest growing economies. Asia's fraction of global goods trade has increased while the share of Europe and North America has declined comparatively (Mehta, Rajesh and Mittal, Diksha, 2021).

Asian economies are gradually doing well and eventually becoming world players. In the aftermath of the global financial crisis, advanced economies like the USA and the UK experienced a vast decline while the Asian countries performed well and remained stable. China has played a lead role in the Asian system and has now become a global player. Asia is also improving in other sectors. A strong middle class has emerged in Asia particularly in South East Asia. According to the Asian Development Bank, around 3 billion Asians are enjoying high living standards similar to those in Europe (Mehta, Rajesh and Mittal, Diksha, 2021). Poverty has tremendously reduced in Asia. The strong presence of Asian people can be seen all over the world. They form a strong Asian community. The Vice-President of the USA, Kamala Harris in Biden's Administration proves that Asians have a strong hold and influential position in America as well.

However, the other side of the coin is blurred. Despite such positivity about Asia, it is also true that Asia has a long history of wars and clashes causing instability and insecurity in the region. It has been engaged in many inter-state bilateral and multilateral disputes which has often given rise to either war or war-like situations. China-Japan tensions and North-South Korea clash has deviated Asia's adventure. The region is divided into many rival political, economic and security blocs. Tensions and border disputes among two giant economies of Asia—India and China—have been very sensitive issues in the region. After the Sino-India war of 1962, there has been a high level of mutual distrust and lack of confidence among each other. In the same way, India-Pakistan rivalry has remained a hot issue for decades. Four Asian countries, namely, China, India, Pakistan and North Korea, are nuclear weapon states. This dangerous nuclearisation of Asia is a biggest security concern in the 21st century. Due to mutual distrust, cultural diversification and lack of Asian identity and affinity as 'Asians', Asia has faced numerous challenges. This narrative highlights that unlike the idea of an American century or the age of European unity, Asia is far behind to have an Asian identity or unity which can lead it towards the centre of power. There are several issues and security concerns due to strategic interests, territorial disputes, democratic values, maritime security issues, external interference in the internal affairs of nations, cyber threats, and dominance of strong nations, and lack of strategic trust between nations causing severe security challenges in the entire region.

Internal and external security has become a prime concern and a major destabilization factor in the region. Interference in internal affairs, attempts to change regimes, creating internal instability and fissure for political gain and geo-political and geo-strategic space has been the great game in the Indo-centric region (Narayan, Rajiv, Major General, 2021). Maritime security issues in the strategically important Asia-Pacific region and the South China Sea are very burning issues in recent times while the conflict in Israel-Palestine, terrorism and bioterrorism are other burning issues which are affecting the entire security network of Asia. There is no regional umbrella able to resolve these challenges and drive a regional economic and security strategy through a common consensus and collective efforts. There are multifarious regional architectures that seem to dominate and over-rule each other, China wants to have the sole leadership of Asia while same democratic countries like India, Japan, South Korea, Indonesia, Malaysia, Singapore and Thailand look towards a multi-polar Asia. There are some major issues and strategic concerns affecting the regional security structure of entire Asia.

Rise of China

Though the rise of any nation is a good sign, as it provides opportunities of development for others and improves living standards of its own people, but in the case of China it is like a threat to the security and stability of the region. China is very aggressive towards its neighbouring countries. China's hostile behaviour and military aggression are increasing day by day throughout the region. It does not respect the sovereignty of other nations. China is flexing its muscles to intimidate and threaten other nations. It became common for China to encroach upon the borders of neighbouring countries. Recently, the India-China face-off in the Galwan valley has triggered acute panic across the world. Its military aggression is not only against India but also against Hong Kong, Taiwan, Vietnam and Japan. In 2002, former Chinese President Jiang Zemin predicted that "within the next twenty years, China would be in a position to exploit America in order to increase its own wealth and power" (Gill, Probhojote, 2020). A similar statement was also given by Chinese President Xi Jinping in the 19th Party Congress in October 2017 which can be considered one of the most authoritative statements of the Party's policy and aims. Xi vowed China would "become a global leader in terms of composite national strength and international influence" and would build a "stable international order" in which China's "national rejuvenation" could be fully achieved (*The Japan Times*, 22 May 2020). The views reflected in the above two speeches are not new in the case of China. Actually, the root cause lies in the Chinese mindset and its ideology having the intention to rule the world and feel superior to others. China's 'Middle Kingdom concept', Mao's belief that "Political power grows out of the barrel of a gun", the 'Five finger theory' which shows the intention of gulping its southern neighbouring countries, Nepal and Bhutan, and some part of Indian territory and the cultural concept of Tian Xia that believes 'Emperor would be the ruler of entire world. It establishes some sort of Chinese supremacy in their minds to rule the world (Dubey, Sarika, 2020). China's strong military power and modernized army, which is able to fight on land, water and air perfectly and its economic power is its real strength which is also working behind the Chinese aggressive behaviour in the entire region.

China's rise over the past two decades has restructured the landscape of global politics. After entering the World Trade Organisation in 2001, China transformed its economy rapidly. It became the world's second largest economy in terms of nominal GDP, and the world's largest economy when measured in terms of Purchasing Power Parity (PPP). It has become the fastest growing economy since 1979 (Gustov, Mel, 2017). Rosemary Foot (2020) thinks that the rise of China has threatened US hegemony in the Asia-Pacific region. It has been observed widely that China is taking political leverage through economic influence. China's economic strategy of the Belt and Road Initiative (BRI) has been a geostrategic push to play a larger role in global affairs. China's debt-trap strategy to entrap states for getting geo-political geo-strategic space is quite dangerous. Now China is ready to gulp small economies through the BRI and will treat them like its colonies. This can be well observed in the case of Pakistan and Sri Lanka. Thus it is quite obvious how China's rise is causing deep security challenges in the Asian region.

US–China Friction

Deterioration in US-China relations is another big concern for the security of Asia. The Trump Administration in the USA had adopted a hardline China policy because of two reasons. First, Xi's 2035 target and second the steps China began to take to surpass the USA. China's Belt and Road Initiative (BRI), a global infrastructure-building project and trade-deficit with the USA were other reasons that had drawn America's attention to every Chinese move and of course if Xi's dream of rejuvenation materializes then definitely it will be the end of America's heyday. Such concerns in the USA have led to concerted efforts to suppress China's ambitions. Xi's revising of the constitution to scrap presidential term limits and his attempts to drive out his political foes through anti-corruption campaigns had also aggravated US tensions which critically impacted US-China relations as it became a life-or-death battle for hegemony between the USA and China.

The story begins in the beginning of 21st century which witnessed remarkable changes in the distribution of global power. Due to lack of strategic vision of the USA, a power crisis emerged in the global arena which accelerated the trends toward new multi-polarity with a number of power structures. When President Trump took office in January 2017, the USA had adopted new foreign policy initiatives and launched its 'America First' policy. He challenged established norms of international relations on many fronts, diminished the US role in global forums and shifted its focus towards China. The one most important issue in this relation is US trade with China.

Trump believed that the USA has long been the victim of bad trade deals and unfair trade practices by China such as undervalued currency and subsidies given to domestic producers to flood US markets with low-cost goods. He believed that these practices created disturbance in the US economy, threatened American jobs, wages and living standards. Therefore, the USA reduced the inflow of Chinese investments, especially those related to acquisition of US companies because it may directly threaten the national security of the USA. According to merger market reports, Chinese investments in US companies have fallen by 94.6 per cent as compared to 2016 (Arezina, Sanza, 2019). The arrest of Mong Wanzhou, Chief Financial Officer and daughter of the founder of high-tech giant, Huawei is an example of the escalation of US-China tensions.

The COVID-19 pandemic has added fuel to fire in US-China relationships. The majority of the countries of the world believe that China is solely responsible for the spread of the COVID-19 pandemic. Some of them believe that it is a deliberate act of China resulting in the entire world facing acute human loss. It has crippled the world, economies have shrunk and unemployment has increased and infected more than 8 million people globally. President Trump termed it a 'Chinese Virus' and a 'worst attack' that the USA had ever experienced. Again, mistrust and rivalries escalated between the two countries in the political gallery and a term 'new cold war' has been floating in the air which was officially first used by Chinese foreign minister Wang Yi in the National People's Congress in Beijing. The reaction was that a "Political Virus" was running rampant in the mind of the USA (Corona Virus Pandemic, 2020).

On the geostrategic level, Washington wanted to control Beijing's activity and its aggressiveness in Asia by supporting its neighbours such as Hong Kong, Taiwan, Japan, India and Tibet. President Trump signed the "Reciprocal Access to Tibet Act" which promotes access to Tibet of US diplomats, journalists and citizens and denies US visas to Chinese officials who were responsible for blocking access to Tibet (Kuo A. Mercy, 2018). In the same way the USA's support to Taiwan and Hong Kong has been a bone of contention between the two countries. China has encroached the borders of Taiwan and Japan and introduced the Hong Kong security law. These initiatives have aggravated the tensions in the entire Asian region and if powerful America jumps into the matter then definitely the situation could become deadly in the region. During the Galwan face-off between India and China, America criticized China's attempt and backed India. India, China and the USA are nuclear powers and no doubt the US army is still advanced in terms of technology and modernized weapons. Thus, if tension escalates in the region, the possibility of war cannot be ignored. Therefore, stressed US-China relations will have a deep impact on the security of Asia.

South China Sea and China's Expansion

China has a long history of claiming the territorial land of its neighbouring countries. It has the largest number of neighbours (14 countries by land and 6 by sea) sharing its 22,000-km land borders, namely, North Korea, Russia, Mongolia, Kazakhstan, Kyrgyzstan, Tajikistan, Afghanistan, Pakistan, India, Nepal, Bhutan, Myanmar, Laos and Vietnam. By sea, it is connected with South Korea, Japan, the Philippines, Brunei, Indonesia and Malaysia and has territorial conflicts with all of them. China's aggressive attitude towards its neighbours and claiming sovereignty over the South China Sea has escalated tension in the region. There are three main principles of Chinese policy on which China claims its right to the land of others that led China towards expansionism. First, in the historical era when the Chinese military power had maximum expansion, China claims sovereignty on all those parts as a part of present-day China, and its Chinese policy to get all its territory back which it had lost in the colonial period. The annexation of Hong Kong and Macau could take place on this ground. Second, China uses folklore, myths and legend as well as history, to bolster greater territory and maritime claims. On this ground China wants to capture Leh-Ladakh and keep an eye on small neighbours like Bhutan, Nepal, etc. Third is the philosophy of Mao-Tse-Tung called antagonistic contradiction that means impossibility of compromise between different social classes and can only be resolved through struggle, which gives a base for Chinese expansionism (*World Focus*, 2020). On the basis of this policy China has annexed several territories into PRC such as Xinjiang, the island of Hainan, Tibet, Yijiangshan island, Dachen island, Aksai Chin, trans Karakoram trait, Zenbao island, Parcel island, Johnson South reef, Skirmish in the South China Sea, etc.

China's aggressiveness in the South China Sea has created a deep concern among Japan and South East Asian countries. Maritime and airspace incidents of encroachment have recently been reported by Taiwan and Vietnam. China's fighter jets have violated the airspace of Taiwan, Japan and Vietnam many times. In 2019, the European Union labelled China a "systematic rival" (*The Economic Times*, 2020). China claims its sovereignty on the entire South China Sea since 1947 on the basis of historical documents and maps which was turned down by a 2016 arbitration ruling but it did not stop China (*World Focus*, 2020). Actually, the South China Sea is one of the world's busiest maritime trade routes that serves as a passage for annual trade worth $ 5 trillion. China is flexing its muscles in this region because it is rich in natural resources and is a strategically important region containing 250 small islands, atolls, cays, shoals, reefs and sandbars. China has maritime border disputes with Taiwan, Brunei, Indonesia, Malaysia, the Philippines and Vietnam in the South China Sea. It has exclusive economic zone disputes with North Korea, South Korea and Japan in the Yellow Sea and the East China Sea. The United States of America deeply criticized all the moves of China against its neighbouring countries. The Trump Administration strongly advocated the freedom of navigation in the South China Sea and criticized Chinese acts of hostility towards all its neighbours especially in the South China Sea, namely, Hong Kong, Vietnam and Taiwan. Amid tensions in US-China relations, the US Navy deployed approximately 300,000 tonne aircraft carriers strike groups in the Pacific Ocean on June 15, 2020, in an unprecedented move aimed to warn China. This is the first biggest deployment of US super carriers *USS Ronald Reagan, USS Theodore Roosevelt* and *USS Nimitz* since 2017 (*Hindustan Times*, 2020). It is quite clear that the US move of deploying troops in the Asia-Pacific is to counter Chinese aggression. The serious impact of all these developments can be seen on the security of Asia. If this situation continues, the region of Asia may turn into a battlefield and we cannot imagine the loss in this situation.

Nuclear Threat: Conflict in Korean Peninsula

The Korea Peninsula is a region located in East Asia. It is divided into two parts—North Korea or the 'Democratic People's Republic of Korea' (DPRK) and South Korea or the 'Republic of Korea'. It drew global attention when North Korea conducted its sixth nuclear weapon test in September 2017 which was its most powerful test to date. North Korea claimed that it has developed the ability to build more powerful higher yield nuclear weapons. Before this test, North Korea had conducted several missile tests and built nuclear warhead-carrying missiles. In July 2017, North Korea conducted its first successful test of an Inter Continental Ballistic Missile (ICBM). After three weeks, it tested another ICBM that could reach the USA (Sang-Hun, Choe, 2017). US intelligence agencies confirmed that North Korea has attained the ability to miniaturize its nuclear weapons to fit inside a missile. All these developments have escalated the tension not only in the entire Korean Peninsula but in Washington too. South Korea and Japan were also worried about this. It has created an unstable environment in the Korean Peninsula. North Korea's nuclear tests increase the possibility of their use against regional states. Tests of ICBM have generated fear across the region and beyond. It has triggered the nuclear arm race again in the Asian region.

Actually, the Korean conflict is based on the division of Korea between North Korea and South Korea and the governments of both the countries claim to be the sole legitimate government of Korea. The problem is the product of the Cold War (Hyung Gu Lynn, 2007, *Bipolar Orders; The two Koreas since 1989*. Zed Books, p. 3). During the Cold War, the Soviet Union backed North Korea and the USA and its allies supported South Korea. The involvement of US military forces in the Korean Peninsula has its roots in the Korean war of the early 1950s in which the USA supported South Korea against the communist forces while North Korea was aided and supported by China and the Soviet Union. At present, the USA is defending South Korea on the ground of a Mutual Defence Treaty between the USA and the Republic of Korea (South Korea). Therefore, it has deployed nearly 29,000 troops in the Korean Peninsula. In addition, an approximate 630,000 troops of South Korea and 1.2 million troops of North Korea are stationed near the demilitarized zone (DMZ), which makes it one of the most heavily armed borders in the world (North Korea crisis, 2021). It means that in case of war with chemical, biological or nuclear weapons, a very huge number of people might be in danger. This could trigger massive bloodshed in the entire Asian region.

In response to the frequent missile tests, the USA has deployed an anti-missile system in South Korea. The Terminal High Altitude Area Defence (THAAD) system is also located in the Seongju region of South Korea. All the three countries—the USA, South Korea and Japan—passed unilateral sanctions against North Korea. In August 2017 the United Nations Security Council unanimously passed tough sanctions on North Korea and targeted its most important sources of revenue including North Korean exports, etc (UN Security Council, 2017). In November 2017, the USA blacklisted North Korea and placed it on a list of state sponsors of terrorism that also enables additional sanctions against it.

There has been a slight change in US policy towards North Korea. In June 2018, President Trump met Kim Jong Un in Singapore and released a joint statement on denuclearization. In late February 2019, they met again in Vietnam but the summit ended without any deal or agreement. Therefore, it is still a tough path towards peace and stability. The present scenario provides enough space for a nuclear arms race in the region and if it is not controlled, the entire Asian region will be in extreme danger.

Turbulence in the Himalayan Region

The Himalayan region of South Asia is one of the most sensitive in terms of Asian security. The region has the greatest geopolitical significance. It is full of natural resources which make it capable of fulfilling the energy demand of the entire region. It connects South Asia to Central Asia through valleys and mountain ranges. Thus, it becomes a strategically important region for trade and commercial activities. The world's two oldest civilizations—China and India—emerged adjacent to each other in the Himalayan region. But the history of the past 75 years indicates that it has not been a peaceful region. Himalayan countries, along with their larger neighbours, have been engaged in Cold War politics. Russia remained present in Afghanistan. The United States of America backed Pakistan while India has been a close friend of Russia. The region has experienced many low intensity conflicts and wars, terrorism and border disputes among neighbouring countries. There are three main determinants of the peace and security of this region. First, India-China relations; second, India-Pakistan relations; and third, stability in Afghanistan.

India shares approximately 3,488 km of border with China. Most of the parts of this border are still disputed between the two countries. India and China fought a war in 1962 and recently they are engaged in a border standoff in the Galwan valley of Leh, Ladakh. The relationships between the two countries are still tense and face a high degree of mutual distrust. Both the countries are strong and atomic power states. The situation is quite different from that of 1962. The escalation of tension between the two nations could be destined to be extremely fatal not only for South Asia but for Asia as a whole.

India and Pakistan have been well known for their rivalry over Kashmir since independence. They fought four wars and have been engaged in low-intensity conflicts. The involvement of Pakistan in state-sponsored terrorism has also been the subject of global condemnation. Due to terrorism and infiltration on its borders by Pakistan, India launched surgical strikes many times. These circumstances are not good for the security of the South Asian region because both the countries are atomic powers and Pakistan is backed by China too. Therefore, escalation in tension and involvement of multiple actors in this region could be deadly.

Another cause of concern is the establishment of peace in Afghanistan. After the 9/11 attack on the USA, the al-Qaeda-Taliban nexus in Afghanistan was clearly observed. To eradicate this nexus, the USA had adopted a three-phase strategy. The first phase begins with toppling the ruling Taliban in Afghanistan. The second phase lasts from 2002 to 2008 in which the US strategy was to defeat the Taliban military and rebuild core institutions of the Afghan states and the third phase belongs to the counter-insurgency doctrine that began in 2008 and was accelerated by President Obama by the decision to temporarily increase US troop presence in Afghanistan to protect the population from Taliban attacks and support efforts to reintegrate insurgents into Afghan society. After a long time, the USA has finally decided to withdraw all its troops from Afghanistan as per US strategy that initiated a conflict resolution diplomacy involving multiple stakeholders to establish peace. After many rounds of peace talks, the USA will withdraw all American troops from war-torn Afghanistan by September 11, 2021. The Biden Administration has rejected the Pentagon's preference for a condition-based exit and insisted on withdrawing the troops without any power-sharing deal between the Taliban and ruling party (Vinay Kaura, 2021). This situation has once again raised severe security concerns in the region because the uncertainty of power sharing and rising level of violence. Though the Taliban has kept the space open for engagement with the Afghan government, yet through acts of violence they are demonstrating that they are capable of seizing power by military force what is not offered to them on the negotiating table. Pakistan has been the most important player in the Afghan conflict and has a history of good relationship with the Taliban. The USA has depended on Pakistan for operational and other support in Afghanistan. Thus, Pakistan will leave no space to exploit this relationship against India in the near future. Afghanistan President Ashraf Ghani has accused Pakistan of running "an organized system of support for the Afghan Taliban. Therefore, there is a strong possibility of rising terrorism once again in the region due to ISI-Taliban connections in case the Taliban is kept out of the democratic process to make a stable government.

Besides such major issues, the Israel-Palestine conflict in western Asia, Iran's nuclear programme and strain in US-Iran relations, unstructured regional formation of Central Asia and lack of cooperation among nations, fragile governments, terrorism, fundamentalism, illegal drug trafficking nexus and a number of economic environmental and societal challenges collectively exist in the security discourses of Asia.

Conclusion

Amid the rapid change and uncertainty of the 21st century and in the time of the COVID-19 pandemic, geopolitical trends in Asia point to the significance of the US role in Asia and its relationship with regional powers. It is required to maintain regional security and balance of power in the region. China's role as a regional power in the corona period has been extremely disappointing and suspicious. China's hostile behaviour towards its neighbouring countries and aggressive, hegemonistic foreign policy approach has been the cause of concern for Asian security. US-China friction, nuclearised North Korea and India-China border dispute have enough potential to disturb the Asian security framework. Asia has always had multi-polar tendencies. Emerging India could play a lead role in balancing power in East Asia. There is a need of promotion of a harmonious relationship between the great powers in Asia. They must develop an open and inclusive architecture for Asian security. The PRC and India can make joint efforts towards improving bilateral relationships and contribute to a peaceful Asia. It will open the door for greater economic cooperation between the eastern subcontinent and the continental ASEAN region. Such a settlement could also open up borders for greater connectivity and inspire cross-border mega projects, including oil and natural gas pipelines as well as rail and road corridors.

The rise of China has played a great role in transforming Asian geopolitics. As the PRC's economic power turns into a strong military power, the region will become a Sino-centric regional order which will lead to regional instability just like Germany's rise in Europe. From current indicators, it is quite clear that the rest of the Asian powers will not accept this Sino-centric regional security order. Some nations might choose to "band wagon" with the PRC but doing so will likely lead to the cessation of their sovereign rights. Therefore, in the current scenario, Asian players would prefer to balance the rise of the PRC with tighter alliances and security cooperation with other powers, especially the USA. There are two main choices at this level—first, to make a strong alliance within the region and erect strong regional institutions having military capabilities to protect each nation of the alliance on the basis of a collective security concept like NATO, and second, to invite external powers, especially the USA, in shaping the security environment in the region. The nature of the Asian response is much closer to the second one which has been already practised in the form of the Quadrilateral Security Dialogue (QUAD) between the USA, Japan, Australia and India. Though the initiative was taken by Japan's Prime Minister Shinzo Abe, it was also in line with America's aspirations because it helped safeguard its strategic interests in the Asia-Pacific region. In a 2021 joint statement, the QUAD members defined the spirit of Quad as a "shared vision for a free and open Indo-Pacific and a rule-based maritime order in the East and South-China Sea which they state is needed to counter Chinese maritime claims. Similar sounds come from ASEAN states on the occasion of the ASEAN regional summit 2021. Vietnam and the Philippines also warned of growing insecurity in South East Asia. In a joint declaration, ASEAN warned China to stop illegal activities and hostile response in the South China Sea. In fact, not Asia but Australia too is feeling the risk of war with China. The new Australian defence minister, Peter Dutton, and his right-hand at the home affairs department, Michael Pezzulo, speculated about the risk of war with China. He argued that people should not discount the risk of conflict over Taiwan and disturbance in Hong Kong (*The Guardian*, 28 April 2021).

In the last five years, the global order has been on the verge of new changes. A unipolar world order led by America is facing a tough challenge from China in every sphere. The prevalent old international order is under threat of the rising economic powers of Asia. Due to strong economic and military capacity, China is in a dominating position in the entire region whereas America's image of a global leader has declined sharply during the Trump period. His foreign policy of threatening to withdraw from the NATO and from the Paris Agreement on Climate Change and abandoning of Trans Pacific partnership has chipped away at the American global supremacy. The world is, as a result, witness to a more decentralized and pluralistic global order with emerging regional players. It has indications towards structural shifts in global power politics. Against the above backdrop, America is willing to regain its previous position. Therefore, the Biden Administration does not want to lose any chance to besiege China. Thus, the USA is pushing the trans-Atlantic military alliance to counter China. In a communiqué of the NATO Summit on 14 June 2021, China was for first time explicitly described as a security risk which was never figured in NATO Summit declarations earlier. It states: "China's stated ambitious and assertive behaviour present systematic challenges to the rule-based international order and to areas relevant to Alliance Security" (*The Hindu*, 2021). Joe Biden has clearly declared his country's policy towards multilateralism, which includes close connection with traditional allies in the Global North. Thus, the Cornwall summit of G7 countries included heads of states from outside the G7, namely, Australia, South Korea and India. In the summit, G7 leaders launched a 'Build Back Better (B3) World' project which pledges hundreds of billions of infrastructure investment in low and middle income countries to counter China's Belt and Road Initiative. In this way, the Biden Administration wants to mobilize regional alliances behind its larger objective of containing China.

Asia is becoming more and more important and grabbing the attention of global powers due to its geopolitical and strategic significance. After NATO and G-7, the European Union is also ready to reinforce its strategic focus, presence and actions to uphold democracy, human rights, the rule of law and respect for international law. The Council of the European

Union approved conclusions on European Union strategy for cooperation in the Indo-Pacific region and declared its aim to promote multilateralism and support ASEAN to contribute to regional stability, prosperity, security and sustainable development (*The Hindu*, 2021). Thus, the current dynamics in the Indo-Pacific region is ready to intense geopolitical competition in addition to increasing tensions on trade and supply chains as well as in technological, political and security areas.

It is quite clear that the Biden Administration has given a clear indication towards deeper global alliances. In the interim government strategy document, he reiterated that his administration would deepen its partnership with India and work alongside New Zealand, Singapore, Vietnam and other associations of South East Asian nations. Biden said that the vital national interests of America compel the deepest connection to the Indo-Pacific, Europe and the western hemisphere. He further said that the USA would support China's neighbours and trading partners to defend their rights (*The Hindu*, 2021). In fact, it is observed that another significant player in Asian geopolitics, Russia, is not willing to accept the entry of the USA in Asia's regional affairs. Russian President Vladimir Putin recently said that India and China are capable enough to resolve their disputes and there is no need for extra-regional powers to interfere in the process. Russia's past history with USA and its interests to keep silent towards Chinese aggression may suit Russia but for India, it is tough to believe. Though India has the potential and capacity to face China and it has proved it in the Doklam standoff and the Galwan faceoff, when India firmly stood against China, yet it would be better for India to be friends with the USA to balance China because India has two-front challenges in the Himalayan region—one from China and the other from Pakistan. Another reason is that Russia is not as strong today as it was in the past to mitigate all the challenges alone in the region. It has also rejected the Indo-Pacific construct in favour of the Asia-Pacific on the ground that it is a purely an American initiative designed to curtail both China and Russia. Russia is against to the Quad grouping. Mr. Lavrov termed it an 'Asian NATO'. Although Russia was not happy about India's role in QUAD, Indian foreign minister S. Jaishankar clearly stated that no country can have a veto on India's participation in the QUAD. Every country has its own fears and strategic interests by which they govern. India's fear and its interests in the current scenario are more visible and secure in connecting with America but this does not mean that there is a lack of mutual understanding between India and Russia.

In the first QUAD leaders' summit, the Biden Administration signified the importance of the Indo-Pacific region and multilateral engagements and declared the Indo-Pacific as their key priority. Biden said, "China was the only competitor potentially capable of combining its economic diplomatic, military and technological power to mount a sustained challenge to a stable and open international system". Yet he clarified that QUAD is something bigger than a grouping centred around the China challenge. "This is an entity forged and formed because we share a common interest. Maritime security is, of course, an important one but our shared interests go well beyond that (*The Hindu*, 2021, 5 March).

The security of Asia has now become quite challenging due to the active presence of global players in the region. It has become a battlefield of interests of the big powers. The USA raised several issues at the Alaska meeting between the two countries such as deep concerns about the treatment of the Uighur minority in Xinjiang, a crackdown in Hong Kong, Chinese economic coercion and Beijing's increasingly aggressive stance towards Taiwan, while China stressed that it would not make concessions to the USA on key issues. Though China has shown an interest to reset the relations which were pitched into turmoil by the Trump's presidency but at the same time warned that it has no room for compromise on issues concerning its sovereignty, security and core interests. Zhao Lijian, a Chinese spokesperson, urged the USA against talking tough and engaging in "Megaphone diplomacy" toward China (*The Hindu* 2021, 19 March). Therefore, it seems the path is difficult to settle all the tensions but it is required to have table talks to resolve all the issues in a peaceful manner. China's aggressiveness may increase the misbalance and counter collective aggression against it by US forces and its allies which will be extremely fatal for the peace and security of the entire region.

There are three main models of peaceful Asia: 1. United Asia; 2. Bipolar Asia; and 3. Multipolar Asia. The first one is idealistic and not possible in reality. The second one is also not possible because of the absence of specific poles, equal to each other in terms of comparative power, within the region. The third one appears to be the most achievable because multiple centres of power are existing in the region having the capacity to balance each other. Therefore, in the Asian context, only the principle of balance of power can prove to be effective for regional security, stability and peace. There is a need of seven pillars of security on which the structure of development and stability of Asia can be built. These pillars are:

S Security of people
E Economic development for all
C Connecting the region
U Unite people to work as on entity of Asians
R Respect for sovereignty and integrity
I Increase trust
T Trigger harmony and mutual respect
Y Yumminess in relationship

In order to achieve these goals, the first step would go towards strengthening regional institutions and a comprehensive conflict resolution mechanism should be evolved through talks to mitigate regional disputes in a peaceful manner.

REFERENCES

Adler, E. (September 1997), "Seizing the Middle Ground: Constructivism in World Politics", *European Journal of International Relations* 3, 45.

Arezina Sanza, 'US-China relations under the Trump Administration': Changes and Challenges; *China Quarterly of International Strategic Studies*, Vol. 5, No. 3.

Badalan, E. (2009), Sisteme globale de securitate. Bucuresti: Editura Centrului Tehnic-Editorial al Armatei.

Baldwin, David A. (1993), 'Neoliberalism, Neorealism and world politics', in David A. Baldwin (ed.) *Neorealism and Neoliberalism*, New York: Columbia University Press: 1-25.

Buzan, Barry. (1991), "New Pattern of Global Security in 21st Century" in *International Affairs [Royal Institute of International Affairs]* pp. 431-451.

Buzan, Barry (1996), 'The timeless wisdom of realism'? in Steve Smith, Ken Booth and Marysia Zalewaski (eds.) *International Theory 'Positivism and Beyond'*, Cambridge University Press: 47:66.

Carr, E.H. (1946), *The Twenty Years Crisis*, London, Macmillan.

Corona Virus Pandemic further strains US-China relations/DW/01.06.2020, www.dw.com https:// www.dw.com/ en/ corona virus - pandemic – further – strains – us -china-relations/a-53650763.

Der Derian, James (1992), Anti-Diplomacy: *Spies, Terror, Speed and War*. Oxford: Blackwell.

Dodds, Klaus (2007), *Geopolitics: A very short introduction*, Oxford: Oxford University Press.

Dodds, Klaus, and David Atkinson (eds.) (2000), *Geopolitical Traditions: A century of Geopolitical Thought*, London: Routledge.

Doyle, M. (1997), *New Thinking in International Relations, Theory*, Boulder: Westview Press.

Dubey, Sarika, 'Realism Shaping India-China Relations', *World Focus*, Research Journal, October 2020.

Dunne, T. and C. Schmidt (2001), *Realism, Globalisation of World Politics*. J. Baylis and S. Smith, Oxford University Press.

Frankel, Benjamin (1996), 'Restating the realist case: an introduction in Benjamin Frankel (ed.) *Realism: Restatements and Renewal*, London: Frank Carr and Company Limited. IX-XX.

Foot Rosemary, (2020), 'China's rise and US hegemony: Renegotiating hegemonic order in East Asia'. *International Politics*, ISSN 17403898, 4.1.2020.

Gill, Prabhjote, 'China's aggression is not only aimed at India but at least four other countries in the region', 17 June, 2020. https://www.businessinsider.in/defence/news https://www.fmprc.gov.cn/mfa-eng/topics-665678/3698-665962/t18872.shtml.

Grygiel, Jakub J. (2006), *Great Powers and Geopolitical Change Baltimore*, MD: The Johns Hopkins University Press.

Gustov Mel, '*Will this be Chinese Century: A Sceptic's view*', Viva Books, 2017.

Herz, J. (1951) 'Idealist Internationalism and Security Dilemma'. *World Politics* 2(2): 24.

Hyung Gu Lynn, (2007), *Bipolar Orders: The two Korean since 1989*. Zed Books, p. 3.

Jackson, R. Howard and Sorensen George, 2010, *Introduction to International Relations: Theories and approaches*, 4th edition, Oxford University Press, p. 166.

John E. Marz, *Beyond Security: Private Perceptions among Arabs and Israelis*. (New York: International Peace Academy, 1980), p. 105.

Kaura Vinay, "A September exit, Afghanistan at the crossroads", *The Hindu*, 25 May, 2021.

Kissinger, Henry (1976), 'Documentation: Foreign Policy and National Security' *International Security* 1/1:182-191.

Kurki Milija, *Causation in International relations: Redeeming Casual Analysis*, Cambridge University Press, 2008, p. 124, n.1.

Kubalkova, V.N. Onuf, et al. (1998), *International Relations in a Constructed World*: New York, M.E. Sharp Inc.

Kuo, A. Mercy, 'Asia's Geopolitical Challenges: Outlook 2019', *The Diplomat, Trans-Pacific View*, 27 December, 2018. https://thediplomat.com/2018/12/asian-geopolitical-challenges-outlook-2019.

Mehta, Rajesh & Mittal, Diksha, 'Is this the Asian Century? Potential and Challenges in Asia Growth'. *The Financial Express*, Mar 25, 2021.

Mohan, Raja. "Emerging geopolitical Trends and Security in the Association of Southeast Asian Nations, *The People's Republic of China and India* (ACI) Region, ADBI Working Paper Series No. 412, March 2013 p. 6.

Morgenthau, Haus J. (1978), *Politics Among Nations: The struggle for power and peace*, 5th edition, New York: Alfred A. Knopp.

Narayan Rajiv, Major General, AVSM, VSM, '*Achieving the Asian Century: Challenges and Options*'. The United Service Institution of India (USI), 4.29.2021. https://usiofindia.org/publication/ usi-journal/achieving-the-asian-century-challenges-and-options.

North Korea Crisis, *Global Conflict Tracker*, 4/29/2021 https://www.cfr.org/global-conflict-tracker/conflict/north-korea-crisis.

Nye, Joseph S., (2009), *Understanding International Conflicts: An Introduction to Theory and History*, 7th Edition, London: Pearson Longman.

Rigakos S., George, *Marxist Legal Theory: Security 2020*. www.criticallegal thinking.com.

Sang-Hun, Choe, "China Suspends All Coal Imports From North Korea", *The New York Times*, February 18, 2017.

Sheehan Michael, (2005), *International Security An Analytical Survey*, Lynne Rienner Publishers, Boulder London, p. 3.

Sloam, G. and Gray, C.S. (19990, "Why Geopolitics?" In C. S. Gray and G. Sloam, (eds.) *Geopolitics*. London: Frank Cass.

The Economic Times, 8.20.2020.

The Guardian, 28 April, 2021.

The Hindu, 5 March, 2021.

The Hindu, 25 May, 2021.

The Hindu, 20 June, 2021.

The Hindustan Times, 20 June, 2020.

The Japan Times, 22 May 2020.

UN Security Council, 2 June 2017, Security Council Unanimously adopts Resolution Extending Number, Scope of Sanctions against Democratic People's Republic of Korea' United Nations.

Waltz, Kenneth. (1959) *Man, the state and war: a Theoretical Analysis*, New York: Columbia University Press.

Waltz, Kenneth. (1988), 'The origin of war in Neorealist Theory', *The Journal of Interdisciplinary History*, 18/4: 615-628.

Weaver, O. (2004 a), Peace and security: The concepts and their relationship. In: Guzzini, and Jung D (eds.) *Contemporary Security, Analysis and Copenhagen Peace Research*. London: Routledge, pp. 53-65.

Wendt, A. (1999), *Social Theory of International Politics*. New York, Cambridge University Press.

Wolfers, A. (1952), "National Security as an Ambiguous Symbol". *Political Science Quarterly*, 67(4): 22.

3

Asia's Nuclear Problematique: Nuclear Contests Impairing Asia's Security Order

Vinod Kumar

Introduction

The ongoing decade, the second of the millennium, had begun on a promising note as far as global nuclear matters are concerned. Having set the tone with a Nobel-winning speech in Prague in April 2009, the then US President, Barack Obama, had spearheaded a handful of initiatives, even if incremental, to progress towards a nuclear weapons-free world.[1] These included the United Nations Security Council (UNSC) Resolution 1887, which resolved to create ideal conditions for disarmament;[2] a Nuclear Security Initiative to secure fissionable materials and nuclear-related resources worldwide;[3] a Nuclear Posture Review (NPR) that sought to reduce the primacy of nuclear weapons in the US national security strategy; and a comparatively successful (Kumar, 2010) Review Conference (RevCon) of the Treaty on the Nuclear Non-Proliferation of Nuclear Weapons (NPT),[4] to name a prominent few (Kumar, 2011). The outcome of these initiatives was the progressive movement towards a condition that could either be termed as a 'nuclear peace dividend' or a 'post-proliferation world' – both characteristically disparate conceptualisations, but commonly signifying lesser risks of nuclear flare-ups, diminishing instances of proliferation, minimal chances of nuclear break-outs and even lesser probability of nuclear weapons or related resources falling into the wrong hands.[5] A reason for these advances, however, has not just been Obama's policies but also the imprint of his predecessor, George W. Bush, whose Administration ran a series of proactive initiatives under the rubric of 'counter-proliferation' which used military tools to track and target proliferation networks especially in countries with a record of such activities (Mauroni, 2019; Kumar 2014).[6] Adding to this momentum were the instances of effective non-proliferation diplomacy during the early half of the decade, particularly the six-party template to engage Iran and North Korea in correcting their nuclear deviance. While the dialogue with North Korea produced mixed results, this multilateral model was successful in carving out a nuclear deal with Iran, in order to ensure complete submission of its civilian nuclear programme to inspections besides terminating suspicious activities at its nuclear facilities in return for the withdrawal of international sanctions.

These encouraging signs in the global nuclear scene, in fact, produced a significant upshot: over 122 nations voted in July 2017 for a Treaty on the Prohibition of Nuclear Weapons (or the ban treaty) as a 'stand-alone' instrument to de-legitimise nuclear weapons.[7] The driving spirit behind this initiative was the broader belief among a majority of nations that the conditions are finally ripe to pursue disarmament and total elimination of nuclear weapons, with the ban treaty emerging as a constructive, if not pragmatic, means towards this end.[8]

Whither 'Nuclear Peace'

While the above-mentioned trends were largely phenomena of the first decade with its splinter effects in the second half, the last few years had seen a sudden and significant reversal to these gains and momentum with a series of events and actions, primarily in the Asian hemisphere, threatening to derail the nuclear 'peace dividend' and push the prospects of a post-proliferation world further away. Foremost among these events was US President Donald Trump's decision to jettison the hard-negotiated deal of 2015 to curb the Iranian nuclear programme, an action seen as bereft of any concrete rationale but for the whimsical behaviour usually identified with the US President.[9] Iran's decision to restart uranium enrichment, after months of hoping for the deal to be salvaged by its European parties, has brought West Asia to the brink of another conflict with increasing skirmishes over sea lanes and trading entities (Mostaghim and Etehad, 2019).

The other zone of nuclear unrest was the Korean Peninsula, which was witness to some unique events that departed from its historical pattern of hostilities, though nowhere near bringing stability to the region. Since the Agreed Framework was first formulated in 1994 to curb its nuclear ambitions, North Korea has had a history of wavering compliance, repeated violations and occasional conciliatory phases that have recurred into predictable cyclic patterns. From the middle years of this decade, Kim-Un Jong, the North Korean leader, had treaded into paths of brinkmanship and rapid expansion of his nuclear arsenal and delivery capabilities. An aggressive response from the Trump Administration to this build-up resulted in months of sabre-rattling threatening to aggravate into full-fledged military hostilities. However, in a dramatic twist, frayed tempers were calmed when the South Korean President, Moon Jae-In, initiated a historic peace move that culminated in a deal with his North Korean counterpart in April 2018.[10] This breakthrough led to another major historical event, the first ever meeting of North Korean and American leadership since the Korean War, with Trump and Kim-Un Jong, confabulating in Singapore on 9 June 2018 (Kim, 2018). Although high on symbolism and sans any agreements, the Summit was instrumental in reducing the tensions in the Peninsula and generating hopes that permanent peace will ultimately blossom in the region, along with its potential de-nuclearisation. A second Trump-Kim Summit in March 2019 did not repeat the optics of the first nor resulted in any deal on curbing Kim's nuclear forays which led to concerns on whether these peace moves will only be a temporary lull before Kim unleashes a fresh onslaught of nuclear one-upmanship hysteria (Sanger and Wong, 2019).

South Asia's status as the foremost nuclear hotspot remained unchanged as the two nuclear-armed neighbours indulged in numerous face-offs that erupt over the low-intensity conflict (LIC) run under a nuclear overhang. Pakistan's attempt to wrest back Jammu and Kashmir since the time of independence through territorial aggrandizement and terror campaigns had resulted in numerous wars and military-level hostilities. Since 1998, nuclear weapons have been introduced in this matrix as a result of major terror attacks and resultant crises raise concerns of an impending nuclear conflagration, triggering international intervention. Though nuclear deterrence has evolved towards maturity in the two decades after the South Asian neighbours went nuclear, Pakistan continued to exploit loopholes in India's nuclear doctrine to effectively implement its LIC by seeking to deter Indian response by projecting ambiguous nuclear use thresholds and nuclear brinkmanship behaviour (Raghavan, 2001; Chari, 2003; Sagan and Waltz, 1995; Ganguly and Kapur, 2010).

However, since the terror attack on Parliament in December 2001, India has been exercising a combination of measures including tactical strike options below the nuclear overhang and technological platforms like missile defence to deny Pakistan the space to exploit the doctrinal space and dominate the escalation mantle. The surgical strikes across the Line of Control (LoC) in September 2016 (after a terror attack at the Uri army camp) followed by an air strike on terror camps in Pakistan's Balakot in February 2019 became demonstrations of India's resolve to undertake military operations under a nuclear overhang, which has, however, raised concerns on how escalation dynamics are likely to turn out in the event of another major terror attack in Indian territory (Singh, 2017).[11] A recent Indian government decision to terminate a special constitutional status for Jammu and Kashmir (J&K) and bifurcate the territory has led to fresh stand-offs that could billow into a new crisis. At the other end of the spectrum, the ongoing strategic competition between the three leading nuclear powers – the USA, China and Russia – has not just the potential to reverse the gains of the nuclear 'peace dividend' but also trigger a new wave of arms race with certain impact on the political dynamics of the Asia-Pacific region. Though the 'hegemonic' powers have been vying for strategic dominance since the end of Cold War, its nuclear imprint had remained curtailed for a brief while with the momentum in favour of reducing the primacy of nuclear weapons in national security strategies and the long-running nuclear reductions by the USA and Russia providing an interregnum. While the Chinese strategic modernisation, which had galloped at a steady pace, has been an aberration to this trend, the recent years are witness to the erstwhile superpowers entering a new era of armament.

Soon after taking office in January 2017, President Donald Trump had declared that he could overhaul the 'archaic' American nuclear weapons complex by initiating the development of new strategic missile platforms (to replace the Minuteman-III) along with overall expansion of strategic weapon capabilities. However, even before this plan could fruitfully take-off, Russian President Vladimir Putin unveiled in March 2018 an array of new-generation weaponry, which, he proclaimed, was primarily intended to negate the American missile defence system, but in its demonstrated intensity comes with unprecedented firepower that could invariably alter global nuclear dynamics.[12] Considering the global reach of these fledging arsenals, the Eurasian hinterland, particularly the Indo-Pacific, will be the key theatre for this strategic competition. What do these developments spell for global nuclear affairs in general and Asian security in particular? Are they embodying a reversal of the nuclear 'peace-dividend' and a new arms race on the anvil, particularly in the Asian nuclear hotspots? What does the shift of the nuclear epicentre to Asia mean for the region? Notwithstanding some of these questions that emerge out of these events, the nuclear problematique[13] in Asia has its own unique dimensions, which, when explored deeply, could provide insights on the varied implications of these events and the larger nuclear gaming in the trans-continental theatres. Through a transient overview of the Asian nuclear enclaves, this paper essays the anatomy of Asia's nuclear problematique and what it bodes for the region's security architectures.

The Nuclear Epicentre, sans any Leverage

Of the 195 nations worldwide, there are nine nuclear-armed states of which five are recognised nuclear weapon states (NWS) under the NPT and the remaining four assumed as States with Nuclear Weapons (SNW), implying they are nuclear-armed but not recognised as such. While China happens to be the only Asian NWS, all the four SNWs – India, Pakistan, Israel and North Korea – are from Asia. Of these four, Israel has refused to confirm or deny its nuclear weapons possession while the remaining three have conducted nuclear weapon tests and have established formal or latent deterrence structures (Cohen, 1998; Karpin, 2006; Farr, 1999). North Korea is the only Asian country that has been a NPT state party and has invoked Article X to withdraw from the treaty, in the process being tagged as a bad example of a state using NPT membership to access civilian nuclear resources and misusing such access to clandestinely develop a nuclear weapons capability (Bermudez, 2015).

India is the only one among these 'outliers' to have gained some kind of legitimacy for its nuclear weapons after its agreement with the USA (widely termed as the India-US nuclear deal)[14] led to its acceptance of many non-proliferation norms in return for greater "integration with the regime" (Kumar, 2014).[15] Having stayed away or resisted many of these norms for a long time, citing their discriminatory nature, the nuclear deal brought India back into the non-proliferation mainstream, enabled its access to nuclear commerce, and positioned it as the only country outside the NPT system which got to keep its nuclear weapons and run its civilian nuclear programme with international participation without having to accede to the treaty.[16] The deal, as the first-of-its-kind arrangement after a rule-based nuclear order came into being, drew ruminations and global attention on the Asian landscape: the high presence of nuclear-armed as well as nuclear-latent states in the region (surpassing the Western hemisphere), the emergence of a nuclear energy industrial base with more countries in the region adopting or expanding their nuclear power infrastructure, and how this complex nuclear dynamic had to be managed, streamlined and controlled within the normative architecture (established by the West). The complexity and enigma have been such that many observers continue to remain inconclusive on pinning the actual rationale behind the India-US nuclear deal.

Pakistan's case has been equally peculiar having followed the Indian nuclear development trajectory, brick-by-brick, yet losing out on the recognition the Indian programme gained through the nuclear deal. The Pakistani nuclear pursuit, particularly its bellicose nuclear behaviour, has been a key element of the Asian nuclear problematique largely because it had adopted nuclear brinkmanship as a core nuclear posturing and had used its nuclear capability as a bulwark in its proxy war against India. The more significant Pakistani imprint on the nuclear landscape, however, was the colossal nuclear proliferation footprint it had created around the globe as also being the hotspot where the international community believed nuclear terrorism could hold its probable genesis. The nuclear black market supposedly spearheaded by A.Q. Khan, described as the 'father' of Pakistan's nuclear programme, was known to have facilitated access to nuclear-related materials and technology for a handful of proliferators spanning the Asian hemisphere (Levy and Scott-Clark, 2007). That Pakistan's nuclear programme also thrived from an active proliferation channel with North Korea, with the tacit involvement of China, also added to the unsavoury dimension in Asian nuclear affairs.

Iran's nuclear deviance of over a decade, along with the North Korean leadership's theatrics, also dominated the discourse over non-proliferation norms for a long period since the end of the Cold War. However, neither Iran's quest for nuclear 'autonomy' nor North Korea's prolonged dilly-dalliance of those years could be seen in isolation as a whole lot of other countries had sought independent nuclear identities and journeys, largely prompted by the uncertainty of the post-Cold War strategic environment and individual security considerations. Notable instances include Brazil, South Korea and Egypt – all of them, subsequently, been cajoled to discard their deviance and return to compliance with non-proliferation norms. The curious dimension is of the Asian actors in this list: South Korea and Egypt happened to be in Asian zones where distinct nuclear dynamics were innately shaping up, namely, the Israeli nuclear capability and its inimical relations with Arab countries in West Asia, and the North Korean quest and the US nuclear umbrella vitiating the security milieu in the Korean Peninsula. While these elements could easily explain why many actors in these regions were self-indulgent in individual nuclear pursuits or latency limits, the fact that only some deviant cases like Egypt and South Korea could be redirected back to normative compliance even as others like Iran and North Korea continued to stick to non-compliance and defiance, was in itself exemplar of other push-and-pull factors in the nuclear domain.

Asia certainly had turned into the nuclear epicentre; yet the ability of Asian nations, both the nuclear-armed and the nuclear-capable ones, to influence and shape global non-proliferation and nuclear trading norms or exercise leverage over the regime's instruments were limited or marginal. In fact, the affairs of the Asian nuclear landscape, like in other regions, were, in effect, controlled by the hegemonic powers based on the norms set by the Western liberal security community (LSC) (Chafetz, 1995). While China happens to be the prominent Asian power at the nuclear high table, as the only Asian NWS at the P-5 groupings and among the three in the Nuclear Suppliers Group (NSG), Beijing is only making gradual inroads in the hegemonic power system that drafts and crafts the global security architectures.[17] China has yet to shape any major policy or normative initiatives in the non-proliferation regime, hitherto devoting a considerable effort on repairing its own past sullied proliferation record, and in recent times, playing supporting roles (like in the six-party talks to resolve the Iran and North Korean nuclear imbroglios) as well as some spoiler roles (blocking India from gaining NSG membership).

Thus, Asia's nuclear actors have been essentially playing the game on the rules set by the Western liberal security community and the great power cliques at their helm. Even a unique template like the India-US nuclear deal had happened only because of the initiative taken by the USA, as the hegemonic power dominating the regime, and had decided to reward countries like India with a decent non-proliferation record (despite being outside the regime) while punishing the violators. That the initiative was backed by the LSC and other great powers (reluctantly by China and Japan) not just demonstrated the influence the hegemon exerted but also the fact that the Asian nuclear enclave had secondary status in the regime's normative ordering, besides having to seek legitimacy from the dominant community. The same imprint could be located in the template used to deal with Iran and North Korea impasses and how the LSC and the hegemonic leadership set the terms and frameworks for these countries to sustain their nuclear pathways. That none of the Asian countries, including 'anti-nuclear' Japan, were prominent participants in the nuclear weapons ban treaty initiative is also testament to how the Asian nuclear enclave, despite its dominant numbers, remains as marginal players in the global nuclear order.

Security Dilemmas and Deficits

Though some literature emanating from Western academic circles have invoked elements like 'power pursuit' and 'prestige' to explain the expansive nuclear imprint in Asia, the actual political characterisation of the Asian nuclear landscape has to invariably revolve around the security relationships in the region. Accordingly, the influence and effects of a security dilemma – wherein the acquisition or expansion of military capabilities by one state could menace its neighbours or rivals – as a constant reverberates on most Asian security interactions, and nuclear decisions in particular. The recurrent frictions in the sub-regional security complexes and the evolution of various nuclear dyads within those complexes are imagery of the actual Asian nuclear landscape and the problematique that organically emerged in the region. Being part of the

Eurasian geo-strategic hinterland, Asian countries have been integral constituents of the nuclear constructs that marked the superpower rivalries during the Cold War. The invocation of the nuclear umbrella (security guarantees) along with the physical placement of nuclear weapons belonging to the superpowers in their territories had essentially implied the inherent nuclearisation of the Asian protagonists of the Cold War within the alliance frameworks.[18] That the purported American nuclear threat during the Korean War and the creeping rivalry with the Soviets had prompted the Chinese leader Mao Zedong to consider development of nuclear weapons, after initially terming them as 'paper tigers', are also historical caricature of the spectre of the security dilemma triggering the initial seeds of the nuclear imprint in the Asian region (Riqiang, 2013; Yunzhu, 2008).

An innate element of the security dilemma phenomenon is the ability to create a domino effect, wherein the response of a 'menaced' rival country to a neighbour's acquisition or expansion of military capability could lead to spiral of similar reactions in the neighbourhood, particularly if the responding actor has other rivals or is also part of another security dyad. While the American nuclear umbrella for its allies in East Asia and the larger impact of superpower arsenals in Asia could have buttressed the Chinese nuclear quest, Beijing's attainment of the capability in 1964 set off reverberations in Southern Asia with the Indian leadership being beset by a clamour within the country to come up with a nuclear weapon riposte to China. It took India a decade more of confabulations as well as many endogenous and exogenous catalysts (including the passage of an imbalanced NPT) to decide (Kumar, 2017) on a similar capability demonstration through the 'Peaceful Nuclear Explosion' in 1974. Pakistan responded instantly by declaring its resolve to pursue a nuclear weapons programme with its leadership having avowed a little earlier to 'eat grass' if needed to do so as a nation to develop nuclear weapons (Khan, 2012).[19] That Pakistan managed to weave a narrative of an 'Islamic bomb' around its nuclear project has had its inevitable reverberations in its extended neighbourhood spreading out into the conflict-ridden and Arab-dominated West Asia, where Israel's nuclear capability and postural ambivalence was already an existential reason for a security dilemma enveloping the region. Much like in Southern Asia, where perennial conflict had fed the nuclear weaponisation impulse, the unending hostilities over the post-colonial redrawing of West Asia political boundaries was perfect conditioning for nuclear ambitions. Since the time of Israel's perceived acquisition of nuclear weapons in 1967, the West Asian strategic environment had been abuzz for decades on which Arab state will take over the gambit of providing a response to the Israeli capability.

Yet, the fact that Israel had not flaunted its arsenal and had preferred to remain opaque on its nuclear capabilities had lessened the gravity of the security dilemma that had troubled the Arab leaderships (Krzyzaniak, 2019; Borger, 2014; Webb, 2019; DePetris, 2019). The dilemma also had a politico-cultural subplot revolving around the Sunni-Shia rivalry in the region that seeded the possibility of nuclear pursuits from the warring intra-faith factions which will be intended not just to counter Israel but also markedly against each other. While Shia-dominated Iran has traversed a path of nuclear latency and raised suspicions, as well as indicative actions, towards building a nuclear weapons capability, the Saudis, as the fountainhead of the Sunni camp, had also expressed their nuclear ambitions in cryptic terms, besides reports that Riyadh had also provided funds to Pakistan's nuclear programme in order to buttress the cause of the 'Islamic bomb', and certainly a Sunni one at that (Urban, 2013; Young, 2018). The spectre of a security dilemma as seen across the Asian theatres may only marginally differ in their fundamental characteristics with that of other regions. For example, unlike in the case of Europe, where the alliance system was a key driver in shaping security relationships and structures, the phenomenon in Asia was more about sub-regional and dyadic political rivalries or territorial contestations that were passed on as post-War and post-colonial legacies. Yet, a closer look at the Asian nuclear problematique points to a deeper conditioning that goes beyond security dilemmas and such conventional constructs of security relationships. Western analyses have largely sought to portray the pursuit of 'prestige' or 'power' as key casual for both vertical and horizontal nuclear proliferation in Asia, whereas the fundamental driver of nuclear pursuits in the Asian dyads and sub-regions has been the enduring pursuit of security, be it for maximising security (often depicted as the power pursuit) or addressing the security deficit.

Security deficit implies a perceptive condition when a state considers major gaps in its capabilities to defend itself against a superior rival, which prompts it to seek options beyond the conventional military means to rectify the asymmetry and gain parity. This quest could encompass a wide extent of possibilities ranging from development of nuclear weapons, engaging in asymmetric warfare methods (insurgency and terrorism), seeking technological alternatives like cyber warfare methods (for subversion and passive offence), and band wagonning with a hegemon for counter-balancing or for security services including a nuclear umbrella, military aid and setting up a diplomatic support base (for international political campaigns). Beyond the condition of a state acquiring a superior capability and menacing its rivals, security deficit as a phenomenon has been glaring in each of the Asian nuclear enclaves. The Chinese leadership's decision to discard their aversion towards nuclear weapons and pursue the capability was not driven by any neighbourhood rival acquiring the capability but by the American nuclear threat in response to the Chinese role in the Korean War. Similarly, the deployment of US nuclear weapons in South Korea, essentially meant to deter the Communist dominance of East Asia, also provided a nuclear umbrella for US allies in the region, Japan and South Korea, thus inherently addressing their security deficit derived by the Chinese acquisition. Decades down the line, North Korea's acquisition of an existential nuclear deterrence had revived the perception of a security deficit for the East Asian countries, which have mulled their own security enhancement options notwithstanding the prevalence of American security guarantees (though US nuclear weapons were withdrawn in 1991) and the expansive deployment of missile defence systems (Kristensen and Norris, 2018).

The Indian example was invariably a classic case of a security dilemma driven by the Chinese acquisition of nuclear weapons, two years after China dealt a humiliating defeat in a border war. However, it has to be noted that despite intense domestic pressure from within the country, the Indian leadership refused to initially respond to the recurring Chinese nuclear tests since 1964 by developing its own nuclear weapons (Jain, 1974).[20] Instead, the political leadership maintained its allegiance to the position of disarmament and the long-held decision not to pursue a weapons programme. In the Indian case, the dilemma was aggravated by the perception of deficit, on how to fulfil its security aspirations without replicating the Chinese action. The leadership initially sought a non-weaponised means to address the deficit while upholding its dogmatic positioning. As a result, India pushed for a comprehensive disarmament instrument that could enable non-proliferation of nuclear weapons, facilitate phased reductions of stockpiles leading to a credible disarmament process and total elimination. While seeking incorporation of these objectives in the NPT, India also sought security guarantees from the nuclear powers to deal with nuclear threats and intervene in the event of a nuclear attack (Noorani, 2001; Kumar, 2014).

It was only when India realised that these objectives were not fulfilled in the NPT text and no insulation provided against the fledging Chinese arsenal that India decided to reject the NPT, and, six years later, demonstrate the capability for a nuclear explosion. Though it has described the test as a 'peaceful nuclear explosion',[21] the test was indisputably a demonstration of nuclear weapon capability, even if India had continued to insist that it will not develop this capability.[22] It was in the early to mid-1980s when indications of Pakistan moving towards a nuclear weapons capability emerged that the decision was apparently taken to exercise the nuclear weapon option, though actual nuclearisation took another decade to happen (Perkovich, 1999).[23] Assuming that the device was supposedly ready by the early 1990s, actual test demonstration of the capability in 1998 was made after a series of developments that essentially complicated India's enduring quest for comprehensive security. These include the indefinite extension of the NPT after its initial period of 25 years and the passage of the Comprehensive Test Ban Treaty (CTBT), both of which, India perceived, could sustain the 'discriminatory' nuclear order, and particularly, allow NWS like China to maintain their arsenals (Ghose, 1997).[24] The 1998 tests and proclamation of a nuclear deterrent were thus deemed to be a permanent solution to address the security deficit.

But for the clandestine nuclear trading through the infamous 'Khan network' and the vitriolic interface with the terror infrastructure, Pakistan's nuclear programme could also be classified as a relentless pursuit of security and addressing a perceived threat to survival as a nation-state (Chakma, 2009; Hassan, 2017). The India-Pakistan strategic matrix has often evoked a sense of being a classic case of security dilemma, wherein their acquisitions and expansion of military capabilities had menaced each other. However, the manner in which Pakistan's nuclear quest has evolved clearly underlines the efforts to address a perennial perception of security deficit—oscillating from security maximalism and asymmetric means to establishing offensive nuclear posturing, all of which, the leadership assumed will secure the nation from threat to its survival. Having originated from a conflictious relationship with India, Pakistan found superpower band wagonning as a reliable means to garner resources for its congenital struggle for political identity, which, it felt, was incomplete without territorial and cultural culmination. The membership with the Western alliance through the Central Treaty Organisation (CENTO) and South East Asian Treaty Organisation (SEATO), and later on as a major non-NATO ally, were expressions to address the security and political deficit it had inherited through colonial legacy. When global strategic transformations put limits to these endeavours, Pakistan found nuclear weapons as a panacea for all strategic challenges: seeking parity with India's conventional superiority, deterring Indian response to its proxy war campaigns, internationalising the Kashmir dispute and indulging in brinkmanship to project the region as a nuclear hotspot.

Pakistan's decision, after its own series of nuclear tests in 1998, to adopt an opaque doctrinal position by keeping its nuclear strike options open and at the same time indulge in ambiguous posturing on the redlines of such usage was a testament to this approach of positioning nuclear weapons as the pivot of its security strategy. For many years after initiating nuclearisation in the early 1980s and after going overt in 1998, Pakistan had managed to largely fulfil its security goals through its nuclear strategy though the strategic transformations in South Asia, mainly India's own capability acquisition and military strategies, had sustained Pakistan's security deficit. As a result, Pakistan is now attempting realignments like 'full-spectrum deterrence' to address the deficit and gain the upper hand in the security maximisation endeavour (Salik, 2016). Unlike in South Asia where nuclear weapons have been conditioning the security environment, West Asia continues to host a complex matrix of security relationships with nuclear capabilities providing a latent backdrop. But for Israel's purported possession, nuclear weapons are yet to make an operational presence in the region; yet, many actors in the region have had, and continue to have, active conversations on nuclear weapons and the means as well as the conditions under which it should be acquired. Iraq under Saddam Hussein was close to achieving the capability in the late 1980s to sharpen his already deadly arsenal of biological and chemical weapons. Egypt was caught with violations in the 1990s while Saudi Arabia is known to have kept its nuclear weapons decision open. Then there is the case of

Iran which had braved international sanctions and economic bankruptcy to persist on a decade-long episode of defiance through violations which were deemed to have brought it closer to breaking out.

What can one make of this West Asian syndrome? National actors in the region do not seem to be menaced by a perceptive capability possessed by one of them; rather their quest seems centred on the objective of addressing the perceived deficit created by the monopolistic and asymmetric acquisition by one state in a region torn by numerous conflicts and contestations. Notwithstanding the fact that Israel has never projected or confirmed its nuclear capability, the gravity of the political conflict and sectarian divide has been such that prominent actors in the region – Saudis and Iran representing conflicting Islamic camps – had to either confine their explorations to some level of latency or risk international angst and violation of NPT through full-fledged nuclearisation. Considering that Israel is politically indemnified by the Americans, Washington's Sunni friends in the region cannot aspire to gain a US security guarantee whereas Russia's political support to Iran also may not translate into a nuclear umbrella nor could be seen as deep enough a relationship to address Teheran's security deficit.

Having denied any nuclear weapon ambitions throughout the whole decade when it engaged in repeated acts of defiance, non-compliance and violations, it was clear from Iran's actions that it was working on a level of latency that could enable it a break-out space as and when needed (Heinonen, 2015). This was amply evident in the manner in which Iran galloped on its nuclear-related infrastructure – particularly the massive centrifuge installation in the second enrichment plant at Fordow, building of the heavy water and reprocessing plant at Arak and the activities at Parchin suspected to have military applications – and sought to be evasive towards inspections and scrutiny by the IAEA. Certainly so, the larger objective of the Joint Comprehensive Plan of Action (JCPOA) agreed between Iran and P5+1 (Germany) on 14 July 2015 was to drastically reduce the intensity and depth of latency by decapitating the accumulated infrastructure.[25] Sample this: IR-1 centrifuges were to be trimmed from over 19000 to around 6000, with 5060 operational ones at Natanz and remaining 1044 in Fordow transitioned to R&D applications; enriched uranium stockpiles cut down to 300 kg of 3.67 per cent enriched UF6 or equivalent in other chemical forms and excess stocks to be sold to international buyers or down-blended to natural uranium level; over 11,000 kg of low-enriched uranium to be shipped to Russia; Arak Heavy Water/Reprocessing Plant to be redesigned for R&D with no scope for any reprocessing or plutonium production; and comprehensive IAEA monitoring and Iran's ratification of Additional Protocol, among others. These measures, the deal enforcers assumed, could drastically increase the break-out time from a few weeks to several months though President Trump, who announced US withdrawal from the deal in May 2018, felt that the provisions of the deal were weak enough to enable the Iranian regime to breakout "in just a short period of time".[26]

After hoping for months that the European troika (UK, France and Germany) would salvage the deal, Iran restarted uranium enrichment beyond 'permissible' limits in September 2019 and declared that it would incrementally take measures to cut nuclear deal commitments until reaching the "desired results" (Dehghanpisheh, 2019). While such actions and statements could be aimed at applying pressure, especially on the European parties, it seems unlikely that Iran might return to a pre-July 2015 condition considering the economic and political costs it had incurred during the decade of defiance and the reason why it had purportedly agreed to the deal. Nonetheless, the fact that the collapse of the nuclear deal has triggered fresh hostilities in West Asia, involving numerous regional and extra-regional actors and spilling into other regions, underlines not just its political ramifications but also how security relationships are being vitiated in the region over these nuclear contestations.[27] That the rumblings over the deal add to the ongoing sectarian tensions rising out of the Saudi action against the Houthi rebels in Yemen, allegedly backed by the Iranians, make it amply evident that not just politico-cultural schisms but also the dilemmas and deficits are destined to endure in the region (Allinson, 2019). With allegations that the spectacular drone strike on Saudi's largest oil plant in Abqaiq in September 2019 was launched from Iran, tensions in West Asia are on the verge of breaking into a full-fledged conflict, with certain implications on its nuclear dynamics.

Conclusion

Asia has been a secondary player in the post-Westphalian world, playing second fiddle to the European powers during the World War and to the superpowers during the Cold War. Despite its civilisational legacies, Asia's quest for identity and security in the post-War and post-colonial world, however diverse that effort has been, was contingent on how the great powers were to shape the post-War global order. Having been forced into political boundaries drawn by the European colonialists, much of the post-War conflict in Asia was among civilisational siblings trying to locate and establish their politico-cultural identities within the nation-states they were structured into. Nuclear weapons were introduced into this milieu by the superpowers – the Soviet arsenal being integral to the Eurasian theatre and the American deployment in the 1950s – thus making it an inevitable element of Asia's political contests and strategic competitions. Unlike the organic assimilation of nuclear weapons into the European strategic scene in the post-War conditioning, in Asia it was more like a forbidden fruit being denied to them for possession or development but flaunted around for their wellbeing by the 'guardians'. These elements are writ large in the psyche of nuclear decision-making in Asia. Having tested before the NPT's cut-off date of 1 January 1967, China ended up as the only recognised nuclear weapon state in Asia, which, in turn, is also a reflection of how global nuclear norms – be it the cornerstone NPT, atoms for peace bargain[28] or the NSG trading guidelines – failed to account for Asian aspirations and were enforced on them top-down. Yet, the fact that the region became home to four nuclear outliers is ample narrative on how many of the Asian nuclear programmes were an enduring resistance to these normative structures and the struggle to attain what has been denied to them through the rules made by the (Western) liberal security community.

When this endeavour got conjoined with the lasting quest for security from the political fissures of the post-War and Cold War years, the Western communities saw the Asian nuclear pursuits as driven by objectives of power and prestige. There were certain exceptions like North Korea where the Kim family sought to use nuclear weapons to also ensure the survival of their dynastic regime, though, also seeking to maintain status quo for the communist system that emerged from the Korean War. Elsewhere, it was all security dilemmas and deficits out in full play and shaping the nuclear dynamics. Individual national notions on the purpose of nuclear weapons, as collectively forged or portrayed through the leadership's thinking, differed only marginally with commonalities of security aspirations and pursuit of dignity and respect on the global stage. The paper concludes with an iteration of two variables that are likely to influence the further course of the Asian nuclear problematique. They are as follows:

Leadership: The current crisis in West Asia flowing from the US withdrawal from the Iran nuclear deal exemplifies a key element – leaderships greatly shape and chart the course of events that lead to either conflict or peace. While Nobel-winner Barack Obama had profoundly contributed to the 'peace dividend' by finding the middle ground and getting Iran to agree on a deal through reasonable restrictions, his successor immensely exercised his personal aversion to this arrangement and initiated an action that has plunged a whole region into turmoil. The same individual, however, charted a diametrically different course of action on North Korea, by leaping into a peace initiative after months of mindless sabre rattling. Trump's differing actions in two Asian theatres begs the question – are not nuclear weapons too serious a business to be left to whimsical leaderships alone? Similarly, the maddening build-up of the North Korean arsenal in the last few years and the brinkmanship of Kim Jong-Un had raised concerns on what it means to have nuclear weapons in the hands of an 'irrational' actor, a question that was earlier posed on Pakistan's nuclear behaviour. Though it is widely assumed that the use of nuclear blackmail is only to leverage the political benefits of nuclear deterrence, it is evident that the extent and limits of 'rationality' exercised by individual leaderships will substantially shape Asia's nuclear landscape in the coming future.

Asian Nuclear Contests have a Global Impact: Many studies constantly point to the huge human consequences, namely the death of millions of people, if India and Pakistan end up in a nuclear war (Toon, et. al, 2019). While this could be the case with a nuclear conflagration in any part of the world, it is also a truism that the world is not any closer to a nuclear conflict but only likely to witness more and more nuclear-related contests and strategic competitions. The implications of these contests, however, are two-fold: one, the billowing of various crises into other regions, and second, the 'Asian century' being halted or hindered. A recent example of how Asian nuclear tussles have spilled out is how a completely unrelated province like Gibraltar became host to the detention of an Iranian ship by British authorities, which led to a reprisal seizure of a British vessel by the Iranians. In both cases, many foreign nationals, who were crew members of these vessels, were detained which led to diplomatic intervention by many countries to get their citizens freed. On the other hand, it is a known fact that global oil prices will spiral out of control at the first hint of conflict in West Asia. The spectacular attack on a Saudi oil plant when contrasted with the constraints placed on Iran's oil infrastructure merely underline how elements like oil and nuclear become building blocks of the larger political and strategic gaming that has been enacted in this region.

Similarly, the girding of loins in the Korean peninsula has had its political and economic impact not just in East Asia but across the whole of the Asia-Pacific, or its latest geo-strategic connotation, the Indo-Pacific. Further, the crisis in the Korean peninsula has had an instant trans-Pacific imprint with North Korea demonstrating the capability to target the US west coast. That Washington, as protector of its East Asian allies, is an integral part of the Korean contests makes its Eurasian competitors in the neighbourhood, China and Russia, having to be actively involved in strategic manoeuvring to counter undue American influence in the region. That China is already locked in a game of supremacy and domination with the USA in the Indo-Pacific further supplements these nuclear tussles. With such an elaborate spread of the strategic imprint within Asia and across other regions, it is worth speculating how these contestations are going to affect the Asian political project or the 'Asian century'. Considering that the nuclear tussles had added to the existing political rivalries and economic competitions among the great powers in various Asian theatres, it would not be inaccurate to infer that the rise of Asia has been slowed in its tracks, even if temporarily (Auslin, 2017; Romei and Reed, 2019).

NOTES

1. Among other things, Obama promised to reduce the role of nuclear weapons in the US national security strategy, pursue a New START agreement with Russia and also ensure the ratification of the Comprehensive Test Ban Treaty (CTBT). See "Remarks by President Barack Obama, Prague, Czech Republic," Office of the Press Secretary, White House, 5 April 2009, available at: https://obamawhitehouse.archives.gov/the-press-office/remarks-president-barack-obama-prague-delivered, accessed in August 2019.
2. See *Resolution 1887, Maintenance of international peace and security: Nuclear non-proliferation and nuclear disarmament*, 24 September 2009, available at: http://unscr.com/en/resolutions/1887, accessed in August 2019.
3. For a glimpse on the nuclear security summits, see "FACT SHEET: The Nuclear Security Summits: Securing the World from Nuclear Terrorism," Office of the Press Secretary, White House, 29 March 2016, https://obamawhitehouse.archives.gov/the-press-office/

2016/03/29/fact-sheet-nuclear-security-summits-securing-world-nuclear-terrorism, accessed in August 2019.

4. Despite promising to strengthen the NPT, the US delegation diluted many disarmament proposals at the RevCon, though, ensuring that a Final Document was issued, unlike in the case of many other post-Cold War RevCon outcomes.
5. These are conceptualizations that have not yet gained definite contours, but are loose descriptions used in different contexts. For a larger paradigm, nuclear 'peace dividend' could be the cumulative results that are accrued from a comprehensive whole of measures and conditions wherein nuclear risks and competitions have lessened and the threat of a nuclear war no longer exists, even if seen as presumptive. A post-proliferation, on the other hand, is a point when no more proliferation is likely to occur, again a presumptive condition. While the prospects of new nuclear break-outs seemed bleak, nuclear arsenals of a few nuclear-armed states have seen expansion.
6. The foremost ventures of Bush's counter-proliferation programme included the Proliferation Security Initiative, Container Security Initiative, Global Nuclear Energy Partnership (GNEP), among others, besides the measures taken to implement key UN Security Council Resolutions like UNSCR 1540 and also the Additional Protocol of the International Atomic Energy Agency (IAEA).
7. Text of the treaty available at: http://www.icanw.org/wp-content/uploads/2018/06/tpnw-info-kit-v2.pdf. For a detailed coverage, see "The Treaty on the Prohibition of Nuclear Weapons At A Glance," *Arms Control Association*, September 2017, available at: https://www.armscontrol.org/factsheets/nuclearprohibition. Also see https://www.icanw.org/status-of-the-treaty-on-the-prohibition-of-nuclear-weapons/ (all links accessed in August 2019).
8. It may not seem pragmatic because none of the nine nuclear-armed states that have joined this initiative.
9. A complete timeline of nuclear diplomacy with Iran is available at: https://www.armscontrol.org/ factsheet/ Timeline-of-Nuclear-Diplomacy-With-Iran, accessed in September 2019.
10. Text of the *Panmunjom Declaration on Peace, Prosperity and Reunification of the Korean Peninsula*, submitted to the United Nations General Assembly (UNGA) on 9 September 2018, available at: https://www.mofa.go.kr/ eng/brd/m_5478/view.do?seq=319130&srchFr=&srchTo=&srchWord=&srchTp=&multi_itm_ seq=0&itm_seq_1=0 &itm_seq_2=0 & company_cd=&company_nm=&page=1&titleNm=, (accessed in September 2019).
11. Also see, "Balakot IAF strike involved 200 hours of planning," *Business Standard*, February 26, 2019.
12. In his address to the Russian Federal Assembly in March 2018, Putin unveiled a series of strategic weapons, which, he claimed, is 'invincible' and could overwhelm US missile defences. The presentation included a description and video-cum-graphical description of the following systems: (a) *Sarmat* inter-continental missile to replace the Soviet-era *Voevoda* system. It weighs over 200 tonnes, has a short-boost phase, and is equipped with a broad range of nuclear warheads, including the hypersonic vehicle and *Kinzhal* air-launched missile; (b) *Avangard* —a manoeuvrable hypersonic glide vehicle with Mach 10 speed. Being nuclear-powered enables it to have non-ballistic trajectories and practically no range restrictions; (c) an unmanned, nuclear-armed submersible, known by various names (Status-6/*Poseidon*/*Kanyon*). Putin declared that this system will be an "entirely new sea-based means to deliver a nuclear weapon," and "simply nothing in the world will be capable of withstanding them"; (d) A nuclear-powered cruise missile that will be a low-flying stealth missile carrying a nuclear warhead and claimed speed

of Mach 20 with inter-continental range and unpredictable trajectory. For more on Putin's presentation, see http://www.thedrive.com/the-war-zone/22270/russia-releases-videos-offering-an-unprecedented-look-at-its-six-new-super-weapons.

13. 'Problematique', derived from French and alternatively referred as 'problematic' in English, is equated with a 'research problem' or with the complex set of issues associated with a problem or topic under examination. The term is largely identified with the Club of Rome and its founder, Aurelio Peccei's conception that major systemic problems of the world cannot be approached or solved in isolation as they are inter-related as 'meta-problems'. In 1970, Hasan Ozbekhan, Erich Jantsch and Alexander Christakis, in their proposal to the Club of Rome titled "The Predicament of Mankind: Quest for Structured Responses to Growing World-wide Complexities and Uncertainties," elaborated on this concept thus: "It seems reasonable to postulate that the fragmentation of reality into closed and well-bounded problems creates a new problem whose solution is clearly beyond the scope of the concepts we customarily employ. It is this generalized meta-problem (or meta-system of problems) which we have called and shall continue to call the "problematique" that inheres in our situation." Text of the proposal available at:https://web.archive.org/web/20140203125912/http://sunsite.utk.edu/FINS/loversofdemocracy/Predicament.PTI.pdf, accessed in September 2019.
14. The reference is to the US-India civilian nuclear energy cooperation agreement, announced by US President George W. Bush and Indian Prime Minister Manmohan Singh on 18 July 2005 in Washington. For a text of the joint statement, see https://www.mea.gov.in/bilateral-documents.htm?dtl/6772/Joint_Statement_IndiaUS, accessed in September 2019.
15. 'Integration with the regime' is a metaphorical description to represent the adherence, membership or synchronisation with normative structures that comprise the non-proliferation regime or system. Following its peaceful nuclear explosion (PNE) of May 1974, India had sought to develop an indigenous nuclear programme following the withdrawal of technological and material assistance by the USA and Canada. Having already refused to sign the NPT, India had in the subsequent years kept itself outside the normative instruments that were floated in the regime.
16. As per the July 2005 joint statement, the US government had committed "to (sic) achieve full civil nuclear energy cooperation with India, adjust U.S. laws and policies to enable this, and to adjust international regimes to enable full civil nuclear energy cooperation and trade with India." The last implied seeking waivers from the Nuclear Suppliers Group (NSG) from its 1991 (Warsaw) guidelines that stipulated that only those non-nuclear weapons states (NNWS) with comprehensive safeguards agreement of the International Atomic Energy Agency (IAEA) can access international nuclear commerce. The NSG granted an India-specific waiver in September 2008.
17. Japan and South Korea are the other Asian members of the NSG. The complete list of the 48 participating governments available at: http://nuclearsuppliersgroup.org/en/about-nsg/participants1, (accessed in September 2019).
18. The concept of 'security guarantees' emerged during the NPT negotiations at the Eighteen Nations Disarmament Committee (ENDC) and the United Nations General Assembly (UNGA) between 1965-68. It implied that the nuclear weapon states will assure non-nuclear weapon states of coming to their aid if threatened with nuclear weapons. The concept was mired in ambiguity from the outset as the conception of guarantee was discussed among the three NWS, namely, the USA, Russia and the UK, while China and France were not part of the deliberations. The NNWS members at ENDC were not convinced that the NWS will risk hostilities with another nuclear power in order to protect them. While the NPT did not incorporate Security Guarantees, the

United Nations Security Council (UNSC) passed Resolution 255 on 19 June 1968, a day after the NPT resolution at the UNGA. Resolution 255 entails that "aggression with nuclear weapons or the threat of such aggression against a NNWS would cause the Security Council, and all its nuclear-weapon State permanent members, to act immediately in accordance with their obligations under the UN Charter; ...certain States will provide or support immediate assistance to any NNWS party to the NPT that is a victim of an act or an object of a threat of aggression in which nuclear weapons are used." See *Resolution 255: Question relating to measures to safeguard non-nuclear-weapon States parties to the Treaty on the Non-Proliferation of Nuclear Weapons*, at http://unscr.com/en/resolutions/255, (accessed in September 2019).

19. Zulfikar Ali Bhutto, then Prime Minister of Pakistan, in an interview with the *Manchester Guardian* in 1965, remarked that if India built the bomb, "we will eat grass, even go hungry, but we will get one of our own."
20. Homi Bhabha, head of India's Atomic Energy Commission (AEC), had declared in an All India Radio address on 24 October 1964 that a nuclear weapon device could be readied in 18 months. Look for "Bhabha: India Can Make Atom Bomb in 18 Months," *National Herald*, 5 October 1964.
21. Devices for 'peaceful nuclear explosions' were extensively tested in the late 1950s and early 1960s through the American Plowshare programme and the Soviets to running a similar programme. The nuclear powers had insisted at the NPT negotiations that a thin line differentiates between a PNE device and a nuclear weapon, and that the technology could be offered to non-nuclear weapon states under safeguards on a commercial basis. India termed this proposal as 'atomic apartheid' and insisted that PNE rights should be part of the inalienable right to access and develop peaceful uses of nuclear energy.
22. India had maintained in its global outreach after the PNE that the test was purely peaceful and that it had no intention to develop nuclear weapons. The complete picture of this outreach and its contents is available in the archival file no. WII/103(18)74, "India's Peaceful Nuclear Explosion 18-5-1974," (Ministry of External Affairs/Americas Division), National Archives of India, New Delhi.
23. There are many narratives on how this decision was arrived at. George Perkovich talks about a high-level committee constituted by Prime Minister Rajiv Gandhi in mid-1980s to examine this question. P. K. Iyengar, a distinguished scientist with the Department of Atomic Energy (DAE) and a member of the 1974 PNE team, told this author that Rajiv Gandhi as PM had mentioned to him about taking a final decision after seeing the response to his Action Plan delivered at the Third Special Session on Disarmament (SSoD) in June 1988 in which he had proposed a three-stage process towards total elimination. Text of Rajiv Gandhi Action Plan available at: Annexure I of the *Report of the Informal Group on Prime Minister Rajiv Gandhi's Action Plan for a Nuclear-Weapon Free and Non-Violent World Order*, http://www.pugwashindia.org/images/uploads/Report.pdf, (last accessed in July 2016).
24. Having advocated a comprehensive test ban instrument since the Limited Test Ban Treaty (LTBT) came into force in 1963, India was also a co-initiator of Resolution 48/70 of 1993 that mandated the CTBT negotiations. However, India disagreed with the final text that proposed a comprehensive ban on testing but did not address existing arsenals and allowed their expansion through simulated methods. However, the treaty had not entered into force, as some of the 44 states (of the Annex II list) are yet to sign and/or ratify the treaty.
25. All documents pertaining to the JCPOA are available at: https://www.consilium.europa.eu/en/policies/ sanctions/iran/jcpoa-restrictive-measures/

26. See *Remarks by President Trump on the Joint Comprehensive Plan of Action*, 8 May 2018 at: https:// www.whitehouse.gov/ briefings-statements/ remarks-president-trump-joint-comprehensive-plan-action/, accessed in October 2019.
27. The events since Iran's decision to restart uranium enrichment include the seizure of an Iranian ship by the British Navy in Gibraltar on 4 July 2019 and Iran retaliating by detaining a British ship in the Strait of Hormuz on the 19th of the same month. Similarly, an American Global Hawk surveillance drone was shot down by Iranian forces on 20 June followed by US claims that it had downed an Iranian drone on 19 July.
28. The Atoms for Peace plan was floated by US president Dwight Eisenhower in a December 1953 speech in which he proposed a grand bargain wherein the nuclear powers were to contribute stockpiles of uranium and other fissionable materials that could be allocated for peaceful pursuits, and that all countries should end the race for armaments. For this purpose, the establishment of the International Atomic Energy Agency (IAEA) was also proposed. See text of speech at: https://www.iaea.org/about/history/atoms-for-peace-speech, accessed in October 2019.

REFERENCES

Abbas, Hassan. (2017): *Pakistan's Nuclear Bomb: A Story of Defiance, Deterrence and Deviance*, Penguin Books, New Delhi.

Allinson, Tom. (2019): "Yemen's Houthi rebels: Who are they and what do they want?" *DW*, 1 October, *https://www.dw.com/*en/yemens-houthi-rebels-who-are-they-and-what-do-they-want/a-50667558, (accessed in October 2019).

Auslin, Michael. (2017): "Is the 'Asian Century' Over Before It has Begun?" *ORF Raisina Debates*, 14 February, https://www.orfonline.org/expert-speak/asian-century-begun/, (accessed in October 2019).

Bermudez, Joseph S. (2015): "North Korea's Development of a Nuclear Weapons Strategy," *North Korea's Nuclear Futures Series*, US-Korea Institute at SAIS, John Hopkins University, https://www.38north.org/wp-content/uploads/2015/08/NKNF_Nuclear-Weapons-Strategy_Bermudez.pdf (accessed in September 2019).

Borger, Julian. (2014): "The truth about Israel secret nuclear arsenal," *The Guardian*, 15 January, https://www.theguardian.com/world/2014/jan/15/truth-israels-secret-nuclear-arsenal, (accessed in September 2019).

Chafetz, Glenn. (1995): "The Political Psychology of the Nuclear Nonproliferation Regime," *The Journal of Politics*. 57(3), August.

Chakma, Bhumitra. (2009): *Pakistan's Nuclear Weapons*, Routledge, London and New York.

Chari, P. R. et.al, (eds.). (2003): *Nuclear Stability in Southern Asia*, Manohar, New Delhi.

Cohen, Avner. (1998): Israel and the Bomb, Columbia University Press, New York.

Dehghanpisheh, Babak. (2019): "Iran to cut nuclear deal commitments until it reaches 'desired result': supreme leader," *Reuters*, 2 October, https://www.reuters.com/article/us-usa-iran-nuclear/iran-to-cut-nuclear-deal-commitments-until-it-reaches-desired-result-supreme-leader-idUSKBN1WH0Y9, (accessed in October 2019).

DePetris, Daniel R. (2019): "Secrets: Everything You Wanted to Know About Israel's Nuclear Weapons," *The National Interest*, 20 July, https://nationalinterest.org/blog/buzz/secrets-everything-you-wanted-know-about-israels-nuclear-weapons-67962, (accessed in September 2019).

Farr, Warner D. (1999) "The Third Temple's Holy of Holies: Israel's Nuclear Weapons," *Counterproliferation Papers (Future Warfare Series)*, No. 2, September, Alabama: Air University.

Ganguly, Sumit and Kapur, Paul S. (2010): *India, Pakistan and the Bomb: Debating Nuclear Stability in South Asia*, Columbia University Press, New York.

Ghose, Arundhati. (1997): "Negotiating the CTBT: India's Security Concerns and Nuclear Disarmament," *Journal of International Affairs*, Vol. 51(1), Summer.

Heinonen, Olli. (2015): "Iran's Nuclear Breakout Time: A Fact Sheet," *The Washington Institute Policywatch 2394*, 28 March, https://www.washingtoninstitute.org/policy-analysis/view/irans-nuclear-breakout-time-a-fact-sheet, (accessed in October 2019).

Jain, J. P. (1974): *Nuclear India*, Volumes I & II, Radiant Publishers, New Delhi.

Karpin, Michael. (2006): *The Bomb in the Basement: How Israel Went Nuclear and What That Means for the World*, Simon and Schuster Paperbacks, New York.

Khan, Feroz Hassan. (2012): *Eating Grass: The Making of the Pakistani Bomb*, Stanford University Press, Stanford, California.

Kim, Victoria. (2018): "Singapore summit: Historic meeting between President Trump and North Korea's Kim Jong Un," *Los Angeles Times*, 9 June, https://www.latimes.com/world/la-fg-trump-kim-north-korea-summit-updates-htmlstory.html, (accessed in September 2019).

Kristensen Hans M. and Norris, Robert S. (2018): "A History of US Nuclear Weapons in South Korea," *Global Research*, 25 June, https://www.globalresearch.ca/a-history-of-us-nuclear-weapons-in-south-korea/5623878, (accessed in September 2019).

Krzyzaniak, John. (2019): "Double Flash: Forty years ago, the Carter administration covered up a presumed Israeli nuclear test," *Bulletin of the Atomic Scientists*, 25 September, https://thebulletin.org/2019/09/double-flash-vela-incident/,(accessed in September 2019).

Kumar, Vinod A. (2010): "Promises, Compromises and a Tie-Breaker: NPT RevCon 2010 was an Otiose Event," *IDSA Issue Brief*, 9 June, https://idsa.in/ system/files/IB_ NPTRevCon2010 _ avkumar.pdf, (accessed in August 2019).

Kumar, Vinod A. (2011): "A Doctrine at Work: Obama's Evolving Nuclear Policy and What it Bodes for India," *Strategic Analysis*, Vol. 35 (2).

Kumar, Vinod A. (2014): *India and the Nuclear Non-Proliferation Regime: The Perennial Outlier*, Cambridge University Press, New Delhi.

Kumar, Vinod A. (2017): "Between Idealism, Activism and the Bomb: Why did India reject the NPT?" in Popp Roland, Liviu Horovitz and Andreas Wenger (eds.), *Negotiating the Nuclear Non-Proliferation Treaty: Origins of the Nuclear Order*, Routledge, London and New York.

Levy, Adrian and Scott-Clark, Catherine. (2007): *Deception: Pakistan, the United States, and the Secret Trade in Nuclear Weapons*, Walker and Company, New York.

Mauroni, Albert. (2019): "The rise and fall of counterproliferation policy," *The Nonproliferation Review*, Vol. 26 (1-2).

Mostaghim, Ramin and Etehad, Melissa. (2019): "Iran backs off more nuclear deal commitments, heightening concern about the agreement's future," *LA Times*, 9 September, https://www.latimes.com/world-nation/story/2019-09-07/iran-breaks-more-nuclear-deal-commitments-raising-concern-that-the-agreement-is-on-verge-of-collapsing, (accessed in September 2019).

Noorani, A. G. (2001): "India's nuclear guarantee episode," *Frontline*, Vol. 18(2), 9-22 June.

Perkovich, George. (1999): *India's Nuclear Bomb: The Impact on Global Proliferation*, The University of California Press, Berkeley.

Raghavan, V. R. (2001): *"Limited War and Nuclear Escalation in South Asia"*, *The Nonproliferation Review*, Vol. 6(3), Fall-Winter.

Riqiang, Wu. (2013): "Certainty of Uncertainty: Nuclear Strategy with Chinese Characteristics," *Journal of Strategic Studies*, Vol. 36 (4), May.

Romei, Valentina and Reed, John. (2019): "The Asian century is set to begin," *Financial Times*, 26 March, https://www.ft.com/content/520cb6f6-2958-11e9-a5ab-ff8ef2b976c7, (accessed in October 2019).

Sagan, Scott D. and Waltz, Kenneth N. (1995): *The Spread of Nuclear Weapons, A Debate*, W. W. Norton, New York.

Salik, Naeem. (2016): "Pakistan's nuclear force structure in 2025," Carnegie Regional Insight, 30 June, https://carnegieendowment.org/2016/06/30/pakistan-s-nuclear-force-structure-in-2025-pub-63912, (accessed in October 2019).

Sanger, David E. and Wong, Edward. (2019): "How the Trump-Kim Summit Failed: Big Threats, Big Egos, Bad Bets," *The New York Times*, 2 March, https://www.nytimes.com/2019/03/02/world/asia/trump-kim-jong-un-summit.html, (accessed in September 2019).

Singh, Surendra. (2017): "This is How 19 Indian Soldiers Did Surgical Strike in PoK, And Avenged the Uri Terror Attack," *India Times*, 9 February.

Toon, Owen B. et. al. (2019): "Rapidly expanding nuclear arsenals in Pakistan and India portend regional and global catastrophe," *Science Advances*, Vol. 5 (10), 2 October, https://advances.sciencemag.org/ content/ 5/10/eaay5478, (accessed in October 2019).

Urban, Mark. (2013): "Saudi nuclear weapons 'on order' from Pakistan," *BBC*, 6 November.

Webb, Whitney. (2019): "Israel's Secretive Nuclear Facility Leaking as Watchdog Finds Israel Has Nearly 100 Nukes," *Mint Press News*, 17 June, https://www.mintpressnews.com/international-watchdog-finds-israel-has-nearly-100-nuclear-weapons/259274/, (accessed in September 2019).

Young, Michael. (2018): "Does Saudi Arabia Intend to Develop a Nuclear Weapons Capability?" *Carnegie Middle East Centre*, 8 March, https://carnegie-mec.org/diwan/75723, (accessed in September 2019).

Yunzhu, Yao. (2008): "Chinese Nuclear Policy and the Future of Minimum Deterrence," in Christopher P. Twomey (ed.), *Perspectives on Sino-American Strategic Nuclear Issues*, Palgrave Macmillan, New York.

4

South China Sea and the Growing Dominance of China: Security Challenges before India and the Region

Chandra Mohan Upadhyay

Introduction

The world is actually facing an existential threat due to COVID-19, incomparable to any of the previous threats like world wars, famines or others faced by humanity in known history. With China's increasing power and the stronger note of aggressiveness in its voice and actions, at the same time, there has been a relative decline in US power in the Asia–Pacific and, under Donald Trump, a good deal of unpredictability in its policy. As its military and economic strength has increased, China has been active in stretching its influence widely—openly through the Belt and Road Initiative and in a more clandestine way through foreign interference operations, border incursions and by other expansionist methods. The rise and domineering behaviour of China has created disequilibrium. China has a great sense of 'History' and is known for its timely moves in international politics. It has chosen the period of the pandemic to put forward its claims forcefully, when the whole world is engaged in self-preservation. Let us not forget that China chose the month of October 1962 to attack India, when both the superpowers were engaged in the deadly Cuba crisis. From Hong Kong to Taiwan and from the South China Sea to the Indian borders, the Chinese government, led by President Xi Jinping, is pursuing more aggressive policies. There is growing concern about Beijing's behaviour, not just in Washington and Delhi but also in Jakarta, London, Tokyo and Canberra. China feels that the corona virus has given it a God-sent opportunity to act while the world is looking away. The turmoil in deeply divided America has made its task look easier, while Europe has already become a confused continent. But the democratic world cannot afford to lose focus on what is happening in East-Asia and the South China Sea or at India's border. A new global crisis could easily break out there, with even graver long-term consequences than the pandemic.

The globally paralysing pandemic has reinforced Xi's efforts to realize his "Chinese dream" by the 2049 centenary of communist rule. Xi said in a speech at Xi'an Jiao Tong University in April 2020 that "great steps in history have always emerged from the crucible of major disasters." Many in the world now believe that the current crisis is crafted within the four walls of China. After 40 years of rapid economic growth, China is now by some measure—the world's largest economy. Its navy has more warships and submarines than that of the USA. Its Internet bubbles with nationalistic chatter about the inexorable rise of the nation. Beijing's growing assertiveness reflects both pride and paranoia. But, alongside the pride, there are plenty of reasons for paranoia at the top levels of government in Beijing. The past 12 months have presented Xi with an unprecedented range of threats and challenges. The pandemic has seen China widely accused of responsibility for a global calamity. This may explain why China has sought to make the most of the pandemic. From breaking Beijing's binding commitment to Hong Kong's autonomy and attempting to police the waters off the Japanese-controlled Senkaku Islands, to picking a nasty border fight with India by encroaching on its territory, Xi has pushed the boundaries.

A regime that used to believe it needed 8 per cent growth a year to maintain social stability now has to deal with a deep economic contraction—compounded by a trade war with the USA. Pro-democracy protests in Hong Kong have continued for more than a year and represent a severe challenge to Communist party authority. And, in January, Taiwan's president, Tsai Ing-wen, won a crushing re-election victory—a humiliation for Beijing, which had worked hard to undermine her. All this seems to be creating a siege mentality in the government. In response, Beijing has intensified its appeal to nationalism. The propaganda goal is to rally the people against external threats and deflect anger about COVID-19 outwards, to the world beyond China. Countries that dare to criticize China over COVID-19 are getting a dose of wolf-warrior diplomacy—Beijing even imposed tariffs on some Australian exports, after Canberra called for an international inquiry.

The growing dominance of a rising China has every potential for global instability in the 21st century. My hypothesis treads cautiously on the premise that China is emerging as a revisionist power. It has security implications and complications for the regional states in particular and the world in general. Any hypothesis, to be sound, should be tested on the basis of facts and not on fancies. I am putting my hypothesis to this rigorous parameter, leaving the judgement to honest readers and critics. By challenging the might of America in South-East Asia, China has given the first major hint of its intentions to dominate the region. China's growing economic and military power has encouraged its initiation of military conflicts. However, the liberal view leads us to expect that China's growth will deepen Asia's economic interdependence, thereby increasing international stability and regional integration. According to this perspective, we should be worrying not about China's rise but about fear of the rise. Given that China is expected to continue growing and eventually equal the USA in terms of the size of its economy, will we also see China become internationally more aggressive. Some scholars have compared the Chinese growth and aggression and have found that China has become more hostile to its opponents in territorial disputes. Their findings support the position that as China gained greater economic capability, it has become more hostile to its opponents. "To test the above hypotheses, let us examine China's practice of initiating militarized conflicts with Asian states and major powers after the death of Mao Zedong, when it began to re-emerge. Using the Militarized Interstate Disputes dataset, which provides information on four types of military action (military threat, military display, use of force, and war, we measure the dependent variable: China's first military action against a particular state in a given year. The dataset contains 55 initiations of militarized conflict by China against Asian and major countries: 22 from 1976 to 1989 and 33 from 1990 to 2001." (Jung, Sung C. and Lee, Kihyun, 2017)

China's greater power has made the country more assertive, rather than cooperative, toward Asian states and major powers. This leads to the hypothesis that China will maintain its current uncompromising and adamant position in the South and East China Seas and elsewhere. Renouncing its earlier charade of peaceful rise, China is now asking others to 'get used to its muscle flexing'. China has searched strategic opportunities everywhere in the world. Now it is time for China to reap the rich dividends and the South-China Sea provides ample opportunities for the realization of its great game ambitions. Belying any reference to history, China claims almost the entire South China Sea, through which about $ 5 trillion worth of trade passes each year. The littoral and regional countries along with the USA have unequivocally criticized Beijing's build-up of military facilities in the sea and expressed concerns they could be used to restrict free movement. China has shown a great deal of disdain towards its neighbouring countries. The claims and counterclaims of territories in the South China Sea continue to fester. China's island-building, construction of facilities, and militarization of features in the area proceed unabated.

The rise of China is not disturbing the least because we once fought a war and are still engaged with China in a deadly fight at the border in 2020, but the implications of resultant dominance are far and wide. What makes the Indian position weaker is the culture of procrastination, whereas China is known for its bold road maps. China has consistently published its Defence-White papers since 1995, whereas India still does not have any. It is appropriate to understand the mindset of China. Noted scholar Lucian Pye points out a strange uniqueness of China, which remains a "civilization pretending to be a nation-state". (Pye, Lucian, 1992) The legendary, former US secretary of state, Henry Kissinger, aptly describes this situation thus, 'the extent and variety of territory bolsters the sense that China is a world unto itself, and its rulers presiding over *tianxia*, or All under Heaven". For China, this is essential for a harmonious world order, where harmony emanates, to quote Confucius 'from knowing your rightful place in the hierarchy' (Kissinger, Henry, *On China*). The multi-polarity of the 21st century is incompatible with this *tianxia* approach. It seems quite plausible that behind all the plans to integrate the world, there is a hidden agenda somewhere down the line to rediscover and regain that Utopian centrality, lost long ago in the vicissitudes of time.

China has initiated a multifarious project, with a pious declaration of connecting the world economy, popularly known as 'One Belt, One Road' or OBOR. The OBOR is basically a smoke-screen to hide its real ambitions of ruling the world. It is part of their cultural front to believe that 'China is a world into itself'. China wants to integrate Eurasia through a trillion dollars of infrastructure. It has rightly been termed by critics as China's New Marshall Plan. In a world of competing economic and trade alliances OBOR needs to be compared with its contemporaries—the most famous European Union has 27 members, OPEC has 13, the Organization of Islamic states (OIC) has 57. OBOR surpasses all with its 60 members. (*Indian Express*, 2017) The initiative has since been widely discussed between policy makers and academics both inside and outside China. Many questions have been asked like 'why did China come up with such a strategy at this point of time when it is already slowing down or what are the real intentions behind it? Is it not Pax-China in disguise? To put simply, it is the long-cherished dream of the Middle-Kingdom or '*zhongguo*' by another name.

India decided not to participate. India was invited to the Beijing conclave. India has got a number of reasons for staying away. None of them was more important than the question of India's sovereignty over Pak-occupied Kashmir (POK), through which an important part of China's OBOR runs. The foreign office in Delhi affirmed that "No country can accept a project that ignores its core concerns on sovereignty and territorial integrity", writes the foreign policy expert, C. Raja Mohan. He further writes, "international isolation is not India's biggest problem...India is too large an economy and political entity to be isolated by another power, occupying a vertical geographical location. India can contribute to the success of China's Belt and Road initiative or create needless complications. India's real challenge is to match its claim on territorial sovereignty with effective action on the ground." (Mohan, C. Raja, 2017)

It is not India alone but the world community at large that is quite concerned with the magnitude of initiatives around the globe. One of the most venerated scholars of international politics, Joseph S. Nye, makes a stinging observation, "Marco Polo would be proud. And if China chooses to use its surplus financial reserves to create important infrastructure that helps poor countries...China's motives are not purely philanthropic. (Nye, Joseph, 2017)

As the *Financial Times* put it, BRI "unfortunately is no more a practical plan for investment than a broad political vision". (May 12, 2017) The financial part of the plan is exposed more than ever. Many countries who earlier enthusiastically participated, like Pakistan and Sri Lanka, are now reeling under the debt burden. Speaking at Shangri-La in Singapore, Prime Minister Modi underlined the deliberate debt-trap in the name of connectivity, "We understand the benefits of connectivity. There are many connectivity initiatives in the region. If these are to succeed, we must not only build infrastructure; we must also build bridges of trust. And for that, these initiatives must be based on respect for sovereignty and territorial integrity, consultation, good governance, transparency, viability and sustainability. They must empower nations, not place them under an impossible debt burden." Finally, all of this is possible if we do not return to the age of great-power rivalries. I have said this before: an Asia of rivalry will hold us all back; an Asia of cooperation will shape this century. So, each nation must ask itself: are its choices building a more united world, or forcing new divisions? It is a responsibility that both existing and rising powers have. Competition is normal, but contests must not turn into conflicts; differences must not be allowed to become disputes. (PM Modi, at Shangri-La Dialogue, 2018)

Asian and particularly South-Asian countries have tried to balance the overbearing presence of China but in the absence of a strong US backing, these countries would fall back on China. As rightly maintained by Samuel P. Huntington, 'a band-wagonning propensity' is likely to exist among Asian powers, which would preclude any US effort at secondary balancing'. (Huntington, 1999) America is aware of this propensity and therefore it is ready with strategy. American defence secretary James Mattis elaborated on it at the 17th Asian Security Summit, Shangri-La, "America's Indo-Pacific strategy is a subset of our broader security strategy, codifying our principles as America continues to 'look west'. In it we see deepening alliances and partnerships as a priority; ASEAN's centrality remains vital; and cooperation with China is welcome wherever possible." (Mattis, James, 2018)

India and the USA both stressed that no nation can or should dominate the Indo-Pacific. The maritime commons is a global good, and sea lanes of communication are the arteries of economic vitality for all. It is in the best interests of the region to preserve that vitality. The USA promised to help regional players build up naval and law-enforcement capabilities and capacities to improve monitoring and protection of maritime borders and interests. So long as littoral nations pool their resources to be a force multiplier for peace, no miracle is going to happen. Therefore, the regional states need to ensure that their military can more easily integrate with others. The strategy is to include Australia and New Zealand also in the ambit of Indo-Pacific security cooperation. The USA values the role India can play in regional and global security and views the US-India relationship as a natural partnership between the world's two largest democracies based on a convergence of strategic interests, shared values and respect for a rule-based international order.

Considering the enormity of the challenge from China, Americans are invoking cooperation from other Pacific allies, such as the United Kingdom, France and Canada, to build a strong and lasting alternative. China on its part has promised several times to play by the rules but never shied away from overt to covert arm-twisting of the regional countries. China's militarization of artificial features in the South China Sea includes the deployment of anti-ship missiles, surface-to-air missiles, electronic jammers and, more recently, the landing of bomber aircraft at Woody Island. Despite China's claims to the contrary, the placement of these weapons systems is tied directly to military use for the purposes of intimidation and coercion. China's militarisation of the Spratlys is also in direct contradiction to President Xi's public assurances. Given the precarious nature of the America leadership, India should take a lead. We must seriously invest in several groupings which are lying dormant like: SAARC, Indian Ocean Rim Countries (IORC) and BIMSTEC, BBIN and Mekong-Ganga Cooperation (MGC), which was conceived more than a decade (year 2000) ago. Our record of translating conceptions into creations is dismal. It is here that our real test lies. It is in this regard a significant development worth mentioning. India and Japan have launched a vision document for the Asia-Africa Growth Corridor (AAGC). The AAGC initiative is part of a Indo-Pacific freedom corridor being put in place by India and Japan with an eye on counterbalancing the Chinese OBOR. It aims at Indo-Japanese collaboration to develop quality infrastructure in Africa, complemented by digital connectivity. It remains to be seen how far this initiative is given flesh and blood or if it remains a paper tiger like its predecessors. It is quite appropriate to examine the ground zero of

Chinese behaviour to comprehend the restructuring taking place under the heavy hammer of China.

China's Domineering Behaviour with the Philippines and other Regional Countries

China's claims, particularly on Scarborough Shoal in the Spratly Islands, have been rejected by the International Tribunal of the Permanent Court of Arbitration (PCA) at the Hague. The PCA at the Hague handed down its historic and sweeping award on maritime entitlements in the South China Sea, overwhelmingly favouring the Philippines over China. The ruling was a major victory for the Philippines, particularly the tribunal's decision on China's "nine-dash line", through which Beijing attempted to lay claim to vast areas of the South China Sea. As expected, Beijing refused to accept the PCA ruling, hardened its legal and diplomatic positions, and. Within hours of the ruling, at least 68 national and local government websites in the Philippines were knocked offline in a massive Distributed Denial of Service attack. The crippling DDOS attacks against the Filipino government networks continued over several days and targeted key government agencies, to include the Department of Foreign Affairs, the Department of National Defence, and the Central Bank. Within a few months after the award, under the huge pressure from China, the Philippines issued a conciliatory statement even as energy officials announced that Manila would soon offer investors new oil and gas blocks at Reed Bank, off the Philippine coast but within the nine-dash line. (*Foreign Affairs*, 2017)

Beijing, for its part, has always made it clear that it regards the tribunal's decision as "null and void" and of 'no binding force.' Statements from the Association of Southeast Asian Nations (ASEAN) states in the wake of the decision were muted. None urged China to adhere to the ruling; the strongest merely called for respecting international law. The real significance of the tribunal's decision was to clarify resource rights. Its main findings were twofold. "First, it ruled that China cannot claim historic rights to resources in the waters within the nine-dash line if those waters are within the EEZs of other coastal states. Such rights were extinguished when China ratified the UN Convention on the Law of the Sea in 1996. Second, the tribunal ruled that none of the features in the Spratlys is entitled to a 200-nautical-mile EEZ. Like Scarborough Shoal, all of the Spratly features are at most rocks entitled to 12-nautical-mile territorial seas". (*Foreign Affairs*, 2017)

Although technically binding only on parties to the arbitration, the tribunal's decision has bolstered the position of ASEAN littoral states in the South China Sea. It has clarified that the EEZ entitlements of the Philippines, as well as Brunei, Indonesia, Malaysia, and Vietnam, are unencumbered by China's nine-dash line or any claimed EEZ from features in the Spratlys. Areas of overlap in the Spratlys are now limited to a 12-nautical-mile ring around rock features. Beyond these areas, China has no claim recognized under international law to fish or to extract oil or gas in the EEZs of other states outside the EEZ generated from China's mainland.

In assessing the impact of the award, what China and ASEAN states do is at least as important as what they say. In official statements issued on the day of and after the judgment, Beijing appeared to expressly assert, for the first time, that China's maritime claims in the South China Sea include "historic rights". It did not specify what it means by this. China is a country whose history is best known to it. It has claims over almost all the neighbouring countries. For centuries Tibet had been an autonomous region, paying tribute to Chinese and adjoining Indian kingdoms. Suddenly, China discovered its forgotten history only to capture Tibet. It still has remnant claims over India after illegally capturing 24,000 sq km of our motherland. Its claims are wide-ranging covering not only land masses but sea areas also. The South-China controversy is nothing but the same kind of historical claim over a number of countries. However, if Beijing is claiming historic rights to resources within the entirety of the nine-dash line (rather than historic fishing rights within territorial seas), its assertion flies in the face of the judgment. In May 2018, Beijing also imposed an annual fishing ban, which overlapped with the EEZs of the Philippines and Vietnam but excluded the Spratlys. The Philippines has been a key ally of the USA and a territorial rival of Beijing in the South China Sea. The impact of Beijing's action could be assessed by the fact that within a few days of this orchestrated drama, the President of the Philippines, Duterte, announced during a visit to China, his "separation" from Washington and realignment with Beijing. This is another form of bandwagoning.

India and the South China Sea

Indian trade and economic linkages in the Pacific are becoming stronger and deeper. Not only are ASEAN and the far-eastern Pacific key target areas of the "Act East" policy, Asia's Eastern commons are increasingly a vital facilitator of India's economic development. With growing dependence on the Malacca Strait for the flow of goods and services, economics is increasingly a factor in India's Pacific policy. China must know that territorial conflicts in the SCS threaten the future trajectory of India's economic development, creating an unacceptable hindrance for regional trade and commerce. India believes that the disputes in the Southeast Asian littorals are a litmus test for international maritime law. In the aftermath of The Hague tribunal's verdict on the South China Sea, New Delhi feels obligated to take a principled stand on the issue of freedom of navigation and commercial access as enshrined in the UNCLOS. "Beijing must know that regardless of the guarantees it seeks from India about staying neutral on the SCS, New Delhi cannot be seen to be condoning the aggression of armed Chinese naval ships, aircraft and submarines in the region." (Singh, Abhijit, 2016)

Beijing must know that New Delhi recognizes the threat that Chinese aggression poses for the wider Asian commons–in particular, the exacerbation of existing power asymmetries. In order to contribute to a fair and equitable regional maritime order, New Delhi must take a stand that restores a strategic balance in maritime Asia. New Delhi's inability or rather the old habit of suppression of information and sometimes denial makes Indian positions unsustainable. Renowned scholar and journalist Arun Shourie has correctly summed up our position as "wishful construction...paste a motive, fling a doubt at the messenger, discredit him...minimize what the adversary has done...manufacture explanations and at each turn summarily pronounce 'But what else could we have been done'." (Shourie, Arun, 2013)

For instance, the correlation Indian maritime analysts discern between aggressive Chinese patrolling in the SCS and its growing deployment in the Indian Ocean Region; or the suspicion in Indian strategic circles that China might use its SCS bases as a springboard for active projection of power in the Indian Ocean and keeping a studied silence. So is the case of India's aggressive encirclement by China, its permanent presence in POK, its calculated incursions in Uttarakhand and Ladakh. Everywhere our response is not only inadequate but at best reactive. New Delhi should really worry about China's reclamation and militarization of features in its possession–particularly the deployment of missiles, fighters and surveillance equipment in its Spratly group of islands, allowing the PLAN (PLA Navy) effective control over the entire range of maritime operations in the SCS. New developments in China's military strategy are also notable. "Recently, Beijing has strengthened its anti-access/area denial (A2/AD) strategy in order to protect its core interests, including Taiwan, from interference by external forces, such as the USA. More specifically, the A2/AD entails changes in military plans and strategies for air, maritime, submarine, space, and cyber warfare. For example, the People's Liberation Army Air Force (PLAAF) has decided to develop long-range mission capabilities and high-tech equipment, such as anti-satellite weapons". (Jung, Sung C. and Lee, Kihyun, 2017)

The People's Liberation Army Navy (PLAN) aims to expand its scope of influence from the first island chain, connecting Okinawa, Taiwan, and the Philippines, to the second island chain, connecting Guam and Saipan. In this regard, PLAN has declared a territorial sea baseline and Air Defence Identification Zone (ADIZ), has conducted regular patrolling of the Diaoyu/Senkaku Islands, and has constructed artificial islands in the South China Sea, among other activities. Such military expansions present challenges to the US-led regional order that has existed in Asia since the end of World War II. Indian experts should also recognize the important role Beijing's militia forces play in achieving its regional objectives. India knows well that the main threat to maritime security in Asia is not so much from the PLA Navy, but China's irregular forces. Chinese surveillance ships, coast guard vessels and fishing fleets are the real force behind Beijing's dominance of the littoral spaces. "With the expansion of Chinese maritime activities in the IOR, New Delhi fears a rise in non-grey hull presence in the Eastern Indian Ocean. Already, China's distant water fishing fleet is now the world's largest, and is a heavily subsidized maritime commercial entity. While an increase in the presence of such ships does not always pose a security threat, India remains wary of Chinese non-military maritime activity in the Eastern Indian Ocean". (Abhijit, 2016)

Beijing's blueprint for maritime operations in the Indian Ocean involves the construction of multiple logistical facilities. China's 10-year agreement with Djibouti in 2015 for the setting up of a naval replenishment facility in the northern Obock region is widely seen as proof of the PLA Navy's strategic ambitions in the IOR. And this anticipation has proven right. Djibouti is a resource-poor nation in the Horn of Africa. Its location also matters greatly to global commerce and energy, due to its vicinity to the Mandeb strait and the Suez-Aden canal, which sees 10 percent of oil and 20 percent of commercial exports annually. According to the *Huffington Post* "The greatest worry is America's diminishing military footprints. It has begun to affect the calculation of allies and rivals alike". (Braude, Joseph and Jiang, Tyler)

The USA has tried to address this fear also. In his brilliant speech at the Shangri-La Dialogue on June 2, 2018, James Mattis was quite forthcoming, "So make no mistake, America is in the Indo-Pacific to stay. This is our priority theatre. Our interests and the region's are inextricably intertwined. In fact, the USA and China are actually playing the role of history. The United States embodies what Huntington considered 'Western civilization'. And tensions between American and Chinese values, traditions, and philosophies will aggravate the fundamental structural stresses that occur whenever a rising power, such as China, threatens to displace an established power, such as the USA. A conflicting situation is envisioned. In the words of famous historian Graham Allison, this is a Thucydides' *trap*. According to Thucydides, "It was the rise of Athens, and the fear that this instilled in Sparta, that made war inevitable." Rising powers understandably feel a growing sense of entitlement and demand greater influence and respect. Established powers, faced with challengers, tend to become fearful, insecure, and defensive." (Allison, Graham, 2017)

With its new-found self-confidence, China is building military bases next door to US AFRICOM in Djibouti. India must learn the right lessons from several such episodes. China is just not any other strong nation satisfied by playing second fiddle. It has its global ambitions and it is unabashed about it. No victim card will fetch security and dignity to India. Long ago, Thucydides reminded succeeding generations through his 'Melian Dialogue' that "standard of justice depends on the equality of power to compel and in fact the strong do what they have the power to do and the weak accept what they have to accept. (Thucydides, 2008)

Our preparedness is not up to the mark and a kind of policy paralysis is visible even today. This is disappointing for a country which harbours the ambitions of attaining great power status. Indian leaders have not articulated the full extent of their anxieties over Chinese maritime operations in Asia. Regardless of the concessions on offer to New Delhi, Beijing must know that India will not agree to a compromise deal with China on the South China Sea.

It is in the light of this situation and Chinese overall aggressive postures in the South China Sea that Indian Prime Minister Narendra Modi's visit to Vietnam in September 2016 and his Japan visit in the second week of November marked an important step forward in their ties. The fact that the PM chose to drop by Vietnam on his way to the G20 Summit in Hangzhou, China, would not be lost on observers and must have ruffled quite a few feathers in Beijing. It also comes in the wake of the July 12 awards handed down by the Permanent Court of Arbitration. Despite the open suggestion to India by China during the recent visit to Japan, Prime Minister Modi went to stress that "India supports freedom of navigation and overflight, unimpeded commerce, based on the principles of international law, as reflected notably in the UNCLOS." (*Indian Express*, 2017) In an age when geopolitics in the region is in a state of flux, it is essential for India to stand by our friends. Just as China has been wading into India's neighbourhood, there is no reason why India should shy away from doing the same in China's extended neighbourhood. With its soft power and lately hard power in full flow in Vietnam and Japan, New Delhi must be careful not to squander the new opportunities.

The Policy Alternative before India and the Region

For China, order is the highest value, and harmony results from a hierarchy. In some ways, Chinese 'exceptionalism' is more sweeping than its American counterpart. "The [Chinese] empire saw itself as the centre of the civilized universe," historian Harry Gilbert wrote in his book, *'Nations Out of Empires'*. (Gilber, Harry, 2001). This notion is buttressed when we come across such assertions from no less a person than the President himself. Xi claimed in his book, *'The Governance of China'*, that "China's continuous civilization is not equal to anything on earth, but a unique achievement in world history." (Xi, 2014) China's treatment of its own citizens provides the script for its relations with weaker neighbours abroad. During a meeting of the Association of Southeast Asian Nations, then Chinese Foreign Minister Yang Jiechi responded to complaints about Chinese assertiveness in the South China Sea by telling his regional counterparts and U.S. Secretary of State Hillary Clinton said that "China is a big country and other countries are small countries, and that's just a fact." (*Indian Express*, June 5, 2010.) China enters the global arena for *shi* or relative advantage. It is against the backdrop of the hegemonic behaviour of China that Japan took the initiative. One of the interesting features of Japan's latest plan to revive the Indo-Pacific quadrilateral dialogue (Quad), is the move to associate the European powers with it. For Prime Minister of Japan, Shinzo Abe, who first discussed the idea of a quad a little over a decade ago, the four-nation forum is, in essence, a coalition of "maritime democracies' '. Abe argued that the maritime democracies have a stake in securing a rule-based global order, liberal trading system and freedom of navigation. 'As a realist Abe is conscious of the fact that the growing power imbalance in Asia amidst the rapid rise of China can't be addressed by America's Asian alliance system alone. Abe has consciously courted special relationships with India, Australia and other regional powers. He also sees the need to keep the QUAD an open-ended organisation that can also benefit from the partnership with European powers.' (Mohan, C. Raja, 2017)

More than 70 per cent of European trade passes through the Indo-Pacific. Both France and Britain have a military presence and security arrangements in the Indian Ocean. France has many military facilities in the Indo-Pacific, including those in Reunion, Djibouti and the United Arab Emirates. Britain continues to control Diego Garcia. It also leads the Five Power Defence Arrangement (involving Singapore, Malaysia, Australia and New Zealand) set up in 1971. France has a variety of coordination mechanisms in the Pacific with the USA, Japan, Australia and New Zealand. As India is concerned about the strategic implications of China's port building in Gwadar (Pakistan) and Hambantota (Sri-Lanka), Canberra too is concerned about the Chinese push for the militarization of Vanuatu islands. Similarly, Japan has also burnt its fingers at Senkaku/Diaoyu islands. Therefore, this convergence of maritime democracies is not coincidental, but rather it is of late recognition of a common-threat. India already has a strong bilateral security engagement with countries like France and Britain. Issues relating to maritime security have been at the top of the agenda. As Delhi prepares to cope with China's rapid naval advances in the Indian Ocean and deploys its ships far from the Indian shores, it needs to bring together its bilateral cooperation with individual

European countries into a comprehensive strategic framework. Japan's plans to bring France and Britain on board quad can only reinforce India's maritime partnerships with Europe.

Freedom of navigation is one of the most essential aspects of maritime cooperation. No wonder Prime Minister Narendra Modi found time during the busy election season to travel all the way south to Male, the capital of the Maldives. Modi's presence at the swearing-in of the new president of the Maldives, Ibrahim Mohamed Solih, underlined the renewed warmth in the relations between the two countries. Under Solih's predecessor, Abdulla Yameen, India's relations with the Maldives rapidly deteriorated even as China's influence began to rise. The intersection of Sino-Indian rivalry with domestic politics has also come to the fore in neighbouring Sri Lanka. India supported Prime Minister Ranil Wickremesinghe, while China openly sided with the former president, Mahinda Rajapaksa. During Rajapaksa's decade-long rule of Sri Lanka (2004-15), Colombo seemed to steadily drift into China's orbit. Symbolising China's new influence in Lanka were the strategic contracts it won to build the Colombo port city and the construction of a new port at Hambantota in the southern part of the island. India, in turn, appeared to lose its historic primacy in the island state. Now we have regained our balance in Sri Lanka also.

Like India in the Indian Ocean, Australia and New Zealand had underestimated the scale and speed of China's power projection into their South Pacific neighbourhood. So, did the USA, which failed to react in time to China's push to gain control of the small rocks and islands of the South China Sea at the beginning of this decade. We cannot allow the historic opportunity, which has come to us in the name of the Indo-Pacific, to be squandered this time. To be sure, the novelty of the Indo-Pacific lies in recognising the growing strategic and economic interdependence of the Pacific and Indian Ocean littorals that we saw as separate theatres until recently. Noted strategic thinker C. Raja Mohan is quite categorical here. "Indo-Pacific is also a sum of its many sub-regions that include the East China Sea, South China Sea and South Pacific to the east of the Malacca Strait as well as the Bay of Bengal, Arabian Sea and the waters of Africa to the west. What India does in these subregions is far more important than the abstract debates on the Indo-Pacific. One such sub-region, the

Andaman Sea—is likely to preoccupy India in the coming years." (Mohan, C. Raja, 2018)

The Andaman Sea is flanked by the Andaman and Nicobar chain of islands in the west, Myanmar to the north, the Thai-Malay peninsula to the east, and Sumatra island to the south. It funnels into the Straits of Malacca that connects the Indian and Pacific Oceans. The large amount of shipping that enters the Andaman Sea from the east heads to Singapore, from where it turns into the Pacific Ocean. After the Second World War, the partition of India and the Cold War between America and Russia, the Andamans became marginal to the new geopolitics. The rise of China and its projection of naval power way beyond its home waters is beginning to put the Andaman Sea back into play. Beijing has signed an agreement with Naypyidaw on building a deep-water port at Kyaukpyu on Myanmar's Arakan coast in the Bay of Bengal. The port will form an important part of the China-Myanmar Economic Corridor, which would connect Kyaukpyu to the Yunnan province in south western China via rail and highways. China is already assessing the cost of building the Kra canal to link the Andaman-Sea to the gulf of Thailand. China is also enhancing its military profile by selling nuclear submarines to Bangladesh and Thailand, and conducting military exercises with Thailand and Malaysia.

For India, the Andaman sea has assumed a new significance. As a sequel to our Look-East Policy, we have conducted the largest ever naval exercise with Singapore, aptly called 'Simbex', in the Andaman Sea. These exercises began 25 years ago. Prime Minister Modi's visits and renaming of three islands on the occasion of the 75th anniversary of Subhash Chandra Bose flying the tricolour in Port Blair has helped highlight the role of the Andaman and Nicobar Islands in India's freedom struggle. New Delhi has decided to end the isolation of the island chain and promote economic development, tighter integration with the mainland, strengthen military infrastructure, regional connectivity and international collaboration. It is in this regard that we can also connect our efforts out of the Malabar exercises. The 22nd rendition of the Malabar naval exercise, held for the first time in waters off the coast of Guam and involving aircraft and ships from the Indian Navy, the U.S. The Navy, and the Japan Maritime Self Defence Force (JMSDF), officially came to an end on June 16, 2018. The Malabar naval exercise began as a joint Indo-U.S. naval exercise in 1992.

Japan became a permanent participant in 2015. India once again refused Australia's bid to take part in the 2018 iteration of the exercise. This is very disappointing, given our penchant particularly for cooperation among maritime democracies. China has successfully studied the Indian mindset, and has decided to downsize India. Chinese stealth incursions in many areas simultaneously like Galwan Valley, Pangong Tso, Hot Springs, Depsang, etc., caught India napping again in 2020. The face-off at Eastern Ladakh's Galwan sector marks the most disturbing period of the Sino-Indian relationship. Galwan valley has never been an area of contention. The unacceptable casualties of Indian soldiers in Galwan have caused irreparable damage to our relations. On the night of 15 June, China just repeated its history of betrayal. What happened in Galwan was waiting to happen for a very long time, as successive Indian governments were ignoring the repeated Chinese ingresses and incursions. The wishful strategic thinking of successive Indian governments that by courting and appeasing China, we could limit Beijing's potential threats to India has resulted in the opposite. The history of appeasements begins with 'Hindi-Chini Bhai-Bhai' and ends with the so-called Jhoola Diplomacy's Plus one and personal' level. After encroaching upon the territory of India, instead of vacating it right now, China is buying time in the protracted negotiations leading nowhere. According to former NSA Shiv Shankar Menon, "Well, I think it's actually dangerous, to speak of disengagement, pullback, withdrawal, buffer zones. These suggest that we are withdrawing from territory which we have controlled consistently, and that we were part of the problem to start with...In fact, we are actually teaching the Chinese the wrong lesson. And this started with Doklam, where we negotiated withdrawals by both sides from the face-off point in 2017. The Chinese then proceeded to establish a very strong, permanent presence on the plateau, leaving the face-off point itself free.". He rightly highlights the Indian government's media management to score some brownie points, where in fact there is nothing to celebrate. "So, frankly, [China] learned the lesson that as long as the Indian [government] could walk away with a propaganda victory, they could actually make gains and change the outcome on the ground in their favour. And I think the risk is that we see the same kind of thing happening now here in Ladakh. I'm not saying it has happened yet, but there is a real risk here". India–China ties will be reset after the LAC standoff. (Menon, Shivshankar, 2020)

The changed dynamics along the LAC will also have repercussions on other aspects of the bilateral relationship. On the economic side, there is bound to be a pushback. At the diplomatic and strategic level, there is bound to be a greater push towards counterbalancing China, something India has traditionally been chary of doing openly. India will have to decide whether to reinforce a failed policy of equidistance with the USA and China, or forge a new one which involves a much closer alliance with the USA.

Now it is heartening to note that India has finally shaken off its needless defensiveness and has decided to invite Australia, along with the USA and Japan to its annual naval exercise. (*Indian Express*, 2020). Way back in 2007, the Indian Navy invited the maritime forces of Japan, Australia and Singapore to join its annual bilateral naval exercises with the USA. Delhi discontinued this unique experiment as China objected and the coalition partner left parties were opposed to engagement with the West for a variety of reasons. China's political and military influence in the island states of the Indian Ocean and the PLAN has emerged as a major strategic actor in the east coast of Africa. As China turns more assertive in the great Himalayas as well as in the Indian Ocean, Delhi is now scrambling to find answers. The decision to invite Australia into the Malabar exercise is a right move at the right time. China is again opposing the evolution of the quad plus Singapore platform. India does not need to be scared of China's band-wagonning. It is not suggested here that India should adopt a confrontational attitude towards China. India has to search every possible opportunity to work and collaborate with China on the one hand and also needs to address the long-term strategic consequences of China's rise and its impact on India's security. India has shown enough maturity and courage by joining the Shanghai Cooperation Organization (SCO) which is also a brainchild of China on the one hand and rightly refused to be part of the Regional Comprehensive Economic Partnership (RCEP), which is dominated by China, on the other. What we want is a dignified presence at the decision-making table. We want respect for our unity, integrity and, of course, the security of our land, air and territorial waters along with the freedom of navigation across various sea routes. The overbearing presence and the domineering behaviour of China has really created a disequilibrium. We have to address this imbalance in right earnest, lest we fall prey to another deceptive design of the devouring 'Dragon'.

Conclusion

Given the Chinese cultural trait of their own ways always, due to their thinking of 'pre-eminence' in the form of '*zhongguo*' the region has reasons to be anxious owing to a colossal initiative in the form of OBOR, and the forceful restructuring of the Global Order, by it. India has always stood for a 'multi-polar' world with meaningful alliances without any kind of hegemony. It is here that we have to match our vision with action. Credibility is an important element of the international order. Credibility for a state is a *sina qua non*. It provides a guarantee that its assurances can be trusted by friends and its threats taken seriously by adversaries. Unfortunately, we have been found wanting at this point. As pointed out earlier, the time has come to impart meaning and significance to some of the regional organizations we have already formed with the active cooperation of like-minded countries. Our success there shall have a reassuring impact on the future and efficacy of the QUAD. India can play a pivotal role here. Because, unlike China which loves *shi* (relative advantage), India wants its rightful place among the comity of nations, with a rule-based global order, freedom of navigation and a liberal trading system. We can supplement our multilateralism with a dynamic bilateralism for a comprehensive strategic framework. Our efforts at different levels are in no way antithetical to China. India is a large country having vast and diverse interests. India can cultivate a very good relationship with China on an equal footing along with the goals of resuscitation and rejuvenation of the aforesaid organizations. It is not a zero-sum game anyway. Both the countries can engage constructively by being creative, which entails the willingness to confront and transcend ambiguities. Chinese actions in the recent border crisis have given a rude shock to our diplomatic and strategic thinking. India now faces her biggest strategic and security challenge in decades. The cruelty at Galwan was premeditated; it must be seen as a deliberate provocation from China to test India's resolve and readiness to protect her territorial integrity. India will have to respond in most emphatic and unambiguous ways. The response is something that not only China will watch, but also India's potential and present allies.

If India continues its policy of appeasing China by camouflaging the issue, like it has done on so many occasions in the past, India will remain a soft target for China. The Chinese will not only keep pushing harder and changing the LAC in their favour by eating away Indian territory inch by inch, but also start dictating what India can and cannot do even in the territory under her control. Other countries will also be watching India's response very closely and carefully to see if India has what it takes to stand up to China and stare it down. Changing that pattern of behaviour will require a more unified and principled response from the world's democracies, perhaps through the formation of a permanent contact group to discuss policy towards China. Given the paranoia and nationalism in Beijing, there is clearly a danger that a tougher, more coordinated response will spark an even more aggressive reaction. But the bigger danger is that the outside world is too distracted, divided and intimidated to respond coherently. That may persuade Beijing to take one risk too many—plunging the world into a new and dangerous crisis. We should also not forget that the desire of *tianxia* may lead China to overreach and ultimately to disintegrate.

REFERENCES

Allison, Graham. *Foreign Affairs*, 2017.

Braude, Joseph and Jiang, Tyler. *Huffington Post*, Online retrieved.

Foreign Affairs, July 2017.

Gilber, Harry. *Nations out of Empires*, Palgrave McMillan, UK, 2001, p. 79.

Huntington. *The Clash of Civilisation and the Remaking of World Order 1999*. Penguin Books, 1999, p. 185.

Indian Express. 16 May, 2017.

Indian Express. 13 July, 2017.

Indian Express. 5 June, 2010.

Jung, C. Sung and Lee, Kihyun. "The Offensive Realists are not wrong". *Pacific Focus*, Inha Journal of International Studies, 2017.

Kissinger, Henry. *On China*.

Mohan Raja, C. "The Politics of Territory", contributed to Carnegie Foundation, May 16, 2017.

Mattis, James. Speech at Shangri-La, June 2, 2018.

Modi, Narendra. Prime Minister of India, at Shangri-La Dialogue, June 1, 2018, Online source.

Nye, Joseph. "Xi Jinping's Marco Polo Strategy", project-syndicate.org, June 12, 2017.

Pye, Lucian. "Social Science Theories in search of Chinese Realities" *China Quarterly*, 132 (1992): 1162.

Shourie, Arun. "Self-Deception", Harper Collins, New Delhi, 2018, pp. 7-8.

Singh Abhijit, IDSA, New Delhi, August 2016.

The Globalisation of World Politics: Oxford University Press, 2008, USA, pp. 70-97.

The Financial Times. May 12, 2017.

Xi: Governance of China, Foreign Language Press, 2014, p. 11.

5

India's Quest for Security: Navigating the Region and the World

Rahul Tripathi

Introduction

India's security dilemma in recent years has focused on two broad parameters. At one level, it has been engaged in confronting the security threats within, which may be having an external dimension, but are largely shaped by domestic variables and outcomes. Low-intensity conflicts, terrorism, naxalite violence, and communal disturbances have been identified as severe internal threats which have seriously undermined security within the country. At the other level, it has had to cope with a challenging external security environment where border disputes, threats to Indian assets and personnel abroad and maritime threats have emerged as major markers shaping our security imperatives from outside. The recent corona crisis opens possibilities of a new intersection between external and internal security. The present paper attempts to map this two-layered security discourse by looking at the complex interplay of the internal and external by looking at India's security threats within the neighbouring region and the world outside and explore whether there is a meeting point between the two. This paper argues that India's security coordinates are linked with local, regional and global and therefore the policy options too reflect this continuum rather than be seen in isolation.

This becomes all the more important now as global politics becomes more uncertain and complex.

Conceptions of India's Security

India's quest for security has been an eternal one, right from independence to the present. Different circumstances and motivations have contributed to the understanding of what is it that would make India secure and political regimes and institutions have grappled with this question at different levels at different points of time. In the process of this search for this fundamental question, new paradigms and frameworks have been suggested at both ideational and policy levels, with relative success or failure of these paradigms being evident in the actual experiences of India's security timeline. In the midst of these deliberations, there has been a quest for what is purported as 'Grand Indian Strategic Thinking' or whether there has been a grand design through which India has tried to meet its security expectations. There is a general presumption that there has not been one and what has emerged as a strategic design therefore is a rather episodic and circumstantial. Besides, India's security thinking often has been segmented and fragmented depending on what the popular political sentiment at a particular point of time is. It is, therefore, ideal to begin first by looking at what these competing conceptions of India's security have been.

Geostrategic Unity and Secure Neighbourhood

In a very classical sense of the term, bordering on continuity of India's colonial past and post-independence evolution, there has been the notion of 'geo strategic unity' of the South Asian subcontinent. The term implies that the security of India is to be seen as linked to the security and well-being of its neighbourhood. As a corollary, any development that imperils our immediate neighbourhood has the potential to disturb the safety and security of the Indian nation itself. It essentially meant that India's security and well-being is intricately linked to the safety and security of its immediate neighbourhood and India must do what it can to ensure the security and protection of its immediate neighbourhood. While this certainly has an external dimension of security associated with it and the internal marker needs a different elaboration, it is worthwhile to explore this argument deeper. India's geopolitical location in South Asia is such that it invariably becomes the focal point of South Asian security. 'Indo-centricity', a term that describes the centrality of India in the South Asian landscape is a matter of geography and history rather than a perception as the country occupies not just a central position within South Asia, but also accounts for nearly three-fourths of the land, resources, and population of the subcontinent. All the countries of the South Asian region, including Pakistan, Nepal, Bangladesh and Bhutan, share land borders and Sri Lanka and the Maldives touch the maritime sphere vis-a-vis India. These borders have had their own legacies and contestations due to the British colonial policy and often been the source of contention between India and her neighbours. To name a few, the line of control between India and Pakistan, open borders with Nepal, exchange of enclaves with Bangladesh, and the maritime border issues with Sri Lanka, all have placed India's geography vis-a-vis her neighbours at some point or the other of contestation. Besides, the very fact that none of these countries have a common border with each other also makes India at times a common transit point for the two South Asian neighbours to connect with each other.

The geopolitical fallout of this location has been that India has traditionally seen any growing external influence in the region as being inimical to its own security and safety. India's desire to remain involved as a key player in the ethnic conflict in Sri Lanka was triggered partly by the desire to keep external powers like the USA out of south Indian shores. India has historically looked at Nepal's act of rebalancing its relationship by having a pro-China tilt as a threat to its own vital interests. Historically, India's attempt to make itself secure has been by securing outcomes in our neighbourhood which would keep the other powers out. This has more often than not, led to situations when smaller neighbours have had a more autonomous perspective of their security needs and that may not always tally with India's conception of the geo-centric unity of the subcontinent. There have been times when political groups in Nepal and Bangladesh, particularly during elections, have raised the pitch about the Indian hand, both visible and invisible, in securing electoral outcomes that favoured it the most. This conception has been reframed by a more 'concentric approach to South Asia's security (Shivshankar Menon, thewire.in).

Collective Security Paradigm for India and South Asia

The other conception of security that encapsulates India's security is the idea of collective security, which has been an important construct in the international relations literature. In its earlier exposition, the idea was seen more as a possible attempt by South Asian countries to feel collectively responsible for their security against threats that were common—an idea that was rooted more in the cold war logic of countering China by being part of a Western alliance (Kennedy, D.E., 1964). The idea of collective security necessitated first a shared perception of a common threat and then the collective will and capability to ensure that the threat is minimized through collective action. The North Atlantic Treaty Organization was perceived as one such example where the member-nations saw a common threat emerging from the Soviet Union and creation of an alliance system that saw a threat to one country as manifesting in a threat to the entire grouping, therefore having a greater deterrent value. There has been an elaboration of this idea in the South Asian context as well, implying whether South Asia, led by India, could have a collective security architecture with her neighbours that could face some of the common threats (not always state-centric) be tackled by them together. But it was argued subsequently that with the complex relationship between India and Pakistan, and China's grand inroads into South Asia which is binding the countries in a pattern of convergent relationships, this model may not hold (Rajan, Saavni, theasiadialogue.com). It is pertinent to note that the idea of cooperation in South Asia, as it germinated in the 1980s, did not base itself on a perceived external threat or challenge, but looked more at the commonalities and convergences that cooperation could build on for collective welfare. Political leadership at the time was far too conscious of the political differences within and the security contentions between the two major partners—India and Pakistan—and therefore SAARC (South Asian Association for Regional Cooperation) was premised on a non-security centric mode of dialogue right from the beginning. As per its Charter, SAARC consciously decided to keep bilateral/political issues out of deliberations and take decisions in the regional spirit with a consensual framework (Iqbal, Jamshed Muhaamad, 2006).

It is quite obvious, with the benefit of hindsight, that the trajectory of SAARC as a potential forum for collective security would have been a non-starter and the concept would need to be applied more in terms of

South Asia being in a position to focus on its internal problems in a such a manner that the political and economic landscape in the region makes the environment conducive for security of the region mutually reinforcing. A more insightful interpretation of security has been given by the 'Human Security' approach, which is seen as a corollary of the human development approach that looks at the concept of security as how it impacts the overall wellbeing of an individual human being rather than the security of the state, defined purely in physical militaristic terms (Chatterjee, Shibashish, 2015). In a way, such an approach to security appeared to be much in tune with the realities in South Asia, which consistently found itself in the bottom quarter of the global human development rankings. While the SAARC process remained painfully slow, caught up mostly in structure rather than substance of cooperation for most of its post-1980s evolution, there were intermittent efforts to inject some momentum into the process so that the essence of this collective/regional security dynamic could at least be given some form from India's side. In the mid-nineties, as part of the so envisioned 'Gujral doctrine', India emphasized on a policy for South Asia where the relationship with smaller neighbours ought to be based on non-reciprocity and extension of unilateral concessions to them without there being similar expectations from the other side. At the same time, smaller states were expected to be sensitive to India's security and political concerns. The logic was simple, given the fact that the geography and history of South Asia had created an asymmetric position for India vis-a-vis other countries, which often had a political fallout and that India reaching the extra mile would be the best way to ensure an environment of trust and friendship that could lead to a mutually beneficial relationship for all. While the doctrine did not see a major departure from previous policies on the ground, it indeed set up a template on good neighbourly relations between India and other South Asian countries which, taken to a logical conclusion, could lead to a more collective security perception through confidence-building (Murthy, Padmaja, 1999). This was also the time when two diplomacies in South Asia were at its glorious best with a number of exchanges between academia, retired diplomats, and media in the region.

The other major instance when India attempted to project a collective security framework through the SAARC mechanism was during its leadership of the 14th Summit in 2007, when it emphasised the themes of regional connectivity as the most important thing in bringing the region together, overcoming the constraints that had been posed to regional infrastructural unity in the post-colonial period. As stated in the summit declaration, "The Heads of State or Government recognised the importance of connectivity in fulfilling these objectives. It was vital to first have better connectivity within South Asia and then with the rest of the world. They agreed to improve intra-regional connectivity, particularly physical, economic, and people-to-people connectivity. They agreed to the vision of a South Asian community, where there was a smooth flow of goods, services, peoples, technologies, knowledge, capital, culture and ideas in the region" (mea.gov.in). While the push did see some significant initiatives on the ground with projects on border areas on integrated container depots, it could not really go beyond in making borders as connecting points rather than dividing lines in South Asia. It would not be wrong to say that the limited accomplishment of a connectivity initiative on the ground, at a time when most of the South Asian economies were growing at a relatively faster pace, and there was a real potential for the region to become more integrated, a big opportunity was lost in making the collective security paradigm work at the grassroots level. In essence, the regional architecture of security, which could have been premised on economic inter-dependencies, was lost sight of and the situation at present remains far more dismal. The way forward for India on the regional front is perhaps to build on the fresh initiatives on connectivity that are being taken both in the maritime and the land border sphere and make them linking points with the sub-regions across the subcontinent, even if it means following a framework different than SAARC. This would also give a continuum between the domestic and regional security dimensions.

India and the Contemporary Global Security: Complexities of an Uncertain World

The complexities of the emergent global political and strategic environment pose a significant policy challenge before India at multiple levels. First and foremost, the uncertainties and unpredictability of global power alliances are more complex than ever before, making partnerships and sustaining them very difficult. Besides the nature of security threats that have emerged from the state as well as non-state actors demand responses that are not just innovative, but also impacting. Finally, institutions that shaped the global security architecture, both organizations and treaty frameworks, are facing a serious threat from nationalist-sovereign assertions by member-states themselves. In such a scenario, India has to deal with a world which is not only changing very fast, but the internal policy making and responses to such global happenings have to have a new flavour, much beyond the idealism-realism binary that India's policy of old and new was often being characterized as. It is imperative to first mark out the nature of the global security environment that has been unfolding in recent years to make a sense of the challenges being faced by India. While it is quite certain that wars and conflicts as they are manifest in the global scenario, have less to do with ideological undercurrents and more to do with geostrategic and geo-economic interests, a system of partnerships and alliances now appear to be more episodic and transient than fixed. For example, during the cold war years, India could take some comfort in the premise that the policy of non-alignment offered us the autonomous space, where we could not only keep ourselves away manifestly from power bloc politics, it also provided us the flexibility to approach any particular player for support as and when the need arose. Thus, while post 1962 war regional dynamics saw India opening up to the USA for assistance, during the 1971 Bangladesh liberation war, it counted on the military and diplomatic support provided by the Soviet Union on its actions. Non-alignment was therefore more a pragmatic policy option than an idealist one that some people would argue (Harshe, Rajan, 1990).

The contemporary global scenario however is far too complex, as the world has moved beyond its post-cold war mainstreaming of democracy and a free market as the carriers of the universal liberal values that were expected to guide the world. In a 'post-globalization' world, which is marked by uncertainty of global economy and resurgence of nation and nationalism as the sovereign space, the contours of global security are going to be defined in terms very different from the earlier premises. In such a situation of perennial flux, nations are being forced to relook at their conventional partnerships and move away from 'isms' in their foreign and strategic policy behaviour. The same approach for India has been outlined in what was described as Non-Alignment 2.0, which emphasized on India creating its own space as it seeks to carve out strategic autonomy in the global sphere (cprindia.org). Some trends in recent years indicate that India will need to enhance such efforts all the more in coming times.

The first very significant pattern unfolding in the global security scenario is that it is difficult to circumscribe a definite view with regard to global security architecture. While the USA would want to retain its position of pre-eminence in the global political economy, it would not want to do it by seeking direct intervention and seek withdrawal from all such involvements that were draining it financially and militarily. The 'Trump' doctrine with all its criticism (Schake, Kori, foreignaffairs.com) would not want to see its allies as free riders and would want them to take on the responsibilities themselves in protecting the US-led regional security architecture. This is manifest in the US potential withdrawal from Afghanistan and its engagement in West Asian hotspots like Libya or Syria. This would still not prevent it from supporting multilateral security frameworks such as the 'Quadrilateral grouping of the USA, Japan, Australia, and India' aimed more at creating a sphere of influence in the Asia-Pacific region. Russia, on the other hand, is playing a balancing act by maintaining its strategic presence in such hotspots and ensuring that its military complex retains a significant presence in the global theatres that matter. At another level, China is gradually but steadily flexing its muscle by riding on its economic power, using its military as a tool in grand continental initiatives such as 'One Belt One Road' of which the China Pakistan Economic Corridor is a showpiece, without actually getting involved in any conflict or conflict-like situations abroad. At another level, one sees trans-regional initiatives like BRICS making their presence felt on the politico-economic landscape showing the effectiveness of the emerging economies in shaping the global policy discourse. In this context, India's best option is to maintain a multiple-level engagement bilaterally and regionally with not just the major players in the system, but also the regional and sub-regional arrangements that may not have had the desired results, but would still have the potential of imparting greater visibility and legitimacy to India's global aspirations. It is pertinent to note that such partnerships may often have overlapping and, at times, competing alignments, but that is the order of the day and the leverages and positioning in these arrangements becomes a handle at times for addressing some core issues of security concerns as well. For instance, while India is a committed partner in the unfolding BRICS (Brazil, Russia, India, China and South Africa), it has maintained a consistent opposition to the Belt and Road Initiative of China stating its geo-strategic concerns and territorial sovereignty arguments. It should be remembered that one major factor that prompted de-escalation of the Doklam standoff between India and China was the fact that the forthcoming BRICS summit at Xiamen in China would have been a non-starter if India had kept away (livemint.com). Similarly, while India will have to keep up the pace of its strategic engagement with the USA, which has made significant strides in recent years, it should have no qualms about maintaining its defence ties intact with the Russians, who have been one of its long-standing partners on defence cooperation. Thus, overlapping and competing partnerships are going to be the norm in the emerging geo-strategic scenario.

The second major issue confronting India's security has been the nature of threat to our internal security which has had deep linkages with external factors, that is, the problem of terrorism. While terrorism over the years has emerged as the most significant global security concern, given its unpredictability and reach, the international outcomes to counter it have remained ineffective. What compounds the problem in the global context is that states which have been instrumental in using terrorism as state policy, often using non-state actors as proxies, are themselves confronting the menace in a manner that destabilizes nations and regions alike. It also has the potential, as it happens in the case of India and Pakistan, to bring two nations to the brink of war (with reference to the recent aerial strikes against Pakistan in response to the Pulwama attack). Unfortunately, though India's stand on terrorism has always found resonance in the global system, it has not translated itself into certain concrete outcomes that it has sought in creating a multi-layered opinion and response on terrorism and its perpetrators. India's call for the UN to adopt a Comprehensive Convention on International Terrorism has not met with appropriate response at the global level, with agreement stuck over 'definition of terrorism'. India's repeated efforts to get Jaish-e-Muhammad chief Maulana Masood Azhar listed as a global terrorist at the UN too have been stalled by China on technicalities (economictimes.indiatimes.com). India has, at the same time, been able to play an active role in getting Pakistan on the terror financing list of the Financial Action Task Force, a global body that has been created to counter money laundering and terror financing (in.reuters.com). India therefore needs to step up its efforts multilaterally to ensure that consensus emerges in the global community on containing terrorism of all kinds.

Finally, it must be realized that the only alternative to the uncertain, unpredictable and often complex global political economy which impinges on security of individual nations is strengthening and not undermining of a more plural-rule based multilateral system. Even though the history of international relations tells us that multilateral or global rules of engagement in global politics are very difficult to adhere to specially when interests of the powerful countries are undermined, that cannot be the pretext for further injecting unilateralism in the global decision-making process. International institutions, no matter how weak they are, if drafted with the spirit of consensus reflect the general will of nations. Whether it is pertaining to the conventions on global security, human rights, or climate change, all are a reflection of the collective will of the global community. There is a need to strengthen these institutions, as they are the only guarantee towards global peace and stability. Strong global institutions provide a reasonable and legitimate framework to address the aberrations that may emerge in the international system. India, as the largest democracy in the world, has to remain committed to the strengthening of a democratic and rule-based multilateral order which would address the complexities of the international system in a more effective way (Swaraj, Sushma,orfonline.org/india).

The COVID Crisis and the New Intersections

The over-engulfing corona crisis which the world finds itself immersed in, poses some radical challenges for looking at the conventional security paradigm discussed so far and has local, national and regional implications. These implications cannot be isolated from each other; rather, they intersect in the following manner. As this is the first major global pandemic of this century, the global community is yet to come to terms with the ways to collectively counter it. Multi-lateral security architectures, whether United Nations or regional arrangements, have not been able to present a counter and more or less left the matters to be addressed by individual states. The external genesis of the crisis notwithstanding, nations are trying to make their national mechanisms stronger and stronger and India is going to be no exception. But the real impact of these measures is going to be felt at ground zero and a country of India's scale and size cannot have a uniform strategy spread across the length and breadth of the nation. Sub-regional—local zones or hot spots—have to become the new theatres of security concern arising out of the pandemic and will have to be addressed.

Conclusion

It is pertinent to note that India confronts a regional and global security environment which is increasingly becoming complex and uncertain. In the region, the security dynamic is complicated by an asymmetric relationship that it has with the neighbours and a divergent security perception. At the global sphere, there exists the challenge of identifying its core security concerns, both military and non-military and being able to build appropriate partnerships that would maximize its security in a growingly uncertain world. The key to this would be its ability to push for a resilient security posture that carries a domestic consensus and at the same time strive for a rule-based multilateral order that counters unilateralism and coercive power projection at the global level. For this, India has to look at its internal and external security matrix as being intertwined and interconnected. Domestic responses to security threats would set our global template and the international environment would provide us greater leverage to take a more decisive action on the security threats back home. In this direction, as a democratic nation, generating internal as well as external consensus would be a key responsibility that the Indian state would have to factor in deeply as part of its domestic and foreign policy.

REFERENCES

Chatterjee, Shibashish. 'The Political Economy of Human Security in South Asia', in *Bhumitra Chakma, South Asia in Transition: Democracy, Political Economy and Security*, Palgrave, New York, 2015.

Harshe, Rajen. *India's Non Alignment:* A Conceptual Reconstruction, *Economic and Political Weekly*, vol. 25, Nos. 7-8, 1990, pp. 399-405.

http://www.*cprindia.org*/research/reports/nonalignment-20-foreign-and-strategic-policy-india-twenty-first-century.

https://thewire.in/diplomacy/india-south-asia-geopolitics-shivshankar-menon.

https://*economictimes.indiatimes.com*/news/defence/china-again-says-no-to-back-indias-bid-to-list-jem-chief-azhar-as-global-terrorist-by-un/articleshow/68006847.cms?from=mdr.

https://*in.reuters.com*/article/india-kashmir/india-presses-for-pakistan-to-stay-on-terrorism-financing-list-idINKCN1QA1US.

https://www.livemint.com/opinion/c4ws2jwOqP7ALa7YORbC1M/Indias-clever-use-of-the-BRICS-card-in-Doklam-standoff-reso.html.

https://www.mea.gov.in/press-release.htm?dtl/2378/Declaration+of+the+fourteenth+SAARC+Summit.

https://*www.orfonline.org*/india-commited-demoratic-rules-based-international-order-says-sushma-swaraj-47282/.

Iqbal, Jamshed Muhaamad: SAARC: Origin, Growth, Potential Achievements, *Pakistan Journal of History and Culture*, vol. 25(2), 2006.

Kennedy, D.E. The Scope of Collective Security in South Asia, *The World Today*, vol. 20, no.10, 1964, pp. 440-448.

Murthy, Padmaja. *The Gujral Doctrine and Beyond, Strategic Analysis*, Routledge Taylor and Frances 1999.

Rajan, Saavni, http://theasiadialogue.com/ 2017/05/25/ would-a-nato-like-security-alliance-work-in-south- asia/.

Schake, Kori. How To Make Right What Trump Gets Wrong, *Foreign Affairs*, https://www.foreignaffairs.com/articles/2019-04-16/back-basics.

With the recent aerial strikes against Pakistan in response to the Pulwama attack on Indian soldiers, the threshold that till now prevented an escalation of conflict between the two nuclear armed neighbours no longer exists.

6

Cultural Conflict and Rise of Extremism: Geopolitical Security Threat in South Asia

Richa Bhatt Ranade

Introduction

Of late, the South Asian region has acquired growing attention, be it due to India's rapid growth as well as geo-political and geo-strategic importance or because it is seen as a theatre where all the major world powers have diverse and at times clashing interests. At times, this engagement with South Asian countries has led to periods of heightened diplomatic and on-ground standoffs. South Asia, while mired in these diplomatic alignments, has seen escalating tensions with proxy wars and a strong emergence of extremism, having global ramifications. Consequently, little is achieved in terms of development and beneficial spin-offs. Global engagement should ideally spur cooperation, trade, and economic development, rather than lead to political tensions and the resultant mass deprivation. All these factors encapsulate the global importance of South Asia. It represents around one quarter of the world's population or 27 per cent of the global population.

The rapid economic growth of this region, especially India, in the beginning of this century as well as a marked rise of extremist Islamist militant groups in both Pakistan and Afghanistan and a growing rivalry between India and China makes South Asia a very relevant subject of study. Apart from focusing on traditional threats in the form of terrorism or extremism, the present paper draws our attention to the non-traditional threats in the form of environmental insecurity, human insecurity, climate change, health insecurity, cyber insecurity and the latest in this series, the Covid crises, which according to experts is perhaps the worst crises which the world has seen after the second world war. In the present paper, an attempt has been made to understand various problems and challenges which are being faced by this region and how the presence of new players like China and Russia further complicates the matter. Despite so many challenges, the leadership of the region is equally concerned about its future and is making all diplomatic efforts to strengthen the economy of South Asia, as well as reduce the challenges and threats coming from unconstitutional players.

Ground for Terrorism

July 2008 saw the Indian embassy in Kabul struck by a suicide car-bombing attack, the deadliest since the fall of the Taliban in 2001. On 26 November 2008, the Mumbai terror attack claimed more than 150 lives. On April 21, 2019, over 300 people were killed and around 500 others injured in eight coordinated attacks on churches and hotels in Sri Lanka on Easter Sunday. The April 21 terror attack in Sri Lanka is among the biggest terror attacks in South Asia in the past 15 years. It comes as a grim reminder of how vulnerable the region is to terrorism. Besides this, the gunning down of nearly 150 people (mostly schoolchildren) at an army-run school in Peshawar, Pakistan, in 2014, and the February 14, 2019 Pulwama terror attack that killed 40 Indian security personnel, are testimony to the fact that South Asia's recent history has been marred by routine terror attacks. "An analysis of terror attacks that took place worldwide between 1970 and 2017 reveals that when it comes to terrorism, South Asia is the second most affected region in the world". (Rawat: 2019)

South Asia faces a grave security threat due to increasing extremism and terrorist activities resulting in the highest regional concentration of militant groups in the world, including some of the most wanted Jihadist groups such as Al Qaeda, the Haqqani Network, the Taliban and Lashkar-e-Taiba, the Afghan Taliban, Tehrik-e-Taliban Pakistan, Lashkar-e-Jhangvi, Jamat-u-Dawa, Student Islamic Movement of India, Indian Mujahedeen, and a number of other groups in neighbouring countries, all involved in terrorist activities in South Asia. All these militant groups have ensured that South Asia has the highest annual number of fatalities attributed to terrorism. It is the common element creating instability and insecurity across the region. The Prime Minister of Pakistan, Imran Khan, in his recent visit to the USA said, "Until we came to power, the government did not have the political will, because when you talk about militant groups, we still have about 30,000-40,000 armed people who have been trained and fought in some part of Afghanistan or Kashmir." At another event, he blamed previous dispensations for the free run terrorists had in Pakistan, saying: "Part of the reason was our governments were not in control. There were 40 different militant groups operating within Pakistan." (*The Times of India*, 2019)

There are many factors that have gone into making this region so vulnerable and volatile. A poor literacy rate, rampant unemployment, growing economic disparity, weak industrialisation, and uneven development patterns in South Asia are among the predominant causes contributing to violence in the region. Besides, with India's emergence as a regional power, Indo-Pak rivalry, Sino-Indian relations, the US presence in Afghanistan, nuclear proliferation, a paradigm shift in international politics, and a transformation from a bipolar to an unipolar world, makes South Asia a classic case for engaging research. It is also true that South Asia is the most densely populated, home to the largest number of poor and malnourished children in the world, facing the problem of climate change, with hundreds of millions of South Asians suffering from serious health issues, hunger, child trafficking, economic disparity, crime, and physical survival. Growing industrialisation and urbanisation has further escalated the demand for precious natural resources such as fossil fuels, agricultural land and freshwater—that are in limited supply and under great strain already. These threats are unfolding within broader socio-economic and political contexts that are underpinned by high levels of inequalities and social injustice. This kind of scenario has provided a fertile ground to the unconstitutional players, external powers, and extra-regional elements to interfere in the region and giving a dangerous tilt to the existing volatile situation.

It is but natural, therefore, that such starkly adverse economic and social conditions would give rise to social tensions and violence. Vanda

Felbab-Brown has succinctly summarised this situation. "Besides the failure of transition to modernity among these South Asian states, the political culture has also led to ethnic solidarities and identification with religion and culture. Pakistan has long been a difficult and disruptive neighbour to Afghanistan, hoping to limit India's influence there, and cultivating radical groups within Afghanistan as proxies. It has augmented Afghanistan's instability by providing intelligence, weapons, and protection to the Afghan Taliban and the Haqqani network". (Felbab-Brown: 2018) Khalid Hussain supports this argument by saying that the Pakistan army considers acting against the Haqqani group as being against Pakistan's national interests. Any such action would be detrimental to the idea of increasing Pakistan's influence in Afghanistan after the US withdrawal. This has been part of Pakistan's 'strategic depth' strategy aimed at countering Indian hegemony in the region. (Hussain: 2012)

Major Players of South Asia: India-Pakistan-Afghanistan

The largest players of this region are India, Pakistan, and Afghanistan whose geo-strategic locations give this region an important position and thus, is extensively observed by the rest of the world. Bilateral relations between these countries are tilted more towards conflicts rather than cooperation. The growing rivalry and mistrust between India and Pakistan and their ambition to control Afghanistan, further push South Asia towards the danger zone. For centuries, Afghanistan, located at the crossroads of south and central Asia, has been at the centre of struggles between big powers for strategic dominance. It has also been the graveyard of great powers. (Subramanian: 2019) India is interested in retaining Afghanistan as a friendly state and has cultivated a significant partnership with it with an aspiration to be seen as a regional power as well as to monitor Pakistan, which is trying to deny India these very opportunities. India faced many security challenges from the Taliban in Afghanistan during the 1990s.

Pakistan, on the other hand, has been instrumental in the birth and continued support of several militant groups like the Lashkar-e-Taiba, Harkat-ul-Mujahideen/Harkat-ul-Ansar, and Harkat-ul-Jihad-al-Islami, which operate in India. It is known that all of these groups have trained in Afghanistan, and enjoy varying degrees of closeness to the Taliban and also the al-Qaeda. Thus, it is in India's interest that Afghanistan should not again become a safe haven for such terrorist groups and syndicates.

Radicalism and fundamentalism inspire and incite the spread of terrorism in this region while becoming a security threat for India. Radical and fundamental Islamic inclinations in Pakistan and Afghanistan are not without their consequential impacts on the domestic social fabric of India. As a natural consequential development, Hindu fundamentalism in India is triggered by such external developments. Bilateral relations between Pakistan and Afghanistan have been strained ever since the formation of Pakistan in August 1947. Afghanistan has the singular distinction of having voted against the admission of Pakistan to the United Nations in 1947. The government of Afghanistan laid claim over Pashtun territory, as well as Baluchistan, due to the presence of deep cultural, ethnic, and historical bonds. On the other hand, the Pakistani military has accused Afghanistan of sheltering various terrorist groups that attack Pakistan. Afghanistan has continuously targeted and held Pakistan's intelligence agency, the ISI, responsible for financial and logistic support to terror outfits and the Taliban. The ISI is accused of the establishment and continual support to terrorist camps within Pakistani territory that frequently attack Afghanistan. There is considerable anti-Pakistan sentiment within Afghanistan, while a strong negative sentiment persists towards the Afghan refugees in Pakistan, even in the Pashtun-dominated regions.

"Pakistan does not want Afghanistan to become a satellite of India", Hillary Clinton said last year, "so it has in the past invested in a certain amount of instability in Afghanistan". Her reference was to the Pashtun Taliban in Northern Waziristan that has been fighting the coalition forces in Afghanistan besides bleeding the Indian economy and tying up her army in Kashmir, the region over which it has a running conflict with Pakistan since 1948. (Hussain: 2012) From 2001 to date, the Taliban has emerged as a key player in the Afghan peace process. Now major players like the USA, Russia and China have accepted this significant position of the Taliban. In fact just a few days ago, the USA has reached a preliminary peace deal with the Taliban that will pave the way for a phased withdrawal of U.S. military forces from Afghanistan and bring an end to America's longest war. "Since only Pakistan has influence over the Taliban, this turn of events can be considered as a diplomatic victory of Pakistan whereas India is increasingly being sidelined in these proceedings". (Sethu Krishnan: 2019)

After more than eighteen years of war in Afghanistan, the USA and the Taliban reached an agreement in February 2020 to end it. Central to the deal is a significant reduction of U.S. troops and guarantees from the Taliban that the country will not become a safe haven for terrorists. The U.S. has reduced the number of troops it has in Afghanistan to 8,600 in accordance with the February deal. The move to reduce America's military presence in Afghanistan is fraught with political and military peril. Critics—including some of Trump's strongest supporters—fear a U.S. withdrawal will open the door for a resurgence of Al-Qaida, as well as other terrorist groups operating in Afghanistan, such as the Islamic State. Nearly 3,500 members of the international coalition forces have died in Afghanistan since the 2001 invasion. The figures for Afghan civilians, militants and government forces are difficult to quantify. In a February 2019 report, the UN said that more than 32,000 civilians had died. The Watson Institute at Brown University says 58,000 security personnel and 42,000 opposition combatants have been killed.

Sen. Lindsey Graham, R-S.C., said in an August 27 interview on *Fox News*, "Al-Qaida is alive and well in Afghanistan. ISIS is stronger today than they've ever been in Afghanistan. There is no substitute for American forces in Afghanistan to protect the American homeland from radical Islam." He and others argue that the Taliban itself is a militant fundamentalist group, and cannot be trusted to keep Afghanistan free of terrorists. "Trump is repeating now the mistakes of Obama: appearing to re-establish artificial deadlines rather than matching conditions," said James Cunningham, who served as the U.S. ambassador to Afghanistan in President Barack Obama's Administration. (Shesgreen, 2019) For the first time, a U.S. administration has recognised and accepted that it cannot effectively stay in Afghanistan indefinitely. Washington has now accepted that the eventual resolution of the conflict will only come from a political process that includes the Taliban. The U.S. has accepted the rationale of the Pakistanis—supported by other regional players such as Iran, Russia, and China—that the Taliban must be part of the government.

Maria J. Stephan, who had served in the US embassy at Kabul from 2009 to 2011, has emphasised the need for civil resistance. She writes, "Nonviolent campaigns using boycotts, protests, strikes and other nonviolent tactics had been twice as effective as violent insurgencies—they achieved their goals 53 per cent of the time compared to 26 per cent for violent campaigns. We also found that political transitions driven by civil resistance led to democratic outcomes 57 per cent of the time, versus 6 per cent for transitions driven by armed insurgencies. Nonviolent resistance was much less likely to lead to civil war compared to violent insurrections, and more likely to advance social and economic development. In both the short and the long term, nonviolent resistance has had a comparative advantage over violence.... Nonviolent campaigns achieved their goals in places where regime violence was brutal, where poverty was high, and where societies were divided. Structural conditions matter, but the strategies and tactics used by the protesters can matter more. While our research focused on campaigns targeting incumbent regimes, other studies of civil resistance to intra-state conflicts in places like Liberia, Nepal, and Colombia, have found that broad-based nonviolent movements have successfully pressured warring parties to end civil wars." (Stephan: 2019)

The withdrawal of the U.S. army from Afghanistan, as well as reducing financial aid to Pakistan would drastically change the internal structure of the entire South Asian region. Overall, the U.S. military aid to Pakistan has decreased by 60 per cent between 2010 and August 2017, without a significant impact on Pakistan's behaviour. Moreover, Pakistan can seek aid from others. Russia awaits an opportunity to undermine the USA. Military cooperation with Pakistan risks alienating India and Russia no longer considers the Afghan Taliban a prime enemy in Afghanistan. Pakistan can also seek military assistance from China. Although China does not want to see a further destabilization in Afghanistan and an export of terrorism outside Afghan borders, it has not been willing to take punitive action against Pakistan's support for the Haqqani and the Afghan Taliban. (Felbab-Brown: 2018)

Apart from this changing scenario and perspective of the world powers in Afghanistan, Pakistan and India are engaged in their own turf war. Both India and Pakistan have historical claims, engagement and influence in Afghanistan. Resolving such earlier geo-political conflicts, therefore, is key to the future of peace in Pakistan and for this, the relations between India and Pakistan must necessarily improve. The end to the war in Afghanistan, therefore, can begin only after peace arrives and is sustainable between India and Pakistan. (Hussain: 2012) The marked nuclear posturing and rivalry between India and Pakistan, followed by numerous armed conflicts, border disputes, further aggravates the situation. The two neighbours after the partition in 1947 have seen wars in 1948, 1965, 1971 and 1999, along with a continual number of low-intensity conflicts. Prolonged, unresolved disputes have resulted in acrimonious relations between the two countries and the pursuit of regional supremacy has increased the instability within the region.

The continual power game between the two major players of the region, India and Pakistan, has provided two perspectives to the countries in the region. According to Stephen P. Cohen, "Classic geopolitics offers them two strategies. One is to ally with the region's dominant power, India, and allow Delhi to limit one's ties with Islamabad, Dhaka, Colombo, Kathmandu and even Male. The other is to maintain ties with India's neighbours as a way of keeping up the pressure on India". The second strategy brings Pakistan close to China. The way China is rapidly expanding its wings over the Indian Ocean Region [IOR] is a cause of worry for India. Chinese naval inroads into the IOR after the People's Liberation Army [PLA] established its first overseas base at Djibouti in the Horn of Africa and continues to have naval turnaround facilities at Karachi can hardly be ignored by India. The growing mistrust between India and Pakistan gives an opportunity to other global powers like the USA and China to make an entry in the region. Stephen P. Cohen says, "I would be the first to note that the policies of the USA have, at times, made things more difficult in South Asia. This is also true of China, and, in the past, the Soviet Union." (Cohen: 1998) Washington built and deployed weapons in obscene numbers and in some cases, with unreliable command and control procedures.

The Narendra Modi government's sweeping constitutional changes in Jammu and Kashmir have come against the backdrop of changing regional dynamics. After New Delhi abrogated the special status to Jammu and Kashmir and bifurcated the state into two Union Territories, Pakistan, reacting to India's move, has not only criticised its neighbour, but has also drastically reduced its diplomatic ties and suspended bilateral trade with India. The American withdrawal of troops from Afghanistan over the next year is expected to leave its impact, especially as it is likely to put the Taliban in the driving seat in Kabul, and Pakistan in a position of influence. This may resonate in the Valley in the same way as the 1989 Soviet pullout fuelled the 1990s militancy. (Ahmed: 2015)

Non-Traditional Security Threats in South Asia: Threat Spectrum Revisited in the form of COVID-19

However, time and developments at the international level proved that security is not static; it evolves with the changing nature of threats. The traditional, interstate security threat perception has been replaced by intrastate, non-traditional security threats like environmental insecurity, human insecurity, climate change, health insecurity, cyber insecurity and many more are a few prominent non-traditional security threats faced by modern states in the 21st century. Along with the traditional concept of security, non-traditional security is also an emerging concern. Comprehensive security, encompassing political, social, economic and environment security is a major agenda. South Asia is the birthplace of numerous traditional and non-traditional security threats.

The non-military causes like illegal cross border movement, population growth, poverty, social inequality, money laundering, transnational terrorism, smuggling, mainly of drugs and arms and environmental degradation are becoming the source of uncertainty at the regional level. The inadequate national security apparatus in countering traditional and non-traditional security threats in South Asia is demanding a cooperative security architecture to mitigate escalating threats for a long time. Corruption is major regional economic security concern in the South Asian region. (Cohen: 1998) Non-military threats are increasing at a much faster rate than ever before and the latest addition in this category is the onset of the corona crises, which has dangerously reversed the path of economic growth all over the world. The worst hit victims of this virus are the poorly developed and densely populated countries of the world. With 1.94 billion people, South Asia is home to almost exactly one-quarter of the world's population, is extremely poor, densely populated and geographically close to China, where the SARS-CoV-2 virus originated. The COVID-19 pandemic was expected to be a "perfect storm", a severe blow for the region, especially their economy and pushed them back into deep poverty.

According to a Hudson Institute think-tank report titled 'Crisis from Kolkata to Kabul: COVID-19's Impact on South Asia', jointly authored by Indian-origin Hudson research scholar Aparna Pande and former Pakistan Ambassador to the USA, Husain Haqqani, the corona virus pandemic threatens not only lives and livelihoods in South Asia; it could also be the precursor of significant political and strategic shifts in the region. China's growing presence in the region is very alarming. Pakistan and Sri Lanka have been the target of Beijing's ambitious Belt and Road (BRI) scheme, criticised for creating 'debt traps' by burdening fiscally weak countries with unsustainable debt. The BRI is Chinese President Xi Jinping's signature global infrastructure policy. First announced in 2013, the project promises to build ports, roads and railways to revive the ancient Silk Road and create new trade corridors linking China to Asia, Africa and Europe. The BRI also includes the China-Pakistan Economic Corridor (CPEC), which India opposed as it goes through Pakistan-occupied Kashmir (PoK).

The report further says, "Pakistan and Sri Lanka will likely move in the direction of negative growth and will need debt relief from their international creditors. Without it, Sri Lanka faces the prospect of a sovereign debt default. Both countries are likely to look to China as their benefactor, as their leaders have tended to do for a while." China will most likely press its advantage by bailing out South Asia's indebted governments, "in exchange for its pound of flesh". There have been considerable concerns in India over China's growing presence in the Indian Ocean region. India has been trying to expand maritime cooperation with countries of the region including Sri Lanka, the Maldives, Indonesia, Thailand, Vietnam, Myanmar and Singapore, primarily to check the growing Chinese assertiveness. The Bangladesh and Indian economies will survive the devastation, but their governments will have to restore growth by protecting and encouraging investment. In a goodwill gesture, the Government of India has provided 10 broad gauge diesel locomotives to Bangladesh. Its Foreign Minister, A.K. Abdul Momen, said that it would help bring both sides even closer and further take the "rock solid" bilateral relations to new heights. Momen said, "We believe 'connectivity is productivity' and our visionary PM (Sheikh Hasina) has been trying to expand our connectivity with our neighbours...Robust railway connectivity is an enabler of economic growth, a platform for uniform development and a catalyst for national integration...". (*The Indian Express*, 2020)

Conclusion

South Asia is the world's fastest-growing region, and is even faster than China. This is explained by strong expansion in countries like India, improving business competition, improved public institutions, improved public health, improved international trade, quality primary education, infrastructure development, increasing foreign investment, transparent financial systems, and economic diversification. The three emerging economic heavyweights in this region are India, Pakistan, and Bangladesh. These three, along with the other countries in South Asia, have unique development challenges but are addressing them through good fiscal and monetary policies and service delivery. (*World Atlas:* 2019)

The COVID-19 crisis has triggered an economic fallout in South Asia that will drive millions into poverty and worsen inequality. Amid the mounting human and economic toll, South Asian countries have ramped up action to curb the health emergency, protect their people, and set the stage for recovery. The impact of the pandemic is so high that it will take years to normalise things. The economic damage will increase the levels of poverty and inequality. In the regional context, it is feared that China could further expand its influence at the expense of India.

"This would come at the expense of India's security and U.S. influence in the region. India and the USA must develop a plan to counter efforts China will likely make to strengthen its position in the Indian Ocean by deepening ties with Pakistan and Sri Lanka, by taking advantage of their economic woes due to the corona virus pandemic." said the Hudson report. It is high time when the South Asian countries', socio-economic problems and human security issues need to be accorded the highest priority by governments. If socio-economic problems and human security issues are properly handled by their respective governments, the region would be marked by fair chances of improvement. Negotiations at both bilateral and multilateral levels would amicably settle inter-state disputes. Each country in South Asia is playing a significant role in the region, irrespective of its size and population. Bhutan and Nepal, both located in the Himalayas, have huge investments in hydroelectric power despite infrastructural challenges.

If South Asia maintains its momentum, the region will most likely achieve economic development and alleviate poverty and economic problems. However, predicting the future in a volatile region remains challenging. Terrorism, jihadist elements and insurgency remain threats to stability and growth. Although Afghanistan and Pakistan are the most affected, these challenges normally affect regional economies. Strategic trends and sound judgement suggest that the two countries may experience future insecurity challenges, as they are part of the epicentre of international terrorism and ideological extremism. (*World Atlas*: 2019) Stephen P. Cohen says, "In addition to the individual state efforts to deal with extremism, the South-Asian countries should come forward and join hands to combat the menace of terrorism and violence. Concerted regional effort is also required as the problem has an additional external dimension to it. There is no shortcut to eradicating regional problems since they are the result of a consistent and gradual failure of the state to deal with the issue of public security and grievances, and also the failure of society to curb tendencies of extremism and intolerance."

Cohen further writes, "To summarise, South Asia can teach the rest of us something about a number of security-related problems. To my mind, the most important of these is the way in which the region has managed its own diversity. My own country benefited enormously from ideas and strategies developed in India, as have a number of other states and regions. There have been some setbacks, but largely, the record is excellent. We have learned that managing social diversity is a labour-intensive activity, that an open, democratic society assists rather than retards this effort, and that one need not be a wealthy, industrialised state to have a functioning democracy." Stephen further gave an emphasis to the Gujral Doctrine, according to which India, being a leading country in the region should be more restrained as well as generous in its approach towards its neighbours." (Cohen: 1998)

South Asian countries should, therefore, focus on strengthening their economies through structural reforms and robust trade regimes, SAARC's agenda should be promoted so that regional trade volume could be enhanced. Emphasis should be placed on diplomatic means, political dialogues and negotiations at both bilateral and multilateral levels to amicably settle inter-state disputes. Global powers should play a proactive role in bridging the divide between disputants by facilitating political engagements between South Asian countries, they underscored, adding that China's Belt and Road Initiative (BRI) offers a vision of common economic development for the entire South Asian region, which may eventually lead to a common security architecture. Rather than attempting to sink this economic initiative in controversy, it should be seen as a means for mutual economic prosperity and development, they recommended. (*The News:* 2018)

REFERENCES

"40,000 terrorists operating from Pak, admits Imran", *The Times of India*, July 25, 2019.

"India, Pakistan, Afghanistan: The new great game", *The Indian Express*, Nirupama Subramanian, Monday, August 12, 2019.

India hands over 10 broad gauge locomotives to Bangladesh, *The Indian Express*, July 28, 2020.

India, Pakistan and Afghanistan: Relations & Implications, by Khalid Hussain, https://www.gsdmagazine.org/india-pakistan-and-afghanistan-relations-implictions/

India, Pakistan and Afghanistan: Relations & Implications, by Khalid Hussain, https://www.gsdmagazine.org/india-pakistan-and-afghanistan-relations-implications/

India, Pakistan and Afghanistan: Relations & Implications, by Khalid Hussain, https://www.gsdmagazine.org/india-pakistan-and-afghanistan-relations-implications/01.2012.

India-Afghanistan Relations—Everything you need to know, Sethu Krishnan M. https://www.clearias.com/india-afghanistan-relations/.

"People Power Can Boost the Afghan Peace Process", Maria J. Stephan, Director, Nonviolent Action, Maria Stephan explains how findings from a book she wrote partly while living in Afghanistan are relevant today. Tuesday, July 23, 2019/by: Maria J. Stephan.

Realm of non-traditional security: 'South Asian countries face multiple common challenges',https://www.thenews.com.pk/print/405197-realm-of-non-traditional-security-south-asian-countries-face-multiple-common-challenges, 13.12.2018.

"Security Architecture of South Asia: A New Framework of Analysis", Raja Qaiser Ahmed, Misbah Arif & Sheryar Khan, *The Dialogue*, Vol. X No. 3, 2015 in https://www.researchgate.net /publication/320191870.

"Security Challenge in South Asia", Stephen P. Cohen, senior research scholar, Brookings Institute, Washington, DC. Excerpted from his keynote lecture delivered at the summer workshop of the Regional Centre for Strategic Studies, Colombo.

"Sri Lanka terror attack: How South Asia emerged as hotbed for terror attacks since 1970", Mukesh Rawat in https://www.indiatoday.in/ world/story/ terror-attacks-sri-lanka-india-pakistan- south-asia-middle-east-1507353-2019-04-22, 22.04.2019.

Stephen P. Cohen, senior research scholar, Brookings Institute, Washington, DC. Excerpted from his keynote lecture delivered at the summer workshop of the Regional Centre for Strategic Studies, Colombo.

Stephen P. Cohen, senior research scholar, Brookings Institute, Washington, DC. Excerpted from his keynote lecture delivered at the summer workshop of the Regional Centre for Strategic Studies, Colombo, 3.12.1998.

"The Poorest Countries in South Asia", Worldatlas, www.worldatlas.com.

The Poorest Countries in South Asia, Worldatlas https://www.worldatlas.com/ articles/the-poorest -countries-in-south-asia.html.

"US Taliban agree to preliminary peace deal", Dierdre Shesgreen, Tom Vanden Brook & Nicholas Wu, Pressreader.com, *US Today*, U.S. edition, 3 September 2019.

Vanda Felbab-Brown, Friday, January 5, 2018, https://www.brookings.edu/blog/order-from-chaos/2018/01/05/ why-pakistan-supports-terrorist-groups-and-why-the-us-finds-it-so-hard-to-induce –change/#cancel, 05.01.2018.

Why Pakistan supports terrorist groups, and why the US finds it so hard to induce change, Vanda Felbab-Brown, Friday, January 5, 2018, https://www.brookings.edu/ blog/order-from-.chaos/ 2018/.01/.05/.why-pakistan-supports-terrorist-groups-and-why-the-us-finds-it-so-hard-to-induce -change/#cancel, 05.01.2018.

7

Trade and Security Issues: Analysing the Challenges of the Chinese Belt and Road Initiative

Bhawana Pokharna

Introduction

The Chinese BRI is one of the most talked about and written topic of international politics nowadays. Political Science scholars around the world are busy analysing the impact and challenges posed by this initiative. The proposed paper aims to analyse One Belt One Road, its inception, its progress and trade and security challenges it has posed with special reference to India. The signature project of Chinese President Xi Jinping is one of its own kind and has ample geo-strategic implications. The project has made an active Chinese presence in most parts of the globe including Latin America and the Arctic region.

The Chinese Belt and Road Initiative is the most ambitious project of the 21st century, which aims to enhance trade and cooperation by connecting three continents of the globe. The project is an attempt to revive the ancient Silk Road stretching from Asia to Europe that gets its name from the silk that was carried along it. The ancient Silk Road flourished during China's Han dynasty (206 BC–AD 220) and famous traveller Marco Polo adventured through it. The great Chinese explorer, Admiral Zheng, accomplished seven expeditions through the maritime silk route during the regime of the Ming dynasty. All these stopped prominently in the Middle East and central Asia and were the developed trade centres of the ancient Silk Route. The present BRI initiative is a policy initiative based on historical practice of Chinese empires, and takes inspiration from Confucian spiritual values. The concept was re-launched by Chinese President Xi Jinping during his visit to Indonesia in October 2013 soon after he assumed office in China. Xi Jinping is a visionary leader of China guided by the mission to enhance Chinese assertiveness and power in the global arena. He advanced his vision of the Chinese dream, which refers to the great rejuvenation of the Chinese nation juxtaposed with regaining the old lost Chinese glory. The Belt and Road Initiative is a combination of the Maritime Silk Road (MSR) with a land-based counterpart, called the Silk Road Economic Belt (SREB). Harkavy (2007) believes that it is a grand Chinese strategy to search for natural resources and develop overland transport networks in order to fulfil its interests. Chaturvedy and Guy (2012) think that China is developing an infrastructure of rail, road, port and energy through its western region, across South Asia and beyond. The enhanced Chinese trade would increase the use of Chinese currency highlighting the increasing Chinese economic assertiveness. A report of CFR (*CFR*, 2019) suggests that besides these physical infrastructures, China will build fifty SEZs based on the Shenzhen Special Economic Zone model, which was launched by China's economic reforms in 1980. The idea of reviving the silk route manifests the Chinese innovative approach and its grand strategy.

More than 70 countries have agreed to participate in the ambitious project which has the prospect to impact 4.4 billion people which is 63 per cent of the world population, and deals with a combined economy of $ 21 trillion which is 29 per cent of the global volume. The BRI comprising the Maritime Silk Route (MSR) and the Silk Road Economic Belt (SREB) aims to reach Europe after originating from China's South Eastern coast. The proposed sea route begins in the South East coast of China and passes through Vietnam, Indonesia, Bangladesh, India, Sri Lanka, the Maldives and East Africa. Along the African coast, China wishes to develop ports in Kenya, Djibouti, Tanzania and Mozambique. The MSR would continue from the African coast to the Red Sea and through the Suez Canal to the Mediterranean Sea. After crossing Athens, the road ends in Venice where it joins the land-based belt route. The land-based route, which starts from the Chinese city of Xian, travels through central Asia, West Asia and the Middle East, before reaching Europe and ending in Venice. The 'Belt Corridors' run along the major Eurasian land bridges, through China-Mongolia-Russia, China-Central and West Asia, The China-Indochina Peninsula, Bangladesh-China-India-Myanmar, and China-Pakistan Belt Corridor comprises a network of planned ports and other coastal infrastructure projects that extends from South and Southeast Asia to East Africa and the northern Mediterranean Sea.

Chinese Foreign Ministry official Hua Chunying while outlining the aims and objectives of the BRI said that China intended to build the Maritime Silk Road of the 21st century while realizing the goals of mutual benefit and common development, peaceful, harmonious co-existence with relevant countries (*NDRF*, 2015). It wishes to enhance people-to-people contacts, mutual trust, joint cooperation and regional integration. China expanded the MSR to the Pacific Ocean while connecting Asia, Africa, Oceania and Europe.

The document emphasised joint development and benefit-sharing among participating countries and wishes to work with the spirit of the plan, develop and share the benefits (*Economic Times*, 2015). The project has been extended to Latin America and the Arctic region also suggesting the giganticness of the project.

Objectives of Launching OBOR

Experts see the BRI as one of the cardinal initiatives of China under President Xi, along with the 'Made in China 2025' economic development strategy. For Xi, the BRI is a strategic initiative in response to the U.S. "pivot to Asia" policy, as well as an attempt for China to get new investment destinations, promote its export market, augment domestic consumption and Chinese income. It denotes Xi's aggressive foreign policy approach which antagonises his predecessor Deng's maxim: "hide your strength, bide your time".

The BRI initiative also has a significant domestic thrust.

- The widespread network will connect China with emerging and developed economies, thereby giving China an opportunity to collaborate with the different economies.

- It is also an attempt to improve the recent decline in the country's growth rate. The Belt and Road Initiative is seen as a way of increasing levels of domestic consumption and diverting China's manufacturing overcapacity.
- The cardinal domestic objectives of the Chinese Communist Party (CCP) are to introduce structural changes and maintain a high growth rate. This is important because the regime's legitimacy and the upholding of the social order in China rely heavily on the CCP's ability to secure the economic prosperity of the country (Seo & Cho, Young, 2013).
- The BRI is therefore seen as a means to ensure domestic stability and maintain the predominance of the Communist party. It also aims to enhance the international stature of China as well as to boost domestic industries.
- China also seeks to address the disparity in economic growth that exists among different provinces in China. The coastal regions have made enough development while the central and western provinces of China are left behind since the economic modernization programme was launched in China in the late seventies. The CCP hopes to produce rapid economic development by connecting provinces such as Xinjiang to Central, South and West Asia through major infrastructure projects (Summers, 2016).
- Removing the economic disparity between Chinese provinces is an important purpose for Beijing as it is understood that the economic gains accrued by the project will help to combat Islamic separatism (Fallon, 2015).

From this, it is clear that although the BRI is the key foreign policy platform of President Xi Jinping, it also has noteworthy domestic objectives that aim to boost the nation's economy, strengthen the CCP's legitimacy and hold the diverse populations of the Chinese state together.

Some scholars believe that China's initiative is to secure its maritime energy supply chain across the Indian Ocean Region and the South China Sea which is the prominent route for seaborne energy. As China increasingly relies on seaborne energy trade, Beijing has come to attach more importance to the security of its sea lines of communication (SLOCs) and has a growing strategic interest in ensuring unhampered access to the energy trade. The importance of the sea lines of communication for China has greatly increased as it opened up to the world economy since the open door policy of the late 1970s. As an export-oriented economy with growing energy demands, which can only be met through imports, China's survival and prosperity is closely tied to the sea-borne trade. Today China's national oil companies have assets across the world in the Middle East, Africa, North America, Latin America and Asia. China relies on seaborne deliveries for much of its oil and natural gas as well as coal. As the majority of China's seaborne energy imports transit through the Indian Ocean Region and the South China Sea, Beijing is aware of the strategic importance of the western SLOCs (Lane, 2015).

Funding the Project

The proposed "One Belt, One Road" (OBOR) is a US$ 1.4 trillion project. China wishes to make a huge financial commitment of US$ 300 billion in infrastructure financing for the project in the future. The BRI is planned to be completed within 35 years, in time for the 100th anniversary of the People's Republic of China in 2049. The Chinese have already kept aside 3 trillion dollars from their foreign exchange surpluses as reserves. The financing for the OBOR initiative will come from many sources. The initial main source of funding the Silk Road Fund was established on December 29, 2014 in Beijing by the Chinese government. In the beginning, funding was procured by the four government entities such as China Investment Corporation, State Administration of Foreign Exchange, Export-Import Bank of China and the China Development Bank. Another important source of direct funding geared towards the BRI was also created in Beijing by the Chinese-led Asian Infrastructure Investment Bank (AIIB). The (AIIB) became effective in January 2016 with 57 founding-member countries as signatories to the articles of agreement.

The BRICS countries, i.e., Brazil, Russia, India, China, and South Africa are significant emerging economies holding meetings annually to promote mutual cooperation concerning political and economic progress. These nations account for about 3.6 billion population, which is nearly fifty per cent of the global population and twenty six per cent of the global land mass. The combined annual GDP of the BRICS countries was 16.6 trillion in 2015, representing approximately twenty-two per cent of the global

GDP. The BRICS countries established a New Development Bank in Shanghai, China for infrastructure development for developing and emerging economies in February 2016 with a 50-billion dollar fund. The money will help to complete BRI projects also. The SCO Development Bank also seemed to be taking part in the project. In total, China has already spent an estimated $ 200 billion on BRI projects.

BRI Summit 2017

The First BRI Summit was held in Beijing, China on May 14-15, 2017. It was inaugurated by Chinese President Xi Jinping. Prior to this meeting, he welcomed UN Secretary-General Antonio Guterres, heads of states/ governments of more than 30 countries and representatives of 100 countries including the USA and North Korea took part in the deliberations.

President Xi Jinping said that China would start the Belt and Road cooperation initiative on trade connectivity together with some 60 countries. He said that the Belt and Road Initiative imbibes the aspiration for inter-civilization exchanges, the desire for peace and stability, the pursuit of common development and the shared dream for a better life. The second summit of the BRI Forum also took place in China in April 2019 where President Xi attempted to assuage the fear of member-countries regarding various aspects of the Initiative.

Security Implications

The BRI initiative is the most talked about project of the 21st century which has attracted the attention of scholars, policy makers and government officials around the globe. Many view the BRI as part of a Chinese attempt to re-order Asia and to contain U. S. influence. Some scholars have cited the programme as "China's Marshall Plan" or "Monroe Doctrine". The Initiative reminds that China under the Communist Party is building a new empire. It seems that China wishes to alter the existing international order. Countries like the USA, Japan, Australia, Singapore, Britain and India are apprehensive about Chinese intentions. Though the BRI proposal looks ambitious and lucrative, it has widespread geo-strategic implications. The unstated strategic objectives of the BRI raise questions about Chinese intentions.

China's attempt to expand its influence in South Asia by developing ports in Sri Lanka, Pakistan and Bangladesh is part of its broader 'String of Pearls' strategy pulling these countries into the Chinese orbit. Chinese presence in the region is detrimental to Indian interests. It presents a challenge to India's supremacy in the Indian subcontinent and jeopardises its interests in the region. Because every Indian neighbour in the IOR littoral already has strong economic ties with mainland China, the perception is that these smaller states are not in a position to come into conflict with China. Since 2006, the China–South Asia trade has increased by 280 per cent to US$ 100 billion (Newsham and Maxie, 2017).

India chose to skip the first and second Belt & Road Forum (BRF) for International Cooperation that was held in Beijing on 14-15 May, 2017 and 25-26 April 2019. Leaders from different countries attended the Forum. India's main concern is with the China-Pakistan Economic Corridor (CPEC), which passes through Pak-occupied Kashmir. It involves the development of roads, railways, pipelines and other infrastructure along a corridor stretching from China's western Xinjiang province to the Chinese-built port of Gwadar (in Balochistan province) on the Indian Ocean. According to its proponents, the CPEC, with a claimed price tag of some $ 54 billion, has the potential to economically transform Pakistan. The project also has the capacity to transform China's regional role by creating a direct transport link between western China and the Indian Ocean. India is protesting against this project because it passes through territories of Gilgit-Baltistan in POK and violates its territorial integrity and sovereignty.

A New Rivalry in the Indian Ocean?

The BRI projects have extended the India-China rivalry to the Indian Ocean and also with the possible fear of involvement of many other countries. The Indian Ocean connects Asia, Africa, the Middle East and Australia through its vast water flow. A major chunk of the global trade passes through the region. The Indian Ocean has rich mineral deposits and fisheries and produces about 40 per cent of the world's offshore petroleum. The BRI project has enhanced Chinese presence in the IOR with its infrastructural projects. That both India and China indulge in a power game to enhance their influence in the region indicates the beginning of a new rivalry in the region. Recently, Beijing also established its first overseas military base in Djibouti.

The Chinese giant company, the Merchants Port Holdings, signed a 99-year lease on Sri Lanka's Hambantota Port in July 2017. It aroused tension in India as China's naval presence would undermine Indian interests in the subcontinent. According to some scholars, Hambantota, in view of a heavy Chinese military build-up, could become another Djibouti. Likewise, the Maldives and Myanmar also have received ample Chinese investments and Chinese naval and military presence cannot be ruled out.

New Delhi, anxious with the thought of Beijing dominating its own backyard, is responding in its own way. In 2015, India's Prime Minister Narendra Modi put forward his concept of security and growth for all in the region (SAGAR) for India's activities in the Indian Ocean. India's objective with this vision is to create an environment of trust and transparency, to try for peaceful conflict resolution and to enhance maritime collaboration, to ensure all countries comply with international maritime rules and norms. In January 2018, during his visit to Oman, Prime Minister Narendra Modi finalised a deal getting access to naval facilities in the Middle Eastern state, which is near the Hormuz Strait. Approximately 30 per cent of seaborne oil exports pass through that narrow waterway daily. The Indian government is striving to strengthen its position in Seychelles and Mauritius. The Indian government signed a pact with Singapore in November 2018 that would boost Indian access to the Changi naval base of Singapore. Simultaneously, in Iran, where India Ports Global is developing the deep-sea Chabahar port, is widely seen as a counter to China's Gwadar port in Pakistan. Future military uses of Chabahar by India cannot be denied. (Nyshka, Chandran, 2018) The Chabahar project, located only about 350 kilometres from Gwadar, expects to create a transit route between India, Iran and Afghanistan. Chinese forays into the Indian Ocean are also a step in the direction of disrupting Regional Security Complex which has serious geo-strategic implications. Again, the security environment of the region is endangered and the plausibility of a new cold war also looming. Indian policy makers need to be more agile and vigilant while dealing with this Chinese mega project.

Debt Trap Diplomacy

China's infrastructure financing programme around the world gets a new name, "Debt trap diplomacy". China is funding projects in partner countries with a hidden wish to secure Chinese access to resources or local markets, rather than to help local economics. As a consequence, these countries are falling prey to the Chinese debt trap and vulnerable to China's influence. For this very reason, Sri Lanka had to hand over its China-financed part to a Chinese merchant company on a 99-year lease. Sri Lanka's struggles to pay back the US$ 8 billion in total, is almost 68 per cent of its GDP to Chinese companies. The Chinese debt trap diplomacy has worried partner countries about the Chinese intention that could result in a revival of neo-colonialism. China's all-weather friend, Pakistan, had to revoke a Chinese project in 2017 to finance and build the Diamer-Bhasha dam over the Indus in the Gilgit–Baltistan region. As China's soft finance to the project was construed to be against Pakistan's interests, Pakistan also cancelled other major road projects and has rejected a demand that the Yuan should be used in the Gwadar free trade zone. (*Strait Times*, 2018)

In Bangladesh also, China invested heavily but recent reports indicated that Bangladesh had cancelled a Chinese project to construct a 214-km. (130 miles) highway from its capital, Dhaka, to its north eastern part. There were allegations of corruption against the state-backed Chinese Harbour Engineering Company (CHEC) amid unhappiness over the project cost of $ 2 billion. That compelled Bangladesh to finance the highway itself at a reduced cost of around $ 1.5 billion. (Dahir, 2019)

Nepal entered BRI in 2018 with great enthusiasm. Nepal and China signed agreements worth US$ 2.4 billion on various infrastructure projects for post-earthquake construction efforts. The highlight of the deals is a plan to build a railway line through the Himalayas. The railway line would connect Kerung in Tibet to Kathmandu. The railway line will boom Nepal's tourism industry as some 2.5 million Chinese tourists are expected to visit Nepal every year. The Chinese government has conducted a pre-feasibility study of the project. The 72.25-km line from the Chinese border to Kathmandu would likely cost US$ 2.25 billion. It is also established that about 98.5 per cent of the line would run through tunnels and across bridges due to the difficult mountainous terrain. The concern in Kathmandu is about the whopping amount of the project. (*Business Standard*, 2019)

In the same way, the Maldives is facing a debt trap of around US$ 92 million that has led to fears of dangerous Chinese actions. In Myanmar, the US$ 7.3 billion Chinese-backed Kyank Pyu deepwater port project was scaled back to US$ 1.3 billion over concerns of being very expensive and the fear of subsequent Chinese control (*Strait Times*, 2019). Simultaneously, in Malaysia, voices were raised against US$ 22 billion worth of BRI projects and Malaysian Prime Minister Mahathir Mohammed criticised China for securing influence while not being able to repay its debt. In August 2018, the East Coast Rail Link (ECRL) and Trans-Sabah Gas Pipeline (TSGP) projects were also cancelled by Prime Minister Mahathir saying his country's top priority was to minimise its debt and loans. Later, an agreement to scale down the cost was signed between the two countries. In Vietnam, public protests against the government's decision to grant Special Economic Zones to a foreign firm with leases of up to 99 years were staged. SEZs would be like giving China access to the Vietnamese territories.

The BRI costs in developing countries have raised serious concerns about debt sustainability. Countries like Tajikistan, Montenegro Djibouti, Kyrgyzstan, Laos, and Mongolia are also at high risk of debt distress due to BRI loans. In most of these countries, rising debts are accounting for more than 50 per cent to GDP ratio with at least 40 per cent of external debt owed to China. These countries will need support to repay BRI loans and will likely move to the IMF and other smaller lenders. (*CISI*, 2017)

In 2011, long before the formal launching of the BRI, Tajikistan handed over land on its disputed border with China to repay some of its debt. China has given loans to tiny nations of Pacific Ocean such as Papua New Guinea, Fiji, Tongo, etc. These countries also fear that if unable to repay their debts, they could fall into debt distress and become vulnerable to diplomatic pressure from China. Chinese investment in Zambia has a marked impact of the Chinese language, symbols and manpower. But the debt is mounting there, with Chinese loans accounting for up to a third of the country's total $ 13 billion national debt. (Fernholz, 2019)

China has only one military base at Djibouti. Chinese money may be putting some countries at risk and Beijing could be using its loans as a strategic tool. Currently, the total Chinese BRI investment is estimated at over $ 1 trillion. Today, many countries are sceptical of Chinese intentions. While the BRI, provides crucial infrastructure funding to developing countries, it also leaves many with irreparable debts. For example, China is funding a high speed rail line in Laos that will cost around half the country's GDP.

Troubles in BRI

Discussing the troubles besetting the OBOR, an article in the *Financial Times* in July 2018 pointed out that 234 out of 1,674 Chinese-invested infrastructure projects announced in 66 Belt and Road countries since 2013 have encountered difficulties. Chinese affairs expert, Oain Benli, in the Border-less Movement website says that the OBOR has created negative effects in foreign countries and led to a neglect of China's domestic consequences including corruption, financial deficiency, and xenophobia. China is to take control of Zambia international airport after a debt instalment default, while Congo is in deep debt due to China-funded projects. The BRI was also aimed at Xi's willingness to consolidate power by sound political and economic accomplishments. They barely ever mention any benefit brought back to the Chinese people. No figure about any relevant increase in terms of jobs, foreign anchorage reserves, or domestic living standards has been found. (*Economic Times*, 2018)

Chinese President Xi Jinping assured partner countries while hosting the second Belt and Road forum in Beijing in May 2019 about Chinese investments in different countries. Xi pledged a debt sustainability framework and to persuade compliance with international infrastructure contracting standards. During the second OBOR summit, China did a lot of clarifying work to quell doubts of the outside world. The BRI project allowed scholars to interpret the aims and objectives of the project differently. Some scholars describe it as new colonialism and to some scholars it is the revival of the dependency theory. The purpose is to establish a system with China at the core, forcing countries to undergo the process of cooperation with China, thus establishing a high dependence on Beijing. Through the implementation of OBOR, China would have the right to formulate rules and regulations and reshape the world structure.

Theoretical Perspective of BRI and New International Order

The Chinese move can be best understood by the offensive realist model first propounded by John Mearsheimer (Mearsheimer, 2014). It brought the two countries into straight conflict. It would also increase the probability of confrontation between the two great powers. Glaser (2011) explains this security dilemma by suggesting that China will ultimately be forced into competition with the USA even if it does not have harsh intentions. And that would instigate Washington to retaliate and lead to a vicious cycle of conflict. Likewise, realists believe that an offensive approach of Chinese foreign policy is a threat to the world. For one, it has embarked unilaterally on a military modernisation programme aimed at strengthening its status as a rising power (Shambaugh, 2015)

Impact of Pandemic Era on BRI

The outbreak of the global pandemic, COVID-19 has shaken the world which has shown the inability of mankind to control a micro organism. The origin of the virus was the Chinese city of Wuhan from where it spread across the globe in various countries. The Chinese dubious role is evident in the whole episode as it kept mum over the initial spread of the disease. Whistleblower Doctor Li Wenliang was admonished and forced to keep silent. Non-cooperation with the international demand to investigate the Wuhan lab or determine the origin of the corona virus, stopped all domestic flights from Wuhan but allowed international flights to operate at the peak of infection.

So the virus spread across the globe in different countries and took the shape of a pandemic of the 21st century but not in other Chinese cities. The massive damage caused to the USA, European, Latin American and Asian countries has exasperated sentiments against China which behaved irresponsibly in the whole episode. Moreover, the Chinese tactics to bully its neighbours and threatening other powers further aggravated anti-Chinese sentiment. The irrational and reckless behaviour of the top Chinese leadership compelled the countries to unite and to form some kind of alliance against China.

The pandemic has adversely affected the BRI project also. Chinese official Wang Xiaolong said that BRI projects in Asia, Africa and Europe had been seriously affected by the pandemic (*Economic Times*, June 28, 2020). Some of the countries that took billions of dollars in loans from China to build infrastructures are now facing economic hardship, asking for debt repayment concessions. Thus, the present global scenario does not augur well for the future of the BRI project.

Conclusion

China's signature project, the BRI, is all set to make China a superpower of the 21st century. Keeping in tune with Chinese President Xi Jinping's Chinese Dream, the project endeavours to revive old Chinese glory by reviving the ancient silk route and equipping it with the latest technologies. The project connects more than 70 countries with 4.4 billion population and deals with an economic aggregate of $ 21 trillion and 29 per cent of the global volume once completed. The gigantic nature of the project is also evident by the fact it spreads across three continents and aims to take South America also into its fold. China has also successfully started the Polar Silk Road to enhance trade with North Atlantic countries. The obvious objective of Chinese diplomacy is to enhance its influence across the globe. Debt trap diplomacy is one of the major impacts of the BRI which has created panic among the partner countries as it is undermining their liberty by putting them in a compromising position. This also reminds us of the revival of neo-colonialism and the dependency theory knitted around the Chinese ambition to become a power bloc. The security implications are also evident as China is getting influence through the trade route. It has already established its first overseas naval base in Djibouti and is trying to access strategic facilities in many more countries. Chinese forays in the Indian Ocean, in South Asian countries, the China-Pakistan Economic Corridor, etc., pose challenges for India. In fact, it has begun India-China rivalry in the Indian Ocean and can be termed as the new 'cold war' which does not augur well for the peace and stability of the region. As China is flexing its muscles for making a New World Order with China at its centre, countries like India, the USA, Australia, Japan, Singapore, etc., would have to strengthen cooperation to thwart the challenges posed by the Belt and Road Initiative. The global pandemic has compelled these countries to unite to contain the irrational, irresponsible attitude and behaviour of China.

REFERENCES

Bretza Gregory John, Financing Belt and Road Initiative available at http:// regionalrapport. Com/ 2017/ 06/ 20/ financing-belt-road-initiative.

Business Standard, available at https://www.business-standard.com/article/news-ani/is-china-s-bri-a-debt-trap-118091800124_1.html, September 18, 2018.

Chaturvedy & Guy M. Snodgrass, 2012, "The Geopolitics of Chinese Access Diplomacy", *German Marshall Fund of the United States Policy Brief*, 29 May.

Chaturvedy Rajiv Ranjan, 2017, The 21st century Maritime Silk Road, 10 February, 2017 available at http://www.orfonline.org/research/the-21st-century-maritime-silk-road/

Chektzi Andrew and Mcbride James, 2019 China's Massive Belt and Road Initiative, *CFR*, https:// www.cfr.org/ backgrounder/chinas-massive-belt-and-road-initiative.

Dahir, Abdi Latif, 2019, China wants to use the power of global media to dispel Belt and Road debt risks, https://qz.com/africa/1604677/china-is-using-african-media-to-back-belt-and-road-initiative/ April 25, 2019.

Dorff, Robert H., 2001, "A Primer in Strategy Development", in Joseph R. Cerami and James F Holcomb, Jr. (eds.), *U.S. Army War College Guide to Strategy,* Carlisle Barracks, P.A., Strategic Studies Institute, p. 12.

Economic Times, http://economictimes.indiatimes.com,18 May 2017

Economic Times available at /economictimes. indiatimes.com/ articleshow/ 69000716.cms? from= mdr& utm_ source =contentofinterest&utm_medium= text&utm_ campaign = cppst.

Fallon, Teresa (2015), "The New Silk Road: Xi Jinping's Grand Strategy for Eurasia", *American Foreign Policy Interests*, 37(3): pp. 140-147.

Fernholz, Tim. Eight countries are falling into Chinese Debt Trap, https://qz.com/1223768/china-debt-trap-these-eight-countries-are-in-danger-of-debt-overloads-from-chinas-belt-and-road-plans/ 8 March 2018.

Ferdinand, Peter, 2016. "Westward ho – the China dream and 'one belt, one road': Chinese foreign policy under Xi Jinping", *International Affairs*, 92(4): pp. 841-957.

Gerstel Dylan, It's a (Debt) Trap! Managing China-IMF Cooperation Across the Belt and Road https://www.csis.org/npfp/its-debt-trap-managing-china-imf-Cooperation across-belt-and-road.

Glaser, Charles (2011), Will China's Rise Lead to War? Why Realism Does Not Mean Pessimism, https://www.foreignaffairs.com/ articles/ asia/ 2011-03-01/ will-chinas-rise-lead-war.

Harkavy, Robert E. (1982), *Great Power Competition for Overseas Bases: The Geopolitics of Access Diplomacy*, Canada: Pergamon Policy Studies on Security Affairs, Pergamon Press Canada Ltd., pp. 14-43.

https://economictimes.indiatimes.com/news/international/ business/majority-of-chinas-bri-projects-abroad-adversely-affected–by-covid-19-pandemic-official/articleshow/76673279.cms?utm_source=contentofinterest&utm_medium=text&utm_campaign=cppst, June 28, 2020.

Kam, Stefanie (2016), "Making China's 'One Belt, One Road' more Turkic", *The Diplomat*, published on (04/ 07/ 16). Accessed (29/ 09/ 16) via: http:// thediplomat.com/ 2016/ 07/ making -chinas-one-belt-one-road-more-turkic/

Lane, Christopher (2015), *China's 21 century Maritime Silk Route and Energy Security, Maritime Affairs*, vol II, no 1, summer, available at www.tandoline.com.

Mearseheimer (2014), Can China Rise Peacefully, Available at https://nationalinterest.org/commentary/can-china-rise-peacefully-10204

National Development and Reform Commission, 2015 Vision and Actions on jointly Building Silk Road Economic Belt and 21st Century Maritime Silk Road, 28 March available at http://en.ndrc.gov.cn/ newsrelease/ 201503/t20150330_669367.html.

Nyshka, Chandran, "Indian military scrambles to keep up after China moves to put forces in Africa", available at https://www.cnbc.com/2018/02/28/military-china-and-india-compete-over-bases-around-indian-ocean.html.

Ruff, Abdul (2017), China's New Silk Road Project: Focus On South Asia, Modern Diplomacy available at http://moderndiplomacy.eu/index.php?option=com_k2&view=item&id=2674:china-s-new-silk-road-project-focus-on-south-asia.

Seo, Jungmin & Cho, Young Chul (2013), "Rethinking Beijing's Geostrategic Sensibilities to Tibet and Xinjiang: Images and Interest", *Pacific Focus*, 28(2), pp. 294-317.

Shambaugh, David (2005), *Power Shift: China and Asia's New Dynamics*, University of California Press.

Strait Times (2019), Belt and Road Initiative not a debt trap, has helped partners grow faster: Chinese foreign minister, available at https://www.straitstimes.com/asia/east-asia/belt-and-road-initiative-not-a-debt-trap-has-helped-partners-grow-faster-says-chinese, March 8, 2019.

Strait Times, China's Belt and Road Initiative Debt Trap or Hope, available at https://www.Straittimes.com/ asia/east-asia/chinas-belt-and-road-initiative-debt-trap-or-hope, 30 September 2018.

Summers, Tim (2016), "China's 'New Silk Routes': Sub-national Regions and Networks of Global Political Economy", *Third World Quarterly*, 37(9): pp. 1628-1643.

Zorawar Daulat Singh, "Indian perception of China's Maritime Silk Road Idea", *Journal of Defence Studies*, vol. 8, no. 4, Oct-Dec 2014, available at www.idsa.in.

8

India and South East Asia: Security Concerns in the Era of Globalization

Anurag Ratna

Introduction

The foreign policy of any country, in one or the other way, relates to its national interests, which is determined by its history, traditions, culture, people's aspirations, moral, ethical, spiritual values and philosophy of life. It is truer in the case of India. The architect of Indian foreign policy, Pt. Nehru, defined Indian foreign policy in the context of national interests in the age of the Cold War (1945-1990). It is based on non-alignment, the temper of peace, friendship with all countries, economic cooperation, stress on U.N. principles and world peace. The basic principles of Nehru's foreign policy continued until the end of the cold war. Some minor changes were introduced by subsequent prime ministers with the changes in nuclear policy, defence policy and policy towards neighbours. These principles gave a strong base to Indian foreign policy.

However, the end of the cold war and the collapse of the Soviet Union changed the dynamics of international politics affecting all nations of the world and India was no exception. India had to define its national interest keeping in view the economic developments and security concerns. India was bound to redefine its relations with developing and developed countries in this regard. P.V. Narasimha Rao, the then Prime Minister, propounded the Look East Policy to develop close economic ties and attend to security concerns. Here, in this paper, I will take up the issue of security concerns in the context of Southeast Asian nations.

South East Asia comprises ten members—Indonesia, Singapore, the Philippines, Malaysia, Brunei, Thailand, Cambodia, Laos PDR, Myanmar and Vietnam. These countries have grouped themselves in a regional organization popularly known as ASEAN (Association of South East Asian Nations). India's focus on a strengthened and multifaceted relationship with ASEAN is an outcome of the significant change in the world's political and economic scenario since the early 1990s and India's own march towards economic liberalization. India's search for economic security resulted in the 'Look East Policy'. The 'Look East Policy' has today matured into a dynamic and action oriented 'Act East Policy'. Indian Prime Minister Narendra Modi at the 12th ASEAN-India summit and the 9th East Asia Summit held in Nay Pyi Tew, Myanmar, in November 2014 formally enunciated the Act East Policy. Apart from economic interests, India's Act East Policy is also concerned with its security issues and strategic partnerships for the region's security. This is the reason that India, apart from ASEAN, has also taken other policy initiatives in the region that involve some members of ASEAN like BIMSTEC, MGC, etc. India is also an active participant in several regional forums ASEAN Defence Ministers Meeting (ADMM) and Expanded ASEAN Maritime Forum. Really, India's relationship with ASEAN is a key pillar of our foreign policy and the foundation of our Act East Policy.

History of India's relations with Southeast Asian countries

With regard to India's approach to Southeast Asia, the narrative has germinated from pictorial, religious and economic perspectives and draw from different resources to buttress the fact that the ties between India and countries of the region have been harmonious and mutually beneficial. The most important narrative starts from the historical perspective and gets amplified with the interactions during the Bandung Conference (Asian African Conference) held in 1955 and the role played by the Asian leaders in creating new camaraderie between the newly-independent nations of Southern Asia. The Indian leadership recognized and promoted the independence of Southeast Asian countries, primarily, Myanmar,

Indonesia and the Philippines, from colonial subjugation. In fact, India conducted the Conference on Indonesia in 1949 that was attended by 15 nations. In the late 1940s and early 1950s, the role of iconic political leadership in Myanmar, Indonesia and Vietnam and the relationships between countries were predicated upon the personal equations or unbridgeable charm between the political leadership because of different views on international cooperation. The charm was apparent between Sukarno and Nehru as well as Mahatir and Indira Gandhi (Jha, P. K., *ASEAN Relations*). India's relations with Southeast Asian countries suffered a setback when these nations along with the USA. and Pakistan decided to sign a Mutual Defence Assistance Pact, the Southeast Asia Treaty Organization (SEATO) and the Baghdad Pact (Mohammad Ayoob, 1990). However, the political understanding between India and ASEAN progressed with phases of discord and divergence.

India's views towards Southeast Asia were shaped by the impact of Indic civilization and the symbiosis of the religious dialogue in the larger Asian context. The influence of Hinduism and Buddhism was felt everywhere and the remnants of the religious influence could be witnessed in the form of architecture in ancient temples, monasteries and religious artefacts (Nicolas, Tasling, 1992). This has formed the bedrock of India-Southeast Asia relations. The Hindu kings and the adoption of Buddhism in subsequent years by Southeast Asian societies were seen as a natural corollary to the interaction among traders, merchants and religious preachers.

In the pre-independence period, the raising of the Azad Hind Fauz (Indian National Army) in Southeast Asia in 1942 and the role played by the popular Indian leader, Subhash Chandra Bose, created a soft affection towards Southeast Asia. In 1967, Indian Foreign Minister, M.C. Chagla paid a visit to Malaysia and Singapore in support of the idea of ASEAN and talked about close trade, economic and commerce cooperation with Singapore (Saxena, K.P., 1986).

But the involvement of the USA in the region and the formation of SEATO created suspicion in the minds of Indian policymakers. India also initiated the formation of the Non-Aligned Movement to safeguard the interests of the developing and newly-independent nations from the influence of power bloc's politics. It was a clear message of the ASEAN countries to join hands with India for their mutual benefit and regional security. In fact, it is perceived that during the anti-communist struggle in the countries of Southeast Asia, India could have developed better relations with Southeast Asian countries such as the Philippines, Singapore and Indonesia, had it not been seen as a partner of the erstwhile Soviet Union. India's Peaceful Nuclear Explosion (PNE) in 1974 was not liked by many countries in the region, but the response to this event was calibrated by India. India was actively involved in Southeast Asian affairs, as illustrated by its recognition of Unified Vietnam and subsequently the Kampuchean government in 1980 (Kripa, Sridharan, 1996). The recognition of the Peoples' Republic of Kampuchea was seen as an irritant in India-ASEAN ties. India's approach towards ASEAN was relatively lukewarm during the time of non-Congress governments (during Janata government rule [1977] and the subsequent coalition government in the late 1980s), (Kripa, Sridharan, 1996). India had to change the contours of its foreign relations and liberalize its economy to have good relations with the Western world. Indian Prime Minister P.V. Narasimha Rao took the initiative and formulated the 'Look East Policy'. He saw larger prospects in ASEAN countries for sustainable economic growth and a lucrative destination for outlining India's economic and strategic priorities. India achieved rich dividends from its 'Look East Policy'. Due to this factor, it is now rechristened as 'Act East Policy'. During a speech in 2017, Secretary (East) Ms. Preeti Saran remarked: "This is an important opportunity for us to assess what we can do further, for a deeper and comprehensive engagement with Southeast Asia, cutting across the three agreed pillars of politics, security, economic and socio-cultural cooperation with the region. Already there are 30 dialogue mechanisms between India and ASEAN including a Summit and seven ministerial meetings on a wide range of sectors such as Foreign Affairs, Commerce, Tourism, Agriculture, Environment, Renewable Energy and Telecommunications. We have taken a number of initiatives including establishing a separate mission in Jakarta in April 2015 to supplement the effects of our bilateral relations in the region (Keynote address by Secretary on India and ASEAN, 2017).

Security Concern for India in ASEAN Region

One of the important aspects of the formation of the ASEAN Regional Forum (ARF) was that it created the necessary institutional set up to discuss issues of larger Asia-Pacific security. ARF, although not very successful, created a platform for discussion on security issues in the ASEAN region.

India's security concerns in Asia are a major issue due to its disputes with its neighbours like China and Pakistan. From this point of view, since independence, the ASEAN region was considered helpful and meaningful for India's security and strategic concerns. K.M. Panikkar in the late fifties and early sixties stressed the need to concentrate on its strategy and define its outlook towards Southeast Asia (Sardar, K.M. Panikkar, 1961). K. Subramanyam also opined that pressure on China should be made from the Indochina region, now a part of ASEAN countries. He stated, "We have a large stake in ensuring that the pressure is contained. That has been our basic policy from the fifties" (Reddy, Ravindranatha, 2009).

During the mid-eighties, many ASEAN nations were worried about the potential threat to their security from India's role in Sri Lanka (Peace Keeping Operations in 1987) and the Maldives (Operation Cactus in 1988 to end an armed coup against the Maumoon Abdul Gayoom government) and even a stalemate with Nepal on trade projected India as a bully for the Southeast Asian nations. Also India's reported plan for building a naval base in the Andaman and Nicobar Islands in the late 1980s perturbed Indonesia and other littoral neighbours about the ramifications of such a base close to their territorial waters. India's naval modernization programme was also seen as a manifestation of India's power projection capabilities in Southeast Asia. Indian leaders had to justify their naval modernization programme though there was no precedence of any untoward behaviour in the past. After the initial dithering, India decided on a damage control exercise. Adopting a more rational approach and sensing it necessary to convincingly articulate its aims in the Indian Ocean region, India offered to hold a joint naval exercise with ASEAN states (Jha P. K., *ASEAN Relations*). Really, India needed the support of ASEAN states for its maritime security in the Indian Ocean. For this, India had to make multiple efforts to assuage the concerns of Southeast Asian nations for their security interests.

The active engagement with ASEAN after 1992 with active support from Singapore and, a decade later, its elevation into a summit-level partnership through the ASEAN India Summit (2002) showed that India has relevance in the neo-liberal and constructivist sphere of international relations. India embarked on getting engaged with the erstwhile small players and engaging the major powers without showing signs of strong affiliation to any one power centre. The strategic configuration was simple:

protect interests and bargain hard. India's commitment to the region's development was articulated through, "ASEAN-India Partnership for Peace Progress and Shared Prosperity (2003)". In the 3rd ASEAN-India-Summit in Vientiane in 2004, a Plan of Action (POA) for the period 2004-2010 was developed to implement the partnership. Again, the POA for 2010-2015 has also been implemented.

In 2012, ASEAN and India commemorated 20 years of dialogue partnership and 10 years of summit-level partnership with ASEAN countries with a Commemorative Summit in New Delhi under the theme ASEAN-India Partnership for Peace and Shared Prosperity on 20-21 December 2012. The Commemorative Summit attended by the leaders of all the 10 ASEAN countries endorsed elevating the partnership to a Strategic Partnership. The leaders also adopted the ASEAN-India Vision Statement, which charts the future of ASEAN-India cooperation. During the Summit, the heads of the Government recommended establishment of an ASEAN-India Centre (AIC) to undertake policy research advocacy and not working activities with organizations and think tanks in India as an ASEAN-India Strategic Partnership.

ASEAN-India connectivity is a matter of strategic priority for India as also the ASEAN countries. In 2013, India became the third dialogue partner of ASEAN to initiate an ASEAN Connectivity Coordinating Committee-India Meeting. India has made considerable progress in implementing the India-Myanmar-Thailand Trilateral Highway and Kaladan Multimodal Project. Later issues related to increasing the maritime and air connectivity between ASEAN and India and transforming the corridors of connectivity into economic corridors were also put up for discussion in the Committee.

India-ASEAN Relations under Narendra Modi

In 2014, Narendra Modi assumed office of Prime Minister with an overwhelming majority. After a 30-year gap, India got a majority-based government and a strong and decisive leader. Expectations were high from him from all quarters. At the international level, much was expected from him to adopt a bold decisive and policy-oriented approach towards key issues particularly on defence and strategic affairs. As India had already adopted the 'Look East Policy' since 1992, ASEAN countries were eagerly awaiting Modi's decision-making. It is true that the 'Look East Policy' had given new colour and dimension to India-ASEAN relations but much was not achieved from either. Perhaps the presence of a coalition government and lack of decisive leadership and proper policy approach and actions were responsible from the Indian side and due to India's not very clear vision approach, ASEAN countries were not paying attention to ASEAN-India relations. Overall, the 'Look East Policy' of India achieved little in 22 years (1992-2014). It was now left to Modi to have a new look at the 'Look East Policy' in view of the rapidly changing international scenario. Narendra Modi responded positively by changing the 'Look East Policy' to the 'Act East Policy' for achieving progress in India-ASEAN relations in various fields—cultural, economic, defence and strategic security, etc. Defence and security issues were key factors of India's ASEAN policy. India's message towards East Asia was made clearer when Indian Foreign Minister Sushama Swaraj visited many East Asian countries including some ASEAN countries and told Indian envoys to Act East not just Look East (*The Economic Times*).

Narendra Modi, in view of security interests, put up his action plan from the very beginning. He participated in the 9th East Asia Summit held at Myanmar which was attended by the representatives of 18 ASEAN countries and India. Other countries were Russia, the USA, China, Australia, Japan, South Korea and New Zealand. In this summit, the stress was laid on the fight against terrorism with a resolution that it could not be related to any religion. In the meantime, Vietnam President Nguyan Tom Derg (October 2014), Myanmar Vice President (January 2015) and the President of Singapore (February 2015) also visited India. They all held discussions on security and strategic issues with Indian P. M. Narendra Modi.

Narendra Modi also visited Kuala Lumpur to participate in the 10th East-Asia Summit and India-ASEAN Summit. He visited Singapore at the invitation of President Lee Hsien Loong to commemorate the 50th year of India-Singapore bilateral relations. All developments were related to security and defence issues. Narendra Modi utilized this opportunity very well. In 2016, many ASEAN heads of state/governments visited India to cement their relations with India. The President of Thailand, Deputy Premier of Malaysia, Myanmar President, Singapore President and Indonesia President were most prominent in this regard (www.wikipedia.com). Their visit made it clear that ASEAN countries are looking up for their active strategic and defence ties and cooperation with India.

Narendra Modi's Vietnam state visit in September 2016 was highly noteworthy. As Vietnam also has security problems with China including border disputes like India so the visit of an Indian P. M. was very significant from the security and defence points of view. Modi signed defence and military pacts with Vietnam in which ASEAN defence armaments, joint naval exercises, exchange of information and the training to combat insurgency. On 16-19 October 2016, BIMSTEC Summit (Bay of Bengal Initiative for Multi Sectoral Technical and Economic Cooperation) was held in which the ASEAN countries Bhutan, Nepal, Bangladesh and Sri Lanka and representatives of Russia and Brazil participated. This was an important summit from the defence and strategic point of view in which major stress was centred around terrorism-related problems and issues. This was a clear message to China and Pakistan which are expanding their illegal activities in Asian politics causing security concerns for India. In the meantime, leaders of many ASEAN countries visited India to hold discussions on security-related issues.

India and ASEAN observed 25 years of their friendship-partnership, 15 years of summit-level interaction and five years of strategic partnership throughout 2017 by undertaking a wide range of over 60 commemorative activities in India and through our missions in ASEAN states which culminated in the ASEAN-India Commemorative Summit on the theme of 'Shared Values Common Destiny' on 25 January 2018 in New Delhi. All heads of state and governments from ASEAN countries participated in the 26 January 2018 Republic Day function (https://mail.google.com). That was the symbol of solidarity of India-ASEAN relations. P. M. Modi also visited Indonesia, Malaysia and Singapore between 29 May and 2 June 2018 to consolidate the relationship with these countries on maritime and defence related issues (*The Pioneer*, 31 May 2018, 1 & 2 June 2018).

Overall, Prime Minister Narendra Modi clearly articulated India's concern regarding regional security in the Southeast region. He said, "In the face of growing traditional and non-traditional challenges, politico-security cooperation is a key emerging pillar of our relationship. Rising export of terror, growing radicalization through ideology of hatred and spread of extreme violence define the landscape of common security threats to our societies. The threat is local, regional and transnational at the same time. Our partnership with ASEAN seeks to craft a response that relies on coordination, cooperation and sharing of experiences at multiple levels (http://mea.gov.in/Speeches).

Impact of Relations with ASEAN Security Perspective

Security concerns are great issues of Southeast Asia and ASEAN countries due to the security problems of the region, i.e., the Indian Ocean and Asia-Pacific region and other global threats like terrorism, environment and rivalry between superpowers. India has also vital security issues in Asia due to rivalry with China and Pakistan expanding terrorism, security of the Indian Ocean region, illegal activities of China in the South-China Sea and South Asia due to its projects like OBOR (One Belt One Road), CPEC (China-Pakistan Economic Corridor) and above all supporting Pakistan-sponsored terrorism. In this regard, the active role of India and its Prime Minister, Narendra Modi, is noteworthy and it has certainly met the defence and security needs of India. Some of its achievements are noteworthy:

1. India has generally improved its ties with the Asian countries. Former prime minister P.V. Narasimha Rao initiated measures to safeguard national interests. A.B. Vajpayee and Dr. Manmohan Singh continued and improved relations with the ASEAN countries. Narendra Modi initiated it in an active manner converting the 'Look East' to the 'Act East Policy'. Due to Modi's active role ASEAN countries also have developed close defence and security ties including maritime security. The upgradation of BIMSTEC by Narendra Modi has given a clear signal to China, Pakistan and other major countries of Asia. The attendance of all ASEAN countries representatives and heads of state/governments for the celebration of 25 years of ASEAN relations and at the 26 January celebration in 2018 has certainly strengthened India's cause of security in the Asian region. In the sphere of defence, over the last 5-7 years India has steadily expanded its ties with the East and Southeast Asian countries. We engage these countries through regional confidence-building and cooperation mechanisms like the ASEAN Regional Forum (A.R.F.) the Regional Cooperation Agreement on combating piracy and armed robbery against ships in Asia (ReCAAP) and the Milan exercises that India holds every alternate year (Sikri, Rajiv,

Southeast Asia Programme, October, 2009).

2. By engaging ASEAN countries in the scope of defence and security interests, India has been successful in maintaining and increasing its presence in the Asia-Pacific region. Narendra Modi has maintained friendly relations with Japan's P.M. Shinze Abe for various interests. He is also ready to cooperate with India on security issues and assist in the nuclear field because Japan is also worried about China's policy of expansion in the South China Sea in particular and Asia in general. Australian P. M. Tony Abbott has also shown his interest in India following his visit in September 2014. As India is highly conscious and sensitive about its security interests in Indian Ocean, it is fruitful to have close relations with countries like Mauritius, Seychelles and Sri Lanka. Narendra Modi visited these countries to maintain close relations with them for cooperation on many fronts including security and strategic issues (Kaur, Harpreet and Kumar, Anupam, *The Pioneer*, 11 August, 2017). The presence of India in the Asia-Pacific region will boost its defence and strategic power and provide it a chance to emerge as a global player in future.
3. China is India's rival and has a belligerent approach towards India. Already, it has captured 38,000 square kilometres of area in Ladakh; it has left no stone unturned to weaken India economically, strategically and on security-related issues. The Doklam incident is the latest effort to weaken and demoralize India as it wants to have a link road in the trifurcation of China, India and Bhutan. China is extending its presence in the South China Sea and the Indian Ocean to pressurize India. So it is a must for India to keep a close watch on the Indian Ocean and the Asia-Pacific region. Due to China's illegal and unwarranted presence in the South-China Sea, ASEAN countries and Asia-Pacific nations are also highly worried. China's Silk Maritime Project is also worrying for India. Due to this factor, India has consolidated its relations with ASEAN and South Pacific nations. (Madhav, Ram, *The Times of India*, 23 December 2016).

   India's efforts to establish close security and strategic ties have put China under diplomatic pressure. It was due to this pressure that China withdrew its troops from Doklam after 73 days of illegal occupation. China's game to build OBOR and CPEC from POK (Pak Occupied Kashmir) is also a challenge for India but with close ties with ASEAN countries, India is in a position to challenge China in the near future to ease it from this undue pressure.

4. India's active role in the ASEAN and India-Pacific region can give a new shape to its relations with Russia and the USA. As U.S. President Donald Trump has followed an 'America first' policy in foreign relations, many countries including India, have tried to balance relations with the USA. The USA's wish to be active in East Asia and the Asia-Pacific region may club India with it if India plays its diplomatic card successfully. As China is a challenge for both the USA and India, India has a great chance to bargain with the USA for its strategic interests. So is the case with Russia. India's association with ASEAN countries will also help it to have close ties with Russia which is a large defence exporter to India.
5. Narendra Modi's approach towards ASEAN countries has given a new dimension to India for its relations with SAARC and South-Asian countries. India has failed to achieve its diplomatic and security target in SAARC due to the suspiciousness of SAARC countries about India and the Pakistani efforts to weaken India via cross-border terrorism. As China is supporting and providing arms and economic aid to SAARC countries Sri Lanka, Bangladesh and Nepal along with Pakistan, it is a cause of great concern for India. China has also supported Pak-sponsored terrorism in India. Due to this factor India has been compelled to develop close security and defence ties with ASEAN countries. It was due to this factor that India organized the BIMSTEC Summit inviting four SAARC countries—Nepal, Bhutan, Sri Lanka and Bangladesh—along with Myanmar and Thailand from ASEAN. India's diplomacy regarding BIMSTEC will certainly put pressure on China and isolate Pakistan in South Asia. The result of this action of India would be seen in the near future.
6. As India is becoming active in East Asia (including ASEAN) and the Asia-Pacific region it will provide a new strategic role to India in future world politics. It will help India to have close relations with the non-aligned and third world countries. India is considered the natural leader of developing countries due to NAM

(Non-Aligned Movement) but failed to provide something new to this organization in the age of globalization. India's rising status as a strategic power in ASEAN and the Asia-Pacific region can also provide a forum to developing countries for their security and development. If India diplomatically shows its activeness in this regard, it may help to raise its status as a world power—strategically and economically.

India's active role and growing position in ASEAN countries and East Asia has provided it a great boost in international politics. The 'Look East Policy' initiated by the late prime minister P.V. Narasimha Rao had certainly opened new avenues for India to be a strategic and economic power. Former prime ministers A.B. Vajpayee and Dr. Manmohan Singh extended this move and the present P.M., Narendra Modi has certainly added a new direction to it by converting the 'Look East Policy' to the 'Act East Policy' for the sake of multifarious interests, security being among one of them. Since the formation of ASEAN and in the last one-and-a-half decades of India's institutional participation in the ASEAN process, dividends in the form of investment, trade and identified core areas of cooperation between business communities, societies and people have been realized. The security concerns are challenging at present but they will soon be realized due to India's determination and close ties with ASEAN countries. Ever since the launch of the 'Look East Policy' and its subsequent avatar as the 'Act East Policy' the India-ASEAN relationship has formed the core of this policy. It will provide its contribution for Asian security in the near future.

In a short period of four-and-a-half years, the faith generated by Modi among leaders of Southeast Asia has certainly produced a hope among them, particularly the victims of Chinese expansionism, that there will be peace in the region in the not too distant future. This faith and hope have all the possibilities of making Modi a leader of Asia and further strengthen his claim of becoming a world leader. There is also a chance of India becoming a world power—strategically and economically—as has been predicted by several international political analysts that the 21st century belongs to India.

REFERENCES

Ayoob, Mohammad, *India and Southeast Asia: Indian Perceptions and Policies* (London: Routledge), 1990, p. 3.

Cited in K. P. Saxena, *Cooperation in Development: Problems and Prospects for India and ASEAN* (Sage Publications), New Delhi, 1986, p. 53.

https://Mail.google.com.

India's *'Look East Policy': A Critical Assessment*, Interview with former Diplomat Rajiv Sikri: Southeast Asia Programme, October 2009.

Jha, P. K., *India-ASEAN Relations*: An Assessment in ASEAN at 50: A Look at Its External Relations.

Kaur, Harpreet and Kumar, Anupam, "A Paradigm Shift in Foreign Policy" *The Pioneer* 11 August 2017.

Keynote Address by Secretary (East) on *India and ASEAN—An Overview at Nehru Memorial Museum and Library*, New Delhi, 2 February 2017.

Madhav, Ram: Pivot to the East, 23 December, 2016.

Opening Statement by Prime Minister at the 14th ASEAN-India Summit (8 September 2016), http://www.mea.gov.in/Speeches-Statements.htm?dtl 27371.

Quoted in Ravindranatha Reddy, *India and Vietnam: Era of Friendship and Cooperation* (1947-1994) (Emerald Publications), Chennai, 2009, p. 36.

Sardar K. M. Panikkar's Annual Day address to the Indian School of International Studies on 13 February 1961.

Sridharan, Kripa, *The ASEAN Region in India's Foreign Policy* (Singapore: Dartmouth) 1996, pp. 34-39.

Sridharan, Kripa, op. cit., pp. 60-75.

Tasling, Nicolas (ed.) *The Cambridge History of Southeast Asia from early Times to 1800*, Vol I Cambridge University Press, 1992, pp. 174-175.

The Economic Times.

The Pioneer, 31 May 2018, Also see *The Pioneer*1 and 2 June 2018.

www.wikipedia.com

9

Bangladesh-India Relations: Problems, Recommendations, and Security Concerns for South Asia

Abu Sayed Md. Nazmul Haider

Introduction

The historical relations between Bangladesh and India was made through blood because during the liberation war the joint force which was formed by freedom fighters and Indian Army personnel dedicated their valuable lives for the independence of Bangladesh. The Indira-Mujib Pact was considered a milestone in the Indo-Bangladesh relationship. At present, the Hasina-Modi Government has opened up a new horizon in the relations between Bangladesh and India. In the standpoint of geo-politics, Bangladesh has some importance of its geo-political stance. India almost engulfed Bangladesh. As a result, Bangladesh has a diplomatic obligation to maintain friendly relations with its neighbouring country, India. On the other hand, Bangladesh has emerged as the emerging tiger of the South Asian economy. Bangladesh is the playground of the India-China geo-political game. The tussle between these two superpowers, India and China, is a significant event for Bangladesh because Bangladesh has gained their economic advantages. On the Rohingya issue, Bangladesh became disappointed with the role of India. Bangladesh is trying to uplift the mutual friendly relations with India. Apart from this, there are some security concerns and issues that affect the relationship between Bangladesh and India. These are water debate, trade issue, transit problem, border management, border killings, insurgency, trafficking, smuggling, etc. These issues are affecting the Bangladesh-India relationship and South Asian security as well. Bangladesh and India are both trying to reduce these problems. Recently, we saw Bangladeshi Prime Minister Sheikh Hasina and Indian Prime Minister Narendra Modi completing collaboration several times. India's relations with Bangladesh are traditionally, cultural, social, and economic. They share the same issues together such as a shared history and common heritage, linguistic and cultural ties, passion for music, literature and the arts. India not only shares a common history of struggle for freedom and liberation but also an enduring feeling of both fraternal as well as familial ties. This commonality is reflected in the multi-dimensional relations with Bangladesh at several levels of interaction. While India played a critical role in 1971 in the birth of Bangladesh, this does not however result in close bilateral ties (Mir, J.A., 2018). Currently, both nations are enjoying extremely good quality relations.

Bangladesh-India Relations in the Past

The relations between Bangladesh and India had emerged in the partition of 1947, which has been blooming since 1971. The present scenario of this relationship is much better than the past decade. From 1971 to the present, we can see some variations of leadership that bring some variation in their relationship. The different leadership periods are given below:

1. Sheikh Mujib-ur Rahman (1971-1975)
2. Zia-ur Rahman (1975-1981)
3. Ershad (1982-1990)
4. Begum Zia (1991-1996)
5. Sheikh Hasina (1996-2001)

The foundation of Bangladesh-India relations was laid in 1971. The Indian government and the people supported us in the great liberation war of Bangladesh. Today, every person of Bangladesh reminisces the great contribution of the Indian government. It is also factual that in the great days of the war of liberation in Bangladesh, the people who defeated the Pakistani military campaign with spirit and determination and established their independence in exchange for immense sacrifice, created a nation of solid self-esteem and self-identity. Some aspects of bilateral relations were visible in the context of the deepening of thought and action between the then government and people of Bangladesh as well as the Indian government and the people. First, India has not delayed accepting the honour and independence of Bangladesh after the War of Liberation. In exchange, Bangladesh also did not show any stigma for its reward. Bangladesh started its journey as a nation using a democratic and secular political structure. India considers democratic and friendly Bangladesh as a partner for its regional interests. As a result, in the context of India's secular interests in the South Asian geopolitical context, in 1972, the long-term friendship and security agreement was enacted. Many people think that this kind of cooperation was true in South Asia's geopolitical context during the independence of Bangladesh. India financially and politically cooperated with war-torn Bangladesh. However, the continuous support of India's internal political and administrative complexity and crisis and the immediate government of Bangladesh have created a separation of the people of Bangladesh. In fact, the seeds of the problem between the two countries were also in the attempt to achieve the self-esteem of the people of Bangladesh. However, it will not be an exaggeration to state that Bangladesh is keen to work with India to achieve India's regional security and strategic goals. But Bangladesh was not willing to accept any kind of obstruction in the way of independence and in this case, hesitant to work out of India's preference as is seen in Bangladesh's strong move to join the OIC Summit in 1974. The political unrest of India and Bangladesh exerted a negative impact on their relations. As an example, two events can be mentioned—one of these is the complexity arising out of the implementation of the land boundary agreement in 1974, (Bhardwaj, S., 2015) and the other is the incident of the 1975 Farakka barrage. India's commitment was that the Farakka barrage would function intermittently (for 41 days). But after the expiry of that period, it remains unfulfilled. As a result, the difference between the views of the two countries has been manifested and negative impacts on the relations between the two countries were at the immediate stage. In 1975, Bangladesh and India started their journey in different ways in both values and interests as a result of government change in Bangladesh. However, the relationship has gradually degraded in the evolution of time and having formalities at the government or policy level.

In the Zia-ur Rahman period, the events of 1976-77 can be remembered. After the collapse of the Congress government in India in 1977, a slight improvement in relations between the two countries was observed. In continuation, the 1979 short-term water sharing agreement of the Ganga and the trade treaty of the two countries of 1980 indicated a similar improvement. (Pant, Harsh V., 2001) During this time both the countries particularly remained focused on their fundamental interests and centred on geo-political issues but there was a marked difference between the two countries on security issues. There are several subtle changes in India's policy regarding Bangladesh at this time. First, the black shadow of Pak-India is over. Secondly, India lost its interest in Bangladesh and thirdly, India also moved away from the idealistic position of Bangladesh and took the basis of real-world cooperation as the basis for the relationship. Despite it, both the countries strengthened regional cooperation.

During the Ershad period in 1985, the establishment of SAARC in Dhaka was one of its manifestations. For this reason, India continued to lose its interest in Bangladesh and the policy makers continued to harbour their position on Bangladesh. India also moved away from the idealistic position of Bangladesh and took the basis of real-world cooperation as the basis for the relationship. Bangladesh could not take any initiative to improve the relations of India if it sought to keep India's position at a tolerable level. Alternatively, Bangladesh tried to build a new structure of relations with India by strengthening regional cooperation. (Datta & Sreeradha, 2012)

In the period of Begum Zia, the return of democratic rule in Bangladesh in 1991 had a positive impact on Bangladesh and India. India's exports to Bangladesh increased significantly. Economic involvement in bilateral relations added a new dimension. The trade relationship between the two countries and the access to Bangladesh's products in India was the main issue in the bilateral relationship of both the political and economic relations of the two countries. But there has not been significant progress about security and other issues. At this time, the bilateral relations remained fairly stable. In the middle of 1995, the initiative had taken by the foreign secretaries of both the countries regarding the issue of water-sharing of the Ganga. As a result, in December 1996, a 30-year agreement was signed between the two countries. Another significant progress was made between Bangladesh and India regarding security issues at this time.

In 1997, in the period of Sheikh Hasina, many people think that the treaty on the Chittagong Hill Tracts was not possible without India's latent support. Needless to say, through this treaty, the atmosphere of peace was established in the Chittagong Hill Tracts though, there were some issues that remained incomplete. Even then, India's indecision over rebels in the northeast provinces remained. A kind of heat was being generated at the border of the two countries, which resulted in bloody clashes between the border guards of the two countries in Padda and Rumari regions in April 2001. In spite of this, Bangladesh's diplomacy was active in India in the nineties and Bangladesh had shown a lot of creativity then.

Contemporary Scenario of Bangladesh-India Relationship (2009 until date)

Since the government of Bangladesh under the rule of Sheikh Hasina in the last ten years, there has been a radical change in relations with India. Both the countries have worked together to strengthen their relationship. Exchange of enclaves, transit of India by road, permission to use the Chittagong and Mongla sea ports, Bangladesh-India Defence Agreement, and Bangladesh's assistance to curb the separatists of India's northeast—all of these have progressed. The transactions in relation to Bangladesh's relations with India in the last ten years were quite significant. Bangladesh was somewhat worried when the BJP government led by Narendra Modi came to power. However, the relations between the two countries have progressed. The progress in these areas over land and sea limits and enclaves are a great achievement. As the number of Bangladeshi nationals in India has increased in recent years, the number of visits from India to Bangladesh has also increased. The Indian government has made it easier for Bangladeshis to get visas than ever before. A section of the people of Bangladesh also had strong anti-India sentiments. But there was a lot of criticism inside Bangladesh particularly over Bangladesh's most exhausted Teesta river water sharing agreement and the issue of India's pressure on Myanmar on the Rohingya issue.

In September 2011, the two countries signed a major accord on border demarcation to end the four-decade old dispute over boundaries. This came to be known as the Tin Bigha Corridor. India also granted 24-hour access to Bangladeshi citizens in the Tin Bigha Corridor. The agreement included the exchange of adversely held enclaves, involving 51,000 people spread over 111 Indian enclaves in Bangladesh and 51 Bangladeshi enclaves in India. The total land involved is reportedly 7,000 acres. On 9 October 2011, the Indian and Bangladeshi armies participated in Sampriti-II (Unity-II), a 14-day-long joint military exercise at Sylhet to increase synergy between their forces. In 2012, Bangladesh allowed India's Oil and Natural Gas Corporation to ferry heavy machinery, turbines and cargo through Ashuganj for the Palatana power project in southern Tripura.

From October 2013, India started exporting 500 megawatts of electricity a day to Bangladesh for a period of 35 years. A 125-kilometre Baharampur-Bheramara transmission line, (40 km of it in Bangladesh), connects the two substations. Bangladeshi officials believe the export would greatly ease the national shortage once 500 MW flows into the national grid. The two prime ministers also unveiled a plaque of the 1,320-MW coal-fired Rampal power plant, a joint venture of the two countries. The link is seen as a major milestone in strengthening the bilateral relationship and comes at a time when India is desperate to make up for its inability to deliver on two key pacts with Bangladesh: one on the Teesta waters and the other on the land boundary pact. From November 2013, a Wagah border-like ceremony is being organised at the Petrapole (in West Bengal, India)–Benapole (Bangladesh) border checkpoint. The ceremony which includes parades, march-past, and lowering of the national flag of both the countries is now a daily routine at sundown on the eastern border. The relations between the countries were definitely moving in a positive direction.

Indian External Affairs Minister Sushama Swaraj visited Bangladesh in her first official overseas trip in June 2014. On 7 May 2015, the Indian Parliament, in the presence of Bangladeshi diplomats, unanimously passed the Land Boundary Agreement (LBA) as its 100th Constitutional Amendment, thereby resolving all 68-year old border disputes since the end of the British Raj. The bill was pending ratification since the 1974 Mujib-Indira accords. In June 2014, during her first official overseas visit, the Foreign Minister of India, Sushama Swaraj, concluded various agreements to boost ties. They include:

- Agreement to send back fugitives accused of murder in India.
- Increase the frequency of the Maitree Express and start buses between Dhaka and Guwahati and Shillong.
- Easing of the visa regime to provide 5 years multiple entry visas to minors below 13 and the elderly above 65.

- Proposal for a special economic zone in Bangladesh.
- Provide an additional 100 MW power from Tripura.
- Bangladesh allowed India to ferry food and grains to the landlocked Northeast India's using its territory and infrastructure.

During Indian Prime Minister Narendra Modi's state visit to Bangladesh in June 2015, as many as 22 agreements were signed by the two sides. During the visit, India extended a US$ 2 billion line of credit to Bangladesh and pledged US$ 5 billion worth of investments. As per the agreements, India's Reliance Power agreed to invest US$ 3 billion to set up a 3,000 MW LNG-based power plant (which is the single largest foreign investment ever made in Bangladesh). Adani Power will also be setting up a 1,600 MW coal-fired power plant at a cost of US$ 1.5 billion. The two countries signed a total of 22 agreements including the ones on maritime safety, co-operation and curbing human trafficking and fake Indian currency. Modi also announced a line of credit of $ 2 billion to Bangladesh. (Memorandum of Understanding, 2016)

On 31 July 2015, around 50,000 people became citizens of India or Bangladesh after living in limbo for decades. Ending a prolonged dispute, the two nations swapped 162 enclaves in the border region, allowing the people living there to stay or opt out to the other country. While 14,214 citizens of Bangladesh residing in 51 enclaves on the Indian side became Indians, a large number of people in the 111 Indian enclaves in Bangladesh preferred to stay with Bangladesh and just 979 opted to move to India. The total number of new Indian citizens will be 15,193. (Memorandum of Understanding, 2016)

This memorandum of understanding is very wide which includes several agreements like Land and Border, Maritime, Trade and Transport, Security and Education, Culture and Development agreements to strengthen bilateral relationships in all walks of life. It tried to demarcate the land boundary between India and Bangladesh according to the 1974 agreement. It also offers the use of Bangladeshi ports like Chittagong and Mongla for the transportation of commodities to and from India via the Agartala, Dawki, and Sutarkandi routes. It foresaw collaboration between the two governments on the blue economy and in the maritime sphere for capacity-building, training, and joint research cooperation. It also enhances trade and transit through land, water, and railways between India and Bangladesh and provides for transit to Northeast India. It permits transportation of Bangladeshi freight through India to its Himalayan neighbours, Nepal and Bhutan. The agreement arranges for the operationalization of passenger buses between Dhaka and Guwahati. It fortifies collaboration in order to prevent all forms human trafficking especially trafficking of women and children and also tries to prevent and control smuggling, production, and circulation of fake currency notes. It also enhances the strength of the Internet available in the Northeast of India through a 22-kilometer optical fibre cable from Brahman aria to the Achaea border. (PF Special Report, June 2016)

In 2018, the leaders of both the countries inaugurated the 130-km long Bangladesh-India Friendship pipeline to supply 4 lakh metric tonnes of diesel to Bangladesh. In September 2018, the Bangladesh cabinet approved the draft of a proposed agreement with India to allow it to use the Chittagong and Mongla sea ports for transporting goods to and from its land-locked north-eastern states.

Bangladeshi Prime Minister Sheikh Hasina visited India in October 2019. The seven pacts and three projects were signed and finalised during this visit in the fields of trade, culture, defence, security, connectivity, etc. Both the countries have attained a great historical best. It is an achievement they are working towards a win-win partnership. (*Economic Times*, 2020)

Issues Affecting Relations

India and Bangladesh share a 4,094-km border with India contiguous to Bangladesh on three sides. Such proximity has contributed to hostilities in the past, and both sides need to resolve certain issues in order for the relationship to move forward. The conflicts of the Bangladesh-India relationship are given below:

Water Debate

Bangladesh and India are South Asian countries. They share 4,094 km of land borders with each other on three sides and another side is open to the Bay of Bengal (Dutta, 2010). There are many conflicting issues between the two countries but the water-sharing issue is one of the most conflicting issues to be resolved (Sood and Mathukmalli, 2011). Most of the time, Bangladesh has no control over the watershed management policy of the river. The water-sharing disputes emerged for two rivers, Ganga and Teesta, between Bangladesh and India. The Ganga runs through the Indian states of Uttarakhand, Uttar Pradesh, Bihar, and West Bengal and reaches Bangladesh where it is known as the Padma. In 1996, the sharing of the Ganga waters was effectively settled by the two countries (Singh, J., 1996). The insufficiency of water is the main reason of these disputes. During floods in Farakka, India gives water to Bangladesh, otherwise India would not like to share Ganga water. Water-sharing remains a critical element in the shaping of India-Bangladesh ties, with the Teesta river dispute and the proposed construction of the Tipaimukh dam at the centre of the controversy. The 1983 Teesta River Agreement allows India and Bangladesh to share 75 per cent of the river water on a 39 and 36 per cent basis. (Mittal, Aruna R., 2016)

In 2011, Indian Prime Minister, Manmohan Singh visited Bangladesh. At that time, it was announced that India would share the remaining 25 per cent of the river water on a 50:50 basis. But Mamata Banerjee opposed that announcement and that is why India has abstained from signing the agreement. The West Bengal government thought that if they share water with Bangladesh, their irrigation projects would be affected. Although resistance from one of the participating states could not have been anticipated, the last-minute cancellation was an "avoidable mess" that damaged India's image as a reliable partner. Therefore, it is a legal right of Bangladesh to get an equitable share with regard to water sharing. This is not benevolence but justice. Bangladesh should take a strong stand during negotiations as the national interest is the cornerstone for any negotiator, and each of the parties will try to ensure its national interest. Freshwater is already a scarce resource and is becoming scarcer day by day, which could be a source of conflict. Therefore, there is no alternative but to cooperate with regard to water sharing. Regional cooperation of the co-riparian countries is crucial for Bangladesh to address her water challenges. Many think that there is another lesson for Bangladeshi negotiators from Kautilya's diplomacy. The Indian mindset and zero-sum gain attitude in negotiations must change to ensure long and healthy Bangladesh-India relationships. Lastly and most importantly, India and Bangladesh should recognise and respect each other's rights, and efforts should be made to firm up regional cooperation to solve the problems of the rivers and the people who depend on them to avoid a water conflict in future.

Trade and Investment

Trade and economic matters between the two countries have made meaningful progress in the past three years. Historically, though trade between Bangladesh and India has favoured India, the trade inequality at a standstill remains high, over US$ 4 billion in 2010-11 against Bangladesh. The Indian government has articulated her commitment to reduce the imbalance in trade. From the commitment, New Delhi has already taken some positive steps towards that. For example, it removed 47 Bangladeshi products from the negative list of imports in order to allow them duty-free access to the Indian market. As a result, exports from Bangladesh to India are anticipated to grow at US$ 1 billion by July 2012 over a period of one year. New Delhi also offered a US$ 1 billion line of credit to Bangladesh for 21 projects during the visit of Sheikh Hasina to India in January 2010. This proved the largest offer of such a line of credit by India to a single country. (Chakma, 2012) India also decided to offer power-starved Bangladesh 250 MW of electricity from its grid, for which the two countries signed a Memorandum of Understanding (MoU) during Sheikh Hasina's visit to New Delhi in January 2010. Eventually, a formal agreement was signed in March 2012 under which Bangladesh would accept 250 megawatts of electricity from the top Indian power utility, NTPC Ltd., and could buy another 250 MW through competitive bidding. Additionally, India has offered its assistance to build a 1,320-MW electricity production plant in Khulna as a joint venture. Given Bangladesh's severe power shortage, India's assistance could play a critical role in meeting the domestic power demand and propelling economic growth. (Chakma, 2012)

Transit

India has long demanded transit amenities from Dhaka to better connect, economically, its remote northeast region with the mainland. Bangladesh refused to accede to this demand considering national security, risks, and infringement on the country's sovereignty. In 2010, when Bangladeshi Prime Minister Sheikh Hasina visited India, a policy shift on the transit issue occurred and changed the country's India policy and relations between the two countries began to progress. Sheikh Hasina decided to allow India (and also Nepal and Bhutan) to use the Bangladeshi sea ports of Chittagong and Mongla and the inland water port of Ashuganj. An agreement was made ready after long efforts, which took more than a year of negotiations for signature during the Indian prime minister's visit to Dhaka in September 2011, but finally could not be signed as Dhaka backed off from signing the treaty due to India's inability to ink the Teesta water agreement. Dhaka gave a condition to sign a transit treaty if New Delhi can deliver a treaty on the Teesta. (Chakma, 2012)

The above discussion on key issues between Bangladesh and India highlights the fact that both Dhaka and New Delhi have altered their policies radically and have sincerely striven to build a new relationship. Notwithstanding considerable domestic opposition in Bangladesh to her government's India policy, Sheikh Hasina has remained persistent with her India policy and the relationship has improved vastly in the past three years. (Chakma, 2012)

Border Management and Border Killings

Bangladesh and India are South Asian countries. After India's partition in 1947, the Indo-Bangladesh border troubles were not inexplicable and gave rise to many questions as to the interpretation and execution of the boundary. There was first an outstanding effort which was made to solve border disputes with erstwhile East Pakistan and the Nehru-Noon Accord was signed in 1958. Though some of the disputes were solved, a number of problems of border management were unsolved since the emergence of Bangladesh in 1971. After independence of Bangladesh, Mrs. Indira Gandhi and Sheikh Mujibur Rahman attempted an Indo-Bangladesh Border Agreement 1974 to solve the border dispute. The agreement listed all kinds of border concerns including enclaves and un-demarcated boundaries with the modalities between two countries. (Singh, 2014) According to this agreement, Southern Berubari was permitted by India to be preserved along with the nearby Muslim enclaves. Bangladesh was left in control of 80 per cent of the Muslim enclaves of Dahagram and Angarpota in exchange. Since the two enclaves were not adjacent to the Bangladesh mainland, India is prepared to lease in eternity to Bangladesh an area of 178 mt. x 185 mt. (Tin Bigha) to unite them with Panbari Mouza of Bangladesh which was ratified in November 1974 but India has still not ratified it. The Government of India argued that ratification needed Border Management: India-Bangladesh Border parliamentary endorsement, which could not be obtained until the entire border had been demarcated, and the areas to be exchanged are identified on the ground. However, Avtar Singh Bhasin argues in *India-Bangladesh Relations 1971-1994 Documents, Volume I* that under the Constitution of India, ratification of an agreement or treaty is an executive prerogative and no legislative approval is required. (Singh, 2014)

On 2 June 2015, Indian Prime Minister Narendra Modi's visit to Bangladesh which was feasible added a new dimension to the strengthening of relations and enhancing bilateral ties. With the declaration of a fresh US$ 2-billion line of credit from India to Bangladesh, the highlight of the visit was the resolution of the 41-year-old boundary dispute between the two countries. Besides, there were 22 Memorandums of Understanding (MoUs) signed between the two countries. During the visit, both heads of the state emphasized the importance of seamless, multi-model connectivity for the wellbeing of regional socio-economic advancement and people-to-people interaction. They had also taken many initiatives such as roadways, railways, and waterways which were the building blocks of an inter-dependent and equally beneficial relationship. Since 2015, the inter-state relations between the countries has been strengthening because of taking mutually outstanding initiatives for the settlement of the boundary dispute. (ORF Special Report, 2016)

The killing of Bangladeshi nationals on the Indian border has been a contentious bilateral issue. Despite Delhi's assurance to bring down border deaths to zero, the situation has improved very little over the years. Officials in Dhaka say cattle smuggling, intrusions, and cutting of the barbed wire border fence are some of the key reasons behind the continuation of border killings. Border Guard Bangladesh (BGB) officials say these reasons were impeding efforts to end the killing of Bangladeshis by their Indian counterparts, insisting that the number of deaths has declined over the years. Government officials say the main agenda in Bangladesh-India bilateral meetings are smuggling of drugs, firearms, and border killings. The issue of border killing is always brought up at each meeting. According to BGB figures, 936 Bangladeshis were killed between 2001 and 2017, by the BSF and Indian nationals. (*Dhaka Tribune*, 27 December 2017)

The Home Minister of Bangladesh, Asaduzzaman Khan Kamal, said in parliament that in the last 10 years, 294 Bangladeshis had been killed by the BSF. (*The Daily Star*, 11 July 2019) Md. Admiral Islam, the MP from

Thakurgaon-2 constituency, said that he had forwarded a number of proposals to curb border killings and smuggling. Most deaths along the border were related to cattle smuggling, the MP added, "Border killings will go down if an arrangement can be made to bring cattle from India through legal corridors." The idea of legalizing the cattle trade has been around for many years. (*Dhaka Tribune*, 27 December 2017). In the December 24 meeting, Iqbalur Rahim, the MP from Dinajpur-3 constituency, said that the number of border deaths had come down. To stop smuggling, he proposed taking more effective measures such as constructing border roads, erecting barbed wire fences, installing CCTV cameras, and creating alternative employment for the smugglers. Kurigram Phulbari Upazila Sadar Union Chairman Harun-ur-Rashid said "In most cases the traders from India cut the fence wires, and create a route for cattle smuggling. The shepherds from Bangladesh are killed while smuggling those cattle, and the main traders from both the countries remain out of reach." Emphasizing the need for creating awareness about border killings, he said: "If we are able to create employment in the border belts, then the shepherds will not engage in such risky work [cattle smuggling], and the number of border killings will come down". (*Dhaka Tribune*, 27 December 2017) Shirin Akhter, Feni-1 constituency MP, said that the proposal she had forwarded was based on the political point of view. She adds, "It is very important to maintain friendly ties with our neighbouring countries. Our relationship with Myanmar is still intact even after such a big incident [the Rohingya influx]." She further said: "Both sides have to be cordial to solve problems whenever they arise. They must sit for talks." Shirin further said, "Raising awareness among the people is important if we want to stop border killings. If we can do that, we will be able to prevent other crimes including smuggling." (*Dhaka Tribune*, 27 December 2017)

When asked why the border killings were continuing, BGB Rangpur regional commander and Additional Director General Brig Gen A.K.M. Saiful Islam explained several reasons: "The BSF insists that they open fire for a couple of reasons, such as whenever someone tries to cut border fences. BSF officials have to face departmental actions if they do not fire in such cases. Another reason is when someone attacks them. They also open fire if any untoward incident occurs during cattle smuggling." Saiful said that the BSF did not usually open fire. "If our people are tolerant and do not behave aggressively, then they [the BSF] do not want to open fire," he added. The BGB official said that there were good relations between the Bangladeshi and Indian border guards. (*Dhaka Tribune*, 27 December 2017) Advocate Abraham Lincoln, Kurigram public prosecutor and lawyer of Bangladesh in the Felani murder case, said: "First of all, our nationals should stay away from the No Man's Land. If the people living in the border areas change their profession, and avoid the borders then there will be no chance of getting killed." (*Dhaka Tribune*, 27 December 2017) "Both the nations should be more tolerant, and they should respect each others' sovereignty," The Kurigram public prosecutor said that border haats should be introduced to increase the supply of products in the area in order to bring down smuggling. He also emphasised on destroying the internal drug business in the border areas. Home Minister Asaduzzaman Khan Kamal declined to comment on government initiatives to curb border killings. "Sixty-eight Bangladeshis were killed along the border in 2008. The number has come down to 21 in 2017. This shows that border killings are gradually going down," he further said, "increasing awareness among the people to curb killings along the border was necessary". (*Dhaka Tribune*, 27 December 2017)

Insurgency

India's north-eastern states, as announced in the press, are tormented by rebellion. It is accepted there are around 175 radical gatherings working in the states encompassing Bangladesh. Bangladesh itself has been battling a revolt throughout the previous couple of decades in its south-eastern part called the Chittagong Slope Tracts, despite the fact that it has been enormously contained as far back as the peace accord with the extremists in 1997. It is likely that there could be an overflow impact of radicals taking sanctuary in each other's nation or utilizing cross-country routes for the transportation of smuggled arms. One Indian source asserts, "Another arms bazaar in the dead zone close to the Bangladesh-Myanmar border town of Naikhangchari has turned out to be home to Indian radical outfits, for example, the Unified Freedom Front of Assam and the National Majority Rule Front of Bodoland. The Harkat-ul-Jihad-al-Islami, a fear-based oppressor in Bangladesh, is known to help these outfits". (Mir, Javid Ahmad, 2018)

In a recent meeting, the head of the fringe security powers traded arrangements of the "culprits" (Bangladesh and India indicating 1,22 and 77 "offenders" individually) covered in their separate nations. Actually, cross-country fear-based oppression, in various structures and indications, is a reality in the entire South Asia. The revolt in northeast India had ended up being an Achilles' Foot for even the English Raj, which neglected to set up its suzerainty over these insurrection-inclined regions. Cross-country psychological warfare or insurrections convey possibilities for firings.

Security Concerns for South Asia

India and Bangladesh are two important countries of South Asia. Both the countries have strategic importance for each other from the perspective of security. Bangladesh is surrounded by India from three sides and shares its land border in the west, north, and east with India, whereas India needs Bangladesh because of the proximity of its northern states. Thus geography plays very important role in shaping India-Bangladesh relations. There are several other issues, which pose severe security threats for the entire region like terrorism, human trafficking, smuggling of drugs and weapons. Terrorism has been one of the major significant threats to the levels of peace and stability in the entire region. It is a remarkable achievement that both the countries are working on a zero tolerance policy on terrorism. During the visit of Prime Minister Sheikh Hasina to New Delhi in 2019, both the leaders—Modi and Hasina—reiterated their faith and strong commitment in order to eliminate all form of terror from their soil and agreed for closer cooperation to fight extremist racial groups and terrorist organisations as a shared priority. (Ministry of External Affairs, GOI, 2019) Both the countries agreed to build counter-terror mechanisms and engage in joint military exercises to enhance cooperation. Another factor is if China and Pakistan make strategic equations with Bangladesh against India it will badly affect the security of the entire region including Bangladesh. Thus, it is quite obvious that friendly India-Bangladesh relations are much required for the security of the South Asian region. It is also helpful to control terrorism, environmental degradation water security, migration, human trafficking, etc.

Recommendations for Indo-Bangladesh Relationship

- To promote harmonious relationship between these two countries in tune with our national interests.

- To be able to contribute effectively towards regional and international steadiness and to possess an effective out-of-the-country contingency capability to prevent destabilisation of the small nations in our immediate neighbourhood that could have unfavourable security implications for us.
- The challenge for India to build on the achievements of neighbouring Bangladesh is to have political determination and to generate consensus to close the big agreements like the Land Boundary Agreement (LBA) and the proposed Teesta water sharing pact.
- Several positive sentiments generated in Indo-Bangla ties during the last few years are undermined by the inability of the Indian polity to come through on the proposed Teesta water sharing pact and LBA. Both Prime Minister Narendra Modi and Chief Minister Mamata Banerjee-led governments need to act quickly in order to wrap up the Teesta pact and implement the Land Boundary Agreement (LBA).
- In order to uphold the national interests, Bangladesh must acquire adequate national power.
- Bangladesh faced general elections in early 2014 and 2018, and the Indian government must engage all political players across Bangladesh's political spectrum, civil society, well-known citizens, media, and key institutions ahead of the polls. A stable Bangladesh is in India's interest.
- Killings along Indo-Bangla boundary by border guards have been an irritant in bilateral ties. The two sides are trying hard to refute this. Border management should be given more importance with emphasis on joint patrolling to prevent border killings.
- Increase access to information: This is not only recommended for the Teesta basin but also recommended for other shared river basins. This access to data is not only for state sharing but also to increase public accessibility to the data.
- During the dialogues and negotiations, consider the entire river basin as a unit of analysis considering that the basin is more important in ecology and economy than a fixed use of it.
- The paradigm is shifting from track-2 processes to track-3 for a new starting of negotiations.
- Discuss the interchange of tradable and sharable benefits in water sharing at the negotiating table: It has already been seen in the negotiations of the Teesta river regime.

- Civil Society Organizations (CSO) should come forward with advocacy and intermediary roles, but trust building is more important to engage in these issues. CSO should have more links with the grassroot people and help to mobilize them for cooperation on shared interests.
- Donor organizations should come forward for capacity building and provide support to the negotiation process as non-state actors.

Conclusion

Greater regional cooperation, especially in the field of economic development to eradicate the poverty trap, may be the ultimate goal for all South Asians. But unless some corrective and ingenious measures are undertaken at this point in time, the situation might move in the opposite direction. That would be extremely disconcerting for the millions of poverty-stricken South Asians. Poverty also gives rise to many other new-fangled crimes, such as women, child and drug trafficking, gun running, and cross-border terrorism, and there is therefore a need to generate greater political will through understanding and dialogue to resolve outstanding issues, some of which may even seem intractable. They may have to go beyond geopolitical compulsions and move towards more concrete regional cooperation like what the Europeans and Southeast Asians are doing. Otherwise, development per se will only elude the South Asians. A change of mindset is a dire necessity for South Asians. Prosperity for all is the way forward. Both Bangladesh and India have much to contribute to this process for the safety and the security of this region.

REFERENCES

Abbas, B. M. (1982). *The Ganga Water Dispute.* Vikas Publishing House: New Delhi.

Arora, N. D. (2016). *Political Science Textbook.* McGraw Hill Publications Pvt. Ltd., New Delhi.

"Bangladesh-India Relations: Past, Present and Future" | 2018-01-26 | *daily-sun.com.*

Bhardwaj, S. (2008). *India-Bangladesh Relations: Are the carrots working*? Institute of Peace and Conflict Studies, New Delhi.

Bhardwaj, S. (2015). "India-Bangladesh Land Boundary Agreement: Ramifications for India's Security", *CLAWS Journal*, pp. 93-110.

C. Rakhahari; Chaudhury Anasua; Basu Ray; Basu, Pratnashree and Banerjee, Sreeparna (2016). *A Year after Modi's Visit. RF Special Report*, June 2016.

Datta & Sreeradha. (2012). "Bangladesh Illegal Migration and Challenges for India". *India's Neighbourhood: Challenges In The Next Two Decades*, (Edited by Dahiya, Rumel and Behuria, Ashok K.) Pentagon Security International, New Delhi, pp. 22.

DCCI Research Department, Report on (2009-2016). *Import Statistics: Bangladesh Bank and Export Statistics: Export Promotion Bureau.*

Dhaka Tribune, 27 December 2017. Why border killing has not stopped, [Online], Website: www. Dhakatribune.com.

Dr. Aruna and Mittal (2016). "India Bangladesh Water Sharing Issues", *International Journal of Humanities and Social Science Research*, pp. 7-11.

Dutta, P. 2010. "India Bangladesh Relations: Issues, Problems and Recent Developments. IPCS Special Report, Institute of Peace And Conflict, India. p. 4.

Economic Times, January 6, 2020.

Emjuddin A. and Nazneen D.R.J.A. (1990). "Islam in Bangladesh: Revivalism or Power Politics?" *Asian Survey* 30: pp. 795-808.

"India-Bangladesh " joint statement during official visit of Prime Minister of Bangladesh to India". (Ministry of External affairs, Government of India. 5 October 2019. Retrieved 29 February 2020).

Javid Ahmad, Mir (2018). "India Bangladesh Relations: A Study of Issues Influencing the Relations and Recent Trends", *Arts and Social Sciences Journal*. 9 (1).

Karim, M. A. (2009). "Bangladesh-India Relations: Some Recent Trends", *ISAS Working Paper*.

Mantoo, S. A. (2015). India-Bangladesh Relationship (1975-1990), *Journal of South Asian Studies* 3: pp. 331-349.

Memorandum of Understanding Sheikh Hasina, Prime Minister, Bangladesh And Narendra Modi, Prime Minister, India, 6 June, 2016. Source: *RF Special Report*, June 2016.

Mir, J. A. (2007). "India Bangladesh Relations". *Arts and Social Sciences Journal*, pp. 9–322.

ORF Special Report, 2016. INDIA – BANGLADESH CONNECTIVITY: A YEAR AFTER MODI'S VISIT, [Online], Website: www. Orfonline.org.

Pant, Harsh V. (2001). "India's relations with Bangladesh". *Handbook of India's International Relation*, (Edited by David Scott), Routledge, New York, p. 88.

Raja, Mohan C. (2004). "Cooperative Security in South Asia". *South Asia Journal*.

Singh, J. (1996). *"National Security An Outline of Our Concerns"*. Lancer Publishers: New Delhi, in association with United Services Institution of India, pp. 59-60.

Singh, Nisha (2014). *India and Development Partnership: Special Reference with Bangladesh in 21st Century*. Procedia-Social and Behavioural Sciences, pp. 157, 137–142, www.sciencedirect.com

Sood, A. and Mathukumalli, B. K. P. 2011. Managing International River Basins: Reviewing India–Bangladesh Trans-Boundary Water Issues. *Int. J. River Basin Manage*. 9 (1): pp. 43-52.

The Daily Star, 11 July 2019. Bangladeshis killed by BSF in 10 years, [Online], Website: www.thedailystar.net.

PART II

Socio-Economic Aspects of Security

10

Non-Traditional Threats to Asian Security in the Post COVID-19 Era: Issues and Challenges

Rumki Basu

Introduction

A security problem may today refer to traditional threats such as inter-state war, intra-state war, and terrorism as well as to non-traditional threats such as economic recession, pandemic, or problems of internal displacement in global politics. The 1994 UNDP Human Development report had argued that the concept of security must shift from the idea of a militaristic safeguarding of state borders to a reduction of insecurity in the daily lives of people. The post COVID-19 era is witnessing a seminal shift in global power relations driven by the newly-emerging powers of the developing world, situated mostly in Asia. China, India, Indonesia, Thailand, South Africa, Malaysia, and Bangladesh have become leading actors on the world stage besides Japan and South Korea. The COVID-19 pandemic, recurring regional conflicts, unexpected alignments among states and cross-border migration involve not just the 'securitization' of certain problems such as economic stability, public health, environmental protection and migration but also the 'internationalization' of domestic problems like organized crime. Asia is the largest and the most populated continent alternating as much by democratic and authoritarian trends as by globalization (integrating) and localization (disintegrating) trends. Asian states have made steady social and economic progress. A strong notion of state-centric security prevailed in Asia for a long time but in the coming decades, a human security model is gradually coming to be accepted by leaders in the region. This is especially relevant for the post COVID-19 era. Asia has a strong potential of becoming the next economic colossus in the 21st century if the countries reduce their military expenditures and increase their human development outcomes by focused public policies and strong governmental action. The need has never been felt as strongly as it is today after the COVID-19 pandemic hit the world and threats to lives and livelihoods became the biggest 'security' issue to all countries of the globe, (developed and developing), in Asia and the rest of the world.

On an average day, until 2019 at least, it was not unusual to see international security issues dominating newspaper headlines such as a terrorist attack, a new state entering the global economic 'hit' list or a cyclone killing thousands of people. With the onset of the COVID-19 pandemic in 2020, public discourse on security has shifted to non-traditional threats like this pandemic, which is the number one threat to people's lives and livelihoods today. Although the international security agenda now virtually includes all of the above crises, our understanding of these issues still varies widely. There are numerous articles on military-related topics of international security, there are much less when we move towards the analysis of non-traditional security threats such as economic crises, infectious diseases and migration, which results in a much lesser perception of these issues as serious threats to international security. However, today after COVID-19, we have a range of new concepts and theories developed to advance our understanding of both traditional and non-traditional security problems.

There are continuing debates among security experts regarding the nature of various threats, the effectiveness of various policy options, as well as the utility of various explanatory frame-works drawn from realism, liberalism, constructivism, and other theories. There can be a question of priorities, which involves values, as in the choice between various objects to be protected (such as national borders versus a vulnerable refugee group), or in the choice between which types of policies to pursue (such as between soft or hard power options). The fact is, true international security is achieved through a host of concurring factors, which some have termed 'complex interdependence' or a 'community of democracies' or a 'zone of liberalism' and possibly, power-balancing dynamics stressed by realists. (Keohane & Nye, 1997)

Today, a 'security' problem may refer to traditional threats such as inter-state war, intra-state war and terrorism (i.e., Russia's annexation of Crimea, Syria's civil war terrorist attacks by Islamic fundamentalist groups or Chinese incursions into Indian territory in 2020) as well as to non-traditional threats such as economic recession, the COVID-19 pandemic and refugees/migration (the Eurozone crisis, the 2013 Ebola outbreak and the Middle East strife-related refugee crisis). It also seems we will have to learn to live with rising cyber security threats as well as with the various problems associated with climate change. At the same time, major international organizations (IOs) involved in global/regional governance and security, such as the United Nations (UN), the World Health Organization (WHO), the World Trade Organization (WTO), and the European Union (EU), seem increasingly overburdened and under-funded to cope with these challenges., e.g., WHO is still struggling with its global efforts to contain COVID-19. Even in Europe, where the EU has worked for decades to manage complex interdependence, the system is under stress from social/economic divides, from domestic and international terrorism, and from the UK's vote to leave the EU, which could destabilize European integration even further. Finally, it is to be seen how the USA and China will manage their increasingly contentious relationship in the light of their bitter confrontations during and after COVID-19, in cyberspace and in the global competitive trade markets.

Herein lies the basic difference between the realist and the liberal approaches to international security: as individuals are at the foundation of all liberal theories, their assumptions about the positive effects of norms, institutions, markets, and democracy are often highly contingent on what might be an unduly optimistic view of human nature. This faith on like-minded, liberal individuals and political regimes can often be taken for granted in prosperous stable states but under more insecure conditions during the ongoing pandemic, for example, liberal assumptions might be very misplaced. In such a scenario, major powers and other stakeholders in the international system facing real or perceived security threats will not necessarily behave peacefully or rationally. Thus, while liberalism and realism can still be seen as ideal types with each one at the end of a hypothetical continuum of the international political spectrum, the oft-recurring violations of international security (traditional or non-traditional threats) have actually fallen somewhere between a pure realist and a pure liberal world dispensation depending on the issues at stake.

An important thing to note is that major international security problems have become more complex since the end of the old Cold War (USA and USSR) and the new one (USA and China). This change largely involves the inclusion of non-traditional threats in international security, often clubbed together as the 'new security agenda' highlighted dramatically during COVID-19. Many such non-traditional problems can be linked to broader globalization processes or to the more specific problem of weak or failed states. The communication revolution in particular has helped to expand a local problem such as a domestic financial crisis to be perceived as an international threat especially if it undermines the national stability of a powerful state. Globalization metaphorically leads to integration of markets; similarly intra-state wars may lead to a 'refugee crises' due to porous borders. This involves not just the 'securitization' of certain problems, such as economic stability, public health, environmental protection, and migration, but also the 'internationalization' of problems that used to remain confined to the borders of a particular state. In 2020, for example, India faced a double security threat—COVID-19 shattered lives and livelihoods at home (non-traditional security threat) and the Chinese incursions into Indian territory in the borders (traditional security threat).

Human Security: Definitions

The 1994 UNDP Human Development report had argued that the concept of security must shift from the idea of a militaristic safeguarding of state borders to a reduction of insecurity in people's daily lives. In every society, human security is undermined by a variety of threats, including hunger, disease, crime, unemployment, human rights violations, and environmental challenges. Let's look at what we understand as economic insecurity. In developed countries there could be millions of young unemployed in post COVID-19 times, while in the developing countries millions of farmers have been unable to earn a decent livelihood from low-priced stagnant agriculture over the years. Closely related is insecurity in food and nutrition. Many households in developing countries, facing high food prices, cannot afford two square meals a day. Another major cause of impoverishment in many countries, rich and poor, is unequal access to affordable health care. Disease and hospitalization are often one of the most important common causes of destitution. Millions of lives have been lost due to COVID-19 in 2020, and millions have been unemployed due to loss of jobs. The pandemic has wreaked more havoc in the world than any other event in a 100 years. Therefore, perspectives regarding security need to shift from an old and exaggerated emphasis on military prowess to a well-rounded, citizen-centric view. In this context, it is pertinent to state that global military expenditures exceeded $ 1,917 billion in 2019, more than the combined GDP of the 50 poorest countries in the world, and 20 times more than the total money given annually as aid to eliminate poverty through multilateral aid The three largest military spenders in the world are the USA, China and India (SIPRI, 2020).

The 21st century is witnessing a seminal shift in global power relations and equations driven by the newly emerging new powers of the developing world. China has become the world's second largest economy, lifting hundreds of millions out of poverty earlier through its planned socialist and now through market economy policies. India has also made slow but steady progress in poverty reduction, (earlier planned economic, now market-driven policies) as well as growth and human development through democratic political regimes in the last seventy years. That Asia has finally arrived is a fact that needs to be celebrated in world politics. Indonesia, Thailand, South Africa, Malaysia, and Bangladesh are becoming leading actors on the world stage. Japan and South Korea had already reached first world levels of growth and development from the 1970s onwards.

Emerging World Scenario

There are narratives of the emergent new world order in popular discourse, which have, for example, announced the arrival of a borderless world, the rise of the South, networked national governance and the emergence of an Asian century. (Heywood, 2014) Such images have been created by the seminal shifts that have occurred in global politics since the closing decades of the last century, e.g., the end of the Cold War, advancement of globalization and the slow but consistent rise of the global South (developing countries) in world affairs. Recurring regional conflicts, unexpected alignments among states, cross-border migration and changing power equations, have surfaced at such a pace that fresh thinking regarding the impact of state and non-state actors in relation to political regimes become an absolute imperative. Turbulence in the Middle East, the 'Arab Spring' and its 'short lived democratizing' effect on the entire region, the rise of new terror axes in different parts of the world, the 'national interest' compulsions of the USA and China to intervene in troubled waters and their trade wars have led to serious global ramifications. The Middle East wars between 2014 and 2017 have left more people displaced and homeless than any period of 20th century history. (UNHCR, 2016) Even after World War II, the 'refugee' crisis had not assumed such major proportions. These global events have had serious repercussions on the domestic politics and governance capacities of Asian states hit by civil war or inter-state conflicts. Then COVID-19 happened in 2020 tearing apart their health and economies.

Laws and constitutions work during 'normal' periods of civil governance; in conflict-hit states these norms do not work and citizens' rights are never fully protected. For citizens living in conflict zones or during times of civil war in Asia, violations, curtailment, or suspension of rights is the norm for both citizens and immigrant populations. The U.N.'s International Migration Report (2017) estimates that there were 258 million migrants in 2017. Between 1990 and 2017, the immigrant population has increased by over 100 million. We now live in a truly 'globalized' world where more and more people are leaving their country of birth for places that have better opportunities and a greater chance of access to higher standards of living. Contrary to popular belief that the West hosts the largest immigrant (legal or illegal) population, it is the developing countries that bear the burden of immigrants worldwide. Although the USA is still home to the greatest number of immigrants in the world, it completely reversed its immigration policy after COVID-19. India hosted the largest number of immigrant populations in 2017. Throughout the greater part of the 20th century, states and public institutions did not deliver the same package of citizen entitlements, which is universally recognized today as a Minimum Agenda of good governance and protection of social, economic, and political rights that are required for human beings to flourish and develop their capabilities. (Basu, 2019)

Today, global politics tilts towards multi-polarity with US-China relations entering a new cold war phase after COVID-19, 'regionalization' of world politics with state and non-state actors both influencing internal polices of states. Religious fundamentalism raises its ugly head every now and then, and although 'democratization' is the current buzzword, it will take decades before the world becomes fully democratic. Across the world, experts lament that democracy is eroding, backsliding, withering, or buckling under authoritarian pressure. If the 21st century is to be dominated by China and India, there are a number of good reasons why this may happen. China and India remain the world's two most populous countries, home to one third of mankind. The recent upsurge in the growth rates of these two countries (till COVID-19 happened), apparently bucking the trend during the financial crisis that spread from the USA in 2007 to most of the developed and developing world, attracted the attention of scholars to the developmental trajectories of Asia's two largest powers. Both are currently undergoing capitalist transformations from socialist/ mixed economy models of growth. China is a 'hard' state, retaining its strong authoritarian one-party regime with above average policy outcomes in most sectors; whereas India's democratic state previously under-performed in most developmental sectors, but over the last two decades, had begun to do much better. (Bagchi & D'Costa, 2012)

The Rise of Asia

By area, Asia is the largest continent at 44,391, 162 sq. km. It is also the largest by population with more than 4 billion people. The ascendance of Asia, which began in the latter half of the 20th century, has been unprecedented in its pace and outcome. Never before in recorded history have the living standards of the average masses changed so rapidly in such a compressed time span. In England, where the Industrial Revolution started, it took 150 years to double its per capita output, while in the USA, which industrialized much later, needed about half a century. Both countries had a population under 10 million when they began to industrialize. In contrast, the current economic resurgence in China and India started with about a billion people in each country. Doubling their output per capita in less than two decades is an economic phenomenon that has made a developmental impact no less radical than the Industrial Revolution in the 19th century. Most developing countries have raised their living standards in the last quarter century, but some have done particularly well-in what can be called the 'rise of Asia'. Some of the largest countries have taken impressive strides, notably China, India, Indonesia, and South Africa.

Over the last two decades, countries from several regions of the world have been converging towards higher levels of human development, as is evident from the UNDP Annual Human Development Index (HDI); a composite measure of indicators involving three dimensions: life expectancy, educational attainment and command over the resources needed for a decent living. All groups and regions around the globe have made notable improvements in relation to HDI components, with greater progress in countries that are ranked low and medium in the HDI range. On this basis, it can be surmised that the world is becoming a better place to live in for most people around the globe. However, national averages often conceal large disparities in living conditions. Disturbing inequalities remain within, and between, countries of Asia. Removing these inequalities will remain the single-most difficult challenge of public governance for Asian states in the 21st century. Let's not forget that for centuries inequality has remained the single-most important destabilizing factor in society.

Development Trajectories in Asia

Some remarkable lessons can be learnt from the diverse and variegated developmental journeys of many Asian states (not necessarily democratic) that have not been imitative of any one model. Their nation-building efforts are dedicated to human development, openness to trade and technological innovation, besides concerns of equity and sustainability incorporated in people-centric policies and strategies. The 'legitimacy' of these states is mainly dependent on their record in development; e.g., China, South Korea, Singapore, Vietnam, Cambodia and Laos. On the other hand, over a number of decades, democratic countries like India, Bangladesh, and South Africa have considered pro-poor patterns of growth as electoral investments. Democracies have to be majoritarian and people-friendly. They need pragmatic political leadership wedded to long-term development, but have to show short-term gains for the electorate as well. In 'soft' democracies, where the demands of various sectors need to be balanced, public investments have to be made in both growth and human development.

In different ways, China is demonstrating that authoritarianism may 'deliver' a better 'growth with equity' outcome than democracy. Both India and China espouse a model of state capitalism in which the strengths of the market are balanced against a strong state, which attempts to reduce the inequities associated with unbridled capitalism. Authoritarian states are usually in a better position than democratic states to take 'hard' decisions, suggesting that Asia may not yet entirely reap the democratic peace dividend, due to the continued coexistence of democratic and authoritarian states in the continent even in the 21st century.

The unexpected turmoil in several Middle Eastern countries and their declining petroleum incomes after the short-lived 'Arab Spring' (signified by pro-democracy movements), is a reminder that the educated young put a high premium on meaningful employment and on their right to expect 'democracy' from their respective governments. A considerable amount of turmoil in Tunisia, Egypt, and Syria was introduced by the urban, educated, Internet-using young, who were disillusioned by the lack of civil and political rights within their countries. Governments can nurture domestic industries (public value based) that would not otherwise emerge because of free market competition. This has enabled several countries of Asia to turn loss-making industries to early drivers of export success, as their economies became more open under the leadership of strong authoritarian regimes, e.g., South Korea and Singapore. Developmental states have experimented with different approaches. However, some features stand out: for instance, expansion of basic social services like health, education with anti-poverty programmes and rapid expansion of employment opportunities are critical features of growth that have promoted human development and created less unequal societies. (Basu, 2019)

Human Security Issues in Asia

My focus here will be to examine the security issues in the Asian context because Asia constitutes more than 60 per cent of the global population. Protecting such a large population and taking them on the path of development is a big challenge. On the scale of economic growth and development, Asia has progressed well so far. It has sufficient resources and economic potential to grow further but there are many problems like political instability, insurgencies, separatism, terrorism, religious extremism, bilateral conflicts, and border disputes that are hindering the development potential of Asia. Though human security is important in Asia, 'national security' also remains an important issue in the light of the instability in North Korea, China's unpredictable behaviour with its neighbours in the South China Sea and increasing defence budget, border disputes between Cambodia, Thailand and India and the ongoing tense relations between India and Pakistan all fall within the realm of traditional security threats.

Asia has a double burden in terms of ensuring the 'national security' of its people, as well as ensuring their human security. The debate on human security is relatively new to Asia. This region has traditionally been associated with the national security paradigm. Two factors, a desire to preserve the sanctity of the new-found sovereignty of the post-colonial 'nation-state', and a relative paucity of sustainable democracies, rendered Asia rather inhospitable to anything but a strictly state-centric agenda of national security. However, now a growing number of academics, scholars, and civil society activists have shown an active interest in promoting this concept in Asia.

Asian Values and the Asian Downturn

In the 1980s, the economic success in Asia was attributed to Asia's intellectual and social traditions, the better known concept of 'Asian Values' that recognised attachment to family as an institution, deference to societal interest, thrift, respect for authority, value of consensus over confrontation and importance of education. Encouraged by their remarkable economic success some Asian political leaders and scholars even began to promote the Asian value-oriented model as an alternative to and superior than capitalism and Western liberal democracy, which has brought about the breakdown of the family, and increased violence and social decay. It was even argued that Western diplomacy focusing on human rights and democracy is simply part of an effort to assert political and economic hegemony over Asia. (Mastume & Chen, 1995)

However in Asia, COVID-19, which wreaked public health and economic losses, will again help to revert to the global debate over human security with much sharper focus. The pandemic-affected large proportions of Asia's population, increasing poverty and destitution, forced migration, food shortages and malnutrition, declining health and education outcomes, precipitating crimes and lack of confidence in existing authoritarian political systems, proving the failure of solving such economic downturns through traditional security approaches. Coping strategies including state and private financial institutional restructuring led to an intolerable political climate, collapse of consumer confidence and recurring instability across the region.

The seminal lesson of the 2020 pandemic was that human rights and democratization thereafter came to be regarded as being indispensable components of human security. To pursue a notion of human security through economic growth and political stability alone without regard to human rights and political participation would be counterproductive. Governments that follow such a path might suffer a dramatic collapse of both political stability and human security. In Asia, state responses to the human security paradigm even today remain cautious. There remains a strong belief that the state will retain a crucial role in promoting human security. Moreover, the notions of physical and territorial security remain an important goal of many governments. As some Asian scholars point out, sometimes the state too faces genuine security challenges, e.g., weak states such as Nepal, Cambodia or Laos, for example, building state capacity is crucial to addressing issues such as poverty, environmental degradation and other threats associated with the human security paradigm. That human security cannot therefore precede state security, is the stated logic.

Due to the above considerations, governments in Asia continue to be ambivalent and divided in their attitude towards human security. Official attitudes of Vietnam, Pakistan and Afghanistan, for example, towards the norms of human security are marked by a fair degree of suspicion. Their representatives stress the need to 'stick to principles', especially those of non-interference and comprehensive security. Their governments view human security as a challenge and financial burden for fragile and weak states. Asian security discourses remain at a flux, reflecting divisions between the traditional statist and the emerging people-oriented conceptions of security. South Asia, for example, is yet to develop a common understanding of human security, which limits its relevance in addressing key security challenges facing the region. Over the long-term, most scholars of Asian security studies do accept that the concept of human security can make an important difference to the regional security environment in Asia. But the need to reconcile political differences and develop a common understanding of the human security paradigm remains an important challenge for Asian governments and their citizens. In a region of ex-colonies where traditional conceptions of sovereignty remain paramount and where the pace of democratisation lags behind other economically dynamic parts of the world, such as Latin America, Asia will take its time in embracing the notion of human security in the 21st century. (Acharya, 2000)

India's Position in Asia and the World

India did score impressive economic progress in the last three decades and was counted as the fastest emerging economies of the world until COVID-19 happened. With a GDP of $ 3.2 trillion, India has emerged as the fifth-largest economy and has diversified her engagements and interests across the globe in tune with her emerging status. India has laid claim to the permanent membership of the Security Council and joined many global mechanisms and groupings like BRICS, Shanghai Cooperation Organisation, G-20 and others to play a larger role in global affairs. India has also cultivated a close strategic partnership with the USA in the post-cold war period—Civil Nuclear Agreement, 2008 (including logistic support agreement) and so on. Yet India has tried to maintain her strategic autonomy between the USA and China in the New Cold War that is emerging between them. In spite of this autonomy India is considered as a close US partner against rising China. Thus, India will not alter the US-led order and will rather try to gain a strategic place in the prevailing global order.

In this international political order the balance of global economic power is gradually tipping in favour of Asia mainly due to the rise of China and India. The extraordinary rise of countries in Asia has generated at least two new dynamics. First, political boundaries are steadily becoming more porous through economic cooperation. Markets are converging across the Eurasian landmass as well as facilitating the geo-economic 'union' of the Indian and Pacific oceans. This has resulted in new integrative dynamics as cultures, markets and communities aspire for development and new opportunities. Second, even though territorial considerations acknowledge economic linkages, political differences are still being reasserted to shape a new political order. Despite border clashes,

China is still India's largest trading partner. Asia is coming together economically but is also threatening to grow apart politically; market-driven globalization in the region coexists with a diverse array of political systems. Within this shifting Asian landscape, India has the opportunity to put in place a new framework for its own security, growth and development, and that of developing countries around the world. As a rising global power, the world's largest democracy and one of the fastest growing economies, India has the economic viability to put together an operational model of human security for its citizens thereby acting as a role model for the developing world. After COVID-19, the Prime Minister has stressed on economic self-reliance, growth with human development and more social sector spending on health and education.

Globalization and localization are both irreversible trends in all Asian societies. Despite the economic homogeneities imposed by a global market, local identities assert themselves everywhere and refuse to be submerged into any kind of cultural homogenization. 'Think globally but act locally' (post COVID-19 philosophy) is the prevalent motto where inter-state conflicts have been replaced by intra-state conflicts in every part of Asia. Domestic insecurities and vulnerabilities have been exposed as never before. In the context of Asia, human rights concerns refer mostly to the challenges of relative poverty and insecure livelihood and employment—challenges that form the basic concerns of human security. Poverty is acknowledged as the biggest violator of human rights. The majority of people in Asia have been yearning to live in peace with their neighbours. But the politics of authoritarian states, the ideologies of the minority elite, the greed of the captains of industry and commerce and transnational financial business and trading institutions have been standing in the way of ordinary people living in their local habitat in peace. Industrialization, Special Economic Zones, dam building or large-scale mining operations in mineral rich zones have led to ecological refugees (local people or tribes becoming internally displaced). Local and trans-border terrorism is another cause of violence throughout Asia leading to the death of innocent civilians from time to time. (Basu, 2017)

In the Asian context, as in many countries of the developing world, the enemies of security are 'within'. Globalization refers to the inevitable conflicts over 'ownership' of local land, water, forests or habitat (globalizers viewed as usurpers). Since inter-state conventional wars have dissipated to a great extent in the Asian context, reaping the peace dividend by reducing military expenditure and fulfilling the Sustainable Development Goals by increasing social sector expenditures would be the most sensible course of policy action. The Human Development paradigm has influenced economic and social development policies in the last 20 years in all the countries of Asia. Well designed and implemented public policies of national governments have brought in successes in key areas of human development. Though maintenance of internal law and order and reasonable defence allocations are nationally accepted as legitimate goals of public policy in all Asian states, it is the success that states can show in giving a human security cover to its citizens that will test the power potential of a state in future. The level of development of a state will be measured not only by its GDP indices and defence expenditure, but also by its Human Development ranking in the 21st century. Small inter-state wars will continue in the post-globalized world but the bigger wars will be intra-state wars among local stakeholders on local issues of hegemony, control of resources or developmental dislocation, e.g., COVID-19 exposed the fact that the greatest impact on lives and livelihoods happened to the lowest and most vulnerable sections of society. There is a great demand for universal health coverage in India now.

Asia represents 60 per cent of the world's population with low literacy rates, health outcomes and per capita income. It contains the largest number of the world's hungry and malnourished children. Most citizens in this continent do not have access to adequate nutrition, housing, universal education or health care. There is a sharp increase in environmental degradation, unemployment, civil wars, drug trafficking, cross-border migration and massive spread of the pandemic in Asia. All these issues pose a far more serious and immediate challenge to the security of human beings than inter-state wars, which have largely been contained. There is a growing realization in Asia of the need to make a paradigm shift in governance from 'state security-centric' models to 'human security-centric' ones. Barry Buzan (1987) argued for broadening the security agenda to include the individual as a referent to security. The causes for this need have been many: the beginning of a period of globalization after the end of the cold war, rise of civil society movements, the spread of democratization, increasing shift of conflicts from inter-state to intra-state ones, etc. This amply demonstrated that new threats were emerging in the globalized world, which could not be solved by militarization alone but by attending to the immediate socio-economic conditions in which citizens live.

All Asian countries have faced border disputes, (the Indo-Pakistan conflict has been the longest and most protracted) and these disputes may continue even in future. These issues have kept the region backward, there is meagre regional trade and perennial suspicion about either Chinese or India's hegemonic role, Asian regional cooperation has never been tapped to its maximum potential. The region is the least integrated in the world. It is time for Asia to collectively work together, concentrate on poverty removal and sustainable development for its citizens by individually focusing on achieving Sustainable Development Goals (SDGs 2015-30) through good governance and collectively working together by learning from each other's best practices in governance.

Concluding Observations

Most Asian states have made steady economic and social progress marked by relatively less interstate wars. However, regional conflicts will not disappear and disproportionate defence budgets will continue, e.g., India and China have the two heaviest defence budgets in Asia. Globalization and localization will continue to remain concurring trends in most Asian societies in the post COVID-19 era. Waves of democratization also toss the continent about as social turmoil often erupts over issues of distributional justice within states. Therefore growth with equity seems to be the best choice for domestic public policy in Asia with enhanced social sector spending on food, education and health. Reaping the peace dividend by improving the distributional aspects of globalization will require strong public action. Civil society groups can play an important role in guiding state actors towards the normative acceptance of human security as a public good guaranteed by the state. The state has to be reinvented and brought right back to the centre of citizen needs and concerns. Asian countries need to learn from each other's success stories in human development outcomes.

Asia has a strong potential of becoming the next economic giant in the 21st century if the incumbent countries reduce their military expenditures and increase their human development outcomes by focused public policies and strong governmental action. The conventional indicators of state power have been size, territory, civil and military technology and nuclear power. All these are necessary to ensure a state's territorial integrity, status and prestige, or, in other words, conventional security would always precede human security. The post COVID-19 era may trigger the biggest paradigm shift in the measurement of the indices of power and security. The biggest *raison-de-etre* of democracy will be the empowerment of citizens though a regime of guaranteed human security for all.

REFERENCES

Acharya, Amitav and Arabinda, Acharya, "*Human Security in the Asia Pacific: Puzzle, Panacea and Peril*", *CANCAPS Bulletin*, December 2000.

Bagchi, A. K. and Anthony, P. D'Costa, *Transformation and Development, the Political Economy of Transition in India and China*, OUP India, 2012.

Basu, Rumki, *Public Administration in the 21st Century: A Global South Perspective,* London, New York, Routledge, 2019.

Reimagining South Asia: Reaping the Peace Dividend from a Human Security Perspective in Minu Jha (ed.) *Ethnicity, Nationalism and State in South Asia*, Delhi, Victorious Publishers 2017.

Buzan, Barry, *People, States, and Fear: The National Security Problem in* International *Relations,* New Delhi Transasia Publishers, 1987.

Heywood, Andrew, *Global Politics*, London, Palgrave 2014, p. 535.

Keohane, Robert and Joseph S. Nye, *Power and Interdependence: World Politics in Transition,* Little, Brown Boston, 1977.

Matsume, Tatsuro and Lincoln C. Chen, (eds.) *Common Security in Asia: New Concepts of Human security*, Tokyo, Tokyo University Press, 1995.

SIPRI Year Book, OUP 2020.

The Sustainable Development Goals, New Delhi, United Nations, 2015.

United Nations Human Development Report, New Delhi, Academic Foundation, 1994.

UNHCR, 2016 data quoted in *The Times of India*, January 18, 2018.

11

Human Security and Linguistic Views: From the Perspective of Japan's International Cooperation

Kenichiro Higuchi

Introduction

Human Security (HS) is becoming one of modern-day Japan's foreign policies. In his speech in 1995 at the 50th anniversary celebration of the founding of the United Nations' (UN), Tomiichi Murayama, Japan's prime minister at the time, referred to HS, revealing his idea of putting more weight on peaceful initiatives such as Official Development Assistance (ODA) for developing countries, humanitarian aid, preventive diplomacy, and disarmament. In 1998, Keizo Obuchi, Japan's prime minister at the time, also proposed the establishment of the UN Trust Fund for Human Security (UNTFHS). As of 2016, Japan has donated roughly 45.3 billion Japanese yen since the establishment of the UNTFHS in 1999[1]. Additionally, as in 2018, Japan has also implemented more than 240 assistance/aid measures, including the assistance required after the Kosovo conflict, and the refugee aid required during the reconstruction of the Democratic Republic of Timor-Leste (East Timor).[2] On top of this, the Commission on Human Security (CHS), whose establishment was announced after the meeting between former UN Secretary-General Kofi Annan and the former

UN High Commissioner for Refugees, Sadako Ogata, in Tokyo in 2001, is focusing on protecting refugees, improving medical care, and strengthening education. The relationship between HS and Language Planning and Policy (LPP), as will be described later on, has an emphasis on literacy. The aim for literacy is not "freedom from fear" by solving social crises or conflicts, but for "freedom from poverty" through prevention/restoration from the perspective of economic empowerment. Japan's government is putting much of its efforts towards these objectives. However, in reality, HS is facing various problems, and from the perspective of LPP, the issues related to literacy will also need a more thorough investigation. This article will look at the relationship between HS and LPP, consider the conflicts between them, and argue the position of LPP in the international perspective.

What is Human Security

Human Security (HS) is a concept that reinforces efforts to resolve various crises that threaten human survival and dignity. This includes not only the destruction of the environment and the violation of human rights, but also topics relating to refugees, poverty, and other humanitarian issues. This concept was originally proposed in the Human Development Report (HDR) by the United Nations Development Program (UNDP) in 1994, suggesting the protection of the security of individuals instead of the more conventional "national security". HS was originally proposed to improve the desperate living conditions seen in developing countries; however, it was later generalized to also include issues relating to human rights, and the treatment of ethnic minorities in developed countries.

To give the background about when this word began to be used frequently—there is a problem relating to how international society; rather than nations which commonly lose their ability to protect their citizen's safety, should protect human safety in countries where conflicts occur, especially in regional conflicts which have frequently occurred since the end of the Cold War. In reality, although the conflicts in countries such as Somalia, Rwanda, and Haiti seemed to be merely different internal disputes or political unrest when HS was proposed in the 1990s, there were still unsolved problems regarding their people's living conditions; such as rapid population growth, low literacy rates, short life expectancies, as well as other issues surrounding poverty, accommodation, education, employment, health and nutrition, etc. Even when national security is ensured, if HS is not, then it is still difficult to say that human safety has been achieved. HDR primarily focuses on seven areas of security, and six of its threats. The seven areas of security are economic, food, health, environmental, personal, community, and political security. The six threats are unchecked population growth, disparities in economic opportunities, excessive international migration, environmental degradation, drug production and trafficking, and international terrorism. (UNDP, 1994: 24-37)

CHS (2003) was later established to meet the demands for achieving the goals of "freedom from shortage" and "freedom from fear". This CHS report examines the issues of safeguarding and expanding people's vital freedoms by shielding individuals from acute threats and empowering them to take charge of their own lives. For this purpose, this report contains the following chapters:

Ch. 2. People caught up in violent conflict
Ch. 3. People on the move
Ch. 4. Recovering from violent conflict
Ch. 5. Economic security—the power to choose among opportunities
Ch. 6. Better health for human security
Ch. 7. Knowledge, skills and values for human security.

We can understand from these issues that the problems related to HS come from many different areas. However, it is also important to note that these issues are not enumerated. Rather, they are mutually complemented through various issues regardless of their differing characteristics, such as short-term/medium- to long-term problems, issues regarding political protection/safety, and issues regarding human development/empowerment.[3]

Human Security and Literacy

The relationship to language policy was also suggested in HDR. Chapter 7 of the CHS report argued that knowledge, skills, and values are needed to support HS. This chapter described the importance of literacy as follows:

> "Basic education has intrinsic value. The capability to read and write improves the quality of life and directly affects people's security, because illiteracy and innumeracy are themselves insecurities. Illiterate people cannot read public notices or bus signs, utility bills

> or newspapers, letters or street signs, wills or loan applications. They must find someone to read for them—and hope that the reader is trustworthy and accurate. The immediate contribution of literacy is to reduce this core insecurity. " (CHS, 2003:115)

Chairman Amartya Sen's idea is clearly shown in this report's message. Sen (2003) points out, "As it happens, widening the coverage and effectiveness of basic education can have a powerfully preventive role in reducing human insecurity of nearly every kind", insisting as below:

> "The most basic issue relates to the elementary fact that illiteracy and innumeracy are forms of insecurity in themselves. Not to be able to read or write or count or communicate is a tremendous deprivation. The extreme case of insecurity is the certainty of deprivation, and the absence of any chance of avoiding that fate. The first and most immediate contribution of successful school education is a direct reduction of this basic deprivation—this extreme insecurity—which continues to ruin the lives of a large part of the global population, not least in the Commonwealth." (Sen, 2003)
>
> "...when people are illiterate, their ability to understand and invoke their legal rights can be very limited, and educational neglect can also lead to other kinds of deprivation. Indeed, this tends to be a persistent problem for people at the bottom of the ladder, whose rights are often effectively alienated because of their inability to read and see what they are entitled to demand and how. The educational gap clearly has a class connection." (Ibid.)

In general, literacy refers to the ability to write, read, and calculate. Below, we look at the world's general literacy situation according to JICA (2012).

There are approximately 796 million people in the world that cannot do simple calculations, read and write letters, or undertake tasks that are necessary for their daily lives. Looking at the statistics by region, illiterate populations are centred around countries in southern and western Asia, Sub-Saharan Africa, and Arabia. The country with the most illiterate population is India, with 283 million of its people being illiterate. Next are China, Pakistan, Bangladesh, Nigeria, and Ethiopia. Two-thirds of those who are illiterate are women. The reasons why these countries have larger illiterate populations are considered to be because a lot of children are at a disadvantage with regard to their opportunities to learn. May be they live far from schools, cannot afford to buy a uniform, and are obliged to farm. Also, some countries are too busy to provide education due to conflict. If their parents have never been educated, then it is hard for them to understand the importance of education. Moreover, even when children start going to school, there is a lack of good-quality education due to language differences among teachers and students. These differences often cause incorrect calculations and an official language of reading and writing. Without literacy and numeracy, people could be deceived by changes in the market. People who work in agriculture could be paid less than what they actually deserve. People who are sick and unable to read may accidentally take an overdose due to not knowing which or how much of a medication should be taken. If they are not able to write their own names, they will miss out on opportunities to receive social security or to vote. (JICA, 2012: 5-6)

Under such recognition, the attention towards literacy in international cooperation has been increasing. At the 1990 World Conference on Education for All (WCEFA) in Thailand, World Declaration of Education For All (EFA) was adopted to confirm that "everyone has a right to education" asserted in the Universal Declaration of Human Rights. It also clarified the facts below and required an expanded vision and a renewed commitment:

- More than 100 million children; including at least 60 million girls, have no access to primary schooling.
- More than 960 million adults; two-thirds of whom are women, are illiterate. Functional illiteracy is a significant problem in all countries; both industrialized and developing.
- More than one-third of adults in the world have no access to printed knowledge, new skills, and technologies, which could improve the quality of their lives and help them to shape/adapt to social and cultural change.
- More than 100 million children and countless adults fail to complete basic education programs; millions more satisfy the attendance requirements but do not acquire essential knowledge and skills.

This program did not go well, however, as the targets were not achieved by the deadline. In accordance with the result, the Dakar Framework for Action was adopted at the 2000 World Education Forum, held in Senegal. In this declaration, new targets were set to be achieved by 2015. The goals were to achieve a 50 per cent improvement in adult literacy levels (especially among women), and to ensure that the learning needs of all young people and adults are met. Moreover, the Millennium Development Goals (MDGs) were adopted at the Millennium Summit held in the same year. The MDGs contained educational goals, which aimed to achieve universal primary education and promote gender equity by empowering women. This action promoted the efforts of EFA. Additionally, The United Nations Literacy Decade was also launched in 2003. (JICA, 2012: 6-7)

JICA has provided much support for basic education since 1990. It has been helping school-age children to receive education by not only building new schools, but also by training teachers, running schools, improving female education, etc. The organization has also been providing literacy education to those who did not receive education during their school-age years through informal education outside the formal education system. As the concrete support for JICA, the enforcement of the administration in charge of informal education has been improved through technical cooperation projects, the adult literacy program as a part of rural development or youth activity from Japan Overseas Cooperation Volunteers (JOCV), the spread of literacy education through the JICA Partnership Program (JPP), among others. (JICA, 2012: 7) Thanks to these efforts, illiteracy has been decreasing. However, according to JICA, over 796 million people still do not have "the least required knowledge, wisdoms, and skills". (JICA, 2012: 7)

Here is a view from a specialist who actually engaged in international cooperation on site. Taro Komatsu; a specialist in educational cooperation, experienced first-hand the challenges of international educational cooperation while participating in the Japan International Cooperation Agency's (JICA) Afghanistan project implemented after the 2001 Afghanistan war. He described how a local school still used textbooks that had been published before the 2001 war; they sought to instil a kind of war-based ethic that had been carried over from earlier war experiences. For example; one textbook presented an arithmetic problem in a casual martial scenario; "There are 30 bullets. If five soldiers share them, how many bullets can each of them get?" Another example included casual violence against Russian enemy soldiers; "I killed three Russian soldiers and you killed five. How many did we kill in total?" This experience led to Komatsu advocating a type of reconstruction that actively seeks to redress oppressive and violence-inducing social values and systems that existed even before the immediate conflict that necessitated intervention arose. According to Komatsu;

> "Reconstruction" in the post war society is not simply to "restore" the society to the one in pre-war days. In the society before or in the middle of conflicts, there exist factors resulting in violence, such as the spread of hatred, the violation of human rights, and social standards which is not fair for specific social groups. The reconstruction would be an opportunity to exclude this kind of factor. Education is a fundamental effort to make a better nation and its people belong there. The way it works possibly changes people's minds toward peace or even the war. [...] Is education equal and is the content not biased or violent? In the very first stage of reconstruction, the local people and those who are engaged in international cooperation need to work together." (Komatsu, 2008)

Komatsu indicated that it was necessary to discuss the methods and standards used to implement education policy. He also suggested that in order for modern nations to function effectively, then improvement in literacy on a mass scale was crucial. In the particular case of Afghanistan; where 70 per cent of the population lacked adequate literacy skills, education, although not often seen as urgent a priority as medical infrastructure or food supply, was the most important concern during reconstruction.

The Agenda of Literacy in International Cooperation

After accepting the significance of literacy in international cooperation, these two questions should be considered from the perspective of language policy: 1) How should illiteracy be defined? 2) Which language should serve as the instrument to administer "literacy"? If literacy is recognized as an ability to read and write, then illiteracy exists in two fundamental forms—an absolute one and a relative one. On the one hand, the former describes a total inability of people to read or write in any language; while the latter describes the inability of people to read or write in certain official or common languages, even when they are able to speak their mother tongue, thus leading to social marginalization legally, politically, and financially.

The concept of literacy for living is based on the idea that attaining the capacity to read and write in a certain language enables individuals to function more effectively in their daily lives. This belief may encourage policy makers to select languages for literacy based on this sole criterion. Such an approach precludes careful consideration of relevant questions pertaining to the linguistic situation, such as the position of marginalized minority languages, or situations where rulers compel populations to learn languages by force. While literacy in the HS may relate to language policy, its logic often prioritizes basic education and in turn fails to take into account issues such as language imperialism, proper language selection, endangered languages, and the costs of implementing the policy.

Chapter 7 of the CHS Report insists upon the realization of human security in the consequences of education: empowering all people with education and knowledge, equipping all people to exercise their rights and responsibilities, and teaching mutual respect (CHS, 2003:124-126). Indeed, education has a profound effect on individual empowerment. But the same is true of language (or linguistic) rights. The choice of an official educational language is a complex problem, one which is inextricable from the right to an education. For example, in India there are more than 800 different spoken languages. Yet the country has 270 million (or more) illiterate citizens. Ethiopia, Chad, and Central Africa have dozens or hundreds of spoken languages, but their literacy rates range from 20 to 40 per cent. In such places, the choice of educational language is inextricable from language rights; and yet, the cost of implementing and maintaining multiple educational languages is prohibitive.

There might be disparities of wealth and academic ability between speakers of an educational language and speakers of minority dialects. But imagine a country such as India or Chad, employing ten educational languages to reduce the shock of difference. The cost of ten educational languages would be larger than the cost of five. Moreover, such a cost would be passed on to international donors, as well as on to the government. Pragmatic as the cost issue may be, it is merely one aspect of the conflict between human security and language policy.

As can be inferred from the above, the realization of language and education rights result in empowerment. Here are a couple of specific examples: Paulo Freire; a Brazilian educator in Recife, taught poor farmers how to read and write, thereby renewing their ability to think about their circumstances and change their lives. The military government of Brazil expelled Freire from his country shortly thereafter.[4] Ngũgĩ wa Thiong'o, a famous writer in Kenya, who has been working on literacy education, said in his book that he stopped writing in English and began to write in Gikuyu, the language of his race, and Kiswahili.[5] The activities of Freire and Ngũgĩ indicate that language choice in literacy is not only a problem of economic survival, but also a problem of identity, spirituality, and politics.

This is also clear in the field of international cooperation. Reviewing his experience as an educational administrator in the United Nations Interim Administration Mission in Kosovo (UNMIK), Komatsu (2006) describes the Shadow Educational System of the Albanians:

> "In Kosovo, where its autonomy was deprived (in 1990), the school education was put under control of Serbian authority. Prior to that, in the elementary schools, pupils were allowed to study in either language of Serbian, Albanian, or Turkish. However, once the unified curriculum in Serbian only was put into practice, Albanians who repelled against it had started their own 'school' at places such as private houses, warehouses, barns, and so on. The 'duplicated educational system' by the 'public education' in Serbian and the "shadow education" in Albanian had lasted nearly a decade until 1999 when the Kosovo war became intensified.
>
> Albanians in Kosovo are proud of the 'Shadow Educational System' even today. They have a huge pride in themselves because they have managed to continue the education as a basis for handing down the ethnic culture by bearing up well against the Serbian authority's pressure. Imagine, however, that the class takes place in a small room of a private house where there is no laboratory, library, sufficient numbers of desks and chairs with probably no stationery. The Serbian police comes around to control the 'illegal education' at the beginning of the new term after a break or during the exam period at the term-end. The class was cancelled each time and the kids had to hide their textbooks written in Albanian. Occasionally, teachers that got caught were beaten in front of the kids, too.
>
> Can these situations be really called "education"? Even if to adults, 'shadow education' might be a sign of ethnic resistance, most likely these would not have been a best environment where kids could learn." (Komatsu, 2006: 13-14)

The pride in education as "the education as a basis for handing down the ethnic culture", and the criticism of "can these situations really be called education?"—questions concerning the idea of 'literacy for existence'. The above sentence; paraphrased from Komatsu, can be linked to experiences within the Japanese education system. It is also a view held by those who have experience as UN staff. Due to their viewpoint of economic efficiency and rationality, however, local populations sometimes hold onto the concept, "I abandon it, neglect it, and positively throw it away." Therefore, the survival and preservation of local or minority languages may be postponed or put in crisis. In such cases, even if a linguist insists that a "language of a mother tongue or an ethnic group, or a language which is in danger of survival, should be protected", the language in question will not necessarily be accepted by local parties. Populations facing persecution or experiencing poverty sometimes wish to learn local languages themselves; such as languages directly linked to work, or languages which can offer them a higher income and improve their quality of life. Discussions of HS are not yet in agreement, and there are a lot of discrepancies among the opinions of those in a position to discuss this matter.[6]

Views on Human Beings and Language through the Perspective of "Human Security"

When we view HS through the lens of language policy, we realize that the problem is comprised of our views on both humans and languages. For example, Amartya Sen provided his view on language in one of his speeches, as below:

> "Later on, particularly in the second half of the 20th century, South Korea, China, Taiwan, Hong Kong, Singapore, and other economies in East Asia followed similar routes and firmly focused on general expansion of education. Widespread participation in a global economy would have been hard to accomplish if people could not read or write, or produce according to specifications or instructions, or to have quality control." (Sen, 2003)

This statement has two significant implications. First, Sen argues that "participation in the global economy" is a result of educational diffusion reinforced by eastern Asian countries. Poverty levels are decreasing across the world, because the global economy has become more aware of economic development in old, developing countries with large populations, such as China and India.[7] However, globalization tends to increase social costs such as environmental destruction and pollution, turmoil and collapse in societies which cannot conform to globalization, and a widening disparity among people. Eastern Asia is currently facing problems such as these. Increasing global economic participation due to an increase in literacy rates is one consequence of HS, and this fact is not beneficial to everyone.

Secondly, Sen's argument might lead to the idea that HS does not exist without national political stability. Therefore, there are no clear guidelines for evaluating one-party dictatorships or the development of dictatorships historically seen in eastern Asian countries. When the overall security of the country and the security of the individual collide with each other, it cannot overcome the realistic idea that "although many people think they should give priority to the security of the individual, this view misses the point because security for human beings is impossible without security for the country."[8] It is important to evaluate what literacy and language contributes to a nation. Regardless of what his intention may have been, Sen's earlier statement may provide the perspective that language is a means to an end, such as a nation's economic development. This is different from the individual empowerment of HS values. In other words, literacy; which was once defined as a means for individual empowerment, may be used as an instrument for sustaining or protecting a political structure that is not necessarily democratic.

One interpretation of Sen's view of language is that it is based on an optimistic take on the term 'human'. Thus, people who receive education, such as reading and writing, are therefore able to take practical action. In this regard, the HS council report states, "In most cases, they (humans) are capable of removing an issue for real by identifying the key to a solution." The subsequent explanation provided by Shimizu (2011) supports this view:

> "The fact that the human security discourse emphasizes individual, political, and economic participation means that it is built—on the premise of so-called liberalism-rational economically-minded people. Indeed, the report from the Commission on Human Security is the first of its kind. When human security decides policies on people's lives, those who are directly affected by such policies should be the most active participants. Autonomous human figures that this person knows best about himself are just typical models of rational economic people based on modern rationalism." (Shimizu, 2011: 97)

HS often emphasizes individual empowerment, making it difficult to identify the relationship between society and community. Detailed discussions of HS not only emphasize individual empowerment, but also the influence that this empowerment can have on society. The influence of the relationship between individuals and their society (for example, the acquisition of a certain language or the economic disparity brought about by the economy) should be included theoretically. When working theoretically, it is necessary to consider literacy such as how to think about economic disparity between those who have learned to read and write and those who, due to various circumstances, have not. When developing theories and working in practice, it is important to recognize the necessity of human security in both diverse and specific cases, such as for minorities and certain ethnic groups within a region, immigrants and refugees, those less physically able, or different genders.

When considering HS, it is important to ensure a consensus during the building process and to consider the legal stability of language policies. Regardless of the maturity of a certain democracy, the language policy decisions of municipalities tend to be arbitrary and technical. This is particularly true in countries where serious intra-regional language conflicts have occurred. It is therefore essential that even widespread intra-regional members are able to participate in the defining of the relationship between individuals and communities concerning language rights and choices. The languages spoken by individuals cannot be changed immediately by changes in policy. Therefore, it is important to have a set of rules previously determined and based on this process in order for legal stability to be ensured. (Higuchi, 2006: 65) It is desirable that such language policy research will be promoted, and the accumulation of language policy research will be utilized in the field of international cooperation.

Concluding Remarks

The field of HS has its own standards regarding safety, a term that carries an intentional meaning. For example, literacy and basic education during peace-building, regarded as a concrete policy, is not necessarily acknowledged directly from the standpoint of language policy research. In HS, although the emphasis is placed on basic education and literacy skills in particular, literacy education should also be offered based on the standpoints of international cooperation and language policy. It is essential to collect such information. For example, the populations of African countries have high proportions of people with hearing difficulties. A shared language may become indispensable as the localization of development progresses such as the level of training for local human resources and the increase of self-procurement. The sign language community should be considered in the language plan for African countries and should be an important issue within the context of their international cooperation. When discussing 'literacy for personal empowerment', the establishment of a sign language system, and the allowing of disabled people to participate in the social economy, may be discussed more in both international cooperation and language policy.

After literacy is established in a population, language education and language planning should be considered next. This has not yet been sufficiently theorized within the context of HS. For example, even though it is based on request principles, the despatching of Japanese language teachers such as JICA, does not lead to an understanding of the actual conditions experienced within a given country or the balancing of local languages and economic disparity after a foreign language has been acquired. This fact is not necessarily consistent with the philosophy of HS, and theoretical refinement is therefore vital.[9] What contribution to HS can LPP studies make? A possible suggestion should be the training and involvement of language experts within discussions on international cooperation. It is also possible through individual, concrete verifications of the validity of literacy education, the maintaining of language ecosystems, the establishing of international sign language systems, the providing of foreign language education for businesses, and the creation of harmonious local language policies. Experts have plenty of room to develop these ideas and assist communities to succeed, as there may be many more ideas on incorporating human resources and language policies into HS-based, international cooperation.

**This is a revised and translated version of Higuchi (2012), originally published in Japanese in 2012.*

NOTES

1. Ministry of Foreign Affairs of Japan. https://www.mofa.go.jp/mofaj/gaiko/oda/bunya/security/statistic.html.
2. Ministry of Foreign Affairs of Japan. https://www.mofa.go.jp/mofaj/gaiko/oda/bunya/ /ah_list.html.
3. There have been controversies over understanding "human freedom" as "freedom from fear" or "freedom from deficiency." For example, Canada and Norway have been

developing foreign policies which focus on "freedom from fear", constituting the Human Security Network (HSN), to deal with matters such as prohibiting anti-personnel landmines and illegal small weapons smuggling, the establishment of the International Criminal Court (ICC), prohibition of child soldiers, prevention of child labour, and the strengthening of international humanitarian law. On the other hand, Japan did not participate in HSN, but rather aimed to realize "human security" via peaceful methods. These methods do not involve arms, and this approach proposes a comprehensive concept that includes aspects of international development assistance. Fukushima (2010) explains that "freedom from fear" is HS' "narrow interpretation." The comprehensive idea includes "freedom from fear", "freedom from deficiency", and "freedom to live with dignity through "a broad interpretation"." In recent years, "signs of convergence" have seen that both interpretations support each other.

4. As to Paulo Freire's thoughts on education, see Freire (1979) and (2001).
5. Ngũgĩ wa Thiong'o (1986). On the literacy education to which Ngũgĩ had a commitment, see also Byam (2000).
6. It has recently been reported that in East Timor (Democratic Republic of Timor-Leste, which became independent from Indonesia in 2002), Portuguese; an official language set by the government, is going through difficulties to become the common tongue of the country. Despite government policies, the majority of the citizens speaks Tetum, and as a result, the policy is accepted as "imposition of a foreign language". However, "it is not easy to develop Tetum which originally had been a spoken language and has not had abstract concepts and academic words to a high-level language for writing and reading." *Yomiuri Shimbun*, June 6, 2012.
7. Kobayashi (2007) says that Xavier Sala iMartin's research dictates that, "The absolute poor, who has an income of less than $ 1 a day, has been reduced to over 200-million people worldwide in 20 years." In response to this view, *The Economist* published an analytical article suggesting that Xavier Sarah Yi Martin's method was different from that of the World Bank's survey, which presented statistics on poverty levels in countries such as China and India. Although the total number of people living in poverty has decreased due to the rapid growth of parts of the country, it does point to issues regarding poverty in sub-Saharan Africa. ("More or less equal?" *The Economist*, March 11, 2004).
8. See Sato (1999: 4-19) and Fukushima (2010: 32).
9. A Korean teacher who taught the Korean language at an Egyptian tourism educational institution during the despatch of the Korea International Cooperation Organization (KOICA) said, "In Egypt; where tourism income is profitable, the tour guide belongs to the high income group. So, among young people there are cases where international cooperation leads to the development of high-income human resources". (Yoon, 2011)

REFERENCES

In English

Byam, L. Dale (2000). *Community in Motion: Theatre for Development in Africa*, Westport: Bergin and Garvey.

CHS (2003). *Human Security Now: Protecting and Empowering People.*

Freire, Paulo (1970). *Pedagogy of the Oppressed*, New York : Herder and Herder (First published in Portuguese in 1968, translated by Myra Bergman Ramos).

——1994 *Pedagogy of Hope: Reliving Pedagogy of the Oppressed*, (First published in Portuguese in 1992, translated by Robert R. Barr).

Ngũgĩ wa Thiong'o (1986). *Decolonising the Mind: The Politics of Language in African Literature*, London: James Currey; Nairobi: Heinemann Kenya; Portsmouth, N. H.
Sen, Amartya (2003). "The Importance of Basic Education" (Speech to the Commonwealth Education Conference, Edinburgh), *The Guardian*, October 28, 2003.
UNDP (1994). *Human Development Report.*

In Japanese

Fukushima, Akiko (2010). *Ningen no anzenhosho: Gurobarukasurutayonakyoi to seisakuhuremuwaku [Rethinking Human Security: Responding to Emerging Global Threats]*, Tokyo: Chikura Shobo.
Higuchi, Ken'ichiro (2006). "Ningen no anzenhosho' to higashiajia no gengoshakai" ["Human Security" and the East Asian Situation of Languages and Societies], Sugita Y. (ed.) *Ajiataiheiy ochiikinio keruhei wakochiku [Peacebuilding in the Asia Pacific Region]* Okayama: Daigaku Kyoiku Shuppan.
——(2012) "Ningen no anzenhosho" togengoseisaku [Human Security and Language Planning and Policy], Matsubara, K. & Yamamoto, T (eds.) Gengo to hinkon [Language and Poverty], Tokyo: Akashi Shoten.
JICA (2012). *JICA's World*, February, 2002.
Kobayashi, Keiichiro (2007). "Gurobaruka to kakusa no kankeiwa" [What is the Relationship between Globalization and Disparity], *The Asahi Shimbun*, March 26, 2007.
Komatsu, Taro (2006). *Kyoiku de heiwawotsukuru [Building Peace through International Educational Cooperation]*, Tokyo: Iwanami Publishing.
Sato, Seizaburo (1999). "Kokubo ganaze 'anzenhosho' ninattanoka" (How the "National Defence" became "National Security"), *Gaiko Forum Special Edition*, Tokyo: Toshi Shuppan.
Shimizu, Kosuke (2011). "'Ningen no anzenhosho' ron: Kozotekiboryokutonokanrennioite" [The Theory of "Human Security": in association with Structural Violence], Odagawa, D., Gonoi, I. & 7 Takahashi, R. (eds.), *Kokusai seijitetsugaku [International Political Philosophy]*, Kyoto: Nakanishiya.

In Korean

Yoon, Seulgi (2011). *Ijipt'ŭesŏHan'gugŏsŏnsaengnimŭrosalgi [Surviving in Egypt as a Korean Language Teacher]*, Seoul: Scenario Chingudeul.
Ministry of Foreign Affairs of Japan. https://www.mofa. go.jp/mofaj/ gaiko/oda/bunya/ security/ statistic.html.
Ministry of Foreign Affairs of Japan.
https://www.mofa.go.jp/mofaj/gaiko/oda/bunya/ /ah_list.html.

There have been controversies over understanding "human freedom" as "freedom from fear" or "freedom from deficiency". For example, Canada and Norway have been developing foreign policies which focus on "freedom from fear", constituting the Human Security Network (HSN), to deal with matters such as prohibiting anti-personnel landmines and illegal small weapons smuggling, the establishment of the International Criminal Court (ICC), prohibition of child soldiers, prevention of child labour, and the strengthening of international humanitarian law. On the other hand, Japan did not participate in HSN, but rather aimed to realize "human security" via peaceful methods. These methods do not involve arms, and this approach proposes a comprehensive concept that includes aspects of international development assistance. Fukushima (2010) explains that "freedom from fear" is HS' "narrow interpretation". The comprehensive idea includes "freedom from fear", "freedom from deficiency", and "freedom to live with dignity through "a broad interpretation". In recent years, "signs of convergence" have seen that both interpretations support each other.

As to Paulo Freire's thought on education, see Freire (1979) and (2001).

Ngũgĩ wa Thiong'o (1986). On the literacy education to which Ngũgĩ had a commitment, see also Byam (2000).

It has recently been reported that in East Timor (Democratic Republic of Timor-Leste, which became independent from Indonesia in 2002), Portuguese; an official language set by the government, is going through difficulties to become the common tongue of the country. Despite government policies, the majority of the citizens speaks Tetum, and as a result, the policy is accepted as "imposition of a foreign language". However, "it is not easy to develop Tetum which originally had been a spoken language and has not had abstract concepts and academic words to a high-level language for writing and reading." *Yomiuri Shimbun*, June 6, 2012.

Kobayashi (2007) says that Xavier Sala i Martin's research dictates that "The absolute poor, who has an income of less than $ 1 a day, has been reduced to over 200-million people worldwide in 20 years." In response to this view, *The Economist* published an analytical article suggesting that Xavier Sarah Yi Martin's method was different from that of the World Bank's survey, which presented statistics on poverty levels in countries such as China and India. Although the total number of people living in poverty has decreased due to the rapid growth of parts of the country, it does point to issues regarding poverty in sub-Saharan Africa. ("More or less equal?" *The Economist*, March 11, 2004).

See Sato (1999:4-19), Fukushima (2010:32).

A Korean teacher who taught the Korean language at an Egyptian tourism educational institution during the despatch of the Korea International Cooperation Organization (KOICA) said, "In Egypt; where tourism income is profitable, the tour guide belongs to the high income group. So, among young people there are cases where international cooperation leads to the development of high-income human resources". (Yoon, 2011).

12

COVID-19 Outbreak and Human Security Concerns

Shalini Saxena

Introduction

The world today is witnessing the havoc of COVID-19. The future will be decided by how countries will react to the current crisis caused by the novel corona virus. The world scenario changed after the Second World War but it was a conventional threat to security. In retrospect, such a threat to security has managed to shake the world order and sometimes even the leading power. The current situation of COVID-19 is a non-conventional threat to security. There are numerous concerns regarding human security amidst this pandemic.

We have witnessed conventional threats to security like wars, balance of power, etc., but now the world is fighting with a non-conventional threat to human security. Amongst the countries, which had the potential to challenge the unipolar world order and will sail through the pandemic without being a victim of considerable damage, will be counted amongst the superpowers. The current pandemic will also affect the process of globalization in the world. We have seen a tremendous trend of globalization after 1990 and we have also seen a sustainable rise in domains ranging from national security to human security concerns. Human security is mainly connected to economic security, food security, health security, political security, environmental security, community security, and personal security. All the main aspects of human security are severely challenged by the outbreak of COVID-19. The human security approach is a proven analytical and planning framework that supports more comprehensive and preventive responses by the United Nations, cutting across sectors, developing contextually relevant solutions, and adopting partnerships to help realize a world free from fear, want, and indignity.

This paper will highlight the threats to human security concerns along with the emerging concerns relating to human security. This issue concerns the globe; therefore, every country becomes a stakeholder in it. This paper will also analyse the possible ways to ensure how to deal with such unprecedented events in the future.

In the 21st century, the term 'security' has become a hot topic of discussion with analysts stating that contemporary state and global relations are being talked and debated upon keeping security in mind. Security is important for the survival of the modern nation-state and is an important aspect of global politics. We are surrounded by issues about security and insecurity by accessing our media outlets and therefore making security an important topic of discussion and debate.

From a social science perspective, security is a disputed topic wherein there is no agreement to its meaning. For many, security is independent in nature while for many others it is the removal of threat. It is a powerful tool for achieving one's political goals, allocation of resources, and achievements (Williams, Paul D., 2013). In a nutshell, there are many approaches to understand the definition of security. As a student of International Relations (IR), one should know different perspectives to form one's definition of security. By doing so, it becomes clear that the field of security is not rigid but flexible in nature. Understanding security is necessary as the questions upon which the field of security revolves around is the same but with time and circumstances, the answers to these questions change with time (Ibid, 2013).

Interest in security has lately increased due to the need for gaining more power than what is already there, information race, key points of history that are being debated upon to create changes in existing social structure, and lastly, material wealth for making the nation-state/ individual more secure. The need to be secure and pursue security came into existence with the coming of the first human society (Ibid, 2013). In the Western world, security gained prominence in the post WW-I and II and Cold War eras.

Security is a subtopic of IR but with it gaining prominence in contemporary times, it has become an important institution on its own. This is evident from the fact that can be seen in educational institutions coming up with departments solely focusing on the study of security and its various aspects. The rising significance of security has prompted significant support from all quarters of human society with non-state actors putting their weight behind the need for security at all levels of human society.

The notion of security has remained a focal point of interest and fundamentally is seen as the utilization of the military strength of a nation-state to defend its borders. And yet, in today's COVID-19 ridden world, it seems that there is a need to focus on other aspects of the security umbrella rather than solely focus on militarization of the national border.

The COVID-19 pandemic is the global outbreak of the corona virus. The virus was first identified in Wuhan (December 2019), China, leading to many names of the virus such as the "Chinese/Wuhan Virus",[1] which, according to many, was seen as an act of racism directed towards the people of Chinese/East Asian origin.[2] On 30 January, the WHO declared the outbreak and labelled it as a health emergency for the international public[3] and on 11 March the virus outbreak was declared a pandemic.[4]. As of now, the global tally of the corona virus cases stands at a whopping 19.1 million infections in 188 nations with more than 710,000 cases resulting in the death of the individual.[5]

According to reports, the virus spread through people being in close proximity to each other and via sneezing, coughing, and talking.[6] The current pandemic situation has led to the shutdown of the day-to-day lives of ordinary individuals and has in turn caused massive problems that have affected the international economy.

Pillars of Security

Security, as a field of study, rest upon the following four key questions: security of what, from what, for what and by what means? (Jackson, Robert, 2000)

The first question, 'the security of what', clearly states that individuals are vulnerable when living in a social or a non-social construct. An individual is prone to attack either from fellow individuals or from nature. Therefore, the security of the individual in IR means being secure and safe from threats emanating either from fellow individuals or from nature itself (Bull, Headley, 1995).

The second question 'security from what' states that every individual is a threat to others either directly or indirectly. There can never arise a situation wherein there is mutual trust and respect and because of such a flawed nature at every level of global politics, security can never prevail in human society. An insecure society leads to the securitization of the state and then the world, as the individual needs to be secure from other fellow beings.

The third question 'security for what' merely states that the opposite of security is defencelessness. Security can be fully achieved when individuals forgo their desires and strive to build a society less insecure. This is, however, not possible due to the simple fact that individuals love to rebel whether that be within themselves or human society. According to subject experts, in spite of the fact that individuals will not control themselves or let anyone control them, security is paramount and can be achieved either by deterrence (Schelling, T., 1980) or by diffidence (Hobbes, Thomas). By being fearful of repercussions, it is possible to secure contemporary human society from threats.

The fourth question 'security by what' is the accumulation of the above three questions. Security is an integral part of human society and if you want to be a part of a group wherein there is communication and interaction, one needs to feel secure. To do so, there is the need for having and implementing various security policies that carry out the job of securing society so that the general public is free and secure to do and pursue their goals and objectives.

Human Security in Security

The security of the individual or, more commonly, Human Security, has gained traction in the field of security studies. Human security is a complicated topic that requires precision when it comes to observing it from many angles/contexts. Human security has become an integral part of international politics with the approach behind it being human-centric

(Kerr, P., 2007), i.e., the main idea behind human security is that security risks need to be assessed from a people-centric viewpoint and that the threat to the individual has greater ramifications on the international security apparatus (Burgess, P. & Grans, J., 2012).

The idea of human security is not new and has existed since the first societies came into existence. For IR, the term came into existence post-Cold War with the focus being on the relocation of resources for the development and security of the individual and society (Kerr, P., 2007). The central thought of human security, with an individual as a point of reference, establishes the framework for an alternative perspective and focuses on how human security is encircled as a perspective. In this regard, human security is comprehended as a method of conceptualizing or moulding a positive vision in an arrangement space, a scholarly plan incorporating dynamic expectation, which helps address squeezing issues from an alternative edge. From this point of view, various parts of the human security idea concerning its definition, scope, and a scientific capacity could either be overlooked or be utilized to help specific political activity.

COVID-19 and Human Security Concerns

The COVID-19 virus has gripped the world. It has shown that something invisible to the human eye has the power to bring the globalized world to its knees. A majority of the world is reeling under the impact of COVID-19. The global economy is in a shambles, people are restrained to their houses, and yet many have not been spared from the wrath of the virus. State and non-state actors are running here and there to produce a viable antidote that has been so far next to nothing. In short, the virus has shown us that a global society is nothing but a mere illusion and the global community tends to veer the individual from the things that require the most attention. COVID-19 has also shown that cracks are emerging in the existing world order and a new world order is on the verge of being created once a viable drug is found for the virus.

From a security view point, we can discuss the implications of the COVID-19 virus on human security:

Security of What: Security of the individual from other individuals because in the case of the COVID-19 virus, human beings are the major carriers of the disease. One infected individual has the potential to affect many others. This has led to insecurity amongst everyone as the threat is not from outside but from inside. A compromised individual is much more of a threat than the virus.

Security from What: In this case, the need to be secured arises from the virus and then secondly from individual threats. Being secure from the virus is doable to a certain degree as one needs to follow some measures/ guidelines. However, the need to be secured from individuals is the most important as one does not know whether those in front of them are compromised or not. Therefore, in COVID-19 era it has become clear that security against the compromised individual is of utmost importance.

Security for What: The opposite of security is defencelessness. People can stop the spread of the COVID-19 virus by keeping a safe distance from each other, wearing a mask, moving out only when needed, sanitizing themselves when they enter their homes, etc. And yet, it is the very opposite that is taking place. Many of the Western, liberalized orders have not paid heed to the warning put forth. People are moving here and there; they are showing their true selves by partaking in rallies and protests aimed at the dismantling of the existing world order and thus putting everyone in harm's way. Therefore, it needs to be understood that in the current pandemic situation there is a need for a security policy, which might be authoritarian, to protect those who are observing the norms.

By What Means: Until a viable cure is found for the COVID-19 virus, it is necessary to implement security by any means possible. There are two ways to go about with the first being the maintenance of existing global relations and repairing those that need repair. Secondly, nation-state security needs to be maintained by the implementation of various security policies that need to be somewhat authoritarian by nature. Fundamental rights need not be usurped but the need to meet and interact with others needs to be curtailed. However, in liberal democracies, it is not possible which is evident from the observation that emerges when one looks at the Western world. However, an authoritarian regime like China, which incidentally is the place of origin for the virus, to some extent maintained its internal security by putting in place strict security measures which the rest of the world has failed to do and are now seeing its repercussions.

COVID-19, like AIDS, spreads from human contact and can only be curtailed when precautionary measures are followed even after the emergence of a cure. Human security in the time of COVID-19 and the post-COVID-19 world order can only be achieved when individuals stop themselves as a threat to others and thereby show self-restraint which in itself is a pipedream as, according to Rousseau "Man is a social animal" and it is this need to interact that either dooms the entire human civilization or creates a world order wherein interactions are kept to the minimum thereby ensuring human security.

COVID-19 and Asia, Europe and America

The COVID-19 virus has spread through the world. Its point of origin is in Wuhan, China, from where the first case was reported. Cases of the virus have been reported throughout the length and breadth of the Asian continent. Nations such as India, Iran, Pakistan, etc., have been cited as the ones that have the highest reported cases. Many nations such as China, South Korea, Vietnam, etc., are believed to have successfully controlled the pandemic though, according to the latest reports, these nations are seeing a resurgence in COVID-19 related cases.[7]

As the virus spread through a globalized transport system, Asian nations such as India, Japan, South Korea and Singapore, to name a few, started to reel under the impact of the corona virus pandemic. India, in order to safeguard its population, ordered a nation-wide lockdown on 22 March 2020, thereby reducing the initial impact of the corona virus pandemic. However, as the initial lockdown period turned from days to weeks to months, the nation also saw a rise in cases. A silver lining here is that the lockdown, termed aggressive by many, was highly praised by the WHO[8] and the UN[9] by stating it as wide-ranging and robust.[10] In regard to the number of corona virus cases in India, WHO puts the number at 2,088,611.[11] To tackle the pandemic, the Indian government invoked the Epidemic Diseases Act, 1897 in which, in accordance with the provisions of the Act, educational and commercial institutions were closed temporarily; the movement of the people was restricted in order to contain the spread of the virus. The Indian government at both central and state levels along with various emergency and surveillance units and experts came up with policy decisions in order to tackle the spread of the virus. India's fatality rate stands at 2.04 per cent and recovery rate stands at 68,32 per cent.[12] India is one of the nations that is at the forefront in terms of developing a COVID-19 vaccine.[13]

South Korea reported its first case on 20 January 2020 and as February 2020 came, there was a rise in corona virus transmissions.[14] In order to control the rate of transmission/contamination, gatherings were prohibited and those infected were put into isolation. Foreigners were not allowed to enter the country. On 9 April 2020 the number of cases was at 10,423[15] cases with a case fatality rate of 1.95 per cent.[16] As of now, South Korea has seen a resurgence of cases[17] with many, including some in the Korean government, stating that the country is undergoing a second wave of infections.[18]

As many Asian nations grapple with the pandemic, the European continent is not far behind. According to the WHO, Europe is the new epicentre of corona virus cases.[19] European nations such as Italy faced the initial brunt of the pandemic. The spread of the virus took place on Italian soil on 31 January 2020 when Chinese tourists visited Rome and, as of now, according to the WHO, 249,756 Italians were infected by the virus.[20] Spain, Great Britain, and other European nations are also plagued by the pandemic.

Cases of corona virus were first detected in January 2020 in the USA and currently the number of cases there has hit the 5 million mark.[21] On 31 January 2020, a public health emergency was declared and on 13 March, Trump declared a nationwide emergency. Similarly, in Brazil, the first COVID-19 case was confirmed on 25 February 2020. Currently, the total number of confirmed cases stands at 3,012,412 according to government sources[22], which includes Brazilian president Jair Bolsonaro.[23]

COVID-19 and Human Security

The impact of the COVID-19 pandemic in terms of human security is varied. From economy to culture to information to society to politics, the COVID-19 pandemic has impacted everything upon which the fabric of the human civilization rests. The COVID-19 pandemic has brought the world to a situation, which many term as the "Corona virus recession"/ "The Great Shutdown/Lockdown" or "The Corona virus crash".[24] The 2020 stock market crash[25] and reports that major G7 nations were in "deep recession"[26] were the early signs of the world entering into a global recession brought about by the virus. The pandemic has brought the world to its knees through the implementation of lockdown mechanisms in order to stop the spread of the virus, thus bringing a stop in consumer activities and leading to an eventual fall in the global economy. The recession has brought in unemployment with the developing half of the global community reeling under the impact of the virus pandemic. The recession has also seen a steep decline in oil prices due to the oil price war that took place between Saudi Arabia and Russia. The collapse of various evergreen industries (tourism, hospitality, energy, etc.) added fuel to the fire.

Social and cultural events were also badly hit. Museums, libraries and various other cultural institutions were closed as the pandemic struck. Religious services were either cancelled or shown to devotees via radio, TV, Internet, etc. Social events that included various and important sporting events such as the 2020 Summer Olympics in Japan were postponed to 2021.[27] Political activity of nations took a massive hit as the pandemic stalled the working of the legislative half of the government; rescheduling elections and lastly many politicians either being admitted to hospital/dying due to the corona virus. Food production also took a heavy hit with many stating that at least 12,000 people can die per day due to the lack of food as a result of the COVID-19 pandemic.[28] The pandemic induced a famine situation that was further intensified due to a locust infestation in various parts of the Asian continent.

The education sector took a hit with many universities and schools being closed.[29] Closures of educational institutions have had far-reaching implications with many social and economic issues coming to light. Issues such as the inability to access digital points of education, Internet issues, etc., have shown gaping holes in every nation's educational infrastructure.[30] The pandemic has brought a rise in mental health issues due to loneliness due to lockdowns and social distancing measures.[31] A decline in global carbon emissions[32] can be seen but at the same time an increase in illegal poaching and deforestation[33] activities has been observed in the current pandemic situation.

COVID-19: China's Expansion Policy

A new cold war-like situation is on the rise due to the COVID-19 pandemic[34] between China and the world, say experts. Many hold that the Chinese government has used the pandemic situation in its favour. The Chinese government has used a two-pronged approach, which consisted of the use of soft and as well as hard power in order to win new allies and deter nations that were enemies according to the Chinese government. The Chinese government supplied the necessary equipment to COVID-19 infested nations[35] thereby furthering China's expansionist policy. Just as there are two sides of a coin, similarly there are two sides to China's expansionist policy in the current COVID-19 pandemic. One can say that the need to supply medical equipment and medicines can be seen as China's face-saving activities. But there are aspects of the nature of the Chinese nation that cannot be kept down for long. China, simultaneously, reared its teeth and fangs at every and any nation it deems a threat. China initiated this by not allowing Taiwan to be a member of the WHO. At a time when the world is reeling under the pandemic, China blocked Taiwan's entry into the WHO by stating that Taiwan is a province of the mainland. The UN toed the Chinese line as it believes in China's "One China Policy" wherein Taiwan is a part of the Chinese mainland and that there is only one Chinese nation in the world.[36]

When it comes to Hong Kong, China is much more aggressive in its policy. Hong Kong, according to its citizens, is an oasis in the desert known as Communist China. Anti-government protests started in February 2019 in Hong Kong when the security bureau proposed an amendment to the law of extradition wherein those guilty will be tried in mainland China. In March 2019, protests by the citizens of Hong Kong were initiated. From April 2019 onwards, the protests intensified between those who supported democracy and those who were loyal to Beijing. The protests continue in 2020 amid the corona virus pandemic with the Chinese parliament implementing national security legislative measures in Hong Kong in order to prevent separation, rebellion, intimidation, and foreign meddling.[37] Many citizens of Hong Kong, as the protests continue, are shifting to the UK. Hong Kong was earlier a British colony and was recovered by China on 1 July 1997. As the anti-government protest grew and the Chinese show of strength increased in Hong Kong, the UK intervened by stating that those who had British National (Overseas) passports and their immediate family could apply for a special UK visa from January 2021 onwards wherein they could emigrate to the UK and look for job and education opportunities and could reside too if the need arose by gaining full British citizenship.[38] As if Taiwan and Hong Kong were not enough, China launched in a new stream of attacks directed towards India. Skirmishes occurred near the India-China border along the Line of Actual Control (LAC). The standoff between the two nations intensified when the Chinese objected to the construction of roads by the Indian government in the Galwan River valley.[39] Following the standoff, the Indian army has increased its deployment and will continue to do so in the coming winter months[40] and the Indian government has ramped up the construction of roads in border areas in order to make the process of deployment in a seamless manner.[41] As diplomatic meetings take place, India has hit China from an economic perspective by cancelling China's entry into the Indian telecom sector and various infrastructure development programs[42] and by banning a number of mobile applications.[43]. Amid the corona virus pandemic, China has reasserted its presence in the South China Sea either through aggression or through harassment. China has been embroiled in territorial disputes with nations such as Malaysia, the Philippines and Brunei over islands that are spread all over the South China Sea.[44] To fuel its ever-increasing appetite, China has shown aggression towards Japan by sending an aircraft carrier, *Liaoning*, between the Japanese islands of Okinawa and Miyako,[45] stating that the Sakteng Wildlife Sanctuary (SWS) near the India-Bhutan-China border is a disputed area[46], and occupying Nepalese villages near the Nepal-China border.[47]

Conclusion

Over the past few decades, new diseases have emerged and thus began to appear on the security agenda. These new diseases are a threat to the security of the individual and are thus changing the very contours of the security paradigm. The current COVID-19 pandemic is being seen as a threat to human as well as national security. This is because a threat to the individual is a threat to the nation-state. The need has risen to incorporate diseases as a threat to the nation-state into the security paradigm. Attention has been provided to the spread of infectious diseases, bioterrorism, etc., which in itself is not enough. An increase in political support and resources need to be taken into consideration but not at the risk of the overall national security architecture.

NOTES

1. Schwartz, Ian (2020). Media called coronavirus "Wuhan" or "Chinese Coronavirus" dozens of times. *Real Clear Politics*. Accessed from: https://www.realclearpolitics.com/video/2020/03/12/ media_called_coronavirus _wuhan_or_chinese _coronavirus_dozens_of_times.html.

2. (2020). Fears of coronavirus trigger anti-China settlement worldwide. *The Korea Times*. Accessed from: www.koreatimes.co.kr/www/world/2020//02/683_282767.html.
3. (2020). Statement of the second meeting of the International Health Regulations (2005) Emergency Committee regarding the outbreak of the novel coronavirus (2019-nCov). World Health Organization. Accessed from: https://www.who.int/news-room/detail/30-01-2020-statement-on-the-second-meeting—of-the-international-health-regulations—(2005)-emergency-committee-regarding-the-outbreak-of-the-novel-coronavirus-(2019-ncov).
4. (2020). WHO Director-General's opening remarks at the media briefing on COVID-19, 11 March 2020. *World Health Organization*. Accessed from: https://www.who.int/dg/speeches/detail/who-director-general-s-opening-remarks-at-the-media-briefing-on-covid-19—11-march-2020.
5. (2020). Coronavirus: which countries have confirmed cases? *Aljazeera*. Accessed from: https://www.aljazeera.com/ news/2020/01/countries-confirmed-cases-coronavirus-200125070959786.html.
6. (2020). How Covi-19 spreads. *Centres for Disease Control and Prevention*. Accessed from: https://www.cdc.gov/ coronavirus/2019-ncov/prevent-getting-sick/how-covid-spreads.html.
7. Feng, Emily; Kuhn, Anthony & Sullivan, Michael. (2020). Coronavirus cases across Asia are again on the rise. *npr*. Accessed from: https://www.npr.org/2020/08/04/898853297/coronavirus-cases-across-asia-are-again-on-the-rise.
8. Agarwal, Nikhil. (2020). WHO praises PM Modi's timely and tough lockdown on corona lockdown 2.0. *livemint*. Accessed from: https://www.livemint.com/news/india//who-praises-pm-modi-s-timely-and-tough-decision-on-corona-lockdown-2-0-1158685150270.html
9. PTI (2020). Coronavirus: United Nation praised India's 'comprehensive' lockdown. *The Week*. Accessed from: https://www.theweek.in/news/india/2020/03/05/coronavirus-united-nations-praises-india-comprehensive-lockdown.html
10. PTI (2020). COVID-19: WHO calls India's lockdown 'comprehensive and robust', UN expresses solidarity. *The New Indian Express*. Accessed from: https://www.newindianexpress.com/world/2020/mar/25/covid-19-who-calls-indias-comprehensive-and-robust-un-expresses-solidarity-2121361.html.
11. World Health Organization. (2020). WHO Coronavirus Disease (Covid-19) Dashboard. *World Health Organization*. Accessed from: https://covid19.who.int.
12. PTI (2020). Covid-19: India's recovery rate rises to 68.32%, fatality rate further dips to 2.04%. *Hindustan Times*. Accessed from: https://www.hindustantimes.com/india-news/covid-19-recovery-rate-rises-to-68-32-fatality-rate-further-dips-to-2-04-centre/story-6T3O1fX28xFgxcHtMSXcgM.html.
13. Ray, Meenakshi (2020). 30 Covid-19 vaccines in different stages of development: Scientists to PM Modi. *Hindustan Times*. Accessed from: https://www.hindustantimes.com/india-news/more-than-30-covid-19-vaccines-different-stages-of-development-scientists-tell-pm-modi/story-cAvTRd5hSkOq9YtHC81UuO.html.
14. Duddu, Praveen. (2020). Coronavirus in South Korea: Covid-19 outbreak, measures and impact. *Pharmaceutical Technology*. Accessed from: https://www.pharmaceutical-technology.com/features/coronavirus-affected-countries-south-korea-covid-19-outbreak-measures-impact/.
15. (2020). S. Korea reports just 39 new covid-19 cases, total 10,423. *KBS World Radio*. Accessed from: https://world.kbs.co.kr/service/news_view.htm?lang=e&Seq_Code=152640.

16. Ranjan, Prashant. (2020). The wounded world: Covid-19, outbreak, responses and future. *Antiques & Collectibles.*
17. Associated Press. (2020). South Korea records 113 new Covid-19 cases, most from overseas. *Hindustan Times*. Accessed from: https://www.hindustantimes.com/world-news/south-korea-records-113-new-covid-19-cases-most-from-overseas/story-J3qGmkaLPu9ku1g7WzYdaJ.hml.
18. BBC. (2020). Coronavirus: South Korea confirms second wave of infections. *BBC*. Accessed from: https://www.bbc.com/news/world-asia-53135626.
19. Fredericks, Bob. (2020). WHO says Europe is new epicentre of coronavirus epidemic. *New York Post*. Accessed from: https://nypost.com/2020/03/13/who-syas-europe-is-new-epicenter-of-coronavirus-pandemic/.
20. World Health Organization. (2020). WHO Coronavirus Disease (COVID-19) Dashboard. *World Health Organization*. Accessed from: https://covid19.who.int.
21. (2020). US hits 5 million Covid-19 case milestone, according to media tallies. *RT*. Accessed from: https://www.google.com/amp/s/www.rt.com/usa//497493-us-coronavirus-cases-record/amp/.
22. Sousa, Marcelo De. (2020). Brazil makes grim milestone—100,000 deaths from Covid-19. *ABC News*. Accessed from: https://www.abcnews.go.com/ International/ wireStory/ brazil-100000- deaths- covid-19-72256747.
23. Reverdosa, Marcia; Pedroso, Rodrigo & John, Tara. (2020). Brazil's Jair Bolsonaro tests positive for Covid-19 after months of dismissing the seriousness of the virus. *CNN*. Accessed from: https://edition.cnn.com/ 2020/07/07/americas/brazil-bolsonaro-positive-coronavirus-intl/index.html.
24. Wolf, Martin. (2020). The world economy is now collapsing. *Financial Times*. Accessed from: https://www.ft.com/content/d5f05b5c-11ea-8fdb-7ec06edeef84.
25. Elliott, Larry. (2020). Great Lockdown to rival Great Depression with 3% hit to global economy, says IMF. *The Guardian*. Accessed from: https://www.theguardian.com/business/2020/apr/14/great-lockdwon-coronavirus-to-rival-great-depression-with-3-hit-to-global-economy-says-imf.
26. Gopinath, Gita. (2020). The great lockdown: Worst economic downturn since the Great Depression. *IMF Blog*. Accessed from: https://blogs.imf.org./2020/04/14/the-great-lockdown-worst-economic-downturn-since-the-great-depression/.
27. BBC Sport. (2020). Tokyo 2020: Olympic and Paralympics Games postponed because of coronavirus. *BBC Sport*. Accessed from: https://www.bbc.com/sport/olympics/52020134.
28. Oxfam. (2020). The hunger virus: how Covid-19 is fuelling hunger in a hungry world. *Oxfam International*. Accessed from: https://oxfamlibrary.openrepository.com/bitstream/handle/10546/621023/mb-the-hunger-virus-090720.en.pdf.
29. UNESCO. (2020). Education: Disruption to Recovery. *UNESCO*. Accessed from: https://e.unesco.org/ covid19/educationresponse.
30. Karp, Paul & McGowan, Michael. (2020). Clear as mud: schools ask for online learning help as coronavirus policy confusion persists. *The Guardian*. Accessed from: https://www.theguardian.com/australia-news/2020/mar/24/clear-as-mud-schools-ask-for-online-learning-help-as-coronavirus-policy-confusion-persists.
31. Brooks, Samantha; Webster, Rebecca; Smith, Louise; Woodland, Lisa; Wessely, Simon; Greenberg, Neil & Rubin, Gideon James. (2020). The psychological impact of quarantine and how to reduce it: rapid review of evidence. *The Lancet*. 395 (10227). Pp. 912-920.
32. Myllyvirta, Lauri. (2020). Analysis: Coronavirus temporarily reduced China's CO_2 emissions by a quarter. *Carbon Brief*. Accessed from: https://www.carbonbrief.org/analysis-coronavirus-has-temporarily-reduced-chinas-co2-emissions-by-a-quarter.

33. Simon, Evan & Castano, Aicha el Hammar. (2020). Deforestation of Amazon rainforest accelerates amid Covid-19 pandemic. *ABC News*. Accessed from: https://abcnews.go.com/International/deforestation-amazon-rainforest-accelerates-amid-covid-19-pandemic/story?id=70526188.
34. Shepherd, Kanchallaiah. (2020). Why India won't be able to compete with China in the post-Covid-19 world. *The Wire*. Accessed from: https://www.thewire.in/political-economy/can-india-compete-with-china-in-the-post-covid-19-world.
35. Mulakala, Anthea & Hongbo, Ji. (2020). Covid-19 and China's soft-power ambitions. *The Asia Foundation*. Accessed from: https://asiafoundation.org/2020/04/29/covid-19-and-chinas-soft-power-ambitions/.
36. Tan, Huileng. (2020). Taipei lashes out at China for blocking Taiwan's access to the World Health Organization. *CNBC*. Accessed from: https://www.cnbc.com/2020/02/06/coronavirus-taiwan-lashes-out-at-china-for-blocking-who-access.html.
37. Reuters. (2020). Timeline: Key dates in Hong Kong's anti-government protests. *Reuters*. Accessed from: https://www.reuters.com/article/us-hongkong-protests-timeline/timeline-key-dates-in-hong-kongs-anti-government-protests-idUSKBN23608O,
38. Lee, Joyce. (2020). How China's security law is pushing Hong Kong citizens to emigrate. *DW*. Accessed from: https://www.dw.com/en/hong-kong-chinas-security-law-emigration/a-54485680.
39. Singh, Sushant. (2020). Chinese intrusions at 3 places in Ladakh, Army chief takes stock. *The Indian Express*. Accessed from: https://indianexpress.com/article/india/m-m-naravane-army-chief-line-of-actual-control-lac-chinese-transgressions-6424478/
40. Singh, Sushant. (2020). Army to retain additional troops in Ladakh for the long haul. *The Indian Express*. Accessed from: https://indianexpress.com/ article/india/india-china- border-dispute-ladakh -indian-army-6533338/.
41. Ray, Kalyan & Bhaumik, Anirban. (2020). Amid border tension, India sends out a strong message to China. *Deccan Herald*. Accessed from: https://www.deccanherald.com/international/amid-border-tension-india-sends-out-a-strong-message-to-china-844496.html.
42. Dastidar, Avishek G. & Tiwari, Ravish. (2020). Chinese firms to lose India business in railways, telecom. *The Indian Express*. Accessed from: https://indianexpress.com/article/business/economy/border-dispute-chinese-firms-india-business-raliways-telecom-6464148/.
43. ET Bureau. (2020). India bans 59 Chinese apps including TikTok, WeChat, Helo. *The Economic Times*. Accessed from: https://economictimes.indiatimes.com/tech/software/india-bans-59-chinese-apps-including-tiktok-helo-wechat/articleshow/76694814.cms.
44. Casiano, Louis. (2020). How China has ramped up aggression in South China sea amid the coronavirus pandemic. *Fox News*. Accessed from: https://www.foxnews.com/world/how-china-has-ramped-up-aggression-in-south-china-sea-amid-coronavirus-pandemic.
45. Gill, Prabhjote. (2020). China's aggression isn't only aimed at India-but at least four other countries in the region. *Business Insider*. Accessed from: https://www.businessinsider.in/defense/news/not-only-india-hong-kong-taiwan-vietnam-and-japan-also-facing-aggression-on-border-issue/sidelist/76418800.cms.
46. Shekhar, Sidharth. (2020). After claim on Galwan, Nepal and Bhutan, China says aggression and expansion not in our genes. *TIMESNOWNEWS*.COM. Accessed from; https://www.timesnownews.com/ international/ article/ after-claim-on -galwan-nepal-bhutan-china-says-aggression-and-expansion-not-in-our-genes/618781.
47. (2020). China occupies Nepal village. *The Tribune*. Accessed from: https://www.tribuneindia.com/ news/nation/ china-occupies-nepal-village-103402.

REFERENCES

Bull, Headley. (1995). *The Anarchical Society*. Macmillan. P. 18.

Burgess, P. & Grans, J. (2012). Human Security. In Snyder, C. A. *Contemporary Security and Strategy*. Palgrave Macmillan. Pp. 89-105.

Hobbes, Thomas. *Leviathan*. p. 81.

Jackson, Robert. (2000). *The Global Covenant: human conduct in a world of states*. Oxford University Press. pp. 190-92.

Kerr, P. (2007). Human Security. In Collins, A. (ed.). *Contemporary Security Studies*. Oxford University Press. pp. 91-108.

Kerr, P. (2007). Human Security. In Collins, A. (ed.). *Contemporary Security Studies*. Oxford University Press. P. 92.

Schelling, T. (1980). *The Strategy of Conflict*. Harvard University Press.

Williams, Paul D. (2013). *Security Studies: An Introduction*. In Williams, Paul D. (ed.). *Security* Routledge, pp. 1-12.

Williams, Paul D., op.cit. pp. 2-12.

13

Safeguarding the Girl Child and Empowering Women in South Asia: Essential for Social Security of the Region

David Sweeny

Introduction

South Asia has a peninsula-like shape that is bordered by three bodies of water: the Indian Ocean to the south, the Bay of Bengal to the east, and the Arabian Sea to the west. The region includes the Indian subcontinent and surrounding countries. South Asia is politically divided into eight autonomous countries: Sri Lanka, Bangladesh, India, Afghanistan, Pakistan, Bhutan, Nepal, and the Maldives. The region covers a total area of roughly two million square miles and has a population size of more than 1.74 billion, which is nearly a quarter of the global population. Additionally, South Asia has the distinction of being the most densely populated area in the world. This paper reflects some of the work of Abused Angels of India (AAoI), a voluntary, not-for-profit organisation which is symbiotic with many, if not all, of the other countries in South Asia; it brings to the fore evidence how the cultures of massive societies across the globe are having to open and change their mindsets about sexual harassment of, and violence towards, every girl and woman; 'developing' countries in South Asia must adopt these standards, ethics and practices if they are to be seen as 'developed' and equal on the world stage on which they aspire to sit.

This chapter will demonstrate how patriarchy can be challenged in South Asia, and how the political silence maintained up to now by governments lacking in vigilance and diligence towards girls and women will soon become a cacophony of noise as the world learns of the perils of being a baby girl, girl child, minor girl or woman living in South Asia. Countries and regions can only be secure if they are stabilised in terms of their citizens both feeling, and actually being, secure as they go about their daily lives. In South Asia, girls and women are marginalised more than anywhere else in the world largely due to the percentage and number of the population suffering rural deprivation. As will be seen later in this paper, the empowerment of women cannot be achieved until girls and women firstly feel 'safe and secure'. Thus, the security of South Asia, in terms of both its citizens and its own economic security, materially rests upon the region meeting the challenges set by the United Nations 2030 Agenda as detailed herein.

Global Developments and Tipping Points

Every one of the South Asian country members of the United Nations has signed up and committed to the United Nations 2030 Agenda. This comprises 17 Sustainable Development Goals (SDGs), and each country has to regularly report on its progress to the United Nations. Each country has to develop national, regional, and global assessment and reporting procedures and, whilst the SDGs are not legally enforceable, evidence of the efficacy of each country's Development Plan will influence how they are perceived in the global community. This paper outlines the 2030 Agenda and its 17 SDGs in greater detail. As defined by the Cambridge English Dictionary, the 'Tipping Point' is the time at which a change or an effect cannot be stopped. Jaha Dukureh, UN Women Regional Goodwill Ambassador for Africa, an outspoken activist leading the UN's global work to end Female Genital Mutilation (FGM) and child marriage, said, "We are at a tipping point in the movement to end Female Genital Mutilation (FGM)". More and more 'tipping points' are developing across the globe, many of which are organized and/or orchestrated by UN Women:

- 25 November 2017 was the International Day for the Elimination of Violence against Women.

- UN Women and partners led hundreds of events worldwide as part of 16 Days of Activism Against Gender-based Violence, concluding 10 December 2017.
- This coincided with the mobilisation of millions behind #MeToo and other movements in an escalating global protest against sexual harassment and assault.
- In the USA, the UK and across Western Europe, myriad movements are working now to support the demolition of sexual harassment of women in many, many working environments.
- Commemoration of International Women's Day (8 March 2018, saw unprecedented global movement for women's rights.
- Through marches of solidarity, viral social media campaigns, cultural efforts and powerful grassroots organizing, people across the world are galvanizing for a future that is gender equal.
- As global mobilization intensified on women's rights, UN's largest meeting on gender equality ran from 12-23 March 2018 (UN Commission on the Status of Women).
- The spotlight on rural women and girls focused on critical issues such as ensuring adequate living standards, food and nutrition, security, access to land, technology, education, health, and ending all forms of violence and harmful practices.
- The recent law change in India, making life sentence and/or capital punishment as mandatory for rape of an under 12, and tight targets to deal with cases, is evidence of the global pressure being brought against India, including pressure from the United Nations to make marital rape illegal.

The 'MeToo movement' has shaken the whole world and 'MosqueMeToo' may well shake Islam. It is far too late for patriarchal powers to turn the clock back and put a lid on these movements and developing 'tipping points'.

Global Snapshot

It is useful to consider the nature and scale of violence against women globally in order to then reflect on the particular problems caused by culture and customs in South Asia:

- In the EU, 45 to 55 per cent of women have experienced sexual harassment since the age of 15 (EU Agency for Fundamental Rights 2014).

- Worldwide, 1 in 3 women have experienced sexual or physical violence – mostly by an intimate partner (WHO 2013).
- Worldwide, 1 in 2 women were killed by their partners or family in 2012 only 1 in 20 men were similarly killed (Global Study on Homicide, UNIDC 2013).
- Thirty-seven countries exempt rape perpetrators from prosecution when they are married to, or subsequently marry, the victim (Iqbal, Sarah, 2015), *Women, Business and the Law*.
- Data from 30 countries found at least 200 million women and girls alive had undergone FGM. In most of these countries, the majority of girls were cut before age 5 (UNICEF 2016).
- Almost 750 million women and girls alive were married before their 18th birthday (UNICEF 2017).
- Seventy-one per cent of all trafficked victims worldwide are girls and women (UNODC 2016).
- Three out of 4 trafficked girls and women are sexually exploited (UNODC 2016).
- Child marriage is legal in almost every state in the USA as of 2014; Over 57,800 minors aged 15-17 years were married. Two states allow girls and boys aged 12 and 14, respectively, to marry (US Community Census Survey 2014).
- Thirty-seven per cent of women in Bihar (India) believe a husband has the right to beat his wife if she argues (NFHS 2017).
- Thirty-eight per cent of rape victims (India) in 2014 were under 18, and rape perpetrators were known to the victim in 87 per cent of the cases (NCRB 2014).

Culture

Many societies seek to explain sexual violence against girls and women and gender inequality by explaining it as their 'culture'. So, what is culture?

- Culture refers to the cumulative deposit of knowledge, experience, beliefs, values, attitudes, meanings, hierarchies, religion, notions of time, roles, spatial relations, concepts of the universe, and material objects and possessions acquired by a group of people in the course of generations through individual and group striving.

- Culture is the systems of knowledge shared by a relatively large group of people.
- Culture is communication, communication is culture.
- Culture in its broadest sense is cultivated behaviour; that is the totality of a person's learned, accumulated experience that is socially transmitted, or more briefly, behaviour through social learning (www.tamu.edu).
- We can see from the above that culture is simply a 'habit'. In many societies, culture is retained at the expense of ethics, morality, and chivalry.
- Ethics: the basic concepts and fundamental principles of decent human contact (dictionary.cambridge.org).
- Morality: conformance to a recognized code, doctrine, or system of rules on what is right or wrong and to behave accordingly (www.dictionary.cambridge.org).
- Chivalry: behaviour system of knights in the medieval period that put a high value on kindness, honour, and courage—especially towards women (www.dictionary.cambridge.org).

AAoI fiercely promotes the belief that boys and men are victims too within a patriarchal society, because patriarchy can only provide an opportunity to control and dominate; control and domination cannot exist alongside care, respect, tenderness, kindness, gentleness, compassion, humility, sacrifice and love. Thus, control and domination render romantic love and the awareness, exchange and release of emotions redundant. In many patriarchal societies, the wife still cannot refer to her husband by his name and she will also be able to eat only after he takes food. The days when the male was the sole provider of food and security while the female was the home-maker are long gone; the male no longer has priority because he is the 'breadwinner'. She works and earns 'bread' too but does so much more. Not everything can have a monetary value as in salary. What she does unpaid, he must do unpaid. We see under SDG5 that women globally do three times as much unpaid care and domestic work as men.

Most of the problems for girls and women in patriarchal societies stem from the fact that they are never taught why they should expect, and how they should recognize a man who believes in gender equality or, if they are forced into an arranged marriage, they are never given such a man. AAoI considers that a man who believes in gender equality will demonstrate that by his actions, not just his words, and he will have the following characteristics and behaviour towards women. He will:

- Never, ever raise his hand to a girl or woman.
- Do the cooking and wash the floor.
- Iron and wash the clothes.
- Care for sick children at home when she has urgency at her work.
- Look after, cook for and entertain the children and take the pressure off her in family life when she is unwell.
- Do or share the shopping and carry the shopping bags.
- Make sure she is served first in restaurants.
- Open doors for her and let her go first.
- Stand up for her against EVERYONE in the world, especially family and villagers who criticise her.
- Put one hand behind his back and fight and beat the whole world for her.
- Shed tears to show his love for her, but be ferocious to those that challenge his tears.

In the pursuit of gender equality, many feminists feel that chivalry is a demeaning behaviour, and many males fail to understand why 'special' treatment should be given to women if we are campaigning for a gender equal society. AAoI is often challenged on these points and, to answer those challenges, reference is made to the following four aspects of parenthood that women face, but men do not: menstruation, pregnancy, childbirth, and menopause. Additionally, and especially within patriarchal societies, women bear the brunt of the daily burden of being nurse, cook, comforter, transport chief, CEO, finance director and, effectively, magician, by somehow resolving seemingly insurmountable problems that arise within families, most of whom live in rural areas.

The 17 Sustainable Development Goals within the UN 2030 Agenda

The eight autonomous countries within South Asia became members of the United Nations on the following dates:

Afghanistan 19/11/1946
Bangladesh 17/9/1974

Bhutan 21/9/1971
India 30/10/1945
The Maldives 21/9/1965
Nepal 14/12/1955
Pakistan 30/9/1947
Sri Lanka 14/12/1955.

Along with the other 185 member-states, these countries signed up to commit to the UN 2030 Agenda in September 2015. The 2030 Agenda for Sustainable Development provides a global blueprint for dignity, peace, and prosperity for people and the planet, now and in the future. Civil society, the private sector, and governments are translating this shared vision into national development plans and strategies. Two of the 17 SDGs, SDG4 (Quality Education) and SDG5 (Gender Equality) are outlined here:

SDG4 Quality Education

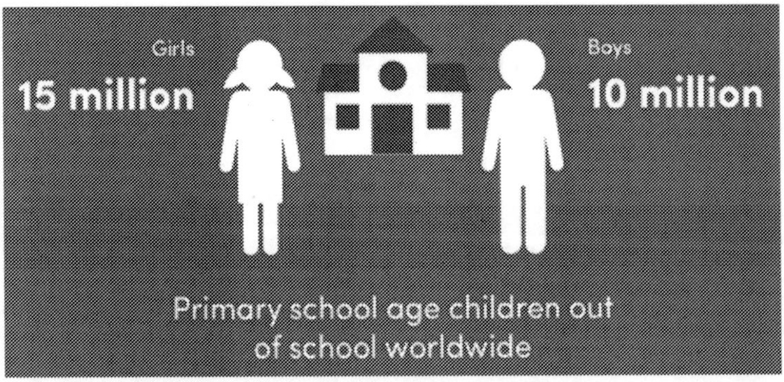

SDG5 Gender Equality

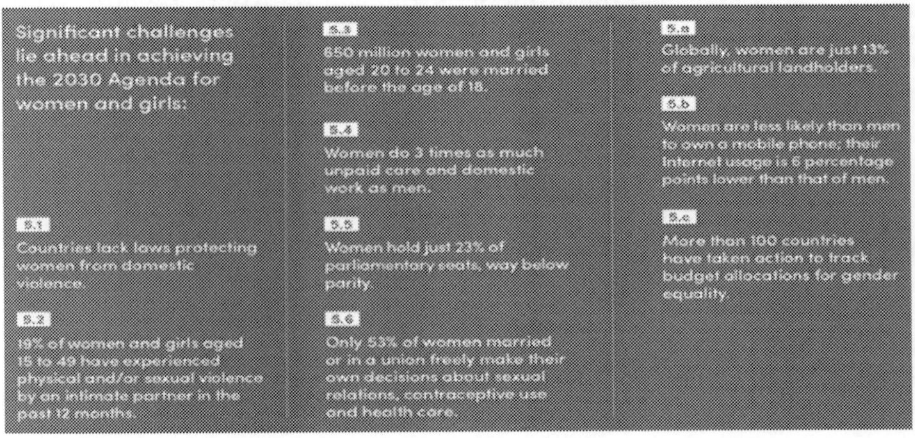

The remaining 15 SDGs are as follows:

SDG1 No Poverty
SDG2 Zero Hunger
SDG3 Good Health and Wellbeing
SDG6 Clean Water and Sanitation
SDG7 Affordable and Clean Energy
SDG8 Decent Work and Economic Growth
SDG9 Industry, Innovation, and Infrastructure
SDG10 Reduced Inequalities
SDG11 Sustainable Cities and Communities
SDG12 Responsible Production and Consumption
SDG13 Climate Action
SDG14 Life below Water
SDG15 Life on Land
SDG16 Peace, Justice, and Strong Institutions
SDG17 Partnerships for the Goals

The statistics against each of the 17 SDGs show just why gender equality matters. Equality is often spoken of, but it is not the same as equity, and equity is the outcome we should strive to attain. Take two people, one who is 5 feet tall, the other 6 feet tall. If they both need to see above a wall that is 7 feet high, and we give each of them a ladder that is 1.5 feet high, they have been treated equally. However, the outcome is not equity as only one can see above the wall.

The importance of membership of the United Nations, and participation within the UN 2030 Agenda, cannot be over-emphasised. Countries that have retained a patriarchally-based culture could have adopted change if they had really wanted to. India is a prime example, following its demonetisation in November 2016 when 86 per cent of its currency was withdrawn overnight and in great secrecy. If a country of 1.4 billion people can do something like that, it can certainly introduce the type of social and educational reforms that will materially eliminate patriarchy and safeguard its most vulnerable citizens...the girl babies. Why did it not do so earlier? Why is it doing it now within the UN 2030 Agenda? We can only speculate it could be because PM Modi was voted third in the list of the world's top 50 leaders in the prestigious Gallup International annual survey 'Opinion of World Leaders' (January 2018), and India wants and needs to be seen as a worthy member of the world's developing nations, a position it cannot hold if it retains prehistoric cultural attitudes on matters such as baby and child rape, gang-rape, child marriage, female genital mutilation and gender inequality. Afghanistan, Bangladesh, and India were the only countries in South Asia to take part in the voting procedure. (Gallup International)

SDG Progress: Asia and the Pacific

Asia and the Pacific are grouped together for the purposes of reporting and assessing their progress with regard to implementing the SDGs. The eight autonomous countries in South Asia are joined by Iran (Islamic Republic of) and Turkey within the South and South West Asia region. The following are key extracts from the 2017 Progress Report for the region as a whole, with South and South West regional area extracts relating specifically to the eight autonomous countries of South Asia.

The Region as a Whole

Despite progress towards some SDGs, the Asia-Pacific region needs to accelerate the pace of change and reverse negative trends in several areas. At the regional level, satisfactory progress has been made towards eradicating poverty (Goal 1) and promoting good health and wellbeing (Goal 3). But at the current rate of progress, only Goal 4 focused on achieving quality education and ensuring that lifelong learning opportunities will be met. While this is a success to celebrate, the region must ensure there are others by 2030. In several areas, the region needs to significantly step up its development reform effort. Inequalities are found to be widening compared to 2000 because rapid economic growth has not always been equitably shared. While progress towards developing industry, innovation and infrastructure (Goal 9) has been relatively successful, efforts to promote decent work and inclusive economic growth (Goal 8) and to reduce inequalities within and among countries (Goal 10) have had limited success. More balanced and equitable growth must remain a priority.

Asia and the Pacific's progress towards SDGs focused on improving environmental stewardship have fallen short across the board. The health of the region's oceans has deteriorated since 2015. There has been no progress towards protecting, restoring, and promoting the sustainable use of terrestrial ecosystems (Goal 15). The protection of forest areas and the reduction in the degradation of natural habitats has weakened at the regional level since 2015. Goal 13, climate action, is unlikely to be met at the current pace of change. Across all these areas, work to find multilateral solutions to overcome these trans-boundary challenges must be enhanced for the benefit of current and future generations. Progress varies significantly from one goal to the next. Out of the 57 targets that are included in this report and which underpin the SDGs, 37 show insufficient progress and seven a deteriorating situation. Where the region has made progress towards certain goals, it has stalled for certain targets. Progress towards SDGs in each Asia-Pacific sub-region and between countries, again varies significantly. In some target areas, regional success may depend on improving the performance of a few countries, while in others, such as those focused on the environment or combating climate change, a reinforced multilateral approach would clearly be more effective. Development strategies must be alive to these differences.

Across the board, the assessment of progress contained in the report is limited by data availability. Only 25 per cent of the official SDG indicators can be used to assess progress in Asia and the Pacific for this reason. Proxy indicators have had to be used to cover goals for which insufficient evidence is available. These large data gaps limit robust progress assessments and impede targeted solutions to overcome development challenges. These data gaps must be plugged by building new partnerships and embracing new data sources across the region. The hope is that the report will galvanise ESCAP (Economic and Social Commission for Asia and the Pacific) countries to do just that, to strengthen the evidence base, to improve the precision of their analysis and the efficacy of their development solutions.

The South and South West Region: Asia-Pacific SDG Progress Report 2017

Some fourteen SDGs will be missed with the current pace of progress. South and South West Asia have made sufficient progress towards Goals 7 and 10. The sub-region nevertheless has huge unfinished work if it aims to achieve all the other SDGs by 2030. By 2017, South and South West Asia have made very little progress towards achieving zero hunger, gender equality, protecting life below water and peace, justice and strong institutions. The sub-region has seen the situation worsen for Goals 8 (decent work and economic growth), 11 (ensuring sustainable cities and communities) and 13 (taking climate action). Compared to other Asia-Pacific sub-regions, South and South West Asia is leading the region in reducing inequalities but are behind the regional average in achieving Goals 5 (gender equality) and 6 (increasing access to clean water and sanitation). South and South West Asia may miss three quarters of the SDG targets. For 12 targets, the direction of travel is negative. Most of the targets South and South West Asia are expected to achieve are under Goals 3 and 4 on good health and well-being and quality education. The region is likely to miss most of the other targets, as indicated by the predominantly yellow and red colour on the SDG dashboard for the sub-region. It is the only Asia-Pacific sub-region that has not made sufficient progress or regressed in all target areas under half of the goals (Goals 8 to 16), except in mobile network coverage.

More than half of the regressions occurred under Goals 8 and 9 on decent work and economic growth and industry, innovation and infrastructure. The sub-region will miss most of the targets with the current pace of progress. For 28 targets, it needs to accelerate progress and a negative trend needs to be reversed for 12.

Empowerment of Women: Global Impact

In January 2016, Ban Ki-Moon (UN Secretary-General) opined that "the empowerment of the world's women is a global imperative". The World Economic Forum Report 2017 stated that, at the rate (or lack) of progress, women will not have equality for 100 years". UN Women, in an update of July 2017, confirmed "when more women work, economies grow. An increase in the female labour force participation—or a reduction in the gap between women's and men's labour force participation—results in faster economic growth".

The Patriarchal Barrier to the Empowerment of Women

With so much weighty opinion and evidence pointing to the global benefits of empowering women, what are the barriers, why do they exist and how can they be overcome? The main barrier can be identified as patriarchy, defined as "a system of society or government in which men hold the power and women are largely excluded from it". (https://en.oxforddictionaries.com). Patriarchy is a term covering many behaviours

Snapshot of SDG progress in 2017: South and South West Asia

GOAL 1	International poverty	Spending on essential services				
GOAL 2	Prevalence of undernourishment	Prevalence of stunting	Prevalence of malnutrition	Agriculture orientation index		
GOAL 3	Maternal mortality	Births attended by skilled personnel	Under-5 mortality	Neonatal mortality	Tuberculosis incidence	Malaria incidence
	Mortality from NCDs	Suicide mortality	Road traffic death	Unintentional poisoning (mortality)	Health worker density	
GOAL 4	Organized learning (before primary)	Inequality indices for education	Organized teacher training			
GOAL 5	Women in parliaments & local governments	Women in managerial positions				
GOAL 6	Safely managed drinking water	Safely managed sanitation				
GOAL 7	Access to electricity	Reliance on clean energy	Renewable energy share	Primary energy supply		
GOAL 8	Real GDP per capita (growth)	Commercial bank & ATM	Real GDP per employed (growth)	Material footprint	Domestic material consumption	Unemployment rate
GOAL 9	Manufacturing value added	Manufacturing employment	CO_2 emissions intensity	R&D expenditure	Medium & high-tech industry VA	Mobile network coverage
GOAL 10	Gini coefficient					
GOAL 11	Economic loss from disasters					
GOAL 12	Material footprint	Domestic material consumption				
GOAL 13	GHG emissions	CO_2 emissions per manufacturing VA				
GOAL 14	Ocean Health Index					
GOAL 15	Forest area (% of land)	Terrestrial & freshwater biodiversity	Mountain biodiversity	Red List Index		
GOAL 16	Intentional homicide	Corruption Perception Index				

- Current rate of progress needs to be MAINTAINED to meet the target
- Need to ACCELERATE current rate of progress to meet the target
- Current trend needs to be REVERSED to meet the target

Dashboard of anticipated progress in 2030: South and South West Asia

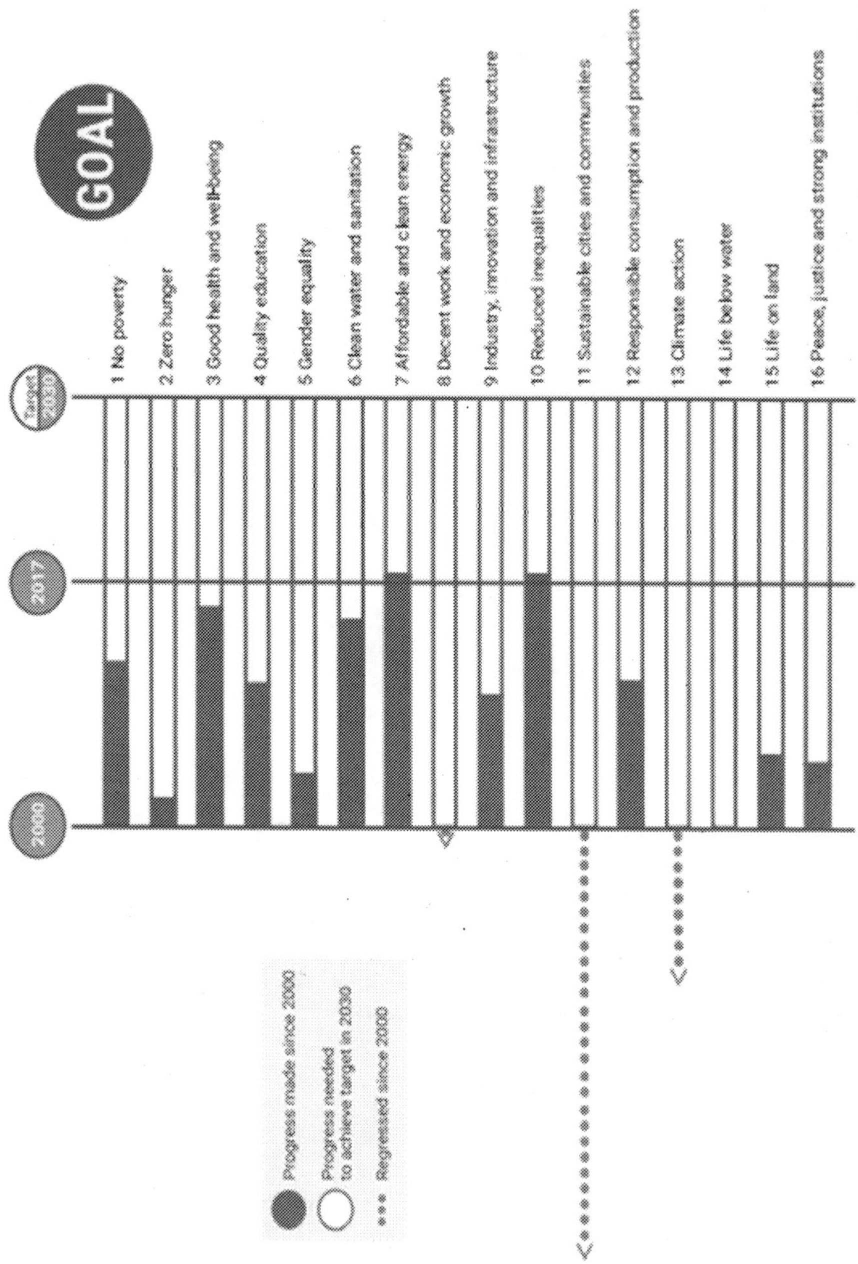

Magnitude of progress gap in SDG target areas: South and South West Asia

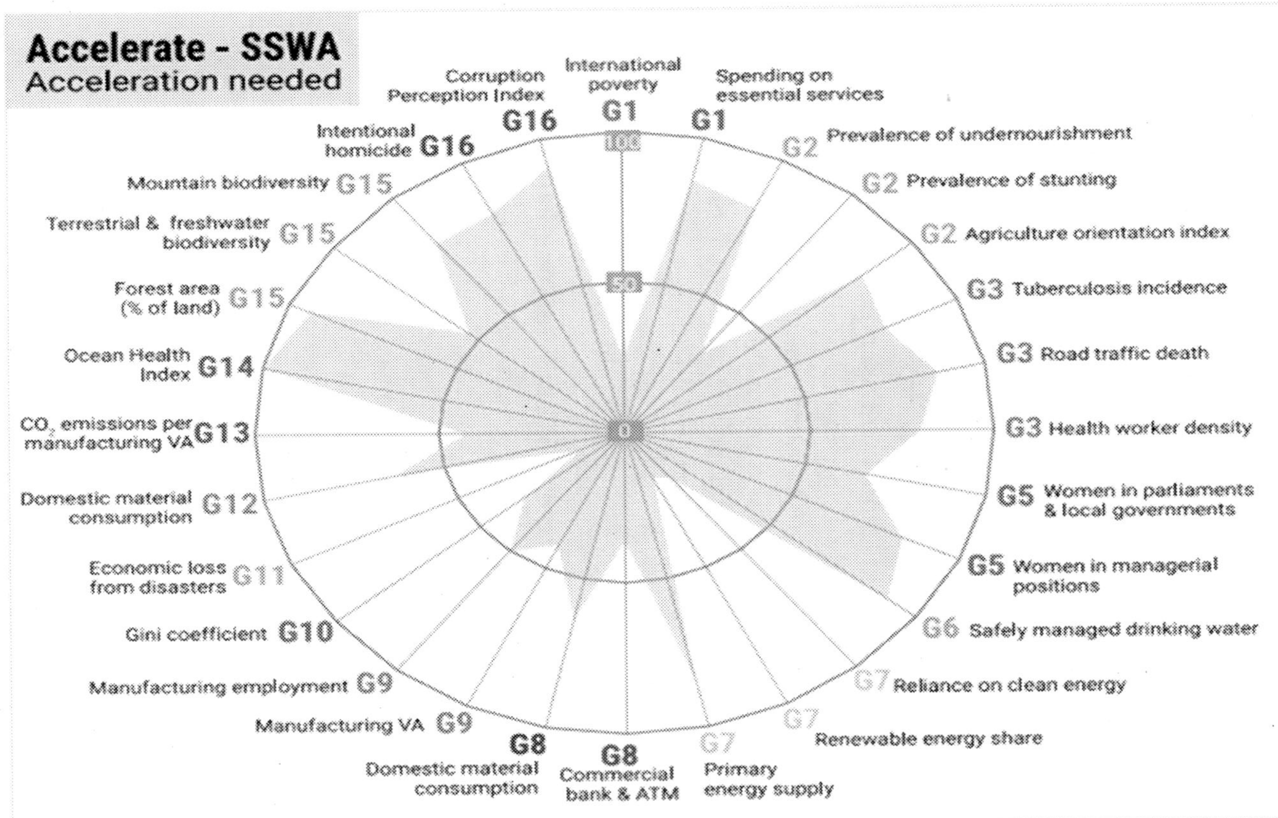

Source: The full report may be accessed at https://www.unescap.org/sites/default/files/Asia-Pacific-SDG-Progress-Report-2017.pdf

and circumstances, from within the home and society, through law enforcement agencies and government. Women who break through the metaphorical 'glass ceiling' often themselves adopt a patriarchal attitude and mode of language.

Questions for Patriarchs

Knowing that the vast majority of girls born will one day become mothers, why does a patriarchal society deny the glorious girl child of a country her God-given right (by all religions) to the equal, fair, respectful and opportunistic life it grants to males simply by virtue that they were not born as females? Why do the leaders in a patriarchal society ignore all the global evidence and indicators that the empowerment of women results in a massive and speedy uplift in the GDP of each country? Why do patriarchal societies cling to the word "culture" as the excuse for ethically and morally (not to mention often constitutionally) unacceptable behaviour? Why do patriarchal societies fail to understand that patriarchy only breeds control and domination, and that such outcomes prevent care, tenderness, gentleness, compassion, kindness, respect, humility and love being at the centre of marriage and family life?

Definition of Empowerment: What Everyone Fails to Understand

The Cambridge English Dictionary defines empowerment as the process of gaining freedom and power to do what you want or control whatever happens to you. 'Empowerment of Women' and 'Women's Empowerment' have become catchphrases, repeated on a mantra-like basis the world over. Due to the focus on abolition of sexual harassment and violence against girls and women, governments, agencies and individuals have lost sight of the fundamental barrier to the empowerment of ANY individual, not just girls and women: how can ANYONE become empowered unless they first feel safe and secure?

The 'baby steps' to empowerment are:

- Safe and Secure
- Confident and Assured
- Respected and Trusted
- Freed and Unchained
- Empowered

Therefore, the process to fully empowering girls and women in South Asia MUST start with safeguarding.

Safeguarding the Girl Child and the Risks Facing Her

In South Asia, the baby and minor (under 18 years) girl child is more marginalised than anywhere else in the world due to (i) the massive rural population, (ii) her time in vulnerable loneliness in communities, both before and after school, (iii) need to use open defecation, (iv) predatory aspects related to sex tourism and child trafficking, (v) pressure for child marriage, and (vi) female genital mutilation. As the girl becomes a woman, the threats to her safety and independence increase as she faces intensive pressure to get married and, within Muslim communities, the incidence of triple *talaq*. As marriage becomes a focus, she then faces the twin threats of dowry crime and honour killings. Female infanticide remains rife in India, and culture-based acts of violence such as honour killings, acid attacks, and stove burnings feature strongly in Pakistan and Bangladesh. Sex tourism is a thriving industry within South Asia, and the trafficking of girls and women from Nepal, Sri Lanka and India to various parts of the world to be forced into prostitution completes the picture of the main threats and dangers facing girls and women in South Asia.

Male vs Female Sex Ratio

Female foetal infanticide, and sex-selective abortions, divides the opinions of scholars as to whether a high or low human sex ratio indicates sex-selective abortions or natural events. Sex-selective abortions arise for a number of reasons, such as cultural preference, dowry or, in the case of the creation of the People's Republic of China in 1949, a one-child policy. Basic health care standards and facilities for men over women also contribute to any imbalance. India's own Finance Ministry Report 2018 states that 63 million women were 'missing' from India's population due to sex-selective abortions, which are illegal in that country. Regardless of their policy on abortion, limited data from other South Asian countries such as Bangladesh, Sri Lanka and Nepal suggests they too have high incidences of such procedures. Aid groups have reported that hardly any steps have been taken in Pakistan for preventing infanticide, especially among poor people. (Karimjee, Mariya, 2014-01-14) In Bhutan, where the State religion is Buddhism, the UN reports that the procedure is probably only allowed to save the life of a pregnant woman. This creates alternative danger, where women will travel to neighbouring India to secure an abortion, often in unsafe conditions. ("Bhutan". *United Nations Abortion*

Policies) The situation would appear to be similar in Afghanistan due to the influence and constraints arising from the national religion, Islam. Turning to the Maldives, the October 2016 data showed a plunge of 90 per cent in its maternal death rate over 25 years. While this does not specifically relate to sex-selection, it does indicate a prioritisation in female well-being and health care. (www.unfpa.org) The development of ultrasound and other techniques has facilitated sex-selection, with more affluent families either opting for abortion or, if a girl child was born, threatening her survival by limiting medical and nutritional care.

Community Conflict Management

Panchayats, or assemblies, are village councils largely within India, Pakistan, Bangladesh, Sri Lanka and Nepal comprising respected elders chosen and accepted by the local community. The Jirga, or council of tribal elders, is a term often used for the panchayat system within Pakistan. Elected representatives are deemed to be wise but, in practice, such judgments would appear to be lacking in any form of common sense. It is very often the case that a tiny girl child of even four years of age will be accused of shaming an entire village if she is gang-raped by several, fully-grown males. The outcome will often be that she and her entire family will be evicted from their village. Kamala Bhasin, Indian feminist and activist, succinctly challenged this backward way of thinking when she asked, "When I'm raped, people say I have lost my honour. How did I lose my honour? My honour is not in my vagina. It is a patriarchal idea that my rape will defile the honour of my community. I'd like to tell everyone: why did you place your community's honour in a woman's vagina? We never did that. It is the rapist who loses his honour, we don't." (https://twitter.com) This form of Community Conflict Management can often result in 'punishments' laid down by panchayats which conflict with the legal framework adopted by the police and judiciary procedures. Severe physical punishment can often be meted out to those found guilty by panchayats of any one of a wide range of deemed 'offences' such as inappropriate choice of marriage partner or unfounded accusation of performing witchcraft, and panchayats will also arbitrarily issue bans on matters such as women wearing nightgowns while doing household chores during the day.

Education: The Road to Safeguarding and Empowerment

Of the 17 SDGs, SDGs 4 (Quality Education) and 5 (Gender Equality) are absolutely pivotal and crucial to safeguarding the girl child, eliminating sexual violence against girls and women, and ultimately empowering women for the benefit of each society. SDG4 clarifies that, for every 10 million boys of primary school age out of schools worldwide, there are 15 million girls. Within South Asia, the UNESCO Gender Equity Monitoring Report (2016) states that 42 per cent of boys and 81 per cent of girls are never expected to enrol in school, 14 per cent and 10 per cent of boys and girls, respectively, enrolled but dropped out and 44 per cent and 9 per cent of boys and girls, respectively, are expected to enrol late. The above data for South Asia makes it clear that getting girls into school is the prime action area. In patriarchal societies, the challenge thereafter is to not only to keep them in school, but ensure they can have the opportunity of higher education and not be pressured into an early marriage. Families often feel it is the girl who should carry the domestic burden as parents get older, so higher education is something of a threat to parents. They think it is far better to get the girl married so she is always there for them as they get older. And, if the first daughter of a family is lucky enough to get a good education, it is so much harder to make families give the same opportunity to second and subsequent daughters.

Essential Educational Reforms

So, what do we define as the educational reforms needed for the South Asian countries committed to the UN 2030 Agenda? There will, of course, be regional and national issues of culture and diversity within each of the separate countries, but the fundamental requirements will include:

- Elimination of political influence within the curriculum so that educators shape the curriculum with the expertise, care, passion and vocation-driven attitude that only they possess.
- Creating effective and active links between home and school by involving home-makers, siblings, etc., in classroom support activities. Not only will this provide a massive, unpaid volunteer force to reduce the ratio of teachers to students (thus improving the quality of teaching and learning), but it will also ensure that children and young people are receiving consistent messages within school and home concerning their personal, social, ethical

and health development. Existing volunteer programmes include support with reading, creative writing, public speaking, play acting, life skills, music and dancing.

- Development of physical education and school sport programmes. These develop the physical, social and moral values of every child and young person, and teach invaluable life skills. Lifelong physical activity aids the fight against obesity and anti-social behaviour.
- Development of programmes that celebrate unity in diversity, showcasing heritage, traditions, culture and customs across each nation, but within an attitude and environment that promotes learning and the sharing and dissemination of best practices and achievements between regions, states, etc.
- Creating gender awareness and equality programmes from pre-KG level; teaching boys and girls it is fine if they want to play cricket or football together. Stereotypical books, curriculum resources that depict girls in the kitchen and boys in the sports field must never feature again. Both boys and girls need to be taught it is fine for them both to display soft and strong characters, and to understand and display emotions. Note: UN collaboration announced on October 17 to incorporate five of its 17 SDGs into the Thomas & Friends storylines, involving 110 countries and 33 languages.
- Gender sensitivity programmes to be compulsory in schools. Distributed through every school in the country, girls should be made aware of their rights under the Indian Penal Code (IPC) should they ever need to attend a police station in connection with molestation or abuse of any kind.

Abolishing Sexual Violence in Society: Sex Offender Registers

Sexual violence exists against males as well as females, all over the world, but the purpose of this paper is only to consider the position as regards girls and women in South Asia. We have already considered how a patriarchally-based society can place the blame on the shoulders of a tiny girl child if she is gang-raped by several, powerful males. This occurs because the thinking skills of supposedly-wise, mature council members are torn into shreds by the perceived fear of someone or something shaming their society. Whilst this perceived shame has historically been used in patriarchal societies to disown, victimise and abandon the very often tiny, baby victims of crimes which their societies should protect them against, the creation of Sex Offender Registers in hitherto patriarchal societies can 'turn the tables' to the benefit of girls and women.

India has one-fifth of the world's child population but also has the largest number of child sex abuse cases registered in the world. According to government figures, a child is sexually abused every 15 minutes—and that is only the cases that have been reported. What about those where the child stays silent, or the parent stays silent for fear of perceived shame after the child has told what has happened? India has become the ninth nation to have such a Register. Crucially, at the moment, the Register will only be accessible by law enforcement agencies—only USA permits access by the general public. This is something that needs to be changed if India is to fully benefit from the Register. India's new National Database on Sexual Offenders (NDSO), has 4.4 lakh entries. It includes offenders convicted under charges of rape, gang rape, POCSO and 'eve teasing'. POCSO stands for Protection of Children from Sexual Offences Act. Each entry has the following information: Name, address, photograph and fingerprint details. A graphic tweeted by the Women and Child Development Ministry said it would also include DNA samples, and PAN and Aadhaar numbers. It is essential that the Register is made available to the general public, with regulations attached to ensure that people cannot misuse the Register for personal grievances against any individual. Only if the Register is made available to the public will the 'perceived shame' factor used against girls for centuries be turned to their benefit. If the personal details of a sex offending male are made public, he will not get a job in sensitive areas such as school bus, security guard in a college, teacher. The outcome will be that parents and communities will start to monitor the behaviour of its male members.

National and International Legislation

Each of the eight autonomous countries in South Asia is governed by a Constitution, which itself is underpinned by national legislation. The effectiveness of any written legislation or verbal or written commitment thereto, can only be assessed by outcomes based on actions arising from the implementation of such legislation. In patriarchal societies, or societies where rampant patriarchy is not applicable but gender equality has yet to be established, the abolition of sexual violence against girls and women, and creation of a gender equal society, requires re-training programmes for those within the police and judiciary, as these are domains where stereotypical gender assumptions are often made by those entrusted to uphold the laws created by Constitutions, adoption of various international conventions and national legislation. Whenever such radical re-training of ideologies is needed, it is often as a result of reactionary statements and policies arising from the political standpoint of self-interest and protection of the state's reputation. A clear example of this was India's response to the infamous 2012 'Nirbhaya' (meaning 'fearless') gang rape of a student on a bus in Delhi. The Criminal Law (Amendment) Act, 2013 (Nirbhaya Act) is an Indian legislation passed by the Lok Sabha on 19 March 2013, and by the Rajya Sabha on 21 March 2013, which provides for amendment of the Indian Penal Code, Indian Evidence Act, and Code of Criminal Procedure, 1973 on laws related to sexual offences. Immediately following this offence, various promises and commitments were made by politicians across India relating to:

- Gender awareness and sensitivity training for the police and judiciary
- Requirement for every mobile phone in India to have a panic button

As on the date of this paper, neither promise nor commitment has been validated by action. One reason for this can be gleaned from the reaction of one politician to this horrific gang rape: when questioned as to why this offence occurred and what should be done to avoid it happening in the future, he opined that it was the duty of mothers to instruct and teach their sons how to behave towards women. Never did it occur to this prehistoric patriarch that it was the father who, by demonstrating actions of care, respect and love towards his wife and the boy's mother, should be responsible for educating the boy. With regard to safeguarding the girl child, and this applying as a base from which to empower women, the UN 2030 Agenda is the most progressive international collaboration since the United Nations Convention on the Rights of the Child (UNCRC). The CRC was adopted by the General Assembly of the United Nations on 20 November 1989 and has been ratified by 195 countries, including Somalia, making it the most widely ratified international human rights treaty in history. As on the date of this paper, only two countries have yet to ratify the landmark treaty—South Sudan and the USA. America signed it in 1995 but never ratified it. The UN Convention on the Rights of the Child (UNCRC) applies to all children and young people under 18. Its aim is to recognise the rights of children and young people and ensure that they grow up in the spirit of peace, dignity, tolerance, freedom, equality and solidarity. The United Nations Convention on the Rights of the Child (UNCRC) is a legally-binding international agreement setting out the civil, political, economic, social and cultural rights of every child, regardless of their race, religion or abilities. However, though legally binding, breaches of the legislation are difficult to prosecute and 29 years after its ratification, the UNCRC is often toothless in the face of ineffective national legislation and attitudes.

Religion and Politics

One very clear example of where religion and politics collide and conflict in the adoption of legislation affecting the girl child is with regard to Female Genital Mutilation (FGM). Jaha Dukureh (UN Women Regional Goodwill Ambassador for Africa) (http://www.unwomen.org) stated on 27 February 2018 that "the biggest challenge standing in our way is this idea that FGM is a religious practice. It is hard to change something that people believe is their religious obligation. We need religious leaders to come out boldly and say that FGM has nothing to do with religion. In Gambia, we organized the first religious leaders' training in 2015. Before the training, I remember how divided the room was...many of the religious leaders who came from Gambia, Senegal and Mauritania supported FGM. By the end of the training, they issued a *fatwa* against FGM." One further area where confusion exists between religion and legislation is in respect of triple *talaq* (or *talaq-e-biddat*), the procedure under which it is thought that a Muslim man may divorce his wife simply by uttering the word "*talaq*" three times. In August 2017, the Supreme Court of India ruled that triple talaq was unconstitutional and not an essential part of Islam. The concept of "Three Divorces" does not exist in the Quran. The concept of "triple talaq in one sitting" or "instant talaq" is alien to the Quran.

Sex Tourism

The World Tourism Organization, a specialized agency of the United Nations, defines sex tourism as "trips organized from within the tourism sector, or from outside this sector but using its structures and networks, with the primary purpose of effecting a commercial sexual relationship by the tourist with residents at the destination". (*Diotallevi, Marina, 1995*) Sex tourism exists in both domestic and international arenas, and provides a valuable source of revenue to associated travel, accommodation, entertainment and other related service sectors globally. Those seeking sexual services are mainly men seeking women, though sex tourism also involves women seeking men, men seeking men and adults seeking children. Due to the essential factor of disposable income to facilitate the associated travel and other costs, sex tourists primarily come from developed European nations as well as the USA. The sex worker is commonly living in poverty, with the provision of sexual services being the main option for earning income and providing for their family. UNICEF (United Nations International Children's Emergency Fund) was created by the United Nations General Assembly on 11 December 1946, to provide emergency food and healthcare to children in countries that had been devastated by World War II. UNICEF has noted that sexual activity is often deemed to be a private matter, thus limiting the action that some communities could otherwise take to deal with sexual exploitation, especially involving children targeted by their local adult community and sex tourists. If there can be a positive aspect to the growth in sex tourism, it is that the decriminalisation in some countries of sex-related work has provided protection and support for prostitutes and other sex workers. Registration to pay tax, join a Chamber of Commerce and access to free health checks are just some of the positive moves as part of integral society.

The USA has very onerous laws governing the involvement of its citizens in prostitution, and those seeking sexual services seek to get around such restrictions by using the global sex tourism industry. Human rights organisations and governments point out that this promotes the trafficking of children and violation of their human rights as noted herein under 4.7 with specific reference to the UNCRC. Within South Asia, prostitution has legal and illegal status. Whereas countries like Afghanistan, Bhutan, the Maldives, Nepal, Pakistan and Sri Lanka label it as illegal; in countries like Bangladesh and India prostitution is totally legal and people are free to step into it without any hesitation and without any legal hassles. In India, related activities including pimping, kerb crawling, child prostitution, prostitution in a hotel, owning or managing a brothel are illegal, while the strict religious profile of Afghanistan brings severe periods of imprisonment, with sex outside of marriage also illegal. While prostitution is legal in Bangladesh, its Constitution provides that the state shall seek to prevent it. In Pakistan, extra-marital sex is held to be immoral and prostitution is illegal. It could be argued that sex tourism and prostitution contribute to gender inequality, and it will be interesting to observe whether the various global movements referred to herein to safeguard the girl child, empower women and bring about gender equality take a specific stance against these global threats to the welfare and human rights of children and women.

Societal Change

It refers to any significant alteration over time in behaviour patterns and cultural values and norms. (https://www.cliffsnotes.com) Any society needs some inherent changes within it. It can be categorised as:

Normalisation: Normalisation refers to social processes through which ideas and actions come to be seen as 'normal' and become taken-for-granted or 'natural' in everyday life.

Denormalisation: Patriarchal societies have 'normalised' all forms of abuse and violence against girls and women. The UN 2030 Agenda and other global initiatives will lead the way for these to be denormalised. The concept of normalisation is found in the work of Michel Foucault, especially *Discipline and Punish* (1975).

Conclusion

It may be seen from the ESCAP (Economic and Social Commission for Asia and the Pacific) Progress Report 2017 that the global movement to achieve gender equality and eradicate violence in all its forms against girls and women has found certain obstacles to progress within South Asia, but this has also been a feature of the assessment of progress across the 193 members of the United Nations. The global movement to change the world for girls and women by accepting their inalienable right to be safe and secure inevitably has its critics and opponents, but many confuse this particular issue with other actual or perceived inequalities, for example, violence against males, treatment of LGBT citizens, etc. There are many inequalities in this world of ours, and every person has the right to be supported in their quest for fairness, respect, opportunity and dignity.

What cannot be challenged is the global evidence that the empowerment of women has an immediate, positive and lasting impact on the economic prosperity of their regions. A peaceful society is a happy society, and mothers the world over are without question the creators of peace in the home and the magicians who somehow find the answers to the daily emotional and financial needs of their families. The security of South Asia, across all the possible threats it faces, will achieve remarkable progress if it focuses on the security threat to its very grassroots: the safety and security of its current and future generations, especially of 50 per cent female population. Societal change and development through education, and individuals challenging their own mindsets and refusing to blindly follow 'culture', provides the pathway for South Asia to follow.

REFERENCES

Bhutan, United Nations Abortion Policies, http://www.un.org/ en/development/ desa/ population/ publications/ pdf/ policy/Abortion Policies ReproductiveHealth.pdf.

Diotallevi Marina, World Tourism Organization, http://ethics.unwto.org/ru/node/29012.

EU Agency for Fundamental Rights (2014), http://interactive.unwomen.org/ multimedia/ infographic/ violenceagainstwomen/ en/index.html.

Foucault, Michel (1975), *Discipline and* Punish, https://monoskop.org/ images/4/ 43/; Foucault, _Michel _Discipline_and_Punish_The_Birth_of_the_Prison_1977_1995. pdf.

Gallup International, https://news.gallup.com/reports/225587/rating-world-leaders-2018.aspx.

https://www.unodc.org/documents/data-and-analysis/statistics/GSH2013/2014_ GLOBAL_ HOMICIDE_BOOK_web.pdf.

https://dictionary.cambridge.org/dictionary/english/ethics.

https://dictionary.cambridge.org/dictionary/english/morals.

https://dictionary.cambridge.org/dictionary/english/chivalry.

https://en.oxforddictionaries.com/definition/patriarchy.

https://twitter.com/shethepeopletv/status/722275049692995584?lang=en.

Iqbal, Sarah (September 2015), *Women, Business and the Law.*

Jaha, Dukureh (UN Women Regional Goodwill Ambassador for Africa) (http:// www.unwomen. org / en/news/stories/2018/3/in-the-words-of-jaha-dukureh.

NFHS (2017), http://rchiips.org/nfhs/pdf/NFHS4/BR_FactSheet.pdf.

NRCB (2014), http://www.ncpcr.gov.in/showfile.php?lang=1&level=2&&sublinkid=1682 &lid=1682.

UNESCAP, https://www.unescap.org/ sites/default/ files/Asia-Pacific-SDG-Progress-Report-2017.pdf

UNICEF (2016), https://data.unicef.org/ topic/child-protection/female-genital-mutilation/

UNICEF (2017), https://www.unicef.org/media/files/Child_Marriage_ Report_ 7_ 17_ LR..pdf

UNFPA (2016), www.unfpa.org/news/stunning-plunge-maternal-deaths-recorded-maldives).

UNODC (2016), https://www.un.org/ sustainabledevelopment/ blog/2016/12/report-majority-of-trafficking-victims-are-women-and-girls-one-third-children/

UNODC (2016) https://www.unodc.org/documents/data-and-analysis/glotip/2016_Global _Report _on_Trafficking_in_Persons.pdf.

US Community Census Survey (2014), https://www.census.gov/ programs-surveys/acs.

World Health Organisation (WHO 2013); https://www.who.int/ news-room/fact-sheets/detail/violence-against-women.

www.tamu.edu/faculty/choudhury/culture.htm.

14

Ensuring Food Security in Asia

Akhilesh Mishra

Introduction

Achieving food security is vital for any nation. However, despite progress in food availability in the post-war period, food insecurity still prevails in many developing countries; with more than half the world's undernourished in Asia. This unacceptable number calls for urgent action. Differences in levels of food security across countries cannot be explained solely by conventional economic arguments, such as resource endowments, country or population size, the level of economic development, and cultural or social differences. The food security as it "exists when all people, at all times, have physical and economic access to sufficient safe and nutritious food to meet their dietary needs and food preferences for a healthy and active life" (World Food Summit, 1996). This definition covers five fundamental aspects, namely, availability, access, stability, nutritional status, and preferences of food. These components are influenced by physical, economic, political, and other conditions within communities and even within households, and are often destabilized by shocks such as natural disasters and conflicts.

Availability and access are two important dimensions of food security. The availability indicates sufficient year-round quantities of quality/ nutritious food available to all individuals in the country. However, the sufficiency of food at the national level cannot assure the availability in areas having armed conflicts, non-availability of arable lands, and confronting prolonged droughts and floods. The distribution of foodstuff in these areas is generally faulty. The access denotes the capacity to produce, buy, and/or acquire appropriate nutritious food by individuals and households (Timmer, 2000). The availability of quality food consistently in sufficient quantities is necessary but may not guarantee food security to all people in the country. Low incomes and lack of required infrastructure could deny access to desired quantities of quality food. Therefore, availability and access elements of food security are inseparably interlinked (Pinstrup-Andersen, 2009).

The access involves both physical access and economic access. The former refers to a place where food is available and requires efficient market infrastructure to have access of people at low cost. The latter denotes entitlement to food (Sen, 1982) that can be ensured either by own production or having food buying capacity or having access/right to other sources of getting the desired food (Staatz et. al., 2009). Thus, there is direct relationship between poverty and food insecurity since the very poor cannot take precautionary measures against food insecurity and thus, they would be the most vulnerable (Cullet, 2003 & Herrmann, 2006).

The third element is stability, which refers to a consistent supply of nutritious food at the national level, household and individual levels, which is directly influenced by the performance of the agriculture sector. Only a small proportion of consumers in developing countries can afford to store food for the whole year. Therefore, stability requires better management of domestic production, food market integration, and rational use of buffer stocks and trade (FAO, 2002). Fluctuations/shortages in food grain production have been very common in South Asia and have recently intensified more because of the climate change phenomenon. In order to tackle unforeseen shortages and save consumers from high food prices, governments have been actively pursuing policies of support/procurement prices, storage and distribution though at a very high cost. Therefore, market infrastructure has a much more role to play.

The definition of food security also alludes to safe and nutritious food, which is required for healthy and active life. For this, the human body has to effectively utilize the available nutrients in the food consumed (Staatz et. al., 2009). Food preparation and health condition of an individual are critical for biological absorption of food, which is influenced by access to improved sanitation and clean drinking water as well as by knowledge of the households regarding proper food storage, processing, and basic nutrition. The preferences for food adds a fifth dimension to food security which relate to social and religious norms. Therefore, foods are to be socially and culturally acceptable and consistent with religious and ethical values (Pinstrup-Andersen, 2009).

The above discussion highlights the fact that achieving food security is a complex and challenging phenomenon. Most of the countries focus on assuring stability in supply of affordable nutritious food and oversight the fundamental issue of 'security'. Food is energy for the human body without which "we are all dead" and thus it should be considered as a "security good". (Fullbrook, 2010, p. 6).

One in nine people around the world are hungry; a total of 821 million people worldwide. But global food security is actually improving, with over 70 per cent of countries strengthening their scores in this year's Global Food Security Index (GFSI). FAO claims that 'unrealistic' goals can be achieved if a worldwide sustainable lifestyle is adopted. According to the FAO report, in a world where lakhs of people suffer from starvation due to poverty every day, another aspect is that 672 million people are suffering from obesity due to unhealthy lifestyle and bad eating habits; 1.3 billion people are overweight.

The Economic Intelligence Unit (EIU) index measures how affordable, available, safe and up-to-standard food is across 113 countries. Only two countries from the Asia-Pacific feature in the index's top 10, with Singapore topping the list for the first time and Australia ranking sixth. At the bottom of the rankings, Laos, Cambodia, Bangladesh and Myanmar are positioned among the world's least food-secure countries, most of which are in Africa.

This chapter approaches the issue of food security in a number of Asian and other countries by highlighting the crucial role played by government and economic institutions and by examining how they influence food availability. It lays down valuable policy initiatives for national governments and international bodies, acting through improved institutions, to reduce poverty and inequality and to achieve higher levels of food security nationally and globally.

Table 1: Rankings and Trends

Rank	*Country*	*Score/100*	*Rank*	*Country*	*Score/100*	*Rank*	*Country*	*Score/100*
1st	Singapore	85.9	**39th**	Brazil	68.4	**77th**	Pakistan	49.1
2nd	Ireland	85.5	**40th**	Malaysia	68.1	**78th**	Venezuela	47.4
3rd	United Kingdom	85	**41st**	Bahrain	67.8	**79th**	Nepal	46
3rd	United States	85	**42nd**	Russia	67	**80th**	Uzbekistan	45.9
5th	Netherlands	84.7	**43rd**	Mexico	66.4	**81st**	Cote d'Ivoire	45.8
6th	Australia	83.7	**44th**	Belarus	65.7	**82nd**	Myanmar	45.7
7th	Switzerland	83.5	**45th**	South Africa	65.5	**83rd**	Bangladesh	43.3
8th	Finland	83.3	**46th**	China	65.1	**84th**	Cameroon	42.4
9th	Canada	83.2	**47th**	Bulgaria	64.5	**85th**	Cambodia	42.3
10th	France	82.9	**48th**	Turkey	64.1	**86th**	Mali	42
11th	Germany	82.7	**49th**	Colombia	63.7	**87th**	Kenya	41.9
12th	Norway	82.2	**50th**	Panama	61.9	**87th**	Senegal	41.9
12th	Sweden	82.2	**51st**	Tunisia	60.9	**89th**	Uganda	41.4
14th	Austria	82.1	**52nd**	Botswana	60.8	**90th**	Benin	41
15th	New Zealand	81.3	**53rd**	Serbia	59.8	**91st**	Tajikistan	40.7
16th	Denmark	80.9	**54th**	Thailand	58.9	**92nd**	Angola	38.6
17th	Belgium	80.2	**55th**	Peru	58.7	**93rd**	Rwanda	38.4
18th	Japan	79.9	**56th**	Azerbaijan	58.2	**93rd**	Togo	38.4
19th	Portugal	79.3	**57th**	Kazakhstan	57.7	**95th**	Laos	38.3
20th	Israel	78.6	**58th**	Dominican Republic	57.2	**96th**	Nigeria	38
21st	Spain	78	**58th**	Paraguay	57.2	**97th**	Burkina Faso	37.9
22nd	Qatar	76.5	**60th**	Jordan	57	**98th**	Tanzania	37.1
23rd	Italy	76.3	**61st**	Egypt	56.3	**99th**	Sudan	36.4
24th	Czech Republic	76.1	**62nd**	Vietnam	56	**100th**	Ethiopia	36
25th	South Korea	75.6	**63rd**	Ukraine	55.7	**101st**	Mozambique	35
26th	Poland	75.4	**64th**	Morocco	55	**102nd**	Guinea	34.9
27th	Chile	75.1	**65th**	Ecuador	54.8	**103rd**	Syria	34.1
28th	Kuwait	74.8	**65th**	Indonesia	54.8	**104th**	Niger	33.7
29th	Oman	74.4	**67th**	Sri Lanka	54.3	**104th**	Zambia	33.7
30th	Hungary	72.8	**68th**	El Salvador	53.7	**106th**	Haiti	33
31st	United Arab Emirates	72.5	**69th**	Algeria	52.1	**107th**	Malawi	32.4
32nd	Saudi Arabia	72.4	**70th**	Philippines	51.5	**108th**	Chad	31.5
33rd	Greece	71.6	**71st**	Guatemala	51.4	**109th**	Sierra Leone	29.2
34th	Uruguay	71.3	**72nd**	Nicaragua	51.1	**110th**	Yemen	28.5
35th	Slovakia	70.3	**73rd**	Ghana	50.9	**111th**	Madagascar	27
36th	Costa Rica	69.3	**74th**	Bolivia	50.7	**112th**	Congo (Dem. Rep.)	26.1
37th	Argentina	69.2	**74th**	Honduras	50.7	**113th**	Burundi	23.9
38th	Romania	68.9	**76th**	India	50.1			

Source: Explore the year-on-year trends for the Global Food Security Index. Figures are from annual baseline model (2018).

Factors and Causes of Food Security

Asia is the largest and most populous of the earth's continents and it is located in both the northern and eastern hemispheres. Asia comprises a full of 30 per cent of world's land area with 60 per cent of the world's current population. It is among the most vulnerable regions in the world being a disaster-prone area accounting for 80 per cent of the total affected population and 86 per cent of the total damage due to droughts (UNEP, 2003; Spijkers, 2011). Climate change has emerged as another significant threat to assuring food security in the region. The temperature is projected to rise in the region by 3–4°C by the end of the 21st century (Spijkers, 2011). Cereal crops are already under heat stress in South Asia (Kelkar and Bhadwal, 2007) and the yields could decrease up to 30 per cent by the end of current century due to change in climate (IPCC, 2007). The monsoon rains are not only delayed in the region but have become more erratic leading to unexpected and unprecedented floods or droughts adversely affecting food production and distribution in the region. The frequency and intensity of floods have increased in Bangladesh, India and Pakistan displacing a large number of people in these countries and adversely affecting their livelihoods and resulting in reduced food production and high food inflation. Thus, ensuring food and nutritional security to the rapidly increasing population of the region remains one of the major challenges that the region would be facing in the coming decades.

The causes of food insecurity in Asia include fast growth in population, fast and unplanned urbanization through rural to urban migration, reduction in arable land, declining average farm size besides skewed distribution, low productivity due to low R&D investments and land degradation, slow process of structural transformations and poor institutions, and changes in climate. The issue of global warming has emerged as a new real threat to food security. The most part of the region is already hot and growing of cereals is already under heat stress. Further increase in temperature could cross the level beyond the optimal for growing some crops, which is expected to reduce the yields significantly. The adverse impacts of climate change on agriculture can be dealt with mitigation and adaptation strategies. The structure of farming and poor resources as well as poverty in rural areas could be major hurdles in adapting to climate change. It is anticipated that Asian countries are likely to face a severe food crisis by 2050 and the issue of food security is going to be a critical issue in the years to come.

In the last few years, infrastructure, food chains, storage houses, and transport facilities have been developed in Asia, yet there is a lot to be done in this direction. In addition to adequate nutritious food items, there is a lack of nutrition education in Asia. Therefore, promoting nutrition education and awareness is needed. We also need to pay attention to agriculture and farmers, especially landless families, workers and small and marginal farmers who are often victims of malnutrition and starvation. Such people are limited to the production of rice, wheat, jowar, and millet and do not think beyond this. Therefore, such farmers should be encouraged to produce fruits and vegetables besides poultry, and goat and cow farming. Landless labourers have been seen to be more affected by the problem of hunger. Therefore, the government should identify the workers and distribute land among them. There has been talk of a minimum support price (MSP) to farmers in Asia and the world for long, but it does not include horticulture, fruits and vegetables. Small and marginal farmers could not get the proper benefit of MSP. Most of the farmers of the world are deprived of MSP benefits.

How to Ensure Food Security

For those working in international development, food security is a complex problem to solve and one that goes beyond hunger alone. With the global population expected to reach 9 billion by 2050, people are asking how we can best address the nature and scale of the challenges that lie ahead. As a research and development-focused organization, the "Association of International Research and Development Centres for Agriculture" believes that science, technology and knowledge sharing can help provide answers. My aim in writing this paper is to do an analysis that can highlight that the opportunities and challenges to create a sustainable food system are concentrated in a small set of crops and places. The following are the measures to be taken for achieving food security for growing population through higher food production:

To Minimize the Yield Gap

Global food production needs to be increased by 60 to 110 per cent between 2005 and 2050 to meet the growing food and feed demand. Intensification and expansion of agriculture are the two main options available to meet the growing crop demands. Land conversion to expand cultivated land increases GHG emissions and impacts biodiversity and ecosystem services. Closing yield gaps to attain potential yields may be a viable option to increase the global crop production. Traditional methods of agricultural intensification often have negative externalities. Therefore, there is a need to explore location-specific methods of sustainable agricultural intensification. By 2050, 120 million hectares of natural habitats will be converted to farming in developing countries, the World Wildlife Fund estimates. In many parts of the world, current agricultural land is not reaching its potential, yielding 50 per cent less than what it could produce. Closing the gap between what is being produced and what could be produced would both reduce the need to clear land for agriculture and feed 850 million people. The next points address how this gap can be diminished.

Crop Diversification

Food availability is a necessary condition for food security. Crop diversification provides farmers with a wider choice in the production of a variety of crops in a given area so as to expand production-related activities on various crops and also to bring down the possible risk. Crop diversification is generally viewed as a shift from traditionally grown less remunerative crops to more remunerative crops. Crop diversification is also taking place due to governmental policies, thrust on some crops, market reforms, infrastructure development, government subsidies, certain other price-related support mechanisms. Higher profitability and stability in production also induces crop diversification. Crop diversification and growing of a large number of crops are practised in dryland areas to reduce the risk factor of crop failures due to recurring droughts. Crop substitution and crop shifts are also taking place in areas suffering with some specific soil-related problems.

Tackling Climate Change

Food security can be achieved by paying higher attention to issues such as climate change, and limiting global warming, including the promotion of climate-smart agricultural production systems and land use policies at a scale to help adapt and mitigate the ill effects of climate change. Climate change affects the livelihoods of poor and rich alike by impacting basic human needs, including food, clothing and shelter requirements. The four components of food security; food availability, food access, food utilization and food production system stability are the heart of the mandate of the Food and Agriculture Organization of the United Nations (FAO). All four components are affected by climate [FAO, 2008(a)] but food availability is most intimately associated with climate and its changes, from crops to animal products, marine and aquaculture products and wood and non-wood products and forests. Urbanization is rapidly taking place in many countries of the world, creating a category of urban poor who do not themselves farm and are very vulnerable to climate change.

Integrated Water Management

Asia needs to produce more crops per unit of land and water resources. Alarming rates of groundwater depletion and increasing environmental and social problems pose acute threats to mankind. Improved management of irrigation water is essential to enhance production and productivity, food security and poverty alleviation. Agriculture is the biggest user of water, accounting for over 80 per cent of water withdrawals. There are pressures for diverting water from agriculture to other sectors. It has been projected that availability of water for agriculture use may be reduced by 21 per cent by 2020, resulting in drop of yields, especially rice, leading to price rise and threat to food security of the poor. The needs of other sectors for water cannot be ignored. As a result, it is necessary that an integrated water use policy is formulated and judiciously implemented. Modern methods of irrigation like sprinkler, drip irrigation, fustigation, among other water efficient tools need to be adopted on a larger scale.

Integrated Nutrient Management

The challenge that the world is facing is to maximize food production to feed the increasing population. Further, agriculture at present encompasses many problems such as stagnating foodgrain production, multi-nutrient deficiency, declining fertilizer response, reduction in land availability for cultivation, environmental pollution and land degradation. To manage long-term soil fertility, productivity as well as environment quality, integration of organic and inorganic fertilizer can be the most sustainable practices to adopt. Several nutrient managements have been practised; however, current studies on long-term experiments indicated that integrated nutrient management proved to be the best approach for sustainable crop production as well as reducing environmental pollution.

Improved Varieties

In most developing countries, the majority of small-scale farmers use traditional crop varieties, which give low yields and may be vulnerable to drought, heat, disease and other stresses. Modern improved varieties offer much higher yields, better quality, and more stable production. Farmers are not able to get information about the availability of new and improved varieties and some are not having access to quality seeds of these varieties, resulting in lesser yields. This situation has to be corrected by developing a national-level network to monitor and coordinate the activities with the various government functionaries working in the area of crop production.

Improved Technology Adoption

One of the best ways to do this is by investing in new technologies that enable farmers to connect with information and institutions that can decrease uncertainty and mitigate risk. Lack of adequate productive resources is one of the most severe causes of food insecurity. Agricultural technologies have a special role because they might boost crop productivity, allowing for higher production and lower food prices and potentially increasing welfare. Adoption of technologies like integrated nutrient management, integrated pest management and integrated weed management need to be made available for adoption to ensure higher production and sustainability of production base.

Awareness of Population Growth

Most of the countries with the highest numbers of people facing food insecurity also have high fertility rates and rapid population growth. This increases the challenge of adequately meeting nutritional needs. The awareness of the pressures of increasing population growth and consumption patterns on ecosystem functioning should be created to sensitize farmers on adoption of sustainable crop cultivation and management practices.

Focus on Small Farmers

Increase in food production in the country does not necessarily ensure food security, if the poor do not have the buying power. Therefore, participation of small farmers in food production is essential to achieve food security. Most of them are illiterate and have failed earlier either in adopting new technologies or repaying loans provided under various development schemes. They need support not only to procure inputs but also to gain confidence. The strategy to enhance food production should address the problems of such small landholding farmers, who constitute over 83 per cent of farmers in the country. They own a small piece of land per family, mostly marginal and non-irrigated. They have been practising low-external input farming and the crop yields have been substantially low. However, their contribution to the national food production is considerable and meets a significant part of their food needs.

Education and Literacy

Role of education in improving farm efficiency and technology adoption has been well established. As agriculture transformed from the subsistence to the commercial level, farmers seek information on a wide range of issues to acquire knowledge or upgrade their skills and entrepreneurial ability. Literacy emerges as an important source of growth in adoption of technology, and use of modern inputs like fertilizers and machines. An educated workforce makes it easier to train and acquire new skills and technologies required for productivity growth. Thus, contribution of literacy will be substantial on yield growth and domestic supply of food.

Agricultural Research Education

The Agricultural education in the whole world is facing one of the biggest challenges. It has to identify its role in equipping human resources for enhanced agricultural productivity and sustainable use of natural resources. Agricultural colleges and universities were initially assigned to disseminate scientific knowledge and skills to the farming community and to train them to use such skills for better output. As a backup for such a mission, agricultural research was encouraged to focus on scientific knowledge to suit the realities of rural societies.

Raise Low Water Productivity

Water is a major issue. Improving irrigation systems and planting crops that use less water would be an effective way to tackle this. For example, rice and sugarcane are among the crops that need the most water. But it is not simple to change the types of crops grown since farmers make decisions of what to grow based on market values, International Food Policy Research Institute Senior Research Fellow, Lawrence Haddad, pointed out to Tree Hugger. One way to encourage change would be to provide economic incentives, but that can change based on regional differences and cultural tastes. With water shortages constraining food production growth, the world needs an effort to raise water productivity similar to the one that nearly tripled land productivity over the last half century.

Since it takes 1,000 tons of water to produce 1 ton of grain, it is not surprising that 70 per cent of world water use is devoted to irrigation. Thus, raising irrigation efficiency is central to raising water productivity overall. Irrigation water efficiency is affected not only by the type and condition of irrigation systems but also by soil type, temperature, and humidity. In hot arid regions, the evaporation of irrigation water is far higher than in cooler humid regions.

Target Food For Direct Consumption

A lot of caloric efficiency is lost when crops are converted for animal feed and other non-food uses. Farmers grow crops that will ensure that they and their family can eat, whether that means eating their own crops or selling them to be able to afford food. "Lots of assumptions are made in this study: that people are willing to change their diets; that people in wealthy countries are willing to take significant measures to reduce food waste; that poor countries have the political and economic means to rectify yield gaps," said Dr. Carol Barford, Director of the Centre for Sustainability and Global Environment at the University of Wisconsin. But, West had a response to this: "It would be very naive to assume that diets could radically shift soon. In fact, the trend toward more meat consumption is happening in many parts of the world. Our main point here is that the amount of calories that we already grow but feed to animals is a 'huge' number of calories. Even small changes in diet can have a profound impact".

Reduce Food Waste

Globally, 30-50 per cent of food production goes to waste because of inefficient preparation or inadequate storage facilities. The USA is one of the biggest culprits for this and needs an agricultural land base that is 7 to 8 times larger than a land base in India to compensate for this waste. Reducing food waste in the USA, India and China could feed 413 million people per year. There are support policies that minimize food waste. In developed countries, most food waste happens as a result of food left unconsumed at home, in restaurants, or in supermarkets. This means that in high-income nations, consumers have the power to significantly reduce food waste by modifying their own eating behaviour and through their collective power to demand that supermarkets and eating venues disclose and take measures to reduce food losses. In contrast, in low-income countries, most food losses occur between the farm and the markets as a result of poor agricultural practices, as well as poor food storage and food distribution systems, including transportation.

Food losses can be substantially reduced by improving the efficiency of agricultural practices through lessons learned from the large-scale commercial and the smaller scale organic farming sectors. From the large-scale commercial sector we have learned how to apply fertilizers and pesticides more precisely, taking into account the nature of the local soil to reduce the use of agriculture's toxic chemicals and to prevent them from leaching into the water supplies. The evolution of organic farming offers lessons as to how to improve the nutritional quality of the soil and to conserve water by using cover crops, mulch, and compost. Consumers in high-income countries could play a key role in fostering sustainable agriculture by reducing their demand for foods that depend on crops that follow unsustainable agricultural practices that erode major ecosystems.

A key strategy for preventing food waste in developed countries is to prevent or use leftovers from foods prepared at home, ordered in restaurants, or purchased in supermarkets, and to develop better recycling systems of food waste. Recycled food waste can then be converted into compost for the production of fruit and vegetables in home gardens or in small community farms. Consumers can also substantially reduce the portion sizes of the meals they consume at home or outside the home and can decide not to buy foods or food ingredients sold in excessive-portion-size presentations. In other words, through the power of their wallets, consumers can apply the pressure needed for the commercial food sector to mitigate the impact of its operations on the environment. On the other hand, by limiting waste and overconsumption, consumers can reduce pressure on producers to supply them with unsustainable food.

Create Careers in Agriculture for Young People and Women

Supporting young people and women in agriculture is not a new challenge, but does need reinvigorated attention. In developing countries, many young people are leaving villages to work in cities, believing there is no future in farming and that there are better prospects in urban areas, yet quite the opposite is true. By 2050, the global food demand is predicted to grow by 60 per cent based on 2005 levels. Nurturing young people's careers in agriculture so that they become part of an effective, efficient and sustainable food production system is a much needed part of safeguarding long-term food security. Supporting women is also central to safeguarding food production. The challenge is finding the means to get the right information to women, as in some cultures they are not always as easy to reach as men. Creating an environment that lets them put information into practice and establish livelihoods in agriculture is important. For this reason, tackling food security must be seen in a much wider context and be treated in a truly concerted manner.

Reduce Income Inequality and Increase Social Justice

Wealth inequities, social injustice, and social exclusion prevent individuals and societies from developing properly. These inequities are major underlying factors that drive the very high rates of food insecurity, poor physical and mental health, and the environmental destruction of our planet. For this reason, it is essential to support the development, implementation, and evaluation of economic, social, and cultural policies that close the huge gaps between the wealthiest and the poorest individuals across the globe.

Promote Sustainable Agriculture

Promote sustainable agriculture technologies and practices that minimize agriculture's carbon footprint and its impact on natural resources, including soil and water. Agriculture is a major contributor to global warming through massive emissions of greenhouse gases. Specifically, agriculture releases more greenhouse gases than all forms of transportation combined. Methane is a greenhouse gas released in large amounts from large-scale commercial cereal agriculture (e.g., rice) and animal husbandry, especially cattle. Large-scale commercial agriculture that decimates tropical forests also leads to massive release of carbon by destroying a major tree-based "carbon sink". Fertilizers that are applied without proper safeguards are also responsible for the release of greenhouse gas nitrous oxide. Agriculture can also negatively affect water supplies as a result of chemical runoff and wasteful irrigation systems. Approximately one-third of all food grown is lost or wasted. Therefore, reducing food loss and waste can significantly reduce the impact of food production on the Earth's ecosystems at the same time that we need to plan on making food available to <"2.5 billion additional individuals between now and 2050.

The red thread linking these issues is the need to put research, technology and knowledge at the heart of creating food and nutritional security. The scientific approach can help frame and structure ways to evaluate or test the impact of interventions. While West's study provides some areas, which need to be considered by policy makers, the study does not delve too far into economics. "The research focuses on food availability, but it would say that most of the problem of hunger is around food access—do people have enough income to purchase food?" Haddad, of IFPRI, said in an email. Haddad writes that a discussion of global food security should also address the different needs of higher and lower income groups, maximize resilience of the food chain in the face of climate change and social conflicts, and minimize greenhouse gas emissions. To be fair, this paper fell short of addressing food access and nutrition, but "It does address many of the key aspects of creating a sustainable food system using low-tech tools, including using fertilizer to boost production in food insecure areas to benefit the people in those areas as well as be less dependent on the major breadbaskets, minimizing waste, as well as reducing the environmental impacts through changes in management practices that increase efficiency. Access, nutrition, and cultural preferences all need to be addressed in concert with the aspects we addressed". The complexity of issues like food security is the reason that hunger is such a prevalent issue in the 21st century. Tackling hunger will take a multi-dimensional and multi-disciplinary approach.

Conclusion

In Asian countries a very slow growth in food production, in comparison to increasing food consumption and population growth, resulted in food insecurity and undernourishment. Nevertheless, Asia still accounts for 62 per cent of all undernourished people of the world and 13.9 per cent of the Asian population remain undernourished. Stunting in children is a major problem. Within Asia, 34.4 per cent of children less than five years of age are stunted and 20.6 per cent are underweight. These numbers are both higher than the global average for low and middle income groups. The current and anticipated environment and economic stresses on agriculture suggest that if the sources of stagnating productivity are not addressed, soaring and volatile food price will return. Addressing Asia's food security challenges therefore requires long-term commitment and finance from the government. The priorities are research and innovations, technology transfer, investment in rural sector infrastructure to raise a higher amount of agriculture production as well as productivity and policy interventions designed to raise agricultural product prices. The policies discussed above are capable of increasing agriculture production. But the investment in infrastructure and skill development of farmers to raise agriculture production and productivity does so without raising food grain prices. The interventions uses increased food prices as its central instrument. If small and marginal farmers are given access to easy processes and subsidized interest credit, and expertise technological training to raise crops by adopting high-yielding varieties, fertilizers, pesticides, insecticides, and other required inputs as per scientific recommendations, and if high-value return on production and, access to markets are available, domestic production will reach at a high to fulfil future food requirements, with quality and quantity while avoiding biotic and abiotic challenges. The result will assure Asia's food security.

REFERENCES

Alur, Ashok. S. & and Maheshwar, D. L. (2013). *Crop Diversification—A strategy to improve Agricultural Production.* http://www.commodityindia.com/publication/magazine/web/crop%20diversificstion%20-20strategy%20to%20improve%20Agricultural % 20Production.html.

Cullet, P. (2003). Food Security and Intellectual Property Rights in Developing Countries. *Geneva: IELRC Working Paper* 2003-3.

FAO (2002). The State of Food Insecurity in the World 2001. *Rome: Food and Agriculture Organization of the United Nations.*

FAO (2008). Climate Change Adaptation and Mitigation in the Food and Agriculture Sector. *Technical Background Document from the Expert Consultation* held on 5-7 March 2008, FAO, ROME. (Fullbrook, 2010; p. 6).

Herrmann, M. (2006). Agricultural Support Measures of Advanced Countries and Food Insecurity in Developing Countries. *UNU-WIDER Research Paper No.* 2006/141.

Karki, L. B. & Bauer, S. (2004). Technology adoption and household food security. Analysing factors determining technology adoption and impact on project intervention: A case of smallholder peasants in Nepal. *The Deutscher Tropentag-1.doc.* pp. 1-8.

Lawrence, J. Haddad, (ed.) (1997). *Achieving Food Security in Southern Africa: New Challenges, and New Opportunities.* p. 334.

Licker, R.; M. Johnston, J. A. Foley, C. L. Barford, C. Monfreda and N. Ramankutty. (2010). Mind the Gap: How do Climate and Agricultural Management Explain the "yield gap" of Croplands around the World? *Global Ecology and Biogeography* 19 (6), 769-782.

Manon, Verchot (2014). Tree Huggers, 5 ways to improve global food security. Source: https://www.treehugger.com/sustainable-agriculture/5-ways-improve-global-food-security.html

IPCC (2007). Climate Change-A Synthesis Report of the IPCC. Technical Report, Intergovernmental Panel on Climate Change.

Kelkar, U. & Bhadwal, S. (2007). South Asian Regional Study on Climate Change Impacts and Adaptation: Implications for Human Development. Human Development Report Office, *Occasional Paper. United Nations Development Programme.*

Orner, M. (2013). Sources: World Food Programme, International Food Policy Research Institute, Asian Development Bank 1, Asian Development Bank 2, *Hunger Notes, UN News Centre.*

Per Pinstrup-Andersen, (2009). Food Security: Definition and Measurement. *Food Security,* (2009) 1:5–7 DOI 10.1007/s12571-008-0002-y.

Pradhan P., Fischer G., Van Velthuzen H., Reusser D. E & Kropp J. P., (2015). Closing Yield Gaps: How Sustainable Can We Be? *PloS ONE10(6): e0129487.*

Sen, A. K., (1982). *Poverty and Famines: An Essay on Entitlement and Deprivation.* New York: Clarendon Press.

Spijkers, M. Ad, (2011). Implications of Climate Change on Agriculture and Food Security in South Asia, Chapter 14 in *Climate Change and Food Security in South Asia* Edited by Rattan Lal Mannava, V. K. Ivakumar, S. M. A. Faiz, A. H. M. Mustafizur Rahman & Khandakar R. Islam. Springer, 2011.

Staatz, J.: M, D. H. Boughton & C. Donovan, (2009). Food Security in Developing Countries. Department of Agricultural, Food and Resource Economics, *MSU,* East Lansing, Michigan. Staff Paper 2009-03.

Timmer, C. P. (2000). The Macro Dimensions of Food Security: Economic Growth, EquiAnnex Distribution, and Food Price Stability, *Food Policy* 25 (2000):283-295.

UNEP (United Nations Environment Programme) (2003). *GEO Year Book* 2003. UNEP, Nairobi.

15

Population, Poverty, Environment and Inter-Relations Effect: The Biggest Security Challenge

Sandeep Kumar

Introduction

An historic agreement to eradicate poverty, improve living standards and well-being, promote peace, reverse the trend of environmental degradation, etc., was signed by governments of the world. The Agenda for Sustainable Development for 2030 commits to promote development in a balanced way—economically, socially and environmentally—throughout the world. Agenda 2030 is according to commitments of the Millennium Development Goals. Agenda identifies 17 sustainable goals and out of these, six critical areas related to poverty and inequalities, demography, environmental damage, etc., were identified. According to a UNDP report, the issue is to assess development and challenges in the mega trends in those six areas for the world countries. It provides a unique scenario to analyse three out of six areas for developing regions in general and Asia in particular. Population, poverty, and environmental degradation and their interaction produce big challenges for developing countries/regions.

The developing world comprises a heterogeneous group of countries, not all of them are at the same stage of economic development or face the same levels of problems. Some countries in this group have been quite successful both in controlling population and maintaining growth. But in the struggle to raise their income and standard of living they achieved it with increasing air and water pollution, more resource depletion, deforestation, soil erosion, over-fishing and damage to marine and ecosystem (Frainer, 1990). For these countries, growth was attained at a significant cost to their natural resources. Because of lopsided income distribution, significant poverty reduction was not attained. It seems that development took place but the poor have not benefitted from the initial development strategy. China, India, Brazil, Argentina, South Africa, etc., belong to this group. On the other hand, many African, Latin American and South East Asian countries are in the second category, having acute problems of population, poverty and environmental degradation. They have failed in controlling population. For 48 least-developed countries, the population is projected to be triple in 2050. In 57 other nations, the population growth could double. In some African and Latin American countries (Zambia, Kenya, Nigeria, El Salvador, Nicaragua, etc.), the population is rising at a rate of 3 to 4 per cent per annum. In the poorest Asian and African countries, the population is growing faster than the GDP. In such countries, the population growth and poverty are exerting dangerous pressure on the carrying capacity of the ecosystem and producing widespread desertification and deforestation (Lewis, 1992; Turner, 1990).

The problem of population and poverty are the problems of developing countries. In the coming future, the biggest challenge for the world is the problem related to global warming and this will be more complex in the Asian region where we have problems of poverty, population and environmental degradation. In the developing world of Asia, except for India and China, the entire region is suffering from problems of population, poverty, environmental degradation and their interrelationship adverse effects, which are acute problems/challenges for the future in the scenario to ensure sustainable development amidst increasing the ill-effects of global warming. Against this background, the present paper is an attempt to understand and explore three major challenges and their interaction effects in the Asian region in the context of the Agenda for Sustainable

Development for 2030 of the UNDP, which commits to promote development in a balanced way economically, socially and environmentally. The challenges discussed in this paper are the most meaningful with severe future implications.

I

Income, Poverty and Inequality

During 1990-2013, income poverty in the world reduced from 1.84 billion to 767 million (almost 10.7 per cent). Due to rapid growth in China and India, there is progress in poverty reduction in East Asia, Pacific and South Asia but poverty reduction is slow in the Sub-Sahara region, i.e., from 54.3 per cent in 1990 to 41 per cent in 2013. In the Asian region, except for growth-oriented India and China, poverty reduction is not fast in other countries. By 2030, poverty will be the biggest challenge in Sub Sahara Africa and then in Asia. During 1990-2013, Africa, Latin America, South Asia, West Asia, etc., have observed a slowdown or reversal in poverty reduction. At the same time, despite considerable growth in the subcontinent, the absolute number of poor living in extreme poverty rose from 276.1 million in 1990 to 388.7 million in 2013 due to rapid population growth. In Asia, Central Asia has managed poverty very well.

Table I reveals that in 1990, the poverty-problem regions were East Asia, South Asia and Sub-Sahara Africa. Poverty was acute in South Asia (44.58 per cent) and Sub-Sahara Africa (54.28 per cent) and the world average was 34.82 per cent. South Asia made progress in poverty reduction but even after 2013 the two most poverty ridden regions were Sub Sahara Africa (40.99 per cent) and South Asia (15.09 per cent) with the world

Table I: Percentage of Population Living Below US$ 1.90 a day (%) (2011 PPP)

Region	*1990*	*2005*	*2013*
East Asia and Pacific	60.23	18.43	3.54
Europe and Central Asia	1.93	4.98	2.15
Latin America and Caribbean	15.84	10.76	5.40
Middle East and North Africa	6.03	3.02	na
South Asia	44.58	33.64	15.09
Sub-Sahara Africa	54.28	50.07	40.99
World	34.82	20.45	10.67

Source: World Bank Calculations from Data Base.

average figure of 10.67 per cent. Hence, the majority of the income poverty of world is localized (almost 56 per cent) in South Asia and Sub-Sahara Africa. The poverty scenario depends upon assumption on pace and incidence of per capita income growth of households. In this regard, poverty will be a big challenge in these regions. Many families and individuals are trapped in poverty due to failure of economic policies, weak institutions, and governance as well as low level of investment in education and health in the poor regions like South Asia and Sub-Sahara Africa.

Multi-Dimensional Poverty

In the multiple dimensions of poverty, sustainable gains have been made in various aspects of poverty but the progress is uneven. In 2015, the child mortality rate was 11 in East Asia, which is in contrast to 86 in Sub-Sahara Africa. This region has also the highest maternal mortality rate, 546 deaths per lakh live births, as against the world average of 216 deaths and only 12 deaths in developed centuries. Multi Poverty Index (MPI) that measures the nature and magnitude of deprivation in health education and living standards counted 1.6 bn people living in such poverty in 2016 with 53 per cent of these in South Asia and 32 per cent in Sub Sahara Africa (Alkine and Robles, 2016). This is nearly twice the number of people living in extreme poverty alone. More than half the Multidimensional Poverty is in the Asian region alone.

Between 1988 and 2013, estimates reveal a declining global inequality. The Ginni Index of global distribution fell from 69.7 in 1988 to 62.5 in 2013. While inequalities between countries have been declining, inequalities within countries are increasing, both for developed and developing. A marked increase in inequalities within countries was observed in some parts of Europe and the Commonwealth of Independent States as well as the Asia and Pacific regions where inequality increased on an average by 13 per cent during the period (UNDP). One of the most challenging forms of inequality to tackle is gender disparity. Although overall gender gaps in education, employment and political representation have narrowed globally, women continue to face disadvantage in access to work, economic assets and participation in private and public decision making. Gender disparities are particularly evident in West Asia and Northern Africa where the unemployment rate is almost double that of men (ILO, 2016). Inequality reduces the impact of growth on poverty reduction and with higher inequality; it is more difficult to reduce poverty.

II

Population Challenge

The growing population is a problem of developing countries. The world population in 1950 was 2.6 bn, which is now 7.6 bn. Region-wise the growing population is a problem of Asia and Sub-Sahara Africa. Table II reveals that in 1990, the population of Asia and Sub-Sahara Africa was 2,921 and 530 million, respectively, with the world population at 5,282 million; hence Asia and the Pacific region together have 55.3 per cent of the world population. In 2015, Asian and world population figures were 4,065 and 7,567 million, respectively, which shows that still 53 per cent of the population of the world is in the Asian region. So, almost more than half of the world population will be in Asia alone in 2025. The problem, according to a study by the Institute of Health Matrices and Evaluation (IHME), is that there is baby boom in developing nations and a 'baby burst' in developed nations. Developed countries have a low fertility and they are not able to maintain the Replacement Fertility level. In the USA and Europe, the fertility rate of 2.05 is below the replacement fertility level. On the other side, in the developing countries specially Asia and Africa, fertility rates are quite higher. According to Mokdad, the population in developing nations is rising and their economies are also growing so this will have a knock on effect which will promote fertility. In Cyprus, the fertility rate is 1 but Nigeria and Afghanistan have 7 and 6, respectively. Between 1990 and 2015, the urban population in Asia and the Pacific increased from 33 per cent to 52 per cent, whereas, it increased from 45 per cent to 59 per cent for the whole world. Such an increasing urban population in Asia is another challenge to handle as it creates pressure on available services, increases air pollution, environmental damage, affects the poor and the quality of life. Top cities, which have maximum air pollution are the populous urbanized cities of China and India (Asian Region).

Asia and Africa are expected to be the largest contributors to the size and distribution of the world population in the coming decades while the population in Europe and a few advanced nations is projected to shrink. Large variations exist in the fertility levels at the regional and country levels. In Brazil, China and the USA, the fertility rate is 2 or less. Countries with intermediate fertility of 2 to 5 are India, Pakistan, Indonesia, etc., whereas, high fertility countries with a fertility rate of 5 and more are Congo, Tanzania, Nigeria, Afghanistan, etc. The most urbanized region today is North America (82 per cent urban population) but African and Asian regions are expected to see the largest and the fastest growth of their urban population in the coming decades with China, India and Nigeria accounting for over 33 per cent of the global urban population growth up to 2050.

Table II: Population by Region

(in millions)

Region	*1990*	*2015*	*2025*	*2050*
Sub-Sahara Africa	530	1099	1378	2082
Asia and Pacific	2921	4065	4467	5192
World	5282	7567	8472	10319

Source: World Bank.

By 2030, Africa and Asia are projected to have 47 per cent and 56 per cent of the urban population. Such population pressure and urbanization is a future challenge because these two problems create many more such as increase in urban poverty, environmental damage, pollution, growing inequalities and exclusion, concerns about security and safety, changes in family patterns, informal jobs and settlements, increased unorganized sector, inadequate housing poor quality services and health risks.

III

Environmental Challenges in Asia

During 1995-2002, industrial production increased 40 per cent against the global increase of 23 per cent. Moreover, environmental regulation and enforcement is weak. During the same period, agricultural production increased 62 per cent due to agro-chemical use. Urban areas will get about 352 million new residents in the next 10 years. Provision of drinking water and waste disposal is lagging. Asia's existing energy supplies are inadequate. This region has access to less than half the per capita global average in energy. Growth in water demand will also place significant pressure on the environment. Extraction from the environment is projected to increase by 25 per cent between 1990 and 2010 (Source: UNESCAP 2005).

The per capita energy consumption in Asia is well under half the global per capita figure but rising. During 1990-2003, the total energy consumption in Asian economics rose by 70 per cent and the share in global consumption rose from 14.7 per cent to 21.7 per cent. China and India together account for 67 per cent of the energy consumption of Asia. China's energy consumption is expected to double between 2002 and 2015 while a 50 per cent increase in consumption is expected in India. China is expected to import 75 per cent of its requirement by 2030 (current import is 45 per cent) and South Asia 95 per cent. Rising energy demand creates a problem in the electricity sector. Potential demand in 2004 exceeds the generating capacity by 10 per cent in China and 7 per cent in India. Failure to meet energy requirements acts as a brake on growth. The Asian region faces three types of energy-related challenges:

- Improvement in efficiency of energy consumption, generation and distribution. On distribution, losses were 38 per cent of total electricity available in India in 2005. Good practices in enhancing energy use efficiency is demonstrated in China.
- To invest in energy security by improving access to and movement of energy resources. There are substantial regional energy resources that remain poorly exploited (natural gas in Bangladesh, hydroelectric power in Lao PDR, Bhutan, and Nepal as well as large resources of oil and gases in Central Asia.
- To meet rising energy requirements without creating environmental damage. Investment in renewable energy (hydro, wind, scalar, biogas, etc.) is desired.

Air pollution is the greatest environmental problem of the Asian region. Rapid and intensive agriculture and industrial growth along with urbanization has increased the environmental problems, e.g. deforestation, desertification, land degradation, pollution from industries are a result of energy generation. Cities are losing their green areas and converting into hot spots due to residential and commercial buildings. Many countries in Asia do not meet the Million Development Goal targets of access to drinking water, sanitation or reversing deforestation. By W.H.O. norms, Asia suffers far more air pollution than any other region. China alone has nine of the world's 10 most polluted cities. Another is in India.

Smoke from forest fires in Indonesia affects Singapore and Malaysia. Very little timber is managed sustainably. Illegal logging is too much.

Groundwater use for agriculture is reaching unsustainable levels in parts of India (World Bank). China and Mongolia suffer from quantity and quality of water. Air quality is the worst in Asia as compared to all other regions of the world. As Table III reveals, that no other region is even near Asia as far as pollutant concentration is concerned. For SO_2 ($\mu g/m^3$) the WHO standard is 50, for NO_2 the standard is 40 and for all suspended particles the WHO standard is 60. As against these, the figures in Asia are 74, 51 and 251, respectively, indicating the worst condition of air quality.

Table III: World Comparison of Air Quality Indicators

Regions	*SO_2 ($\mu g/m^3$)*	*NO_2 ($\mu g/m^3$)*	*Total Suspended Particles*
WHO Standards	50	40	60
Africa	35	44	89
Europe	12	42	58
North America	13	39	21
Latin America	41	46	187
Asia	74	51	251
Oceania	4	18	43

Disasters due to natural hazards have become more frequent during 1996-2015. An Emergency data base (EM-DAT) reveals a total of 8,014 disasters relating to natural hazards in the world affecting 4.1 bn people during 1996-2015 which is almost twice as the figure between 1976 and 1995. The financial cost of disasters was US$ 2.1 trillion during 1996-2015. Looking at the geographical distribution, Asia was hit the most often (3,093 occurrences) followed by the USA (1,831) and Africa (1,781).

IV

Population, Poverty, Environment: Interrelation Challenge

As explained till now, the problems of population, poverty and emission degradation are important challenges to Asia. But their interrelation is much more dangerous and severe with cumulative harmful effects. It has significant implications on the economy of Asia and the quality of life in the context of Agenda 2030 of the UNDP for sustainable development. It is not only the number of people but also their lifestyle, political system and social structures that define the relationship between humans and their environment. It is not the economic growth but the way development takes place that is important in poverty alleviation and environmental degradation. The status of women is an important variable in population poverty environment interactions. Structural adjustment and programmed macro economic reforms and globalization can be important in stimulating overall eco-growth and greater economic efficiency. On the other hand, such developments may place poor countries in a situation where they have to over-exploit natural resources in order to handle BOP problems or deal with changing global conditions. Reforms of governance structure are a prerequisite in developing countries to promote the sustainable use of environmental resources.

In the Asian region, asset-based poverty is more meaningful in examining poverty environment interaction. Asset-based poverty is more prevalent in Asia and it is further pushed up due to population growth. Here, poverty refers to lack of sufficient income to generate assets needed to be able to provide an adequate level of basic necessities (UNDP). Assets may include natural capital (ownership of land), human capital (work skills) social capital (human relations), physical capital (tools of trade), and financial capital (cash savings). For the poor, individual ownership of these assets may be beyond their reach. Unfortunately, pro-poor public policies in the Asian region do not focus on how to better allocate and manage these assets on a sustainable basis so that the economic circumstances of the poor can be improved. There is a difference in the relationship between environmental, rural and urban poor. The rural poor have very few assets; they are marginalized and depend upon natural resources, and common property resources for their life and livelihood. They live in regions where the natural ecosystem is already fragile with an overloaded carrying capacity. Here, pressure from population growth is expressed in territorial expansion that creates deforestation and ecological encroachments or migration to urban areas. For alleviation of rural poverty, it is essential to improve the poor people's ability to derive sustenance income from more productive sustainably managed natural resources. To avoid the tragedy of commons and for upliftment of the rural poor and marginalized tribes, Common Property Resource Management is essential.

On the other hand, the urban poor live in densely populated regions with sub-standard housing and surroundings, polluted water, and indoor and outdoor air pollution. It increases health risks. Environmental conditions affect the poor and affect their productivity and income-earning ability. Improvement in the environment of urban poor areas and planned urbanization can reduce urban poverty. Unfortunately, population and urbanization are both increasing in the Asian region. Along with fast industrialization, managing urban poverty is a big challenge. The poor create environmental degradation and they are also affected by the poor environment. In Asia, cities are unable to improve their infrastructure and services fast enough to keep pace with urban population growth. Urbanization encroaches farm land, destroys wildlife habitats and threatens sensitive and inshore fisheries. The rural and urban poor are interdependent groups. A worsening condition of the natural environment of the rural poor promotes migration to urban poor areas and creates further deterioration in their living conditions. So management of environmental degradation and common Property Resources are not only beneficial for this group but also for the urban poor.

V

Policy Failures of Past

In the decade of the 1960s, many developing countries were engaged in a desperate struggle for a transition from colonialism to political independence. A serious push was made to raise the standard of living of these countries (Bandhopadhyay & Shiva, 1989). The motivation for this was the poverty scenario in the newly-independent nations of Africa and South East Asia. The United Nations also started several development programmes with growth as the development strategy. It was hypothesized that growth of GDP not only alleviates poverty in developing nations by creating jobs but could also create surplus which can be used to clean up the environment and control crime and violence (Homer-Diason et. al, 1993). Moreover, according to the theory of Demographic Transition, a higher standard of living will reduce the fertility rate and higher growth will reduce environmental damage as per the Environment Kuznets Curve. Using the traditional model of development, capital accumulation was chosen as a catalyst for economic growth (Todaro, 1989). Hence, all the development projects of the 1960s to the 1980s focused upon capital formation for promoting growth which included large-scale capital-intensive projects. In the 1980s, it became clear that the traditional approach to development, depending on capital accumulation and free trade, was not successful. It failed to improve productivity; more people in the developing world were found poorer than earlier, environmental damage reached a crisis, political instability and the burden of international debt existed. So what went wrong? Actually, in the developing regions of Asia and Africa, any policy of development for poverty and environment can only be successful when it incorporates the prevailing scenario of the political system and stability, social institutions, land tenures, women empowerment, economic and environmental dimensions, governance status, reforms, etc.

Environment and Development

Considering the environment, there are two main weaknesses of previously adopted strategies:

- Conventional measure of GDP does not account for depreciation of natural capital. Empirical evidence reveals a decline in natural capital with accumulation of various forms of capital (OECD; 2002). The natural resource base is a pre-condition to sustainability as revealed by the sustainability approach of Hartwick-Solow, ecological economics and the strong sustainability indicator of Pearce and Atkinson. Hence, earlier growth strategy increased environmental damage rather than protect it. Some fast-growing countries of Asia developed fast but at the cost of their natural capital and environment. It is the biggest challenge for the Asian region which has maximum population and large numbers of the poor. If environmental degradation increases, then their interrelation has dangerous implications.
- Capital-intensive projects, e.g. dams, highways, power plants, etc., were not pro-poor. It has not encouraged development or technology that benefits the poor or the environment. Such projects created benefits for the urban class and no Trickle-Down Effect was realized. Moreover, such projects increased degradation, deforestation, soil erosion, damage to coastal and marine ecosystem, development of coral reefs, etc. Protecting the environment should be an integral part of poverty alleviation strategy.

Development, Environment and Trade

Trade is viewed as a vehicle for economic growth in developing countries (Bhagwati, 1993) but empirical evidence suggests that commercialization and international trade is an important factor for a rapid rate of tropical deforestation and extinction of some valuable plant species worldwide (Repetto &Homer, 1983; Rudel, 1989). Trade with developed countries accelerated deforestation in Latin America and South East Asia and intensified the desertification and extinction of animals and plant species (Rudel, 1989). The implication to note is that contrary to earlier beliefs, free trade has not been consistent with environmentally sustainable trade (Daly, 1993). Under free trade, the value of all international exchanges is assessed on the basis of market prices. Two factors have been responsible for price distortions of natural resources for developing countries during 1960-1990:

- In the populous Asian and African regions, the economies of many countries are weak and unstable. In the desperate attempt to finance international debt, they offer their natural resources for sale at a discount (Kerlen, 1991). Brazil in the 1970s and the 1980s aggressively adopted economic policies that encouraged cattle ranching and in doing so accelerated the rate of deforestation.
- The second reason for price distractions was market failure because market prices do not take into account externality (H. Daly, 1993; Ekins, 1993), e.g., when lumber is exported from a country in South East Asia to Japan and France, the importing country paid the market price which does not include externalities. Free trade based on market prices leads to undue exploitation of natural resources upon which a vast number of people in poor countries of developing regions depend for their livelihood. Past experiences suggest that the free trade policy leads to environmentally unsustainable and economically inefficient appropriation of resources on a global scale (Daly, 1993; Ekins, 1993). Moreover, international trade works against the poor for many reasons. Resources that have been used for local consumption can suddenly be overexploited for exports as happened in the case of the shrimp industry in South East Asia (UHDP, 1999). Structural adjustment programmes imposed by IMF may limit the ability of countries to provide subsidies to the poor.

Growth, Poverty, Environment and Governance

Political, social and economic institutions constitute the focus of governance. Good governance promotes integrity, transparency and accountability in the management of natural resources (2002; OECD). These key institutional elements are lacking in many poor developing countries. In the past, economic growth in these countries was pushed with little or no security to global exposure. The main culprits of lack of good governance in poor regions of Asia have been political instability, land tenure system, widespread corruption, insufficient experience, etc. In the past, for most developing countries, political instability and insecure tenure over many valuable remarkable resources such as forests, fisheries and arable lands continually negate public policy efforts to stabilise the population, control pollution and conserve resources. (Turner *et. al.* 1993). The countries of Africa, South East Asia, and Central and North America, which face internal disputes leading to tribal conflicts and civil war, are examples of political unrest. In such a political climate, it is impossible to implement effective population and environmental policies. The ultimate effect of an inappropriate regulatory framework for environment and its poor implementation, corruption and poor land reforms is responsible for the rapid degradation of valuable environmental assets in Asia.

Therefore, the development strategy of economic growth based on capital accumulation and free trade adopted during 1960-80 in the newly-independent countries of Asia failed in alleviating poverty and controlling degradation. During 1960-80, the population in the Asian region increased which increased the problem of poverty and degradation there. In the current scenario of the growing problem of global warming, these issues are significant with dangerous implications for the future in Asia. It requires learning from past policy mistakes and taking up new initiatives in a realistic scenario for sustainable development.

VI

Conclusion and Suggestions

An analysis of global demographic trends reveals that the world population problem is one of developing nations, specially the Asian and African regions. The Asian region countries suffer from three problems: 1) population and multidimensional poverty; 2) increasing environmental degradation; and 3) intermixing cumulative effect of the above two. In recent times, it has been realized from past experiences that not only have past development policies failed but the problems of population poverty and environmental degradation are interrelated which must be solved in the realistic conditions of Asian countries. An understanding of the interaction among population, poverty and environmental degradation is essential and it is required that a new development strategy be prepared by keeping in mind the other related scenarios/conditions of countries of the Asian region. The future policy options to tackle the challenges in this regard are:

- Increase holding of assets for the poor through pro-poor strategies because asset-based poverty is important in the context of population, poverty, and environment.
- More investment in government programmes on environment and biodiversity conservation.
- Since environmental regulation is weak in the Asian region so effective environment policies should be prepared and enforced with effective implementation. Since most of the regulations are of the Command and Control type so Market Based Regulations should also be applied as it creates incentives to pollution control and investments in controlling technologies, e.g., pollution tax, subsidies, pollution permits, etc.
- Realizing the unconditional endorsement of the special role women play in population control, poverty reduction and management of the environment, improvement in the economic and social status of women and gender equality should be the top priority.
- To tackle rural poverty, improvement in utilization and management of natural resources/CPRs is essential. Since the rural poor depend heavily on environment, so conservation and management of environment should be an integral part of the strategy of poverty alleviation.
- There are examples of resource management projects and development programs that failed miserably in the implementation process due to lack of good governance systems. The Government, private sector and institutions should be accountable for environmental performance.
- Decentralization and transparency in decision-making should be encouraged and participation of all stakeholders should be ensured.
- Since a highly unequal distribution of income and assets often

> has a tendency to suppress rates of economic growth (UNDP 1999), reforms of asset distribution are justified on the grounds of both equity and efficiency. Pro-poor asset reforms would lead to improved management and conservation of environment resources. Such reforms give the poor entitlement to assets.

The problems of population, poverty and environmental degradation and their interrelation is an extremely serious challenge for the Asian region, which requires immediate action. Even if we start today, the fruits will not be realized at once. Solutions need a long-term vision and much sacrifice from right now. Countries cannot tackle these problems without stable governments, political peace, proper land tenure system, asset reforms, good governance, gender equality, empowerment, environmental awareness and effective environment regulation policies. Last, but not the least, by strict measures, it is most essential to control the birth rate. Even the most effective policies will be useless if population growth is not checked. So checking, population growth should be a top priority.

REFERENCES

Ahmad, M. Hussen. (2011). *Principles of Environmental Economics and Sustainability*, 3rd edn. Routledge Taylor and Francis Group.

Allen, J.C. & Barrens, D. F. (1995). *The Census of Deforestation*, Annals of Association of American Geographers 75, 2: 163-184.

Bandhopadhyaya, J. & Shiva V. (1989). Development Poverty and Growth of the Green Movement in India, *The Ecologists*, 111-17.

Bhagwati, J. (1993). The Case of Free Trade, *Scientific American*, 269.

Bremmer, J, Carr David. (November 2010). Population, Poverty, Environment, and Climate Dynamics in Developing World, *Inter Disciplinary, Environmental Review*, USA.

Farrington, John. (June 2006). Growth and Poverty in Asia: where Next?, *Working Paper* 267, Overseas Development Institute, London, UK.

Global Trends, "UNRISED", *UNDP*.

Hardin, G. (1968). The Tragedy of Commons, *Science* 162: 1243-8. Population Research Bureau, Population Trends, Washington, D.C.

Jodha, N. S. (1990). Rural Common Property Resources: Contributions and Crisis, June 30, *EPW*.

Karpagam, M. (2006). *Environmental Economics*, Sterling Publishing Pvt. Ltd.

Kolstad, D. Charles. (2005). *Environmental Economics*, Oxford University Press.

Repelto R. & Holmes T. (1983). The Role of Population Resource Depletion in Developing Countries, *Population and Development Review*, 9, 4: 609-32.

Stephen, D. Mink. (WDP 189). Poverty, Population and the Environment, *World Bank Discussion Paper*, 1992.

Todaro, M. P. (1989). *Economic Development in the Third World*. 4th edn. Longman.

Trainer, F. E. (1990). Environmental Significance of Development Theory, *Ecological Economics* 2: 277-86.

16

BRICS, Renewable Energy and India's Energy Security

Manisha Ashish Mehrotra

Introduction

The world saw a global financial crisis in 2008, which started from the USA and spread across globe. It was the greatest economic upheaval after the Great Depression of 1929-30. It had badly affected the global economy. The disaster paved the way for rethinking on changes in the architecture of global governance. The fragile political and economic global situation triggered by the crisis led to the emergence of a regional power confederacy, particularly within the developing world. Consequently, the importance of Brazil, Russia, India, China, and South Africa (BRICS) within the global governance structure went up and a new shift in world power emerged amongst the developing nations. The five member-countries, namely, Brazil, Russia, India, China and South Africa (BRICS), started work with concrete proposals for reform of global financial governance structures, in line with the increase in the relative weight of emerging countries in the world economy. The role played by BRICS was instrumental in the reform of the IMF quotas approved in Seoul in 2010. The launch of the New Development Bank (NDB) marked a milestone in BRICS co-operation and international development. The Contingent Reserve Agreement (CRA) was set up to give support, strength and principal stability to other nations. The steps of the NDB and CRA show the strength of BRICS in market and policy space. Through the NDB and CRA, BRICS offered a alternate option to the IMF to other countries in respect of global energy sector finances. In Renewable Energy, BRICS provided vast potential for collaboration amongst its member-nations with other outside nations However, the energy intensity of the world's GDP varies on natural, climatic and economic conditions. Problems of energy efficiency are considered particularly relevant, since they affect the efficiency of the economy development as a whole. Increasing the energy efficiency of the economy is important for the government, business and society as a whole One of the primary challenges facing BRICS countries in terms of implementing renewable energy solutions has been the leveraging of finances and strengthening energy cooperation among them to ensure global energy security and reduce price volatility in the global energy markets.

India's power sector is one of the most diversified in the world from conventional sources such as coal, lignite, natural gas, oil, hydro and nuclear power to viable non-conventional sources such as wind, solar, and agricultural and domestic waste. India has emerged as a big player in New and Renewable Energy with tremendous potential in solar and wind energy. There is a huge market for renewable energy within BRICS member-countries and beyond. India is attracting large-scale investments in the renewable energy sector. Major transformations are underway in the global energy sector, from growing electrification to the expansion of renewable energy, upheavals in oil production and globalization of natural gas markets. Major challenges like carbon emissions, air pollution, and energy access outline different possible future scenarios for energy security. India needs to ensure long-term planning to ensure universal energy access and meeting its commitment under the Paris Agreement to ensure sustainable and inclusive growth. India is setting up a web of energy relationships in the extended neighbourhood covering Myanmar and Vietnam in the east, with Central Asian countries like Kazakhstan and Gulf countries in the west. The Indo-US nuclear deal opened up new vistas for India in the field of nuclear energy facilitating cutting-edge technology and nuclear fuel. India has started to engage with China, Kazakhstan and Australia for nuclear fuel, especially Green Energy.

It is in the light of the background that this paper tries to review the role played by BRICS nations in various areas of the energy sector and evaluate the possibilities of renewable energy exploration with major concerns of India in energy security within BRICS. The main objective of the paper is to analyze the position of the BRICS countries in the global energy sector, energy security and explore new areas of Renewable Energy based on the statistical data of the US government's Energy Information Administration, BP Statistical Review of World Energy 2019 and 2017 and Global Energy Architecture Performance Index 2017. Further, the paper also attempts to show how India has unlimited capability in the growth of Renewable Energy and if explored and utilized properly it can have a dominant position not only in Asia but also in the world energy sector overcoming its major challenges. Indicators of the level of production and consumption for oil, natural gas, coal, and renewable energy has been calculated and compared with BRICS and other countries to evaluate the position of BRICS.

Conceptual Background of BRICS

The BRICS nations are all leading developing or newly industrialised nations. BRICS was formed to encourage cultural, commercial and political operations among BRICS nations. It was named BRICS after South Africa joined the group in 2010. Earlier it was just BRIC. It was formed in 2006. The global financial crisis that had erupted in the USA during 2008 battered the global economy. The disaster paved the way for rethinking on changes in the architecture of global governance. The fragile political and economic global situation triggered by the crisis led to the emergence of a regional power confederacy, particularly within the developing world. Consequently, the importance of Brazil, Russia, India, China, and South Africa (BRICS) within the global governance structure has gone up and a new shift in the world power is emerging amongst the developing nations. The steady emergence of BRICS in global politics has been mainly based on their excellent economic performances. This development on the economic front coincides with increasing cooperation and coordination and formulating common positions on global political issues. BRICS, as a united entity, is expected to shape global governance in the twenty-first century. In 2011, at the Sonya Summit, South Africa became part of the grouping, adding the "S" to the acronym, BRIC. In the last 10 years, 11 summits have taken place, with the presence of all the leaders with its first summit held at Yekaterinburg, Russia, in June 2009 and the last being in Brasília, Brazil, in November 2019 at Palácio Itamaraty, under the theme "BRICS: economic growth for an innovative future". The priority areas of BRICS are (i) strengthening cooperation in science, technology and innovation; (ii) strengthening cooperation in digital economy; (iii) increased cooperation in combating transnational crime, in particular, organized crime, money laundering and drug trafficking; and (iv) encouraging rapprochement between the New Development Bank and the Business Council.

BRICS has significantly expanded its activities in several fields since its first summit in 2009, but it was the financial field that guaranteed greater group visibility from the outset. The role played by BRICS was instrumental in the reform of the IMF quotas approved in Seoul in 2010. BRICS cooperation led to the launching of the first two institutions of the mechanism: the New Development Bank (NDB) and the Reserve Contingent Arrangement (RCA). The creation of the bank was aimed at responding to the global problem of the scarcity of resources for the financing of infrastructure projects.

BRICS began to seek new areas of cooperation since 2015 and kept the need of the priority areas of the five member-countries in line with the global need to obtain tangible benefits for the five countries; for example, Brazil kept the areas of health, science, technology and innovation, digital economy and cooperation in the fight against transnational crime as priority in this effort to advance new areas of action.

BRICS together represents 3 billion people and a combined GDP of 16 trillion dollars. The group is the 'third giant' after the EU and the USA but BRICS member-nations are too different and have few synergies to represent a solid economic and political power. The level of economic development is still well below that of industrialized economies such as of Germany or the USA. Even Russia and Brazil, which currently reach the highest GDP per capita values of all BRICS countries, only touch one-sixth of the corresponding value of the USA. Emerging countries like China and India occupy places at the bottom of the Globalization Index ranking. South Africa has a higher index amongst BRICS nations.

BRICS Concerns in Renewable Energy

One of the primary challenges facing BRICS countries in terms of implementing renewable energy solutions has been the leveraging of finances and strengthening energy cooperation among the BRICS countries to ensure global energy security and reduce price volatility in the global energy markets (Putin, Vladimir, 2019). This was one of the critical talking points during the tenth BRICS Academic Forum panel held in Sandton, South Africa, on energy research. BRICS Think Tanks Council (BTTC) has proposed the establishment of an Energy Research Platform. In order to limit temperature increases to 2°C, an additional investment of between $ 780 billion and $ 2.3 trillion will be required by 2035. The solution to this challenge lies with private capital. However, currently there are $ 100 trillion assets under management available across the world but institutional investors seeing slow returns between 0.15 per cent and 3.45 per cent have stagnated over the past decade. Further, banks are subject to international regulations such as the Basel Norms, which affect how they lend money. Basel III specifically makes lending for a project like renewable energy more difficult. The reason for this is that certain projects—including those in certain geographies, those that are long-term in nature and those that use special purpose vehicles—are considered by the Basel laws to be more risky. However, to circumvent these challenges, there is a need to incorporate climate risk into the equation, thereby, giving banks a disincentive to invest in projects that are not green. Another option would be to formulate an alternative credit rating system. Green bonds, which are tax exempt and used to fund green projects can play a key role in helping to fund climate projects. BRICS countries have already had considerable involvement in the green bond market.

Global Energy Nation-wise Status

Power is one of the most critical components of infrastructure crucial for the economic growth and welfare of nations. The existence and development of adequate infrastructure is essential for the sustained growth of the economy.

Energy reserves in the world are placed unevenly. Currently, Venezuela, Saudi Arabia, Canada, Iran, Iraq, and Kuwait have the largest reserves of oil in the world; Russia is only at the seventh position with 6 per cent of the world's reserves. The total share of BRICS, EU and NAFTA countries together is only about 20 per cent of the world's oil reserves, about 30 per cent of the world's natural gas reserves and about 75 per cent of the world's coal reserves. (Table 1).

Table 1

NAFTA, EU and BRICS countries' share of world reserves and primary energy consumption, at the beginning of 2017 Region, country	*Oil reserves (%)*	*Natural gas reserves (%)*	*Coal reserves (%)*	*Primary energy sources consumption (%)*
NAFTA, including:	**13.3**	**6.0**	**22.8**	**21.0**
USA	2.8	4.7	22.1	17.1
Canada	10.0	1.2	0.6	2.5
Mexico	0.5	0.1	0.1	1.4
EU, including:	0.3	0.7	6.6	12.4
UK	0.1	0.1	0.0	1.4
Germany	0.0	0.0	3.2	2.4
BRICS, including:	**8.9**	**21.1**	**45.3**	**36.9**
Brazil	0.7	0.2	0.6	2.2
Russia	6.4	17.3	14.1	5.1
India	0.3	0.7	8.3	5.5
China	1.5	2.9	21.4	23.2
South Africa	0.0	0.0	0.9	0.9

Source: Rodionovaa, Irina; Shuvalovab, Olga; & Mareevac, Maria, 2018.

Table 1 shows that the largest share of oil reserves among the NAFTA countries belongs to Canada (about 10 per cent of the world). The total oil reserves in the BRICS countries are not very significant (8.9 per cent of the world) even less than in the NAFTA countries (13 per cent). The BRICS countries clearly outstrip the EU and NAFTA countries in terms of natural gas and coal reserves. At the same time, China and India alone account for over 2.5 billion people and indicators of oil reserves per capita in NAFTA are 10 times higher than those for BRICS (*BP Statistical Review of World Energy* June 2017).

Global primary energy demand grew by 2.9 per cent and carbon emissions from energy use grew by 2.0 per cent in 2018, which was the fastest rate since 2010/11 due to the increasing number of passenger cars on the planet and mainly due to the effects of weather. This growth was largely driven by China, the USA, and India, which together accounted for around two-thirds of the growth. (Dudley, Bob, 2019). The most striking growth was in the USA, where energy consumption increased by a whopping 3.5 per cent, the fastest growth seen in 30 years and in sharp contrast to the decline trend seen over the previous 10 years. This acceleration was particularly pronounced in natural gas demand, which increased 5.3 per cent, one of its strongest growth rates in over 30 years, accounting for almost 45 per cent of the entire growth in global energy consumption. Coal demand (1.4 per cent) also increased for the second consecutive year, following three years of decline. Growth in renewable energy (14.5 per cent) remained by far the world's fastest growing energy source. The world is on an unsustainable path, the longer carbon emissions continue to rise, the harder and more costly will be the eventual adjustment to net-zero carbon emissions.

Global Energy Sector-wise Status

Oil

2018 was another rollercoaster year for oil markets, with prices starting the year on a steady upward trend, reaching the height of $ 85/bbl in October, before plunging in the final quarter to end the year at close to $50/bbl. The growth in demand was dominated by the developing world, with China (0.7 Mb/d) and India (0.3 Mb/d) accounting for almost two-thirds of the global increase. But relative to the past 10 years or so, the big outlier was the USA, where oil demand grew by 0.5 Mb/d in 2018, its largest increase in well over 10 years, boosted by an increased demand for ethane as new production capacity came on stream.

Natural Gas

2018 was a bonanza year for natural gas, with both global consumption and production increasing by over 5 per cent, one of the strongest growth rates in either gas demand or output in over 30 years. The main actor here was the USA, accounting for almost 40 per cent of global demand growth and over 45 per cent of the increase in production. US gas production increased by 86 bcm, an increase of almost 12 per cent, driven by shale gas plays in Marcellus, Haynesville and Permian. Indeed, the USA achieved a unique double first last year, recording the single largest-ever annual increase by any country in both oil and gas production. The gains in global gas production were supported by Russia (34 bcm), Iran (19 bcm) and Australia (17 bcm). China's gas consumption grew by an astonishing 18 per cent last year. This strength stemmed largely from a continuation of environmental policies encouraging coal-to-gas switching in industry and buildings in order to improve local air quality, together with robust growth in industrial activity during the first half of the year.

Coal

2018 saw a further bounce back in coal—building on the slight pickup seen in the previous year—with both consumption (1.4 per cent) and production (4.3 per cent) increasing at their fastest rates for five years. This strength was concentrated in Asia, with India and China together accounting for the vast majority of the gains in both consumption and production. The growth in coal demand was the second consecutive year of increases, following three years of falling consumption. The growth in coal consumption was more than accounted for by increasing use in the power sector. This is despite continuing strong growth in renewable energy which increased by over 25 per cent in both India and China last year, which together accounted for around half of the global growth in renewable energy but even this was not sufficient to keep pace with the strong gains in power demand, with coal being sucked into the power sector as the balancing fuel. This highlights an obvious but important point: even if renewables are growing at truly exceptional rates, the pace of growth of power demand, particularly in developing Asia, limits the pace at which the power sector can decarbonize.

Power Sector

The power sector needs to play a central role in any transition to a low carbon energy system. It is the single largest source of carbon emissions within the energy system and it is where much of the effort and hope lie for reducing carbon emissions over the next 20 years. Global power demand grew by 3.7 per cent, which is one of the strongest growth rates seen in 20 years, absorbing around half of the growth in primary energy. The developing world continued to drive the vast majority (81 per cent) of this growth, led by China and India who together accounted for around two-thirds of the increase in power demand. But the particularly strong growth of the power demand in 2018 owed much to the USA, where it grew by a bumper 3.7 per cent, boosted by weather effects.

On the supply side, the growth in power generation was led by renewable energy, which grew by 14.5 per cent, contributing around a third of the growth, followed by coal (3.0 per cent) and natural gas (3.9 per cent). Solar generation grew by 30 mtoe, just below the increase in wind (32 mtoe), and provided more than 40 per cent of renewable growth. Hydroelectric generation increased by an above-average 3.1 per cent, with

European generation rebounding by 9.8 per cent (12.9 mtoe), almost offsetting its steep decline in the previous year. Nuclear generation rose by 2.4 per cent, its fastest growth since 2010. China (10 mtoe) contributed almost three quarters of global growth, with Japan (5 mtoe) registering the second largest increase. China continued to lead the way in renewable energy growth, accounting for 45 per cent of the global growth in renewable power generation, more than the entire OECD combined.

Renewable Energy

Despite renewable energy increasing at a very fast rate, penetration of the fuel mix in the global power system remains stagnant, with the shares of both non-fossil fuels (36 per cent) and coal (38 per cent) in 2018 unchanged from their levels 20 years ago. This persistence in the fuel mix highlights a point that the International Energy Agency (IEA) and others have stressed recently, namely, that a shift towards greater electrification helps as a pathway to a lower carbon energy system only if it goes hand-in-hand with a decarbonization of the power sector. Electrification without decarbonizing power is of little use. Carbon emissions from the power sector are estimated to have increased by 2.7 per cent in 2018, their highest rate of growth in seven years, accounting for around half of the growth in global carbon emissions in spite of the growth in renewable energy. If we focus solely on renewable energy, given the profile of demand growth, to maintain the level of carbon emissions from the power sector at its 2015 level, renewable generation would be needed to grow more than twice as quickly than it actually did, by over 1800 TWh over the past three years, rather than its actual growth of a little over 800 TWh. This poses a serious challenge for China and India on the one hand and the USA and Russia on the other.

Measures to Enhance Energy Security: Increasing Accessibility to Clean Energy and Security

In November 2016, the Paris Agreement on climate change came into force—a landmark moment for the international community committed to collectively accelerating the transition to a clean-energy economy. The adoption of the United Nations 2030 Agenda for Sustainable Development and the Sustainable Development Goals also signalled renewed emphasis on the need for affordable, clean energy.

Countries have increasingly looked to drive security through exploiting indigenous renewable and fossil fuel energy sources. The United States' shale boom has placed the country in a position where it is expected to become a net exporter of gas this decade, having lifted its 40-year ban on crude oil exports in 2016. Liquefied natural gas (LNG) has gained a share in the world energy market, coinciding with regional shifts in trade and historical importers becoming exporters, and vice versa. The leading countries for installed renewable energy in 2018 were China, the USA, and Brazil. China was leading in renewable energy installations with a capacity of around 696 gigawatts. The USA, in second place, had a capacity of around 245 gigawatts. Renewable energy is an important step in mitigating climate change and reducing the consequences caused by the phenomenon (Wang, T., 2019).

Switzerland tops the rankings for the third consecutive year, benefiting from a diverse supply mix, low-energy intensity and low carbon dioxide (CO_2) emissions from electricity production followed by Norway (2nd), Sweden (3rd), Denmark (4th) and France (5th), cementing their position as the top five countries on the EAPI from last year with France and Denmark switching ranks· Major energy consumers continue to struggle to take leading positions such as China ranks first by consuming 3,164 mtoe, USA is second by using 2,258 mtoe, followed by India in the third position consuming 929 mtoe, Russia in the fourth place with 800 mtoe and Japan in the fifth position with 424 mtoe and Brazil in the ninth place with 290 mtoe energy consumption (*Global Energy Statistical Yearbook*, 2019). To curb the consumption of fossil fuel, Renewable energy sources are increasingly being introduced especially consumption of solar and wind energy. The world leaders in solar energy consumption—solar are: China (about 20 per cent), the USA (about 17 per cent), Japan (about 15 per cent) and Germany (over 11 per cent). By comparison, BRICS countries account for almost 25 per cent of the world's solar energy consumption, NAFTA - 18 per cent, total for all EU countries - 33.5 per cent. The world's leaders in wind energy consumption (Terawatt-hours) in 2016 were: China - 25.1 per cent of the world consumption, the USA - 23.8 per cent Germany - 8.1 per cent, Spain - 5.1 per cent, India - 4.7 per cent, the United Kingdom - 3.9 per cent, and Brazil - 3.4 per cent. Comparisons: BRICS - 33.6 per cent, NAFTA - 28.8 per cent, and EU - 31.3 per cent (Global Energy Architecture Performance Index Report, 2017).

India's Energy Sector Current Status

India's power sector is one of the most diversified in the world. Sources of power generation range from conventional sources such as coal, lignite, natural gas, oil, hydro and nuclear power to viable non-conventional sources such as wind, solar, and agricultural and domestic waste. Electricity demand in the country has increased rapidly and is expected to rise further in the years to come. In order to meet the increasing demand for electricity in the country, massive addition to the installed generating capacity is required. In May 2018, India ranked fourth in the Asia Pacific region out of 25 nations on an index that measures their overall power. Between April 2000 and March 2019, the industry attracted US$ 14.32 billion in Foreign Direct Investment (FDI), accounting for 3.41 per cent of total FDI inflows in India.

India imports 80 per cent of its oil needs and is the third largest oil consumer in the entire world. India's energy consumption is expected to grow 4.5 per cent every year for the next 25 years. Recently due to high international crude oil prices, the Current Account Deficit (CAD) inflated because of higher cost of oil import, raising concerns about long-term economic stability in India, highlighting the importance of energy security.

Energy Security

Renewable energy is defined as the uninterrupted availability of energy at an affordable price. Long-term energy security deals with timely investments to supply energy in line with economic developments and environmental needs. Short-term energy security focuses on the ability of the energy system to respond promptly to sudden changes in the supply-demand balance. India aims to become a leading global economic power, which will fuel energy needs for providing infrastructure, provisioning of basic necessities, developing human skill, employment generation and manufacturing abilities. India's economic fortunes continue to be tied to the sharply fluctuating international price of oil.

Challenges for India's Energy Security: Policy Challenges

India's major challenges are:

- Failure to attract international investment in domestic hydrocarbon exploration, e.g., NELP failed to attract the interest of large international energy corporations.

- Major investments will have to be made to acquire hydrocarbon reserves abroad.
- Coal mining in India suffers from delays due to regulatory and environmental clearances.
- Indo-US nuclear deal helped fuel domestic power plants and give India access to critical technologies in strategic areas but it did not lead to India setting up foreign-built reactors.

Accessibility Challenge

- The household sector is one of the largest consumers of energy in India. It is responsible for about 45 per cent of the total primary energy use.
- In rural areas, biomass accounts for 90 per cent of total primary fuel consumption for cooking. This has serious health impacts on the rural people.
- Presently, 304 million Indians do not have access to electricity and around 500 million Indians are dependent on solid biomass for cooking.

Infrastructure and Skill Related Challenges

- Lack of skilled manpower and poorly developed infrastructure for developing conventional and unconventional energy.
- India lacks transportation infrastructure for making energy accessible, e.g., pipelines can be a useful way to boost the total supply of gas in the country.
- Gas will play a major role in the Indian energy mix because it can be used effectively in several demand sectors.

Economic Challenges

- Coal, oil and natural gas are the most important sources of primary energy in India. Inadequate domestic supplies of these hydrocarbons are forcing the country to increase its import bill.
- Rising fuel subsidies and rising CAD creates difficult conditions for the economy.

External Challenges

India's fragile energy security is under severe pressure from its rising dependence on imported oil, regulatory uncertainty, international monopolies, and opaque natural gas pricing policies:

- India seeks to achieve its energy security through multiple partners, e.g., the Indo-USA nuclear deal, oil imports from the Middle East, etc.
- However, in recent times, due to conflict among India's energy partners, e.g., the USA and Iran; India had to reduce oil imports from Iran.
- In the wake of its difficult geographic location in South Asia, India faces strategic challenges to meet its energy needs. China's One Belt One Road Initiative can give China a definitive advantage if any conflict ensues between countries, by disturbing India's access to energy.
- Failure to get onboard all interested parties in the IPI (Iran-Pakistan-India) gas pipeline and TAPI (Turkmenistan, Afghanistan, Pakistan and India) gas pipeline for assured supply of natural gas.

Policy Changes

India has already committed itself to bring electricity to every household by 2022. An even more ambitious goal would be to provide "electricity to all households" on a 24×7 basis. To bring clean fuel in rural areas, the Pradhan Mantri Ujjwala Yojana should be complemented by setting up of biomass pelletizing units and distribution of 'efficient biomass chullahs'. On the agricultural front, the solar irrigation pump distribution target must be stepped up and financed through credit support from NABARD and government subsidies. The potential non-conventional energy sources must be explored and researched to make them technologically economical and accessible, like geothermal energy, tidal energy, etc.

Enhancing Efficiency

The National Mission for Enhanced Energy Efficiency (NMEEE) should conduct a thorough cost-benefit analysis of the available energy-efficient technologies and products across all the sectors, especially agriculture, housing and transportation. At the institutional level, the national and state designated agencies working in the area of energy efficiency should be strengthened. To enhance vehicle fuel efficiency gains, auto fuel quality should be upgraded to BS VI norms for nation-wide launch in 2020. India's

Energy Security Scenarios, 2047 (IESS) has been developed as an energy scenario building tool. The guiding ambition of this is to develop energy pathways leading up to the year 2047, comprising of likely energy demand and supply scenarios. NITI Aayog launched the India Energy Security Scenarios 2047 calculator (IESS 2047), as an open source web-based tool. The tool aims to explore a range of potential future energy scenarios for India, for diverse energy demand and supply sectors leading up to 2047. It explores India's possible energy scenarios across energy supply sectors such as solar, wind, bio fuels, oil, gas, coal and nuclear and energy demand sectors such as transport, industry, agriculture, cooking, and lighting appliances.

Infrastructure

India should sustain its export capacity of refined products by setting up new refineries and augment refining and distribution of oil and gas. At present, 31 companies are developing City Gas Distribution (CGD) networks in 21 states for transportation or distribution of natural gas to consumers in domestic, commercial or industrial and transport sectors through a network of pipelines. For the hydro projects, the government will need to make efforts to expedite progress on capacity under construction through satisfactory Rehabilitation & Resettlement implementation. India has also built its strategic petroleum reserves in order to meet any supply shocks due to external exigencies like wars, natural disasters, etc. Indian Strategic Petroleum Reserves Ltd., a special purpose vehicle under the Oil and Gas Ministry, has constructed three strategic petroleum reserves in huge underground rock caverns at Visakhapatnam on the East Coast, and at Mangaluru and Padur on the West Coast. These facilities, with a total capacity of 5.33 million tonnes, can meet about 10 days of India's crude oil requirements. India now plans to build another 6.5 million tonnes of storage at Padur and Chandikhol in Odisha, which will augment its supply to 22 days.

India's Energy Diplomacy

India is setting up a web of energy relationships in the extended neighbourhood covering Myanmar and Vietnam in the east, with Central Asian countries like Kazakhstan and Gulf countries in the west. The Indo-US Nuclear Deal opened up new vistas for India in the field of nuclear energy facilitating cutting-edge technology and nuclear fuel. India has started to engage with China, Kazakhstan and Australia for nuclear fuel. India's SCO membership could now play a bigger role in ensuring greater energy cooperation between energy producers and consumers by linking Central Asia and South Asia.

Promotion of Renewable Energy

The Ministry of New and Renewable Energy (MNRE) is the nodal ministry at the central level for all matters relating to new and renewable energy. It has been facilitating the implementation of broad spectrum programs including harnessing renewable power, renewable energy to rural areas for lighting, cooking and motive power, use of renewable energy in urban, industrial and commercial applications and development of alternative fuels and applications. Over the years, the renewable energy sector in India has emerged as a significant player in the grid connected power generation capacity. A renewable energy capacity of 100 GW should be achieved by 2019-20 so as to contribute to achievement of the 175 GW target by 2022.

There has been a visible impact of renewable energy in the Indian energy scenario during the last five years. Apart from contributing about 12.96 per cent to the national electricity installed capacity, renewable energy based decentralized and distributed applications have benefited millions of people in Indian villages by meeting their cooking, lighting and other energy needs in an environment friendly manner by introduction of solar stoves, by initiating coordinated research and development activities in solar PV and thermal, second generation bio fuels, hydrogen energy and fuel cells, etc. Emphasis on the Jawaharlal Nehru National Solar Mission clearly show cases the vision and ambition for the future along with the launching of the Renewable Energy Certificate (REC) mechanism, which helps in the creation of a pan-India renewable energy market.

Renewable Energy Achievements and Potential

India attains global fourth and fifth positions in wind and solar power installed capacities; it now at the fifth 5th global position for overall installed renewable energy capacity. A total of 101.83 billion units of power was generated in the country during the year 2017-18 from renewable energy. The Government has declared the trajectory of bidding for 60 GW capacity of solar energy and 20 GW capacity of wind energy by March 2020, leaving two years' time for execution of projects.

As per the Paris Accord on Climate Change, India made a pledge that by 2030, 40 per cent of installed power generation capacity shall be based on clean sources; it was determined that 175 GW of renewable energy capacity will be installed by 2022. This includes 100 GW from solar, 60 GW from wind, 10 GW from bio-power and 5 GW from small hydropower. Table 2 below shows the share of renewable energy in the overall installed capacity in the country as on 31.10.2018.

Table 2

Source	*Installed Capacity (GW)*	*Percentage*
Thermal	221.76 GW	(63.84%)
Nuclear	6.78 GW	(1.95%)
Hydro	45.48 GW	(13.09%)
Renewable	73.35 GW	(21.12%)
Total	**347.37 GW**	(100%)

Source: Achievements of Ministry of New & Renewable Energy 2018, PIB, Govt. of India.

It has been further estimated that India has a renewable energy potential of about 900 GW from commercially exploitable sources, viz., wind – 100 GW (at 80 metre mast height), small hydro – 20 GW, bio-energy – 25 GW and 750 GW solar power, assuming 3 per cent wasteland is made available. (Ministry of New and Renewable Energy, Annual Report, 2014-15).

In addition, there exists significant potential from decentralized distributed applications for meeting hot water requirements for residential, commercial and industrial sectors through solar energy and also for meeting cooking energy needs in rural areas through biogas. Around 1.1 million households are using solar energy to meet their lighting energy needs and an almost similar number of the households meet their cooking energy needs from biogas plants. Solar Photovoltaic (PV) power systems are being used for a variety of applications such as rural electrification, railway signalling, microwave repeaters, TV transmission and reception and for providing power to border outposts. Over 10,000 remote and inaccessible villages and hamlets have been provided with basic electricity services through distributed renewable power systems. The Solar Energy Corporation of India Limited (SECI) should develop storage solutions within the next three years to help bring down prices through demand aggregation of both household and grid scale batteries. A large programme should be launched to tap at least 50 per cent of the biogas potential in the country by supporting technology and credit support through NABARD by 2020.

Core Drivers for Development and Deployment of New and Renewable Energy in India have been

(a) Energy Security: At present around 60 per cent of India's power generation capacity is based on coal. Net coal import dependency has risen from a negligible percentage in 1990 to nearly 23 per cent in 2014. This, in addition to India's increasing dependence on imported oil, is leading to imports of around 28 per cent of India's total energy needs.

(b) Electricity Shortages: Despite increase in installed capacity by more than 110 times in 62 years, India is still not in a position to meet its peak electricity demand as well as energy requirement. The peak power deficit during the financial year 2001-02 was 12.2 per cent, approximately 9,252 MW, which has reduced at the end of financial year 2013-14 to 4.5 per cent and in absolute terms peak deficit was at 6,103 MW.

(c) Energy Access: India faces a challenge to ensure availability of reliable and modern forms of energy for all its citizens. Almost 85 per cent of rural households depend on solid fuel for their cooking needs and only 55 per cent of all rural households have access to electricity.

(d) Climate Change: India has taken a voluntary commitment of reducing emission intensity of its GDP by 20-25 per cent from 2005 levels by 2020. In the recently concluded 20th Conference of the Parties to the United Nations Framework Convention on Climate Change (UNFCCC) held at Lima, Peru, all parties to the Convention were invited to communicate Intended Nationally Determined Contributions (INDCs) towards climate change mitigation.

India and BRICS Energy Security

Speaking at the informal BRICS leaders' meeting in Osaka, Prime Minister of India, Sri Narendra Modi, laid emphasis on ensuring energy security and low priced energy resources like oil and gas for economic development. Modi put forward a five-point approach to address common challenges facing the world, including protectionism and unilateralism at global financial organisations like the WTO and terrorism. He said there was an immediate need to strengthen the WTO, fighting protectionism, ensuring energy security and work together to fight terrorism.

There are three major challenges in the area of India's outlook towards BRICS. First, the recession and uncertainty in the world economy. Unilateral decisions and rivalries are overshadowing rule-based multilateral international trade systems. On the other hand, the lack of resources is reflected in the fact that there is a shortage of an estimated USD 1.3 trillion in investment for emerging market economies. Making development and progress inclusive and sustainable is the second major challenge as rapidly changing technologies such as digitalization and climate change are concerns not just for the present generation but also for future generations. Development can be called sustainable when it reduces inequality and contributes to empowerment for the common masses. The third biggest issue is global terror, which is the biggest threat to all humanity. Talking about Modiji's five-point approach to tackle these challenges, the ill effects of unilateral decisions can be addressed to an extent by the coordination between BRICS countries. He said, "We need to emphasize on the necessary reforms in international financial and business institutions and organisations for improving multilateralism," (Modi, N., 2019).

For sustainable and inclusive development, the New Development Bank should give priority to investment in the physical and social infrastructure and renewable energy programmes of member-countries which is a very important issue in energy security. India's initiative for Coalition for Disaster Resilient Infrastructure will help in the development of appropriate infrastructure in developed and developing countries to face natural calamities. The Prime Minister had invited all the member-nations to join for mutual cooperation. Thus, India is looking towards BRICS with a very positive and friendly outlook.

Conclusion

India's Gain from BRICS Collaboration

India's power sector is one of the most diversified in the world. Sources of power generation range from conventional sources such as coal, lignite, natural gas, oil, hydro and nuclear power to viable non-conventional sources such as wind, solar, and agricultural and domestic waste. India has emerged as a big player in New and Renewable Energy with tremendous potential in solar and wind energy. There is a huge market for renewable energy within BRICS member-countries and beyond.

Secondly, major transformations are underway in the global energy sector, from growing electrification to the expansion of renewable energy, upheavals in oil production and globalization of natural gas markets. Recently, the Ministry of New and Renewable Energy, Government of India, organized the first Renewable Energy Global Investors Meet & Expo (Re-Invest) between 15 and 17 February 2015 in New Delhi, as a follow-up to the 'Make in India' initiative launched by Prime Minister Shri Narendra Modi. The central theme of RE-Invest was to attract large-scale investments for the renewable energy sector in India. India needs to build its capacity in research and skill building to deal with these transformations in the energy sector.

Thirdly, major challenges like carbon emissions, air pollution, and energy access outline different possible future scenarios for energy security. The dynamic scenarios foreseen by India Energy Security Scenarios, 2047 (IESS) should guide policy makers in the energy sector.

Fourthly, India needs to ensure long-term planning to ensure universal energy access and meeting its commitment under the Paris Agreement to ensure sustainable and inclusive growth.

Lastly, India is setting up a web of energy relationships in the extended neighbourhood covering Myanmar and Vietnam in the east, with Central Asian countries like Kazakhstan and Gulf countries in the west. The Indo-US Nuclear Deal opened up new vistas for India in the field of nuclear energy facilitating cutting-edge technology and nuclear fuel. India has started to engage with China, Kazakhstan and Australia for nuclear fuel especially Green Energy. Therefore, it can be summed up that tremendous potential exists between India and BRICS nations and strategic planning and willpower is required for bringing clean energy available for our future generations for sustainable development.

REFERENCES

BP Statistical Review of World Energy, June 2017 Available at: https://www.bp.com.

Dudley, Bob (2019), Group Chief Executive, *BP Statistical Review of World Energy*, 68th edition Available at: https://www.bp.com/content/ dam/bp/business-sites/en/global/corporate/ pdf/energy-economics/statistical-review/bp-stats-review-2019-full-report.pdf

Global Energy Statistical Yearbook, 2019, Enerdata.

Global Energy Architecture Performance Index Report 2017, *World Economic Forum.*

https://www.spglobal.com/platts/en/market-insights/latest-news/oil/062819-putin-calls-for-greater-brics-cooperation-in-energy-security-reducing-price-volatility.

India Brand Equity Foundation Report, October 2019, Available at: https://www.ibef.org/industry/ power-sector-india.aspx.

Ministry of New and Renewable Energy, Annual Report 2014-15.

Rodionovaa, Irina; Shuvalovab, Olga; and Mareevac, Maria, (2018) BRICS in the World energy sector development trends, Proceedings of Ecos 2018 - The 31st International Conference on Efficiency, Cost, Optimization, Simulation and Environmental Impact of Energy Systems, June, 17-22, Guimarães, Portugal.

T. Wang (2019) Renewable energy capacity - country ranking 2018, Available at: https://www. Statista.com/ statistics/267233/ renewable-energy-capacity-worldwide-by-country.

PART III

Environmental, Cultural, and Other Aspects of Security

17

A Model of Sustainable Livelihood Security Based on Community-Based Tourism Initiative

Chai Ching Tan

Introduction

Livelihood security is widely recognized to take root in sustainable human and social development, which relies on developing the capabilities and knowledgeable use of necessary resources (Chambers & Conway, 1992) to grow the economics (Tao & Wall, 2009). Nevertheless, livelihood security is constantly under different forms of external and internal pressures, such as the policy defect (Biggs et. al., 2018) and ecological deterioration (Field, 2012), natural disaster (Yang et. al., 2018). This research applies the livelihood security concept and conducts an exploratory research to suggest to rural communities, which are usually remote from major metropolitan centres (Robinson, 1990), in developing their capacities to improve their economic aspect of livelihood security. In addition, the communities should also recognize beyond the anthropocentric view of their livelihood security development (Cobanglu & Karakaya, 2009) by extending their understanding to the web of relationships among the developments and maintenances in economics, socio-cultural and ecological domains. The non-anthropocentric emphasis shares the Vedic view, which acknowledges the universal duty of human mankind towards the resources they rely upon for livelihood. In other words, while implementing livelihood-earning initiatives, such as community-based tourism (CBT) initiatives studied in this research, the communities should take to heart an ethical duty (deontological duty) pursued for their own sake (a positive view of ethics). The ethical and Vedic principles, as narrated, thus become the ethical base for livelihood security development. Apart from the positive root of ethics, Vedic literature also actively promotes an instrumental view in which righteous methods would lead to the positive development of society or communities, which is interpreted at the karmic level in that what is sowed is reaped (Ashok Kumar, 2014). As it was understood in the above, efforts of development should provide a broad influence to the communities and should be implemented in a well-planned intervention manner. Morse and McNamara (2013) categorize these developments into immanent and intentional characteristics, respectively. The immanent element would be illuminated by the socio-psychological theory in this research, whereas the planned intervention is depicted in a sustainable livelihood structure that is supported by CBT initiatives. It is thus assumed that the suggested sustainable livelihood mechanism would lead to positive sustainable impacts in domains of economics, socio-culture, and ecological environment.

To obtain an empirically validated picture of a sustainable livelihood approach (SLA) in remote communities, the objective of this research is to embed into the existing sustainable livelihood approach (SLA) a socio-psychological base and empirically test the validity utility of the model for remote communities in highlands, which exploit concepts of CBT as additional capacities and incomes of sustainable livelihood. Tourism is an important economic development option and change agent for rural community development (Su et. al. 2019), in reducing poverty (Lee & Jan, 2019), and along this view, CBT initiatives are developed around the world as an additional livelihood option for rural residents (Kheiri & Nashikatkon, 2016). To succeed in CBT, the sustainability concept is an important driving force as tourism activities seldom occur in isolation, and it requires a sustainable use of scarce resources such as "land, water, labour, energy, and waste assimilation capacity" (Tao & Wall, 2009), without jeopardizing the ability of the downstream stakeholders to share some of the ecological resources such as water. The SLA acknowledges the diversity necessity of livelihood in terms of multiple activities (Scoones, 1998) that extends beyond agricultural practices (Dias et. al., 2018). Many suggestions can be found in extant literature pertaining to SLA; for instance Tao and Wall (2009) propose both empowerment-driven strategies and participation strategies, which centralizes on assimilating new initiatives into the community over time. These two strategies are operationalized by two important constructs, namely, community development and stakeholder support. The former involves developing community leaders and tour guides, human capitalization, and organization and the development aspects of the community in preparation for the CBT initiatives. The latter involves stakeholder support from private organizations, academic institutions, and NGOs, including governmental assistance.

Literature Review

The literature review is presented in two sections. First, relevant socio-psychological theories provide an additional base to the concept of a sustainable livelihood approach and its literature. Underpinning the socio-psychological base, the SLA framework is presented in the section that follows:

The Socio-Psychological Underpinning SLA

Although concepts and research publications on sustainable livelihoods are widely available (Quandt, 2018), which focuses mainly on development-oriented mechanisms comprising the capabilities, assets and activities required to make a living (Su et. al., 2019), the empirical research that study the perceptions of the residents in highland-communities and incorporating the experiences of tourists are limited. To fill this gap, some fundamental but relevant socio-psychological theories are adapted in this research. For instance, according to the social representation theory, identity is an important construct, which the communities could use to help them create order in their livelihood mechanisms (Pachmayer et. al., 2005) based on matching the initiatives to their cultural and social values passing from generation to generation (Pearce et. al., 1996). Community identity thus can help community members shape their roles and responsibility. A deeper analysis of the extant literature highlights the fact that identity plays numerous important roles; for instance, identity provides a conceptual boundary, which can also help the community to distinguish between alternative tourism options in the markets (Gnoth & Matteucci, 2014); and shared identity (Peters & Waterman, 1982) and can strengthen a sense of belonging of community members (Sufi & Lyons 2003; Tajfel, 1972), which can further improve the motivational drive and investments in new initiatives that the community suggests. Identity is also often treated as a base for product and service differentiation (Rampersad, 2001), and provides a base for brand development (Sun & Jiang, 2014).

In addition, the developmental commitment and investment of the community, in aspects of community leadership, the organization and development of the community, tour guide development and human capitalization of the community, should gradually be phased in improve the self-confidence strength of community members, which is an important theme in the theory of planned behaviour (TPB, Ajzen, 1991). When the residents develop their capabilities and make use of the resources, they will gradually improve their attitudes, and at the same time, will be more confident in their identity-differentiated direction, and thus can better involve external stakeholders for support. From the view of TPB, identity is also an indication of the attitude and stakeholder support provides a behavioural representation of social norms, which is obvious if it is explained by the insight of the self-schemata theory, stating that identity is a cognitive generalization of the community that is attributable to the influence of past accumulated experiences and has a robust belief system adherence playing in the background. In other words, from the view of the self-schemata theory, community identity has the capacity of serving as an "organizing context", which is referred to as "an interactively enacted shared reality that is historically and culturally embedded' (Johannisson, 2007). In this way, community identity is a social resource for sustainable livelihood. Thus, the SLA model, to be deductively developed in the sequel, should embed in it an explanatory ability of the theory of planned behaviour. Besides, any activities deviating from the community identity indicates that the community has crossed over the sustainability-driven boundary, and the dissonance that arises thus can continue to facilitate the sustainable livelihood development. The dissonance-induced commitment and CBT development efforts can be inferred from the self-discrepancy theory or, alternatively known as the cognitive dissonance theory (Festinger, 1957), which postulates that "people experience psychological discomfort when there is an inconsistency between cognitions (i.e. attitude, beliefs, values, opinions, knowledge) about themselves, about their behaviours and about their surroundings" (p. 9).

The Sustainable Livelihood Approach (SLA) Framework

To form a sustainable livelihood, the concept of a sustainable livelihood approach (SLA) is widely acknowledged. SLA is aimed as an integrationist in the sustainable livelihood design and implementation (Shen et. al., 2008), which should incorporate a careful reflective process and systematic planning that is beyond "technical fix", and is all-embracing, joined-up, beyond monetary income, by integrating the intangible or less tangible aspects of livelihood (Morse & McNamara, 2013). The SLA model is shown in Figure 1, which sees the roles of two types of resources, namely, of socio-psychological and capabilities and assets development, in CBT management for accomplishing a positive sustainability achievement. CBT management is shown side by side with the community' agricultural base and the products and services the communities offer. Since the 1960-1980s, the Thai government has been active in promoting export-oriented cash crop monoculture practices or intensive agricultural practices, but such practices have generated many environmental challenges such as soil

Figure 1: A Sustainable Livelihood Approach (SLA) Enabled by CBT

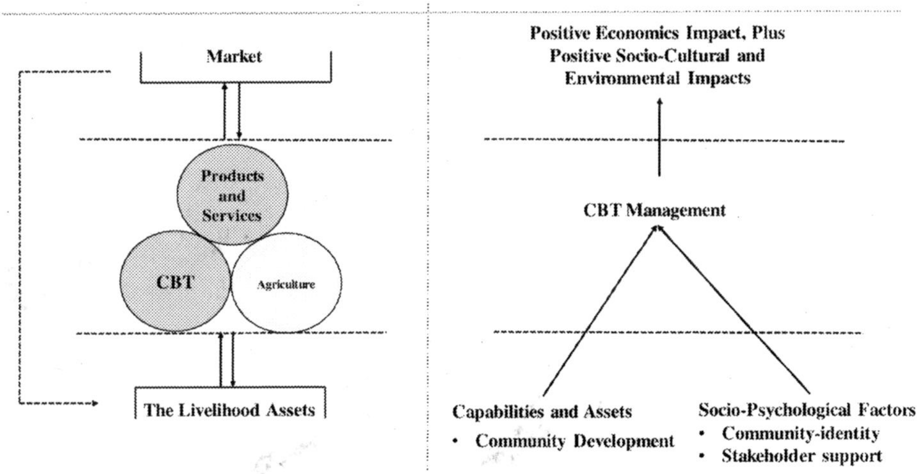

condition deterioration, pollution, farmers' debt and health damage, as a result of the corresponding intensive use of pesticide (Niemmanee et. al., 2015). To overcome these challenges, practices such as organic farming, which uses organic matter as the only fertilizer while pests and weeds are controlled by organic chemicals made from herbs, etc., and alternatively, agro-forestry, sufficiency thinking (Avery & Bergsteiner, 2016) and sustainable business practices (Grossman, 2017), are also widely implemented and policy-supported. The concept of sustainability, as explained in Grossman (2017), is "first and foremost a mindset based on a belief in the values, social benefits, and business opportunities that applying its principles will create" (p. 28).

Specifically, as a holistic approach, the SLA integrates the community-based tourism (CBT) initiative and agriculture and products and services offered. CBT is an alternative form of tourism and it provides the opportunity avenue for additional income, and also creates spaces for improving the community, its knowledge and understanding, socially and culturally, and of the ecological environment, through engagement with external stakeholders and internal community dialogues. The "capabilities and assets" element highlights the developmental theme of SLA (Bebbington, 1999). Apart from agricultural income, rural communities in Thailand often offer handicraft products (Sitabutr & Pimdee, 2017), and the OTOP (One Village One Product) campaigns, started in the early 1990s and until today, have shown some evidence of success in developing sustainable livelihood security (Sura, 2017). With the globalization influence widely becoming the norm in a nation's industry and market development, OTOP initiatives have become an avenue for extending the influence of SLA beyond the local. In other words, communities can preserve their local identity and yet be global in their mindsets and strategies (DFID, 1999). Overall, sustainable livelihood security is an important governmental policy in Thailand, which relies on the communities to develop their self-reliance capabilities to improve community solidarity (Sundramedhi, 2016) and economic self-sufficiency (Prayukvong, 2007). Figure 1 can also be reckoned as an entrepreneurship mechanism that exploits resources to match the opportunities for revenue-earning. The socio-psychological factors shown in Figure 1 are important livelihood assets, and communities rely on their cultural and livelihood identities to create related themes for CBT (Pongpattanaurak, 2018).

Community identity is a widely recognized social capital (Suebvises, 2018). Apart from the economic impact, the socio-cultural and ecological environment sustainability achievements are considered. The socio-cultural element of the community is an obvious element, as community is, by definition, a social organization (Paredo & Chrisman, 2006). A definition given in Boonratana (2010) clearly articulates the sustainability holism, namely, "CBT is defined as an economically, environmentally, socially and culturally responsible visitation to local indigenous communities to enjoy and appreciate their cultural and natural heritage, whose tourism resources, products and services are developed and managed with their active participation" (p. 286). In other words, the use of CBT as a means for sustainable livelihood should enable communities to make a living in an economically, ecologically and socially sustainable manner, and should be regarded as the ultimate goal for them (Bull, 2015). Ultimately, as suggested in Figure 1, SLA should ultimately be able to contribute to develop the economic, socio-cultural and ecological aspects of sustainability, for instance in improving facilities and road conditions (Lee & Jan, 2019) and quality of life and respect of others on the community's cultures (Brunt & Courtney, 1999). On the other hand, without proper CBT management and capability building, tourism development may eventually lead to deterioration in aspects of community economics, socio-cultural improvements, and environmental sustainability (Teh & Cabanban, 2007).

Method

Research Instrument

A survey questionnaire was designed based on the information of the literature reviews, fieldtrip observations and in-depth interviews, using latent variables, including the residents' perceptions of the sustainability achievement domains under CBT initiatives, and the tourist perceptions and attitude that resulted from CBT experiences. The residents' perceptions were aimed to provide validity support to the proposed SLA by use of CBT, and the tourist perceptions provide insights to suggest to the communities in areas they have done well in and the whereabouts of improvements needed. The overlapping of the supply-side and the demand-side would provide a more holistic approach to SLA. On the residents' perceptions aspect, surveys were organized in two parts: Part I deals with the basic background of the community and the second part involves the variables illustrated in the SLA framework. Community identity is a construct that represents "what the community is to themselves and what they are to others" (Crisp, 2011), and reflects a shared norm of the community (Tan, 2016). In the view of cybernetics sciences, identity is an autogenesis force, which provides direction and logic to shape CBT initiatives (Poutheir et. al., 2013). The community identity adapts the two rules, namely, the feeling rule and the framing rule, in accordance with the identity theory suggested in Stets and Burke (2014). The instrument thus reflects the two rules; for instance, when community members feel loyal to the community (feeling rules), and in introducing tourism as an expansion of what the community can offer as livelihood, it will not dilute the community's identity (framing rules). To some extent, the community identity construct shares the essential theme of the Affect Control Theory (ACT: Heise, 1979; 2007), which proposes that the communities construct and interpret their social interactions in the direction of confirming established cultural sentiments for the operative identities and actions, and thus the commitment is devoted to ensure cybernetic stability, by following the autogenesis rules (i.e., sustainability goals, sustainable livelihood security goals).

There are many variations in operationalizing the community development construct, which depends on the uniqueness of the communities studied. Al-Ramiah and Hewstone (2013) consider active participation, intergroup membership development and psychological interdependency in the group membership. Kline et. al., (2015) and instead advocate a processual approach, comprising development group, community awareness and value identification, organizational structure, product and development and marketing, implementation, monitoring and evaluation, and process catalyst. In this study, community development is operationalized in tune with the sustainable livelihood approach, comprising the community leadership variable, the organization and development (i.e., in aspects of rules and regulations, residency involvement, performance monitoring and controls, and job distribution), tour guide development, and human capital investment. The CBT management construct intercepts the elements of both the supply-side and demand-side activities, including design and implementation of the values offered to tourists and visitors. Thus, the CBT management construct depicts the concept of a business model (Aung & Tan, 2016), comprising tourism resource management, market demand identification and marketing strategy development, and values proposition design and implementation. The sustainability constructs are important as the nature of CBT actually relies on environmental and socio-cultural resources for the ability to succeed. Commitment to sustainability is a sense of responsibility and respect for nature, cultural heritage, society and the income-generating capacity of the community. The concept of sustainability is no longer a niche topic, but relevant for today's business and livelihood, which requires the community as a business entity to make the necessary effort in conserving and preserving the ecological health, social justice and harmony, cultural heritage, and economic generation capacity. Thus, the "sustainability" theme requires the communities to form a clear conscience of what they would need to do in areas of culture, economics, and social and ecological aspects. The instrument of the above constructs follows the validity and reliability assurance suggestions, for instance, in Forza (2002) and Nunnally (1978).

Sampling Target

Data was collected in 2017-2018, during the non-rainy seasons and hot summers, when harvesting of coffee cherries and tea leaves was possible. To ensure more homogenous statistics of the data, the sampling was targeted to two communities who have had relied upon coffee and tea cultivations as their main livelihood sources of income. The two communities are located in the highlands and share similar ethnicity backgrounds (Aka tribe and Lahu tribe) and ecological resources and landscapes, and face no mobility or fluidity issues leading to fluctuation of population. The respondents at the household level were used for questionnaire-based data collection, which form the bases for providing insights, as suggested by common research on sustainable community livelihoods (Su et. al., 2016), at the community level. With the help of a Thai Royal initiative, back in the early 1980s, farmers of the two communities started to plant Arabica coffee, while tea cultivations had a much longer history, and many tea plants are a hundred years old, planted in shaded forests. The rich soil in the north of Thailand and the cool weather has helped coffee and tea cultivation to flourish (Migrationology, 2017).

Results and Discussion

This section presents the statistical results in validating the SLA framework, which can suggest to other similar communities to plan their interventions in accordance with a sustainable livelihood approach, to initiate community-based tourism in support of their agricultural livelihood sources. The interviews provide rich information on the variables studied and the context, which help illuminate the understanding of the theoretical and validated structural equation model. A total of 88 community members were surveyed, and the profiles of the participants in the questionnaire-based surveys are shown in Table 1. The interviews were sourced from community members who hold leadership positions in various duties of the community, such as the overall community performance, agricultural cultivation, agricultural products, cultural products and services, homestays, and community-based tourism.

Table 1: The Respondent Profiles

Profile Variables	*Percentages*
Gender	38.6% male, 61.4% female.
Ages	3.4% of age less than 20, 13.6% in between 20-less than 30, 19.3% in between 30-less than 40, 23.9% in between 40 and less than 60, and 39.8% more than 60.
Education	45.5% with primary education, 27.3% with secondary education, 4.5% college graduates, 10.2% Bachelor, and 12.5% unspecified.
Main livelihood sources	28.4% depend on tea, 37% on coffee, and 31.8% in combination, and 2.3% unspecified.
Income	33% less than 5,000 Baht/month, 34.1% between 5 and 9k Baht/month, 17% 10k-15k Baht/month, 3.4% 15k-30k Baht/month, 4.5% more than 30k Baht/month, 8% unspecified.
CBT role	11.4% serving as CBT head in one way or another, 10.2% involved in some CBT committee, 3.4% responsible for CBT marketing, 2.3% planners for CBT, 29.5% homestay providers, 2.3% transportation providers, 11.4% responsible for cultural shows, 9.1% responsible for food, 5.7% on medicinal products and services, 6.8% on heritage management, 4.5% on infrastructure management, 5.7% on flower farming, 38.6% involved in other aspects of CBT.
Years of experience in CBT	31.8% less than 2 years, 47.7% 2-3 years, 4.5% 3-5 years, 2.3% over 5 years, and 13.7% unspecified.
Family members	6.8% has two family members, 12.5% has three members, 29.5% has four members, 26.1% has five members, 11.4% has six members, 4.5% has seven members, 2.3% has eight members, 2.3% has nine members, and 1.1% has 10, others unspecified.
Ownership	94.5% own agricultural farms, 35.2% own homestay services, 13.6% own some types of retail business in the community and elsewhere, and 79.5% are income-earners.

The eight important constructs shown in Table 2 were evidenced with the validity and reliability aspects of the measurement instrument. Each of the constructs has a factor loading of the items and inter-item consistency over the 0.70 threshold, and total variance explained (TVE) is larger than the 0.50 threshold, signifying divergence or discriminant validity of the constructs. In addition, as the square-root of the TVE in the diagonal is shown larger than the cross-correlational coefficients, convergent validity is also established. For further information, one can refer to Fornell and Larker (1981) and Hooper et. al. (2008).

Table 2: Reliability and Validity Assessments of the Constructs

	V1	V2	V3	V4	V5	V6	V7	V8	Mean	Std. Dev.	TVE	Cronbach Alpha
V1	0.843564								4.267	0.66393	0.7116	0.864
V2	0.289	0.815187							3.5309	0.61034	0.66453	0.857
V3		0.571	0.776801						2.9823	0.81404	0.86855	0.843
V4	0.687	0.717	0.426	0.776801					3.7727	0.46699	0.60342	0.884
V5	0.548	0.571		0.751	0.750986				4.0256	0.56177	0.56398	0.901
V6	0.578	0.549		0.718	0.672	0.893085			4.0085	0.52948	0.7976	0.848
V7	0.451	0.659		0.721	0.596	0.741	0.821511		3.8813	0.52015	0.67488	0.843
V8	0.647	0.678	0.379	0.744	0.668	0.712	0.698	0.816578	3.8587	0.58553	0.6668	0.897

Note: V1 = community identity, V2 = community development, V3 = stakeholder support, V4 = CBT management, V5 = economics impact, V6 = cultural impact, V7 = social impact and V8 = environmental impact. The bivariate correlations are significant at 0.001 level (2-tailed).

The SLA framework is shown valid from the result of the structural equation modelling (SEM) in Figure 2. The three fundamental bases of sustainable livelihood are represented by community development, identity and stakeholder support, which can explain the CBT management efforts in 78 per cent of the variance and, in turn, influence the level of economics impact, with 56 per cent of variance explained. Economics impact is positively related to cultural impact, at 0.578**, social impact at 0.451** and environmental impact at 0.647** of bivariate coefficients. In other words, when incomes are positively rewarded from CBT initiatives, positive results are also obvious in the domains of socio-cultural and ecology. Thus, the SLA framework is an effective mechanism conforming to a sustainable livelihood theme connoting "the means of living against further poverty which require necessary capabilities, assets and activities to maintain an economically, ecologically, and socially sustainable manner" (Chambers & Conway, 1992; You & Zhang, 2017). The structural equation modelling statistics show a perfect fit of the SLA framework, which are indicated by Chi-square/df at 0.850, p insignificant at 0.467, and NFI (normed fit index) at 0.990, RFI (relative fit index) at 0.966, TLI (Tucker Lewis index) at 1.006, CFI (comparative fit index) at 1.000, and RMSEA at 0.000.

Figure 2: Economic Impact of the SLA

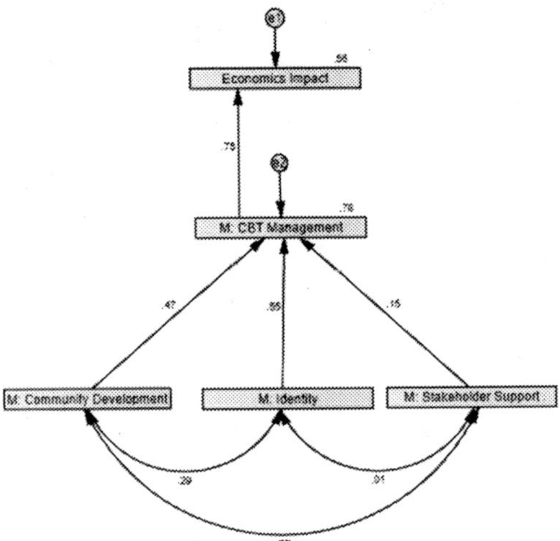

Model Fit Summary

CMIN

Model	NPAR	CMIN	DF	P	CMIN/DF
Default model	17	2.549	3	.467	.850
Saturated model	20	.000	0		
Independence model	10	252.095	10	.000	25.209

Baseline Comparisons

Model	NFI Delta1	RFI rho1	IFI Delta2	TLI rho2	CFI
Default model	.990	.966	1.002	1.006	1.000
Saturated model	1.000		1.000		1.000
Independence model	.000	.000	.000	.000	.000

RMSEA

Model	RMSEA	LO 90	HI 90	PCLOSE
Default model	.000	.000	.170	.558
Independence model	.528	.472	.585	.000

The community identity, which explains a sense of belonging linking it to the community's unique cultural heritage, ethnicity, and farming-centred livelihood, is repeatedly illuminated by the respondents in the interviewing sessions. One respondent reinforced the significance of identity-driven CBT activities that takes root in environmental sustainability and authenticity as reflected in the ways of life. When tourists feel and perceive they experience something authentic, they will be loyal in the sense of providing positive suggestions to other potential tourists (Casteran & Roederer, 2013), which implies a positive economic impact for CBT-supported sustainable livelihoods. It is not necessary to derive authenticity from the natural heritage and original lifestyles; even the non-fixed elements, i.e., furniture and building construction can be included as representing the authentic showpieces of the communities. "Sustainability" characteristics of livelihood is an important identity of the communities, especially those that rely on ecological resources for sustainable livelihood security. The sustainability identity can easily be observable and shown to tourists and visitors in the sense that agricultural cultivation does not need fertilizers and even water, which indicates the sustainable treatment and capacity of the forests, and the ways tea and coffee are shadow-grown in the forest, as the pictures taken at the communities show in Figure 3. As a result, the costs and uncertainties induced by environmental pressures are alleviated to the minimum, which results in positive economic benefits, including quality agricultural products. To be exact, the community's sustainability measures, as a part of the CBT management, comprising tourism resources management, tourism activities and product design and realization, and market demand identification and tourist value management, have shown capable to create the so-called "ecological health", as shown in Figure 3 and the correlations relationships of the sustainability domains, in Table 2, in supporting the "goal of living within the environment's ability to support life over the long run" (Worley & Lawler, 2010). The ecological health of the community lands is shown in Figure 3.

Figure 3: Ecological Health of the Environment

Community development is another important capacity and asset-utilization driver, which occupies a specific standard regression weight of 0.47, second only after the role of community identity in influencing the management of community-based tourism. While community identity has a mean perceptual value of 4.267, in five-Likert scale response, the developmental effort has a much lower value, receiving 3.53, with standard deviation of 0.610, which signifies that more systematic efforts should still be needed. The research conducted by Kline et. al., (2015) also indicates a need to properly plan for community development in order to ensure a sustainable option for the local community. Kline et. al., (2015) shed light by use of stakeholder theory with the basic premise that "if there is interest in the product or organization, they should have the right to be involved"

(p. 80). Five important areas are implemented in the survey instrument to measure community development, namely, tour guide development, community leadership, organization and development of the community, and human capital investment. Tour guides are important bridging means to connect to the tourists, as their various facets of roles, such as social roles, interactional role, communicative role, instrumental role, and care-taking role, can offer the interaction opportunities to share with the visitors and help them gain experiences at a memorable level (Tan, 2017). The leadership element of community development is operationalized in terms of the leadership quality or characteristics such as the ability to inspire members and local people to participate in tourism development, and take the necessary leading responsibility in addressing needs, interests and issues of the communities. According to Onyx and Leonard (2011) and Uhl-Bien et. al., (2007), community leadership is usually less hierarchical and more of having an emergent, interactive dynamic connotation, and its significant role is the ability to create and utilize social capital to benefit the communities, for instance, in grassroot innovation; in other words, to benefit the design and implementation of CBT management for positive returns economically, ecologically, and socio-culturally, as shown in Figure 2.

To some extent, the development orientation could be an important characteristic of the community, signifying a linkage with the identity of the community. The bi-variate correlation strength is shown in Table 2, at 0.289, significant to 0.001 level (2-tailed). One of the community members who were interviewed stated, "It is our development-oriented spirit and competence that continue to enable us to obtain funding support from the government. Based on our community's development commitment, with systematic problem-solving brainstorming, we can continue to improve our products and services, such as the quality shown in the Cymbidium flowers and the coffee qualities, (in Figure 4), including the creation of souvenir products, and shops for the tourists or visitors to relax."

Through concerted group efforts, brotherhood strength is further strengthened, leading ultimately to develop social cohesion and positive social impacts, i.e., CBT gives pride to the community, and enhances the social conditions of the community households. One respondent stated, "When the community is absorbed in brotherhood, it can establish

Figure 4: Cymbidium Flower and Café Projects of the Community

collective awareness of sustainability orientation in everything we do, so that positive environmental and social impacts can be seen, including, of course, economics returns." Brainstorming and leadership-followership relationships are also important strategies of human capital investments, which, as conveyed by the interviewees, suggest a holistic approach such as in areas of environmental conservation and training in CBT services. One respondent stated, "The knowledge shared eventually becomes our standard practices. We also segregate our responsibilities into different zones, which make management easier, communication simple and moreover, it creates an internal competitive spirit that actually benefits the entire community". By referring to the SEM structure, what the respondent stated describes the propagating effect of the efforts at the development and socio-psychological levels to the tourism activities designed and implemented, and the sustainability outcome improvements. Thus, the development process is directly or indirectly facilitated by simultaneous formal and informal knowledge-sharing and conversion, and internalization processes as described in Nonaka and Takeuchi (1995), and the learning is very much driven by motivation to resolve issues that emerge in day-to-day operations and creation of new initiatives (Argyris & Schon, 1978; Tan, 2018).

The validated SLA framework in the SEM configuration, shown in Figure 2, presents a 78 per cent of variation in the CBT management being explained by the sustainable livelihood determinants, namely, community identity, community development and stakeholder support. The level of efforts at the CBT management has a mean of 3.7727, with, nevertheless, narrower standard deviation, valued at 0.470. The CBT management involves both the supply-side and demand-side activities, comprising tourism resource management (of the resources available, such as natural resources, cultural resources, historical sites, and involves waste management, rules and regulations on natural resource conservation, monitoring and controls, and tourist capacity planning for preventing natural depletion and causing tourist dissatisfaction), tourist value designs and memorable experience deliverables, and careful identification of market needs and strategies development in the aspects of marketing, communication and community identity promotion. The respondents address some important challenges that can cause the CBT management not up to expectations, for instance, lack of basic infrastructure in terms of electricity and telecommunication facilities, muddy road and safety issues, information availability and contact accessibility. Respondents address the significant values of resources that can be used and transformed into products and services. There are various spectacular and unique cultural and natural resources, and heritage that can be exploited, such as for herbal use of medicinal benefits, and cultural food offers to tourists and visitors, and ecotourism tracks of the community's surrounding ecological environment. The communities offer agricultural products such as Macadamia, coffees and teas and flowers, and cultural handicrafts and coffee-based or tea-based by-products such as shampoos and soaps, and services are generally home stays and community tours to familiarize with the lifestyles, the cultural practices, the experiences of cultural foods, farming learning and agricultural product-making processes. Figure 5 presents examples of the products and services at one of the two communities surveyed.

The last picture in Figure 5 illustrates the introduction to tourists of Akha's unique medicinal knowledge passed from generation to generation. The Akha communities exploit the diverse use of herbal plant parts, bark and steam, and leaves, and their traditional botanical knowledge of the medicinal plants, for medicinal benefits in alleviating

Figure 5: In sequence: Ecotourism site, Lisu leader explaining Lisu culture. Macadamia products and their processing illustration. Cultural lunch enjoyment, coffee tasting, coffee products, and village handicrafts, and traditional coffee roasting, Akha handicrafts, farm tours, Akha ethnicity, and medicinal product introduction

system disorders, skin and subcutaneous cellular tissue disorders, digestive system disorders and injuries, and metabolic disorders.

Conclusion and Implications

The sustainable livelihood approach (SLA) framework, which depicts integrating the capability and socio-psychological determinants in explaining the level of efforts in CBT initiatives, and in turn influence the sustainability domains, has been shown valid by use of structural equation modelling (SEM). Besides the quantitative statistics evidence, the qualitative richness is made possible by interviews and observations, which support the subtle details for each of the constructs and their relationships. The three sustainable livelihood determinants, namely, community identity, community development and stakeholder support, are shown to be important in influencing the levels and scope of the CBT management efforts. The community identity has been demonstrated with both the framing and feeling rules, which is established by sharing the insights of the identity theory advocated in Stets and Burke (2014). Based on the cybernetics sciences, the determinants also show the autogenesis and autopoiesis functions, namely, the directional guidance of community identity, and the combined community development and stakeholder support, respectively. Community identity is an elaborate idea of how the community members think about themselves, which represents "who they are to themselves, and who they are to others" (Crisp, 2011), and can serve as a boundary reference point to guide the community in developing community-based tourism (CBT) initiatives.

It can be inferred that the values offered to tourists and visitors should be aligned with the business model on the horizontal, and the ecological and socio-cultural assets and sustainability outcomes on the vertical, in Figure 6, which sees how values can be derived from the innovative works on the four domains—the supply side, the demand-side, and the socio-culture and ecology. In this way, the tourist value proposition design is SLV driven. Figure 6 can be an important bridging framework to understand tourist behaviour and attitudes towards the experiences with community-based tourism. The business model is fundamentally a logic of integrating both the supply-side and the demand-side activities, which manifest steps and processes of value design, value creation, value manufacture, value delivery and value capture, or, in terms of value segment (to whom the community offers CBT), value configuration (how does the community develop and attribute the offering cost effectively), value network (who collaborates with the community in order to develop, distribute and sell the offering), and value capture (how much, and in what way, does the community generate revenues) (Jabreel et. al., 2017).

Based on Figure 6, which exploits the community destination personality (i.e., competence and femininity) and the CBT destination

Figure 6: The Value Proposition Alignments to Sustainable Livelihood Resources and Business Model

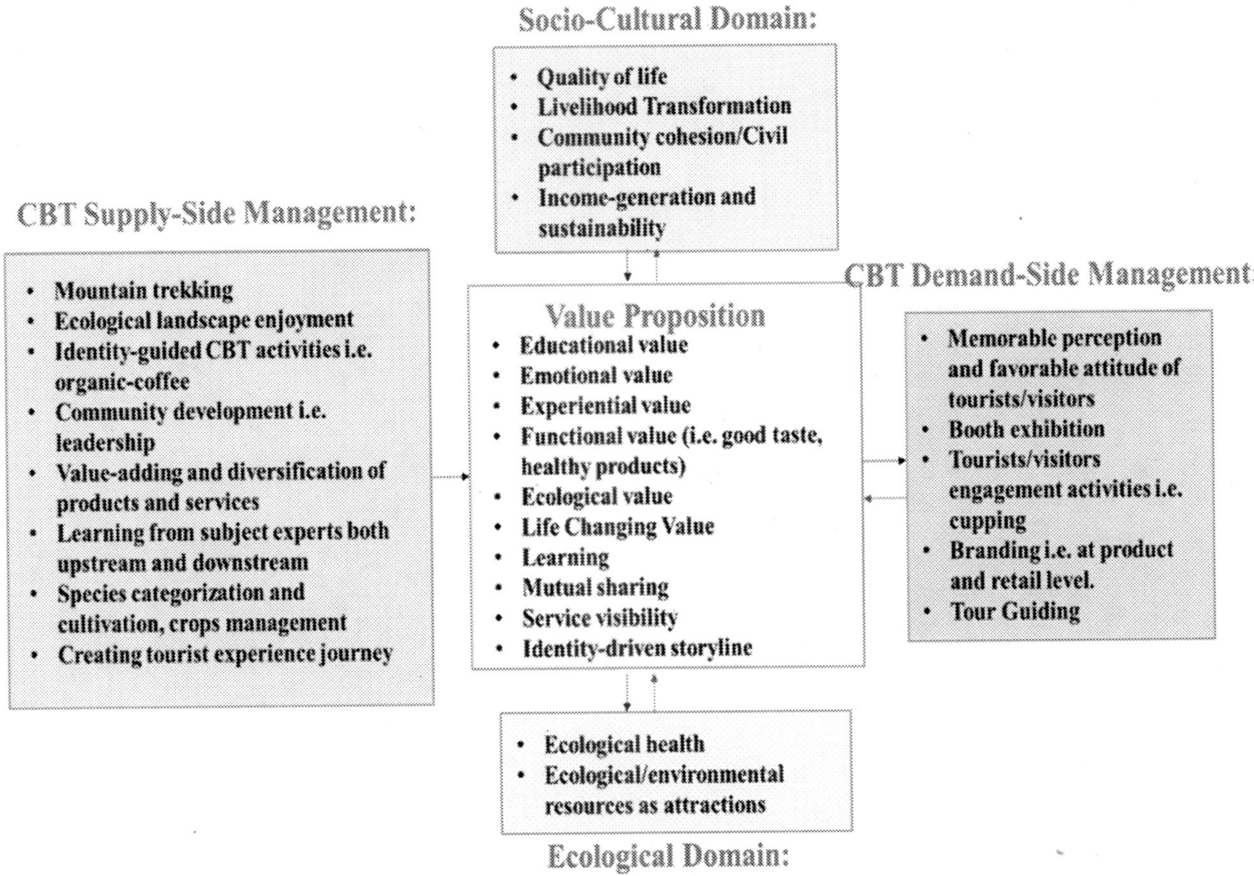

quality, and the community-as-a-brand image at the supply-side, and the tourist self-congruency (i.e., the destination personality is congruent with the tourists) on the demand-side, together with tour guide facilitation, a 106-sample size SEM statistics show a perfect tourist behaviour model fit in Figure 7, with Chi-square at 29.276, df = 22, Chi-square / df = 1.331, p. insignificant (p = 0.137), and NFI (normed fit index) at 0.974, RFI (relative fit index) at 0.934, TLI (Tucker Lewis Index) at 0.983, CFI (comparative fit index) at 0.993, and RMSEA (root mean square error of approximation) at 0.056. Figure 7 depicts a stimulus-organism-response (SOR) model configuration to describe how tourists and visitors perceive of their experiences towards CBT, which sees the mediating role of tourist values in influencing tourists and visitors to engage in learning, which results, further, in tourist satisfaction, forms loyalty attitudes and engages in positive word-of-mouth (WOM).

Figure 7: The SEM (Structural Equation Model) on the Demand-Side Manifested in SOR Configuration

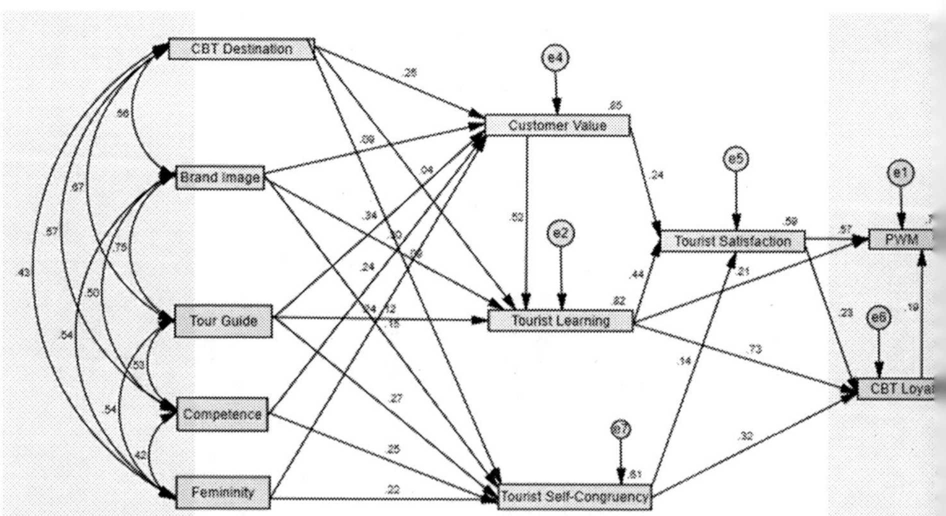

Thus, to sustain livelihood security by means of CBT, it is important that tourist values are appropriately designed to match the personality of the given destination resources and attractions. Figure 7 is a face-based approach in the design of tourist value as part of the CBT management in the SLA model. In other words, the stimuli should be designed so that sensory order (Hayek, 1976) is in place to form favourable cognition (i.e., the brand image of the community, the tourist values), and support tourist learning. Community-as-a-brand is associated with an image, which is about the expression of the experiences (i.e., sensory experiences, Crompton, 1979), the knowledge, and impressions formed of the community (Sun et. al., 2013) and the CBT experiences. Brand destination personality, shown in Figure 7, is operationalized with similar human traits, such as competence, sacredness, vibrancy, femininity and excitement. For the communities visited and studied, only competence and femininity personality traits are significantly important in influencing tourist perceptions of destination experience values. CBT destinations quality adapt the technical service quality (refers to experience outcome, being unique, educational and valuable), and functional service quality in terms of activity assortments (Grönroos, 1984). Based on the social learning theory (SLT) advocated in Tajfel and Turner (1986), tourists can create meaningful connection between the community as a brand and themselves when they have identity-congruence. Identity-congruent tourists are indicators of an important tourist segment for community-based tourism experiences. In favourable identity-fit situation, the uncertainty of tourist perception towards the community can thus be reduced, which leads to loyalty. Values indicated in Figure 7 can reflect the worth of a tourist experience (Zeithaml, 1988), or the benefits received (Bojanic, 1996), which are operationalized for this study as comprising functional value (Sweeney et. al., 1996), emotional or hedonic value (Hirschman & Holbrook, 1982), educational value, experiential value, and life-changing value.

Both educational and experiential values stand out significantly when compared with other types of values, at respectively 4.12 and 4.06 mean values, with a standard deviation at 0.65 and 0.58, as shown in Table 3.

Table 3: The Value Perceptions

	N	*Minimum*	*Maximum*	*Mean*	*Std. Deviation*
Functional Value	106	2.47	5.00	3.7463	.61723
Emotional Value	106	2.33	5.00	3.9780	.69923
Educational Value	106	2.00	5.00	4.1258	.65458
Experiential Value	106	2.75	5.00	4.0623	.58311
Life Changing Value	106	2.75	5.00	3.9434	.57038
Vaoild N (listwise)	106				

According to Pine and Gilmore (1990), educational value is a part of the experiential value, especially when tourists and visitors are absorbed in the experiences actively, as shown in Figure 8. On the passive experience aspects, tourists and visitors can experience the beauty of the destination (aesthetic), or by passively engaging in the tourism activities organized by the community (entertainment), as shown in Figure 8.

Figure 8: The Experiential 4E-Realm (Source: Pine and Gilmore, 1990)

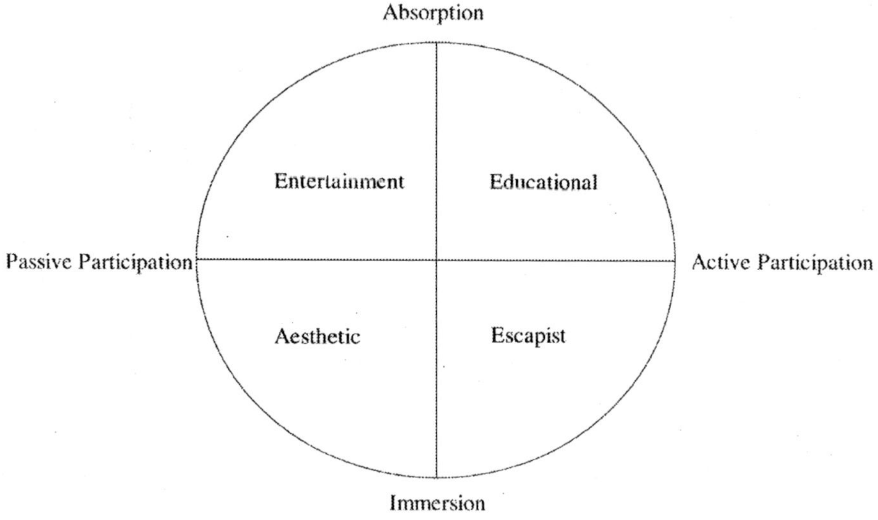

Further Research

Obviously from the qualitative interviews, there are some unique elements that could be included in questionnaire-based surveys. For instance, one community head addressed the need to develop the community according to a "sustainable neighbourhood and community" theme, which they believe has significant impacts on their livelihoods. This research is cross-sectional in nature. Due to the continuing evolution and social emergence of the community, a longitudinal method is suggested as it can allow a closer examination of the different perceptual and actual developmental pictures at different stages of the developments, including observing the stability of the SLA dynamics and the changes at the community's social-structure level.

REFERENCES

Aaker, D. (1996). *Building Strong Brands*. New York: The Free Press.

Ajzen, I. (1991). *The Theory of Planned Behaviour*. Organizational Behaviour and Human Decision Processes. Amsterdan, 50, pp. 179-211.

Al-Ramiah, A. & Hewstone, M. (2013). Intergroup Contact as a Tool for Reducing, Resolving and Preventing Intergroup Conflict. *American Psychologist*, 68(7), pp. 527-542.

Argyris, C. & Schon, D. A. (1978). *Organizational Learning: A Theory of Action Perspective.* Reading, MA: Addison-Wesley.

Ashok Kumar, S. (2014). Thoughts on Business Ethics and Corporate Social Responsibility from Vedic Literature. *Procedia Economics and Finance*, 11, pp. 15-22.

Aung, Z. M. and Tan, C. C. (2016). Using the Business Model Concept as a Broad-based S-O-R (Stimulating-Organism-Response) Consumer Behaviour Model for Tourism Industry: The Case of Bagan, Myanmar. *Journal of Mekong Societies*, 12(2), pp. 21-44.

Avery, G. C. & Bergsteiner, H. (2016). Sufficiency Thinking: Thailand's Gift to An Unsustainable World. *NSW*, Australia: Allen & Unwin.

Bebbington, A. (1999). Capitals and Capabilities: A Framework for Analyzing Peasant Viability, Rural Livelihoods and Poverty. *World Development*, 21(12), pp. 2021-2044.

Biggs, E. M.; Gupta, N.; Saika, S. & Duncan, J. M. A. (2018). The Tea Landscape of Assam: Multi-Stakeholder Insights into Sustainable Livelihoods under a Changing Climate. *Environmental Science and Policy*, 82, pp. 9-18.

Bojanic, D. C. (1996). Consumer perceptions of price, value and satisfaction in the hotel industry: An exploratory study. *Journal of Hospitality and Leisure Marketing*, 4(1), pp. 5-22.

Boonratana, R. (2010). Community-based Tourism in Thailand: The Need and Justification for an Operational Definition. *Kasetsart Journal of Social Sciences*, 31, pp. 280-289.

Brunt, P. & Courtney, P. (1999). Host Perceptions of Socio-cultural Impacts. *Annals of Tourism Research*, 26(3), pp. 493-515.

Bull, K. (2015). Improving Rural Livelihoods and Environments in Developing Countries. Report. Institute for Land, Water and Society, Charles Sturt University. Http://www.csu.edu.au/ research/ ilws/research/ sra-rurallive.

Casteran, H. & Roederer, C. (2013). Does Authenticity Really Affect Behaviour? The Case of The Strasbourg Christmas Market. *Tourism Management*, 36, pp. 153-163.

Chambers, R. (1988). *Sustainable Livelihood Thinking – An Approach to Poverty*. Brighton, UK: Institute of Development Studies, University of Sussex.

Chambers, R. and Conway, G. (1992). Sustainable Rural Livelihoods: Practical Concepts for the 21st Century. *IDS Discussion Paper* 296. Brighton, UK: Institute of Development Studies, University of Sussex.

Cobanoglu, E. O. & Karakaya, C. (2009). The Viewpoints of Primary Education Pre-Service Science Teachers about the Environment According to Anthropocentric and Non-Anthropocentric Approaches. *Procedia Social and Behavioural Sciences*, 1, pp. 2513-2518.

Crisp, R. J. (2011). Introduction. In R. J. Crisp (ed.), *Social Psychology: Critical Concepts in Psychology* (pp. 1-4). New York, NY: Routledge.

Crompton, J. L. (1979). An assessment of the image of Mexico as a vocation destination and the influence of geographical location upon that image. *Journal of Travel Research*, 17(4), pp. 18-23.

DFID (1999). *Sustainable Livelihoods Guidance Sheets*. London: Department for International Development.

Dias, C. S. L.: Rodrigues, R. G. & Ferreira, J. J. (2018). What's New in the Research on Agricultural Entrepreneurship. *Journal of Rural Studies*. Http://doi.org/10.1016/j.jrursud.2018.11.003.

Festinger, L. (1957). *A Theory of Cognitive Dissonance*. Stanford, CA: Stanford University Press

Field, C. B. (2012). Managing the Risks of Extreme Events and Disasters to Advance Climate Change Adaptation: *Special Report of the Intergovernmental Panel on Climate Change*. UK Cambridge University Press.

Fornell, C. G. & Larcker, D. F. (1981). Evaluating Structural Equation Models with Unobservable Variables and Measurement Error. *Journal of Marketing Research*, 18(1) pp. 39-50.

Forza, C. (2002). Survey Research in Operations Management: A Process-based Perspective *International Journal of Operations & Production Management*, 22(2), pp. 152-194.

Gnoth, J. & Matteucci, X. (2014). A Phenomenological View of the Behavioural Tourism Research Literature. *International Journal of Culture, Tourism and Hospitality Research*, 8(1), pp. 3-21.

Grönroos, C. (1984). A service quality model and its market implications. *European Journal of Marketing*, 18(4), pp. 36-44.

Grossman, N. (2017). *Thailand's Sustainable Business Guide*. Bangkok, Thailand: Didier Millet (EDM).

Hayek, F. A. (1976). *The Sensory Order*. Chicago, IL: University of Chicago Press.

Heise, D. R. (1979). *Understanding Events: Affect and the Construction of Social Action*. Cambridge: Cambridge University Press.

Heise, D. R. (2007). *Expressive Order: Confirming Sentiments in Social Actions*. New York, NY: Springer.

Hirschman, E. C. & Holbrook, M. B. (1982). Hedonic consumption: Emerging concepts, methods and propositions. *Journal of Marketing*, 46, pp. 92-101.

Hayek, F. A. (1976). *The Sensory Order*. Chicago, IL: University of Chicago Press.

Hooper, D.; Coughlan, J. & Mullen, M. (2008). Structural Equation Modelling: Guidelines for Determining Model Fit. *Electronic Journal of Business Methods*, 6(1), pp. 53-60.

Jabreel, M.; Moreno, A. & Huertas, A. (2017). Semantic Comparison of the Emotional Values Communicated by Destinations and Tourists on Social Media. *Journal of Destination Marketing & Management*, 6, pp. 170-183.

Johannisson, B. (2017). Enacting Local Economic Development – Theoretical and Methodological Challenges. *Journal of Enterprising Communities: People and Places in the Global Economy*, 1(1), pp. 7-26.

Kheiri, J. & Nashihatkon, B. (2016). The Effects of Rural Tourism on Sustainable Livelihoods (Case Study: Lavij Rural, Iran). *Modern Applied Science*, 10(10), pp. 10-22.

Kline, C. S.; Cardenas, D.' Viren, P. P. & Swanson, J. R. (2015). Using a Community Tourism Development Model to Explore Equestrian Trail Tourism Potential in Virginia. *Journal of Destination Marketing & Management*, 4, pp. 79-87.

Lee, T. H. & Jan, F. H. (2019). Can Community-based Tourism Contribute to Sustainable Development? Evidence from Residents' Perceptions of the Sustainability. *Tourism Management*, 70, pp. 368-380.

Lordkipandize, M.; Brezet, H. & Backman, M. (2005). The Entrepreneurship Factor in Sustainable Tourism Development. *Journal of Cleaner Production*, 13, pp. 787-798.

Migrationology (2017). Doi Chaang: How to Visit Thailand's Coffee Paradise. Retrieved from https://migrationology.com/visiting-doi-chaang-coffee-thailand, on 27 November, 2017.

Morse, S. & McNamara, N. (2013). Sustainable Livelihood Approach. Dordrecht: Springer.

Niemmanee, T.; Kaveeta, R. & Potchanasio, C. (2015). Assessing the Economic, Social and Environmental Condition for the Sustainable Agricultural System Planning in Ban Phaeo District, SamutSakhonn Province, Thailand. *Procedia – Social and Behavioural Sciences*, 197, pp. 1554-1560.

Nonaka, I. & Takeuchi, H. (1995). *The Knowledge-Creating Company: How Japanese Companies Create the Dynamics of Innovation*. New York: Oxford University Press.

Nunnally, J. C. (1978). *Psychometric Theory*. New York, NY: McGraw-Hill.

Onyx, J. & Leonard, J. R. (2011). Complex Systems Leadership in Emergent Community Projects. *Community Development Journal*, 46, pp. 493-510.

Pachmayer, A.; Zhao, S. & Andereck, K. (2005). Theoretical Perspectives in the Study of Community Residents and Tourism. In K. S. Bricker & H. Donohoe (eds.). *Demystifying Theories in Tourism Research*, Boston, MA: CABI., pp. 118-127.

Parredo, A. & Chrisman, J. (2006). Toward a Theory of Community-based Enterprise. *Academic Management Review*, 31(2), pp. 309-328.

Pearce, P. L.; Moscardo, G. & Ross, G. F. (1996). *Tourism Community Relationships*. Bingley, UK: Emerald Group

Peters, T. J. & Waterman, R. H. (1982). *In Search of Excellence*. New York, NY: Harper and Row.

Pine, B. J. & Gilmore, J. H. (1990). *The Experience Economy: Work is Theatre and Every Business a Stage*. Boston: Harvard Business School Press.

Pongpattanaurak, N. (2018). Impacts from Tourism Development and Agriculture on Forest Degradation in Thap Lan National Park and Adjacent Areas. Agriculture and National Resources. http://doi/.org/10.1016/j.anres.2018.09.013, pp. 1-8.

Pouthier, V.; Steele, C. W. J. & Ocasio, W. (2013). From Agents to Principles: The Changing Relationship between Hospitalist Identity and Logics of Health Care. *Institutional Logics in Action, Part A. Research in the Sociology of Organizations*, 39A, pp. 203-241.

Prayukvong, W. (2007). A Buddhist Economic Approach to Happiness and Capability Linkage in OTOP Craftsmen in Southern Thailand. *Kasetsart Journal of Social Sciences*, 28, pp. 161-176.

Rampersad, H. K. (2001). A Visionary Management Model. *The TQM Magazine*, 13(4), pp. 211-223.

Robinson, G. M. (1990). *Conflict and Change in the Countryside*. London: Belhaven Press.

Quandt, A. (2018). Measuring Livelihood Resilience: The Household Livelihood Approach (HLRA). *World Development*, 107, pp. 253-263.

Shen, F.; Hughey, F. D. & Simmons, D. G. (2008). Connecting the Sustainable Livelihoods Approach and Tourism: A Review of the Literature. *Journal of Hospitality and Tourism Management*, 15, pp. 19-31.

Scoones, I. (1998). *Sustainable Rural Livelihoods: A Framework for Analysis*. Brighton, U.K.: Institute of Development Studies, University of Sussex.

Sitabutr, V. & Pimdee, P. (2017). Thai Entrepreneur and Community-based Enterprises' OTOP Branded Handicraft Export Performance: A SEM Analysis. *SAGE Open Journal*, Jan-March, pp. 1-15.

Stets, J. E. & Burke, P. J. (2014). The Development of Identity Theory. *Advances in Group Processes*, 31, pp. 57-97.

Su, M. M.; Wall, G. & Jin, M. (2016). Island Livelihoods: Tourism and Fishing at Long Islands, Shandong Province, China. *Ocean & Coastal Management*, 122, pp. 20-29.

Su, M. M.; Wall, G.; Wang, Y. & Jin, M. (2019). Livelihood Sustainability in a Rural Tourism Destination – Hetu Town, Anhui Province, China. *Tourism Management*, 71, pp. 272-281.

Suebvises, P. (2018). Social Capital, Citizen Participation in Public Administration, and Public Sector Performance in Thailand. *World Development*, 109, pp. 236-248.

Sufi, T. & Lyons, H. (2003). Mission Statements Exposed. *International Journal of Contemporary Hospitality Management*, 1595), pp. 255-262.

Sun, X. X.; Chi, C. G. Q. & Xu, H. G. (2013). Developing destination loyalty: The case of

Hainan island. *Annals of Tourism Research*, 43, pp. 547-577.

Sun, Y. and Jiang, J. (2014). Metaphor Use in Chinese and US Corporate Mission Statements A Cognitive Sociolinguistic Analysis. *English for Specific Purposes*, 33, pp. 4-14.

Sundramedhi, S. (2016). The development of community enterprise: A case study of Moku Moku farm in Mie prefecture. *Rangsit Journal of Social Sciences and Humanities*, 11(6) pp. 23-47.

Sura, K. (2017). OTOP Leaders in Chiang Mai Province of Thailand. *Journal of South Studies* 34(2), pp. 176-196.

Sweeney, J. C.; Soutar, G. N.; Whiteley, A. & Johnson, L. W. (1996). Generating consumption value items: A parallel interviewing process approach. *Asia Pacific Advances in Consumer Research*, 2, pp.108-115.

Tajfel, H. (1972). Social Categorization. English Manuscript of La Categorization Sociale. In S. Moscovici (ed.). *Introduction a la Psychologie Sociale* (vol. 1, pp. 272-302). Paris: Larouse.

Tajfel, H. & Turner, J. C. (1986). Social identity theory of intergroup behaviour. In W. G. Austin &S. Worchel (eds.), *The Social Psychology of Intergroup Behaviour* (vol. 2, pp. 7-24). Monterey, CA: Brooks/Cole.

Tan, C. C. (2016). *Towards a Phenomenological Theory of Corporate Social Responsibility and its Spirited Services*. Ibrahimpatnam, Krishna Dt, A.P., India: IMRF Publication House.

Tan, C. C. (2017). A Field Trip Approach to Studying the Role of Tour Guides in Shaping the Tourist Experience. *Journal of Mekong Societies*, 13(2), pp. 23-44.

Tan, C. C. (2018). Stimulate Changes of Views, and Measures to Learn to Transform Organizational Performance: *An Action Research Case. Advanced Science Letters*, 24(7), pp. 5080-5085.

Tao, T. C. H. & Wall, G. (2009). Tourism as a Sustainable Livelihood Strategy. *Tourism Management*, 30, pp. 90-98.

Teh, L. & Cabanban, A. S. (2007). Planning for Sustainable Tourism in Southern Pulau Banggi: An Assessment of Biophysical Conditions and Their Implications for Future Tourism Development. *Journal of Environment Management*, 85(4), pp. 999-1008.

Uhl-Bien, M.; Marion, R. & McKelvey, B. (2007). Complexity Leadership Theory: Shifting Leadership from the Industrial Age to the Knowledge Era. *Leadership Quarterly*, 18, pp. 298-318.

Worley, C. G. & Lawler, E. E. III. (2010). Built to Change Organizations and Responsible Progress: Twin Pillars of Sustainable Success. *Research in Organizational Change and Development*, 18, pp. 1-49.

Yang, H.; Dietz, T.; Yang, W.; Zhang, J. & Liu, J. (2018). Changes in Human Well-Being and Rural Livelihoods under Natural Disasters. *Ecological Economics*, 151, pp. 184-194.

You, H. and Zhang, X. (2017). Sustainable Livelihoods and Rural Sustainability in China: Ecologically Secure, Economically Efficient or Socially Equitable? *Resources, Conservation and Recycling*, 120, pp. 1-13.

Zeithaml, V. A. (1988). Consumer perceptions of price, quality and value: A means-end model and synthesis of evidence. *Journal of Marketing*, 52 (July), pp. 2-22.

18

Environmental Security is Essential to Combat Global Catastrophic Risks

Sarika Dubey

Introduction

In the last fifty years, the world has witnessed an unprecedented increase in the human population, due to which existing resources have been under tremendous pressure and their carrying capacity has decreased. The world had 3.2 billion people in 1965, which rose to 7.32 billion in 2015. By 2050, it is estimated that this number could rise to more than a billion (FAO, 2009). Due to rapid increase in the human impact on the environment the global climate change and environmental degradation has emerged as a complex challenge to human wellbeing and survival. It has now become a million-dollar question that with limited resources, how long can we survive on this planet. We all know that the Earth, our home, is the only place in the entire universe where life is found and the only planet known to have an atmosphere containing free oxygen. It is possible because the Earth lies in a 'Goldilocks Zone' which denotes its appropriate distance from the sun that makes it not too hot and not too cold. But human impacts are now playing a leading role in environmental degradation, having severe irreversible impacts on nature and the living conditions of all species on the planet. It has threatened life and endangered the existence of not only humans but all living beings. Earlier, man used to live in harmony with nature. They balanced their lives with the environment. In fact, cultural values believe in peaceful coexistence that promotes life through love and respect for the natural world. But later, the blind race for development has changed our entire value system and the pattern of life on a large scale. Several researches were being conducted in early 2000 that proved that it was human activities that is solely responsible behind the breakdown of our ecosystem (IPCC, Fifth Assessment Report, 2013). It caused deleterious changes that resulted in the current idea of climate change. The report highlighted that between 1880 and 2012, the average global temperature increased by 0.85°C. The IPCC has warned and focused on the requirement of rapid, far-reaching and unprecedented changes in all aspects of society to limit global warning to 1.5°C. (IPCC Special Report 2018) It can be best observed during the current COVID pandemic when human activities were largely stopped due to lockdown in most of the places in the whole world. Reports from all over the world are indicating that after the outbreak of COVID-19, environmental conditions have improved dramatically. The quality of air and water is improving and started supporting wildlife and aquatic life. We could see the 200 km away Himalayan range from Jalandhar, Punjab. When Delhi's 11 million registered cars were stopped and factories were closed, the Air Quality Index (AQI) of Delhi suddenly improves and the pollution level decreases to 49 per cent. Dolphins appear after 30 years at the Ganga ghat of Kolkata Flamingo birds appear in thousands in Navi Mumbai. The water of the Ganga in Haridwar becomes drinkable and supports aquatic life. Nitrate concentration falls and the level of dissolved oxygen increases which reduced the biological oxygen demand of water. This was noticed not only in India; the same trends appeared all over the world during the lockdown period. It has been observed that the emissions of greenhouse gases fall at the global level (Zambrano Monserrate et. al., 2020). The lockdown has improved the air quality at a high scale because of the dramatic decrease in industrial activities, road traffic, and tourism. There was a marked decline in air pollution as its NO_2 concentration and PM 2.5 decreased. Anthropogenic activities like industrial projects, vehicular movement, construction projects, tourism, and other common transportation activities are the main source of environmental degradation which has now become a silent killer for human beings.

According to the World Health Organization (WHO), around 7 million people die every year from exposure to fine particles in polluted air (World Health Organization, 2018). The States of India Environment (SOE) Report 2019 declared that 12.5 per cent of all deaths in India are due to air pollution (*India Today*, 2020). It proves how human impacts lead to large-scale degradation of the environment. It has crossed global concern on environmental issues in recent years and demands environmental security at the utmost priority to combat global catastrophes.

The environment has now become a security issue which is directly linked to human survival. It has received more attention than any other issue in the ambit of security. Myers (1993) termed it "ultimate security" and it has also been called "pollution" of true security (Deudney, 1990).

Environmental Degradation: Cause for Concern

The problem of environmental degradation has brought us to a dangerous point today. It has become a common concern for humankind over the past few decades. It is an umbrella concept that covers a variety of issues including climate change, global warming, pollution, over-population, deforestation, etc., and is one of the ten threats that were officially cautioned against by the high-level panel on Threats, Challenges and Change of the United Nations. The United Nations international strategy for Disaster Reduction defines environmental degradation as "the reduction of the capacity of the environment to meet social and ecological objectives and needs (*UNISDR Terminology*, 2009). The problem of environmental degradation is serious today because it has become anthropogenic rather than natural phenomena. The impact of environmental degradation can be seen in several forms which are as follows.

Loss of Biodiversity

Variety of biodiversity generally refers to the existence of species on Earth. After the emergence of *Homo sapiens*, biodiversity has been facing severe challenges. Currently, biodiversity is on the verge of extreme danger because the relationship of humanity with nature has been broken. The *Living Planet Report* 2020 by the Wildlife Fund reveals the fact that human activity, specifically, population, overconsumption of resources and intensive farming, has destroyed 68 per cent of vertebrate wildlife since

1970. (*Living Planet Report*, 2020) The American Museum of Natural History announced the results of a nationwide survey titled 'Biodiversity in the next millennium' that we are in the midst of a mass extinction of living things and it will be a major threat to human existence in the next century. It believed that the Earth is currently in the early stages of a human-caused mass extinction known as the 'Holocene Extinction'. They termed it as the Sixth extinction and stated that this mass extinction is the fastest in the Earth's 4.5 billion-year history (American Museum of Natural History, press release, April 1998). In the same way, the United Nation's Global Assessment Report on Biodiversity and Ecosystem Services, 2019 reveals that roughly one million species of plants and animals face extinction due to anthropogenic causes, such as expanding human land use for industry, agriculture, and be overfishing, deforestation, etc. (*IPBES Global Assessment Report*, 2019) It is now clear how dangerous the situation is.

Global Warming and Climate Change

Planet Earth, which is known as "a jewel in space" is facing several catastrophic risks such as global warming, deforestation, lifeless rivers, and land sterilized by humans resulting in climate change, desert expansion, loss of biodiversity, extinction of species, etc. Over the last 50 years, Mother Earth is suffering from a fever called global warming. The average global temperature has increased at the fastest rate in recorded history and this trend is still continuing. Global warming is mainly the result of increasing atmospheric carbon dioxide (CO_2) concentrations due to the combustion of fossil energy sources such as petroleum, coal, and natural gas. Global warming occurs when carbon dioxide (CO_2) and other air pollutants including greenhouse gases in the atmosphere absorb sunlight and solar radiation that have bounced off from the surface of the Earth. According to IPCC's special report on Global Warming of 1.5°C (2018):

> "Human activities are estimated to have caused approximately 1.0°C of global warming above pre-industrial levels, with a likely range of 0.8°C to 1.2°C. Global warming is likely to reach 1.5°C between 2030 and 2052 if it continues to increase at the current rate."

The report indicates an alarming situation caused by global warming. We have already seen the consequences of 1°C of global warming in the form of extreme weather, rising sea levels, diminishing Arctic Sea ice, etc. So it is just a wake-up call to the world to understand how bad the situation is.

Another deadly impact of global warming is climate change which is running faster than we are. It is one of the most serious global threats of the 21st century. It refers to any change in climate over time whether due to natural variability or as a result of human activity. In this context, it is taken to mean the average weather. The impact of climate change can be seen on water resources, energy resources, transportation, wildlife, agriculture, ecosystem and, most importantly, on human health. It reflects in the form of intense rainfall, decrease in snow cover and sea ice, more frequent and intense heat waves, rising sea levels, melting of glaciers, deadly floods, droughts, etc. The melting of glaciers and polar ice-caps in the Antarctica has become a cause of grave concern. The dense snows of Kilimanjaro have melted more than 80 per cent since 1912. Glaciers in the Garhwal Himalaya region in India are melting fast. It is believed that mostly the central and eastern Himalayan glaciers could virtually disappear by 2035 (*World Focus*, January 2020) resulting in rising sea levels.

Around 250 million people live along the coast that lies less than five metres above the sea level. Changes in sea level affect people through flooding. The IPCC's Special Report on Ocean and Cryosphere in a Changing Climate (SROCC) finds that "global mean sea levels will most likely rise between 0.95 feet (0.29 m) and 3.61 feet (1.1 m) by the end of this century" (*IPCC Report*, 2019). The existence of many islands and island countries like the Maldives, Srilanka, etc., are in danger due to sea level changes. Despite this, drinkable water shortage which is an existential requirement for living beings, mostly humans, has exacerbated through climate change. It has another adverse impact on human health. The changing pattern of the climate has increased a huge number of infectious diseases affecting human life in a big way (Mc Michael, 2003).

Rapid Growth of Human Population

According to the United Nation's Report 2019, the world population increased from 1 billion in 1800 to 7.8 billion today. It is expected to increase by 2 billion persons in the next 30 years (*United Nation's Report*, 2019). It is concluded that the world's population could reach its peak around the end of the current century at a level of 11 billion. According to David Attenborough, the famed British naturalist and television presenter, human population on the planet is a multiplier of all other environmental problems. He described humanity "as a plague on the Earth" that needs to be controlled on a very urgent basis (*The Telegraph*, 2013). There are several thinkers having similar views on overpopulation. They tried to warn through harsh statements and believe that overpopulation has been the primary driver behind most of the ecological and societal threats. Overpopulation includes several problems like overconsumption, overexploitation of resources, pollution, and deforestation that curtailed the bearing capacity of the Earth.

Deforestation

Trees are being uprooted at an alarming rate to settle or accommodate the growing population causing the problem of deforestation which is a rapidly growing problem in areas like Africa and Central and South America. Several other serious challenges have emerged due to rapid deforestation like less cleansing oxygen, displacement of wildlife, floods, soil erosion, the most important being global warming. It also leads to much drier climates because trees extract groundwater to release into the air. Our tropical rainforests, which are very important for stabilizing the climate and human survival, are being chopped at a fast pace. About 50 per cent of rainforests are being cut and if this continues, we will lose it completely in the next 40 years.

Pollution

Pollution is directly proportional to population and means "more population more pollution". Pollution is the presence of harmful materials called pollutants in the environment. Human activity plays a great role in increasing pollution in the form of air, water, sound and nuclear pollution which is very dangerous for human life. It is directly linked to our lifestyle. Pollution has got so out of control these days because our desire for more things has led to our old things being thrown away at an alarming and unnecessary rate. It leads to air and water pollution. Today we are not able to have clean air and clean water due to pollution. Low Air Quality Index shows the pitiable conditions of most of the cities of the world. Air pollution is the fifth leading risk factor for mortality worldwide in 2017 (*State of Global Air*, 2019). Almost the same situation can be seen in the case of water pollution, etc. The impact on the environment during the COVID-19 pandemic has proved how human activities have affected the entire universe.

The implications of environmental degradation and climate change can also be observed in terms of food security, water security, energy demand, human health, biodiversity, economy and large-scale migration due to climate disasters like floods, droughts, cyclones, etc. The great scientist, Stephen Hawking, said, "We are in danger of destroying ourselves by our greed and stupidity. We cannot remain on this Earth for many years. I don't think the human will survive the next thousand years, unless we spread into space" (*Daily Telegraph*, 2001).

Global Catastrophic Risks

Global catastrophic risks are those risks that seriously threaten human existence and well-being on a global scale. It includes a diverse collection of events ranging from anthropogenic to non-anthropogenic risks like global war, nuclear holocaust, bioterrorism, civil war, hostile artificial intelligence, global warming, cosmic threats, volcanic eruptions, asteroid impact events, etc. Global catastrophic risks not only threaten the present generations but future generations also. Technological advancements and economic forces have aggravated these challenges manifold and also created new risks, such as anthropogenic climate change, 20th century nuclear arms race and bio-weapons and bioterrorism. Global catastrophic risks have a long history. There are several disasters causing more than 10 million deaths such as the An Shi Rebellion (756-763), the Taiping Rebellion (1851-1864), famine of the Great Leap Forward in China, the Black Death in Europe, the Spanish flu pandemic, the two world wars, Nazi genocides, the famines in British India and the very fatal current COVID-19 pandemic behind which there is sharp noise among political galleries that the COVID-19 pandemic originated in Wuhan Lab, China, causing the deaths of millions of people around the world.

Global catastrophic risk focuses on the risks that are global in scope and may kill the vast majority of life on Earth. The Global Challenges Foundation defines global catastrophe as a "possible event or process that, were it to occur, would end the lives of approximately 10 per cent or more of the global population, or do comparable damage (*Global Catastrophic Risks*, 2016). There are some catastrophic risks that led human civilization towards extinction risk, which is a subset of global catastrophic risk, which would end the human race. Bostrom and Cirkovic (2008) conclude that all risks having the potential to cause serious harm on a global scale are global catastrophic risks. Such catastrophic risks may have some bad direct effects like the deaths of many people, technological capabilities being greatly reduced, destabilizing political systems, etc. Richard Posner (2006) identified the events that may either overthrow or ruin life on a global, rather than on a local or regional scale. He emphasized on the need to pay special attention to such events on cost-benefit grounds because they could threaten the survival of the human race as a whole.

In terms of origin, global catastrophic risks can be divided into two broad categories—anthropogenic risks and non-anthropogenic risks. Anthropogenic risks are caused by humans which are of three types (1) Technology related like hostile artificial intelligence, experimental technology accident, etc.; (2) Governance related like global war, nuclear holocaust, civil war, bioterrorism, etc.; and (3) Climate changes like global warming, environmental degradation, extinction of species, deforestation, water crisis, crop failures, etc., while non-anthropogenic risks include cosmic threats, asteroid impact events, super volcanic eruptions, etc.

In the current scenario, these global catastrophic risks are further categorized as ongoing risks and emerging risks. Ongoing risks could occur in any given year. The most significant ongoing risks are catastrophic climate change and nuclear war, whereas emerging risks are those risks that can emerge in the near future like catastrophic climate change, extinction of species, unknown diseases, etc. The world today is at the verge of global catastrophic risks. In the twentieth century, human civilization faced the most fatal Spanish influenza pandemic (1918) which may have killed as much as 5 per cent of the world population. In the 21st century, the world has witnessed the current COVID-19 pandemic in which more than millions of people have died. The invention of nuclear weapons has pushed human civilization towards a new era of risks created by human action. Alone in Asia, most of the countries are nuclear powers, some others are ready to become nuclear powers while some countries are undeclared nuclear powers. North Korea's nuclear programmes and Iran's nuclear-related activity under the 2015 deal have aggravated the tension in the USA and these countries many times over. Any nuclear war between the major powers may kill tens or hundreds of millions in the initial conflict. Climate change is also one of the most leading anthropogenic risks in the current global arena which received little attention by governments. Emerging technologies are able to create unprecedented risks in the near future which is unknown or hidden right now. Challenges through artificial intelligence and biotechnology could enable the creation of pathogens, which can be far more damaging and fatal than those found in nature.

Environmental Security

Environmental security is very essential to combat global catastrophes. It is the most important step to secure the survival of humanity. Today human civilization stands on the verge of peril. The securitization of the environment has become inevitable due to severe climatic challenges. The 21st century has witnessed many natural disasters and pandemics. In its very beginning, we cannot forget the painful Kedar tragedy of 2013 and the Uttarakhand floods due to a cloud burst. The year 2020 has seen many natural disasters that brought catastrophic results for millions across the world. It not only caused millions of deaths but also tens of billions of dollars in losses. The most deadly ever known to mankind, the corona virus, the Australian bushfire, devastating floods in Indonesia, hurricane in the USA, volcano eruption in the Philippines, earthquakes in Turkey, the Caribbean; China; Iran; Russia; the Philippines and India, locust swarms in East Africa and parts of India and Asia, cyclone Amphan in India and Bangladesh, Europe windstorm, floods in India, Japan and China, Antarctica snow turning green are the most destructive climate disasters of the year which led to heavy damage to humans and the economy (Natural Disasters of 2020). Thus, it becomes a necessity to address the environmental issue in the broadened security concepts.

The United Nations Security Council on January 31, 1992 declared that threats to international peace and security emerge from "non-military sources of instability in the economic, social, humanitarian, and ecological fields" (Michael Sheehan, 2005). It has grabbed political attention and environment has been taken as a policy issue on the international agenda for a long time. Though fears and damage to the environment were being voiced in the 1960s and early 1970s, they gained momentum during the Stockholm Conference in 1972 organised by the United Nations on human environment and the event can be seen as having begun a process "that has resulted in the piecemeal construction of a number of environmental institutions, the steady expansion of the security agenda, and increasing acceptance by states of international monitoring of environmental standards" (Minget & Karns, 1995: 127).

Environmental security has become one of the most important aspects of security these days. It examines threats posed by environmental events, anthropogenic activities, and collective actions of individuals, communities, and nations. It focuses on conflicts among nations, international relations, development processes and its impact on the environment, or on how environmental problems cross state borders. Environment is a transnational issue because it affects human well-being to a great extent; thus, its security is an important dimension of peace, national security, and human rights. Environmental security is central to national security because of having interconnections among the nature resource base, the social fabric of the state and the economic engine for local and regional stability. It is defined as concerning "the maintenance of the local and planetary biosphere as the essential support system on which all other human enterprises depend" (Buzan, 1991a: 19). Thus, it clearly falls within the ambit of security studies. It encompasses several other issues of state action which may affect human civilization like wars, nuclear issues, conflict among nations, role of international bodies, etc. Much of the environment security literature is equated with environmental protection; however, it is much wider and does not relate to a novel conception of security. After the Stockholm conference during the 1970s and 1980s, most scholars highlighted the inability of national governments to manage common environmental problems that threatened international stability and national wellbeing. Then, in 1987, the World Commission on Environment and Development released its landmark report titled 'Our common Future', which stressed on the concept of sustainable development and introduced the term 'Environmental Security' (J. Barnett, 2009). According to Barnett, J. (1997), "Environmental security is the proactive minimization of anthropogenic threats to the functional integrity of the biosphere and thus to its interdependent human component." Belluek, D. A. et. al. (2006) define "by ensuring environmental security we mean guarding against environmental degradation in order to preserve or protect human, material and natural resources at scales ranging from global to local". The millennium Project defined environmental security as viability for life support with the sub elements: first, restoration of environmental damage by military action and, second, preventing and responding to environmentally caused conflicts and third protecting the environment (J. Barnett, 2009). Gusyn Prins (1993) defined environment security as "threats without enemies". Thus, it is quite clear from the above analysis that security must be accessed both objectively and subjectively. It is value-laden and values are an integral part of our normative system. Thus, study material of environmental security covers the entire activity of human aspects, development process and all kinds of climatic impact on the environment.

The Environmental Security Issues

There are wide ranges of environmental security issues that can be grouped into a number of sub categories. First, disruption of ecosystems such as climate change, depletion of ozone layer, loss of biodiversity, desertification, soil erosion, deforestation and various forms of pollution. Second is the energy issue including depletion of natural resources, problems of energy scarcity and uneven distribution, Third, human population growth comprises problems such as major population movement, migration, excessive consumption, overuse of natural resources, livelihood restoration and reducing ability to adopt to climate change, increasing hazardous waste, unbalanced living standards, poverty and social intensity, food security, uneven food distribution, Fifth, national and international instability such as fight for sovereignty, growing resentment and distrust in the industrialized world, social movements, weak governments and corruption, militarization of strategic natural resources, arms races, wars, conflicts among nations, military operations in land, oceans, mountains, etc. Sixth is emergence and convergence of technology like new weapons and weaponizable technologies, destructive technologies, use of bio-weapons, hostile artificial intelligence, and bioterrorism. Most of the analysts believe that the entire problem is rooted in excessive population growth but Simon Dolby (1998) has strongly criticized this approach. He argues that "Pressures of globalization and the operation of postmodern capitalism are the main culprits rather than population growth", as it has interconnected the world's economies and cultures, promoted market capitalism and consumerism and resulted in excessive use of natural resources that changed the life pattern of the common people. It is believed these days that humanity is living beyond the "carrying capacity" of the Earth which is defined as "the total patterns of consumption that the Earth's natural systems can support without undergoing degradation" (Buzan, Weaver & De Wilde, 1998: 81).

Environmental Security Approaches

Securitizing the environment has always remained a controversial issue among thinkers, analysts, and policy makers. Traditional military analysts and particularly realists have largely ignored the idea due to limiting development projects and human activity for the long-term environmental and human security. But in socio-academic circles, it has been the matter of grave concern to securitize the environment. There are a few main approaches of environmental security. The first group is composed of military security specialists who see environmental issues in the form of 'resource shortage problem' and focused on natural resources as a potential course of future interstate conflict and war. It believes that the scarcity of natural resources and their geo-political importance had always been the cause of conflict. For example, relative shortage of water in the Middle East was a major contributor that led to tensions in the region (Bulloch & Darwish, 1993). This group also believes that deliberate manipulation of the environment for military purposes and its use as a weapon had always increased tensions among nations. The Gulf War could be seen as an example of ecological warfare (Gleick, 1991), China's aggression in the South China Sea, Turkey's pressure on the Syrian government to withdraw its support for Kurdish separatists through control over the headwaters of the Euphrates are examples of manipulation of the environment for political and military reasons.

The second environmental security approach is the "Toronto school". This school focuses on the links between renewable resources scarcities and violent conflict. It stresses upon issues such as scarcities of cropland, forest, fish stocks, and water rather than the traditional environmental issues like global warming, climate change, etc. Michael Sheehan (2005) identified three types of scarcity. First, supply induced scarcity which is caused by degradation and depletion of environmental resources such an erosion of cropland. Second, demand-induced scarcity which is an outcome of population growth within a region that increased per capita consumption of a resource and creates more demand. Third is a structural scarcity that arises from an unequal social distribution of a resource that concentrates in the hands of a few people. Thus, according to this group, the environmental issue has been an integral part of international and regional conflicts, so it becomes important to deal with it under the broader security framework.

The third approach belongs to the realist-environmentalist school which believes that the environment can be a future cause of war. China wants to build a hydropower project on the river Brahmaputra which has triggered concerns in both India and Bangladesh. In the same way, the construction of the Farakka Barrage in India along the river Ganga had created water stress in Bangladesh. The Indus Water Treaty is a water distribution treaty between India and Pakistan. All these issues have affected bilateral relations largely. Reidulf Molvaer (1991) argued that "environmentally induced food shortages have been a major contributor to conflict in the Horn of Africa".

The fourth group of analysts is 'environmentalist protectionist' which believes that the threat to the environment itself is the problem. Therefore, protection of the environment is very essential for many reasons such as to maintain biodiversity and biosphere as a life support system for the human race. It is very crucial to protect the environment for a variety of reasons because it believes in the argument that life runs on the principle of mutual dependence. Thus, it becomes necessary to protect plants and other creatures for the sake of our own survival. For example, loss of biodiversity might threaten the development of medicinal drugs and medicines. Thus, it is quite necessary to preserve the biosphere and protect the environment to sustain life.

What is Required Now

There are several ways to combat global catastrophes and to save life on the Earth. But the most important thing is to understand why they occur. It is deeply rooted in our changing lifestyle patterns and individualism-based belief systems. Over-aspiration and fast pace of development is another reason for environmental degradation. It has been observed that countries are victims of such unbalanced growth of development. They cannot be blamed for global environmental problems because they are far less demanding on global resources and are the most vulnerable to its consequences. Their energy consumption is ten times lesser than that of industrialized countries. Sometimes, damage to the environment is described as a planetary problem but actually the problem is regional rather than global. It works on the very basic principle "mistakes individual but punishment collective". This raises very crucial issues for international relations. Who is paying the cost of this damage? Who is responsible for damaging the environment? Who should take the lead in dealing with the problem? It becomes difficult to tackle because often the countries that suffer the most are the least able in technological and financial terms to deal with the problem but they are sufferers and the most at risk. Thus, a kind of blame game begins that creates problems to tackle the situation.

Another interesting aspect of environmental security is to identify the provider of security. In the cold war discourse, the state was the main agent in the role of security provider and its instrument was the armed forces. But when it comes to the environment, each and every individual becomes the agent of security. In fact, civil society, non-governmental organizations, epistemic communities such as scientists, and social and religious groups should take the responsibility for enhancing environmental security. The footprints of environmental problems are visible on various aspects of human life. Thus, it becomes inevitable to realize the close connection between environment and security. International organizations, governments and the general public have taken cognizance to securitize the environment because today, security is not confined to military threats. The environment is one of the most important components of security. Therefore, it is necessary to address all the environmental issues under the border security framework.

There are following measures that can be adopted to preserve and protect the environment.

- Promote cooperation among states; this builds confidence and leads to an integral mechanism of peace building and security policy.
- Establish innovative institutional arrangements.
- Move towards sustainable use of natural resources; overexploitation should be avoided.
- Strengthen environmental ethics.
- Encourage sustainable development.
- Preserve biodiversity.
- Avoid wastage of anything.
- Use biodegradable products.
- Change lifestyle pattern.
- Create harmony with nature.
- Focus on the renewable energy principle of life and minimize requirements.
- Move from consumerism to spiritualism.

By adopting such measures, we can make a better world tomorrow for our next generations.

REFERENCES

Barnett, J. (2009), *International Encyclopaedia of Human Geography*. https://www.sciencedirect.com/ topics/ earth-and-planetary-sciences/environmental-security.

Barnett, J. (1997), Environmental Security: Now What? Seminar, Department of International Relations, Keele University, 4 December 1997.

Belluck, D.A.; Hull, R.N.; Benjamin, S.L.; Alcorn, J, & Linkov, I. (2006), Environmental security, critical infrastructure and risk assessment: Definition and current trends. In Moral, B. and Linkov, I. (eds.) *Environmental Security and Environmental Management*, pp.3-16. Dordrecht: Springer.

Biodiversity in the next Millennium, A survey by the American Museum of Natural History, in conjunction with Louis Harris and Associates Inc. April 1998. http://www.mysterium.com/ amnn.html.

Bostrom, Nick & Milan, Cirkovic (2008), *Global Catastrophic Risks*, Oxford University Press.

Bulloch, John & Darwish, Adel (1993), *Water Wars: Coming Conflicts in the Middle East*. London: Victor Gollancz.

Buzan, Barry; Weaver, Ole & De Wilde, Jaap (1998), *Security: A New Framework for Analysis*. Boulder: Lynne Reinner.

Buzan, Barry (1991a), *People, States and Fear*, 2nd edn. Boulder: Lynne Rienner.

Dalby, Simon (1998), "Human Security: Environmental Dimensions of a Contested Concept". Paper presented at the 1998 Meech Lake conference on Taking Human Security Seriously.

David Attenborough, "Humans are a plague on the Earth" *The Telegraph*, 22 January 2013. http:// www.telegraph.co.uk/news/earth/earthnews/9815862/Humans-are-plague-on-Earth-Attenborough.html.

Daily Telegraph, 16 October 2001.

Deudney, Daniel (1990), "The case against linking environmental degradation and National Security". *Millennium: Journal of International Studies* 19, pp. 461-476.

FAO (2009), FAO's Director-General on How to Feed the World in 2050. *Population and Development Review*, vol. 35, issue 4, pp. 837-839. Doi:10.1111/j.1728-4457.2009.00312.X

Gleick, Peter H. (1991), "Environment and Security: The clear connections". *Bulletin of the Atomic Scientists*, 47, no. 3, pp. 16-22.

Environment and Climate Adoption, *World Focus*, January 2020, www.worldfocus.in

https://knowledge.unccd.int/publications/ipbes-2019-global-assessment-report-biodiversity-and-ecosystem-services.

India Today (2020), www.indiatoday.in/education-today/latest-studies/story/air-pollution-india-deaths-children-five-years-report-center-for science-and-environment-1543779-2019-06-06.

IPBES's The Global Assessment Report on Biodiversity and Ecosystem Services: summary for policy makers, 2019, https://ipbes.net/global_assessment.

IPCC Report: Sea Level Rise Is a Present and Future Danger, 2019. https: www.nrdc.org/experts/rob-moore/new-ipcc-report-sea-level-rise-challenges-are-growing# :~: text = The % 20 Special % 20Report %20 on % the, ever.

IPCC's Special report on, Global Warming of 1.5°C 2010. https://www.ipcc.ch/sr15/ and https://wmo.int/ en/resources/bulletin/ipcc-issue-special-report-global-warming-of-1.5-%c2%BOc

Living Planet Report: Bonding the curve of Biodiversity Loss, Wild Life Fund and Zoological Society of London, September 2020.

McMichael, A.J. (2003), Global Climate Change: Will it affect vector-borne infectious diseases? *Internal Medicine Journal* 33: 554-555; doi: 10.1111/j.1445-5994.2003.00492.X.

Minget, Karen & Karns, Margaret (1995), *The United Nations in the Post-Cold War Era*. Boulder: Westview.

Molvaer, Reidulf (1991), "Environmentally Induced conflicts? A Discussion based on studies from the Horn of Africa". *Bulletin of Peace Proposals* 22, pp. 175-188.

Myers, Norman (1989), "Environment and Security", *Foreign Policy* 74, pp. 23-41. 1993 Ultimate Security, New York: W. W. Norton.

Posner, Richard A. (2006), *Catastrophe: Risk and Response*, Oxford University Press, ISBN 978-0195306477, Introduction, "What is Catastrophe?"

Prins, Gusyn, (ed.) (1993), *Threats without Enemies: Facing Environmental Insecurities*. London: Earthscan.

Sheehan, Michael (2005), *International Security, An Analytical Survey*, Lynne Rienner Publishers, Boulder London.

State of Global Air 2019: Air Pollution a significant risk factor worldwide, http://healtheffects.org/announcement/state-global-air-2019-airpollution-significant-risk-factor-worldwide.

Ten biggest natural disasters of 2020 that shook the world costing money and lives/curly tales, https://curlytales.com/9-natural-disasters-that-have-already-happened-in-just-5months-of-2020/

UNISDR Terminology and Disaster Risk Reduction, Geneva, Switzerland, May 2009, www.unisdr.org/publications and on prevention web at www.preventionweb.net.

United Nation's Report, "The world population prospects 2019", published by population division of the UN Department of Economic and Social Affairs. https://www.un.org/development/desa/ publications / world-population-prospects-2019-highlights.html.

World Health Organization, press release on 2 May 2018. www.who.int/news-room/detail/02-05-2018-9-out-of-10 people-worldwide-breathe-polluted-air-but-more-countries-are-taking-action.

Zambrano–Monserrate, M.A. & Sanchez–Alcalde, A. Indirect effect of COVID-19 on the environment. *Sci. Total Environ. 2020*; 728:138813. doi: 10.1016/j.scitotenu.2020.138813.

19

Terrorism in Asia: Challenges for Security and Human Rights

Ashima Ghosh

Introduction

The scourge of terrorism has become a major security threat for countries all over the world. Terrorism is no more a regional phenomenon. Terrorist organizations have spread their tentacles to much wider areas. Modern technology and networking have made the operations of terrorist organizations more deadly, operating on trans-national and global levels. This challenge of trans-national terrorism requires concerted and coordinated response from the global community.

Acts of violence and subversion by terrorists create fear and panic among the people. Through their violent acts, they try to prove that the government is powerless to prevent terrorism and they seek publicity for their cause. Agreement and co-operation amongst the states is essential to fight against terrorism, so that their sources of funding, procurement of arms, and training camps can be curbed and those involved in acts of terror can be extradited for trial according to law.

The Asian continent, which has seen economic growth and progress in the 21st century, has been facing the challenge of terrorism. Terrorism has emerged as a major security threat for most of the countries in Asia.

Terrorism is not a new phenomenon. But with time, its nature and capacity to inflict damage and loss through violence has undergone change. There is the fear of terrorist groups acquiring nuclear material. Bio-terrorism is emerging as a new potent threat for the world community. Cyber-terrorism has also emerged as a grave security challenge. There is also the problem of state-sponsored terrorism and passive and tactical support to extremist groups and terror organizations. This paper has largely focussed on the problem of terrorism in West Asia and the Indian sub-continent.

Evolution

There are historical evidences that show that terror groups were active even in the ancient and medieval period. In the first half of the 20th century, terror groups were active among the Nazis and the Fascists. The 'Contras', opposed to the communists, were operating in Nicaragua. The Irish Republican Army (IRA) carried out a number of attacks against the British authorities. The 'Irgun' which sought to defend Jews from attacks by Arabs also indulged in acts of sabotage and bombing. 'Black Hand', a Palestinian national militia was using bombs and firearms to kill Jews. It inspired a number of terror groups in the Middle East like the Hamas.

During the second half of the 20th century, the number of terror groups and organizations multiplied manifold. Acts of violence have been attributed to the Jewish Defence League (JDL) which was founded in 1969. The Japanese Red Army, founded in 1971, indulged in acts of sabotage, hijacking, and assassination. The Liberation Tigers of Tamil Eelam (LTTE) was founded in 1976. It was a militant Tamil organization based in northern Sri Lanka. 'Aum Shrinko', a Japanese religious group founded in 1984, later began to militarize and resorted to bioterrorism. The Babbar Khalsa Khalistan movement, another militant group with headquarters in Canada, indulged in acts of terrorism to carve out an independent Khalistan in the Punjab region of India. One of the deadliest acts of terrorism carried out by this group was blowing up of Air India Flight 182 while it was in Irish airspace. With the rise of Islamic fundamentalism in several Muslim countries in the 1980s, there was rise in what has been termed as 'Islamic Terrorism'.

The emergence of 'New Terrorism' in the form of 'global jihad' feeds on the view that there is oppression of Muslims worldwide. They believe that the West's military strength and military dominance and their economic strength are the main reasons of oppression of Muslims. They reject Western cultural values. The terrorist groups use religion as a motivation with the purpose of using violence to obtain political power so as to establish order based on the Sharia Law. The operations of terror groups in Asia like Al-Qaeda, Ansar-ul-Sunn, and Islamic State of Iraq and Syria (ISIS) have caused immense damage to the peace and stability in a large part of Asia. Militant outfits like the Lashkar-e-Toiba (LeT) and Jaish-e-Mohammad (JeM) have been provided tacit support by Pakistan in funding, recruitment and training activities. The 'Mujahideens' and 'Taliban' were prominent among other terror groups, which have caused political, economic and social instability in Afghanistan.

The impact of terrorist acts which were previously limited to national boundaries became a trans-national phenomenon during the second half of the twentieth century and by the end of the century, it became a global phenomenon. The expansion of air traffic, popular use of television, as well as convergence of extremist groups with similar political or ideological goals led to the growth of trans-national terrorism. The Iranian 'Islamic Revolution' of 1979 was a watershed event in trans-national terrorism (Baylis, Smith & Owens, 2008, p. 375).

The main target of Islamic terror groups was Israel and its supporter, the USA. The attacks became more sophisticated and deadlier. Terror groups were frequently resorting to suicide attacks. With the end of the Cold War, trans-national terrorism amongst the Left-leaning terrorist groups was waning but militant Islamic terrorism was transforming into a global phenomenon.

'New terrorism' has gained much strength with globalization. The ultimate purpose of the extremists who supported militant Islam was to obtain political power and thereby establish political, social, economic and religious order as per the Sharia Law. Technological advancements in the global world further helped terrorist groups to improve their capabilities and plan devastating operations. The use of the Internet, wireless technologies, modern software, sophisticated electronic gadgets, creation of their own websites, videography, and modern fast communication have all helped the terrorist groups to integrate their activities on a global scale, to raise and transfer funds, procure arms and also to radicalize and select new recruits.

War on Terrorism

The attack on Washington and New York on 11 September 2001 brought terrorism to the centre of security issues. It triggered a global, US-led military offensive against terrorism. On 20 September 2001, President George Bush in a televised address to a joint session of Congress said, "Our war on terror begins with Al Qaeda but does not end there, it will not end there. It will not end until every terrorist groups of global reach has been found, stopped and defeated." He made it clear that the enemy is a radical network of terrorists and every government that supports them (*The Washington Post* online, 20 September 2001).

The United States of America-led military offensive against militant Islamic groups was mainly in the Middle-East, South-West Asia and Horn of Africa. The U.S.-led invasion in Iraq led to violent sectarian struggles which brought down the rule of Saddam Hussein in 2003. The U.S. intervention in Afghanistan, which began in late 2001, crushed the Taliban regime. But the Taliban regrouped and continued their offensive against the Afghanistan government and U.S. forces in Afghanistan. The U.S. government also gave assistance to the Philippines government to defeat the Muslim rebels who were fighting for autonomy in the southern islands. The USA also began to put pressure on Pakistan to initiate action against terror outfits operating from its land. The USA extended support to the 'moderate' Somali government to counter extremist groups operating there. There are also instances where U.S. intervention has led to escalation of conflict in many parts of the world. The U.S.-led global 'war on terror' interacted with local and regional tensions to create major instability in Iraq, Afghanistan, Pakistan, and the Horn of Africa (Burnell, 2008, p. 253).

Terrorism in West Asia

Issue of Palestine: In West Asia, both Jews and the Arabs increasingly resorted to militancy. Terrorist attacks became more and more frequent in this part of the world. The Munich massacre during the Summer Olympics in 1972 and the assassination of Anwar Sadat, the President of Egypt in Cairo on 6 October 1981, attracted international attention. After the Arab armies were defeated by Israel in the six-day war in June 1967, religiously motivated terror groups gained prominence in the Middle East. Organizations like Hamas, Palestine Islamic Jihad and Hezbollah continued their struggle against Israel and its supporters by increasingly resorting to acts of terrorism. Syria and Iran constantly tried to give aid and support to such groups fighting against Israel. During the Arab-Israel wars, Israel not only defeated the Arab forces but also occupied parts of Arab territories. A large number of Palestinians were forced to flee from the occupied land and live in refugee camps in pathetic conditions.

The conflicts between Israel and Palestinians have continued over the years. Several attempts have been made by the USA and the international community to bring peace to this part of the world. In 1993, under the Oslo Accords, the Israel and Palestine Liberation Organisation (PLO) agreed to officially recognize each other and renounce the use of violence. The Oslo Accord also established the Palestinian Authority which received limited autonomy in the Gaza Strip and parts of the West Bank. In 2014, the United Nations Human Rights Council (UNHRC) passed a resolution to probe Israel's human rights violation in Gaza. Despite the attempts to resolve the dispute, violence by terror groups supported by both the opposing parties have continued. The Joe Biden government in the USA has said it intended to "restore credible U.S. engagement with Palestinians as well as Israel"; Russia has backed a Palestinian proposal for a West Asia Peace Conference.

Iraq: Radical Muslim groups in West Asia received support from Pakistan and Saudi Arabia. The World Islamic Front for Jihad against Jews and Crusaders (WIFJAJC) was formed in 1996. It later developed into the Al-Qaeda led by Osama Bin Laden. Saudi Arabia also supported militant Islamic groups opposed to the rising power of the 'Shia Crescent' under the leadership of Iran. The Shia-Sunni conflict has spread to many countries of West Asia. This has led to a lot of bloodshed, untold suffering and gross violation of human rights of innocent people.

The U.S. intervention in Iraq in 2003 and subsequent dismantling of the government of Saddam Hussein also led to an increase in insurgency in this region. U.S. forces invaded Iraq on the ground that it possessed Weapons of Mass Destruction (WMDs), which it could not ever clearly prove. There was a surge of anger against the USA amongst Muslims around the world. It was during this time that the Al-Qaeda started to operate in Iraq. Later, some of these military officers broke away from Al-Qaeda to form the Islamic State. The new extremist outfit's objective was to establish an Islamic 'Caliphate' in northern Iraq and Syria. Very soon, it gained much strength as many disenchanted Muslims from around the world joined its ranks to carry out terrorist attacks against Western nations.

ISIS: On 29 June 2014, the establishment of the Islamic State of Iraq and Syria (ISIS) with Abu Baker Al Baghdadi as its Caliph was announced. It claimed religious authority over all the Muslims. Later, the name was change to Islamic State (IS). It became a well funded terrorist organization in the world. In 2015, the ISIS claimed responsibility for the suicide bombing in Beirut which killed about 40 Shia Muslims. It was responsible for downing a Russian airliner over Egypt killing 234 people. From its inception in 2014 until 2018, more than 140 terrorist attacks were carried out in as many as 29 countries, other than Iraq and Syria, have been attributed to the IS. Those attacks have killed at least 2,043 people and injured thousands of others (CNN World online, 2018, February 12).

As the ISIS conquered large parts of Iraq and Syria, even the survival of the Iraqi government was at stake. The USA adopted a "limited liability, limited risk" strategy to defeat the ISIS. The U.S. military and its coalition partners gave critical air support to the Iraq and Syria ground operations. The coalition airpower which provided essential intelligence and strategic air strikes halted the ISIS offensive. The coalition air strike began to target ISIS cash reserves and destroy ISIS's oil business. It has been estimated that the air strikes caused ISIS losses amounting to more than $ 500 million by August 2016. This, along with its territorial losses, weakened the organization considerably. The ISIS which held about a third of Syria and 40 per cent of Iraq lost 95 per cent of its territory by December 2017, including Mosul and Raqqa.

In 2018, Syrian Kurds and Arabs known as the Syrian Democratic Forces (SDF) backed by US forces captured key ISIS positions in eastern Syria. The town of Hajin was recaptured by the SDF. In March 2019, Baghauz, the last holdout of the ISIS, was captured which formally ended the Caliphate's claim to any territory. Finally, Baghadadi was killed in a US raid in northern Syria on 26 October 2019.

Effects of Terrorism: According to the Global Terrorism Database (GTD) 2018, the highest number of casualties caused by terrorism since 2001 has been concentrated in the Middle East.

Large-scale violence and murders leading to fear and uncertainty among the people of this region has adversely affected the economic progress and social fabric here. It has resulted in large-scale migration of people to other parts of the world to save their lives. An increased number of terrorist incidents also resulted in capital flight. The government's expenditure on public services and public welfare was drastically reduced as more funds are diverted to combat terrorists. In the meanwhile, the IS fighters, who withdrew from the frontline, formed cells in the mountainous and desert region of the hinterland of conflict-ridden countries might again become active.

Thus, it is essential that priority be given to resolve political disputes and establish stable governments in this region. Weak governments and political instability would invite outside interference and strengthen the terror groups. The global community needs to come together for a peaceful solution, which is essential for political stability, economic growth and social progress in this part of the world.

Terrorism in South Asia

South Asia has been facing serious challenges of terrorism, religious extremism, separatism, ethnic violence, and right-wing and left-wing terrorism. The existence of international terror organizations and their supporters in South Asia is identified as a threat to peace, prosperity and political stability of the countries of this region. Except for Bhutan and the Maldives, most of the countries of this region have been facing the challenge of some form of terrorism or the other for quite some time. Afghanistan, India, Pakistan and Sri Lanka have been largely been affected by acts of violence by terrorists and separatists. Terror groups have also become active in Bangladesh and Nepal. A large population of the people in South Asia is poor and illiterate. There is unequal wealth distribution in society. These factors have helped in the growth of terrorists with a political agenda, to find support and recruits.

Afghanistan: The ethnic, sectarian, regional and tribal identities are strong amongst Afghanistan's overwhelming Muslim population. Lack of a strong, stable and central government and institutional and internal factionalism were the root causes of external interference in Afghanistan. Saudi Arabia, Pakistan, the Soviet Union and the USA have intervened in the affairs of Afghanistan. Saudi Arabia and Pakistan helped in the growth of the Mujahideens (those who engage in 'jihad') and Sunni organizations.

The Soviet intervention in 1979 in Afghanistan fuelled the growth of groups espousing the cause of Islamic jihad. Terrorist organizations like the Taliban and Al-Qaeda gained strength and engaged in war with the Soviet forces. The mujahideens fighting Soviet occupation received a large quantity of arms and war material from countries opposed to Soviet occupation.

After the fall of the Soviet-backed Najibullah government in 1992, when Soviet forces withdrew, there was a state of civil war in Afghanistan. In 1994, the Taliban was able to conquer Kandahar city and by 1995, it was in control of 12 Afghan provinces. The Taliban was backed by Pakistan's Inter-Services Intelligence Agency (ISI). The Taliban held power from 1996 to 2001 and enforced a strict interpretation of 'Sharia' or Islamic Law. The Talibans committed systematic massacres against civilians, imposed severe restrictions on women, resorted to killing and violence, and engaged in cultural genocide. They destroyed numerous monuments including the Buddhas of Bamiyan. The Taliban regime had the support of the Al-Qaeda.

According to the USA, the leader of Al-Qaeda, Osama-bin-Laden was the mastermind of the 11 September attacks on the World Trade Centre and the Pentagon. The USA and allied forces initiated military action in October 2001 by bombing Taliban and Al-Qaeda related camps in Afghanistan. The ISI of Pakistan helped to evacuate a large number of Taliban militias and Al-Qaeda combatants from the conflict zones. Osama-bin-Laden, who was initially hiding in the Tora-Bora mountains, later escaped to Pakistan, after the fall of Taliban, and an interim government headed by Hamid Karzai of the Northern Alliance came to power in Afghanistan and a number of senior Al-Qaeda members were either captured or eliminated.

American intervention in Afghanistan and Iraq scattered the Al-Qaeda network and increased anti-Americanism amongst the Muslims. It helped in the spread of militant Islam. The IS-Khorasan (IS-K), an offshoot of the Islamic State (IS), has gained ground in Afghanistan. The Afghan Talibans have again regained ground in Afghanistan. The Doha deal between Washington and the Taliban in February 2020 bypassed the Afghan state. It has granted legitimacy to the Taliban and justification for the withdrawal of US forces from Afghanistan. Pakistan-based terror organizations such as the Tehrik-e-Taliban Pakistan, Lashkar-e-Toiba and other have a close relationship with the Taliban. The militants have no faith in the democratic process and rule of law. They strongly support a totalitarian system based on a narrow interpretation of the Sharia.

The return of the Taliban in Afghanistan has once again escalated acts of violence and violation of human rights. It has adverse security implications for neighbouring countries. It is feared that the U.S. troop withdrawal would escalate incidents of terror in Afghanistan. This may lead to an influx of refugees in Pakistan, increase cross-border terrorism and drug trafficking. The return of a pro-Pakistan Taliban is also a cause of concern for India as the jihadis operating against India have links with the Talibans.

India-Pakistan and Cross-Border Terrorism

The challenge of terrorism has been a major security issue before the Indian state. India has faced terror attacks from Islamic groups in Kashmir, Sikh separatists in Punjab, Naxalism in parts of Central India and a separatist movement in the eastern part of the country. India has lost two prime ministers due to acts of terrorism.

India has long been a victim of 'cross-border terrorism'. A large number of terror incidents, India has alleged, have been sponsored by the Pakistani military and the ISI. Numerous attacks on civilian and military personnel in Kashmir and various Indian cities have been attributed to the Lashkar-e-Toiba (LeT). Some prominent terror incidents linked to terror groups operating from Pakistan soil are the hijacking of an Indian Airlines flight in 1999, attack on the Red Fort in Delhi on 22 December 2000, attack on the Indian Parliament in December 2001 and the Mumbai attacks that killed about 200 people on 26 November 2008. India is also concerned about links between domestic terror groups such as SIMI and similar fundamentalist groups in Bangladesh, Nepal and Pakistan (Malone, 2019).

On February 14, 2019, a terror attack was carried out in Pulwama in Jammu and Kashmir by a suicide bomber belonging to the Jaish-e-Mohammad (JeM) which killed about 40 CRPF personnel. The United Nations Organization (UNO) and countries from across the globe condemned the brutal terror attack (*The Hindu*). On 26 February, about 12 days after the Pulwama incident, Indian Air Force jets bombed a JeM camp in Balakot, in Pakistan. India also launched diplomatic efforts to get JeM chief Masood Azhar designated as a global terrorist (*The Economic Times* online, 14 February 2020).

Naxalites are responsible for a high percentage of terror deaths in India. Many innocent people and a large number of security personnel have been killed due to such acts of terrorism. They have targeted industrial plants, transport systems, bridges, markets and religious places.

In Kashmir, the radical Islamic terrorist group perpetuated horrendous acts of brutality and human rights violations. Kashmiri Hindus of the Kashmir Valley were selectively targeted. They were killed, their houses burnt, shops looted, and women kidnapped and raped. They were given the option to leave or be killed. These atrocities and inhuman acts forced the Kashmiri Hindus to leave their homes and livelihood and flee to other parts of India. The pathetic part is that they are like refugees in their own country.

India has been consistently trying to fight the menace of terrorism, both at the global level and on the national front. It has proposed a 'Comprehensive Convention on International Terrorism (CCIT)' at the United Nations General Assembly, which would provide a legal basis to criminalize terrorist activities. India has supported the USA and the UNO in their efforts to curb international terrorism.

A number of laws have been passed by the Government of India to tackle the menace of terrorism. Some of them are:

- Unlawful Activities Prevention Act, 1967.
- Terrorist and Disruptive Activities (Prevention) Act (TADA), 1987. (TADA lapsed in 1995)
- The Maharashtra Control of Organised Crime Act (MCOCA), 1999.
- Prevention of Terrorism Act (POTA), 2002.

The abrogation of Articles 370 and 35(A) on 5 August 2019 was made to withdraw the special autonomous status given to the state of Jammu and Kashmir which will help the Government of India to integrate Kashmir with India in a meaningful manner and curb terrorism in the state.

Counter-terrorism measures require the co-operation of the countries of the Indian subcontinent. But the role of Pakistan to encourage subversive acts by terrorists in India, its nexus with the Taliban in Afghanistan, its policy to provide safe haven to international terrorists like Osama bin Laden and Maulana Masood Azhar have proved to be bottlenecks. The US Country Reports on Terrorism describe Pakistan as a "Terrorist Safe Haven", where terrorists are able to organize, plan, raise funds, communicate, recruit, train, transit and operate in relative security because of inadequate governance capacity, political will or both. Pakistan's involvement in providing logistics support to terrorist organisations led to the suspension of military aid to Pakistan by the Trump Administration. The US military aid to Pakistan decreased by 60 per cent between 2010 and August 2017 (Brown, 2018).

Osama bin Laden, the fugitive leader of Al-Qaeda was hiding in Abbottabad, Pakistan. His compound was raided by US Naval SEALs in a special operation in which Osama was killed on May 2, 2011.

The international community's concern and doubts about Pakistan's superficial efforts to check terrorist groups operating from its land has kept Islamabad in the 'grey list' of the Financial Action Task Force (FATF). This would make it difficult for the Pakistan Government to get financial aid from international lending agencies such as the International Monetary Fund (IMF) (*The Economic Times* online, 19 October 2019).

Sri Lanka: Sri Lanka has also been facing the challenge of terrorism for a long time. Ethno-nationalistic separation and religious extremism have been largely responsible for the growth of terrorism in Sri Lanka.

The Janatha Vinukthi Peranuna (JVP) and Liberation Tigers of Tamil Eelam (LTTE) have mainly been accused of causing immense destruction through acts of terrorism and subversion. The country faced some of the worst known acts of terrorism including massacres of civilians and assassination of political leaders. The JVP launched insurrections against the government in the 1970s and in the 1980s. The government used brutal force to crack down on the JVP. Government forces were involved in armed conflict with the LTTE which was fighting to create an independent Tamil state. Beginning from 1983, the war lasted for nearly three decades. During the course of the war, nearly one lakh people were killed. The LTTE was listed as a terror organization in 32 countries, including the USA, Canada, India and the European Union (EU). The LTTE's attacks on the Temple of the Tooth, a highly sacred Buddhist shrine in 1998 led to its proscription by the government. In May 2009, the government declared an end to the 25-year civil war after the army took control of the entire island and the death of Velupillai Prabhakaran, the leader of the LTTE.

Islamic terrorist organizations have also gained ground in Sri Lanka. The National Tawahujja Jama'ath (NTJ) is a Sri Lankan Islamic terrorist group responsible for the 21 April 2019 Sunday Easter bombings in Sri Lanka in which more than 260 people were killed. It is believed to have ties with the Islamic State (IS). The group was also responsible for killing Buddhists and Sufis. The government imposed an emergency shortly after the Easter bombings. The emergency laws gave the military and police sweeping powers to arrest and detain suspects without a court order. The two local Muslim groups that were responsible for the attacks claimed allegiance to the IS. The Sri Lankan authorities hunted down the members of these groups and announced that those directly responsible for the suicide bombing had either been killed or arrested.

Counter-terrorism measures have been used by the Sri Lankan government to deal with acts of terror on the island. The Prevention of Terrorism Act was enacted in 1978. It was a temporary law, which was made permanent in 1982. It provides the police with broad powers to search, arrest and detain suspects. In 1983, the Special Task Force (STF) was formed which specializes in counter-terrorism and counter-insurgency operations. The counter terrorism laws gave enormous discretionary powers to the security forces who have often been accused of blatantly misusing them.

Terrorism in South Asia: The Road Ahead: Religious extremism and terrorism has also emerged as a threat in Bangladesh. Militant groups are actively involved in criminal activities. The convergence of radical religious groups with organized crime syndicates is a growing challenge and threatens to trouble the South Asian region and beyond. The Harkat-ul-Jehad-al-Islami (HUJI), a designated terrorist outfit, has been running camps in different parts of the country to impart training to terror groups operating in India and Myanmar. The government in Bangladesh is acting against Islamic radical groups like the Jamat-ul-Mujahideen Bangladesh (JMB) and HUJI. A host of factors that are conducive for the spread of terrorism in Bangladesh include unemployment, poverty, rising religious fundamentalism and easy availability of firearms.

Bhutan also faces a threat from Maoist groups who are active in India and Nepal. Bhutan has not allowed separatist organizations from the northeastern region of India like the ULFA to set up camps in Bhutan.

Islamic fundamentalist groups have now become active even in the Maldives. Though the problem of terrorism is not acute, it may grow in times to come. There have been reports of some Maldivians having joined Al-Qaeda cadres.

The rise in growth in religious fundamentalism and support for such fundamentalists from political parties and groups is a major problem in South Asia. The activities of the terror groups are not confined to national boundaries. The required political will and cooperation amongst the countries of South Asia to effectively tackle this problem is lacking.

The UN General Assembly adopted the UN Global Counter-Terrorism Strategy for South Asia in the light of the problem of terrorism faced by South Asia. The strategy has broad-based political support which may offer states in the region the opportunity to develop a coherent and holistic response to the threat of terrorism in South Asia (Rosand, Fink & Ipe, 2009).

Regional organisations like the South Asian Association of Regional Cooperation (SAARC) and the Bay of Bengal Initiative for Multi-Sectoral Technical and Economic Cooperation (BIMSTEC) have devised potentially useful counter-terrorism instruments but unfortunately only a few have been translated into action by the member-countries. The SAARC Regional Convention on Suppression of Terrorism was signed at Kathmandu on 4 November 1987. SAARC also created the Terrorist Offences Monitoring Desk (STOMD) and the Drug Offences Monitoring Desk (SDOMD). But tensions between India and Pakistan have inhibited necessary cooperation for effective implementation of measures suggested by SAARC. BIMSTEC faces limitations in promoting regional counter-terrorism cooperation, as Pakistan is not its member (Rosand, Fink & Ipe, 2009, pp. 1-8).

Terrorism in South-East Asia and other parts of Asia

Terrorism has affected regional security in South-East Asia since the 1990s. In the 21st century, the threat has amplified as there has been a growing consolidation of diverse terrorist groups operating on regional and international bases. Networks of terror groups linked with the Al-Qaeda and the IS gained a foothold in South-East Asia. Through their decentralization strategy, they have not only managed to establish links with smaller local terrorist groups operating in South-East Asia but have also created financial opportunities that help them to carry out and expand their operations in this region.

Some of the terror groups operating in South-East Asia are the Jemaah Islamiyah (JI), and Indonesia-based groups called Jamaat Ansharut Daulat (JAD), Abu Sayyaf group (ASG), and Maute group. In 2018, there was a series of coordinated suicide bombing in Indonesia. The process of radicalisation and the growing number of ISIS sympathisers in Malaysia is also a cause of concern.

South-East Asian countries realize the threat to peace and security of this region from terrorism. The Association of South East Asian Nations (ASEAN) has come together to tackle this problem. The role of the Shanghai Cooperation Organisation (SCO) in countering the threat of terrorism is important. In its summit meeting held in Astana, Kazakhstan, in June 2017, the SCO resolved to develop a permanent body, the Regional Anti-Terrorist Structure (RATS). This has helped SCO member-states to prevent a number of terrorist attacks while still in the planning stage.

China has been facing terror attacks carried out by Uighur separatists in the Xinjiang province. They are fighting for an independent state in the north-western province of Xinjiang which they call 'Eastern Turkestan'.

In Russia, terrorist threats are presented by the Islamic insurgents in the North Caucasus, especially in Chechnya, Dagestan, Ingushetia, and Kabardino-Balkariya. The Chechen terrorist groups have increasingly resorted to random attacks on military installations, on tourists and deliberate killings of foreign-aid workers, kidnapping and hostage taking. They were responsible for the raid on Beslan's school in September 2004 in which 334 people were killed, including 186 children.

The greatest threat to the Central Asian States is from groups like the Islamic Movement of Uzbekistan (IMU), an Islamic terrorist organization and the Hizb-ut-Tahris (HT), an international pan-Islamist fundamental political organization. The governments of Russia, Azerbaijan, Kazakhstan, Turkmenistan and Iran participated in an anti-terrorism conference on 14 July 2005 focussing on preventing attacks against oil and natural gas pipelines in the Caspian Sea.

How to Counter Terrorism

The growth of terrorism has created not only security problems but endangered the lives of the people. In 1994, the General Assembly of the UNO passed a resolution condemning "all acts, methods and practices of terrorism, as criminal and unjustifiable, wherever and by whomever committed, including those which jeopardize the friendly relations among states and peoples and threaten the territorial integrity and security of States". The resolution also urged states to refrain from organizing, instigating, facilitating, financing, encouraging or tolerating terrorist activities. After the 9/11 attacks, the United Nations Security Council (UNSC) passed resolution 1373 which imposed several obligations on member-states including efforts to prevent and suppress the financing of terrorist acts, freezing of funds, financial assets and economic resources of persons committing or participating in commission or facilitating terrorist activities (Ghosh, 2016).

The United Nations has emphasized on four pillars of counter-terrorist strategy:

- Measures to address conditions conducive to the spread of terrorism.
- Measures to prevent and combat terrorism.
- Measures to build capacity of the states to prevent and combat terrorism and strengthen the role of the United Nations in this regard.
- Measures to ensure respect for Human Rights for all and the Rule of Law as the fundamental basis of the fight against terrorism (Rosand et. al., 2009, pp. 11-23).

To counter the menace of terrorism, the states have to be alert and vigilant to such threats. Co-operation and co-ordination amongst them at the regional and international levels is imperative to counter terrorism. Countries need to upgrade and invest in security measures to protect people and organizations that become targets of terror attacks. They should have a mechanism that monitors potential terrorists and promptly identifies individuals who may become radicalized. Websites that use hate speech or call for violence or discrimination should be taken down. Governments should take measures to combat terror financing. There should be systematic sharing of information amongst the countries to combat trans-national organized crime and terrorism.

There should be sufficient safeguards in anti-terrorism laws so that they are not misused. Some of the root causes that breed terrorism like poverty, unemployment and political instability should be looked into and resolved through political will. It is increasingly acknowledged that unless social economic and political contexts are addressed and othe tactics such as diplomacy and intelligence are deployed, problems wil not disappear and global terrorism could escalate (Burnel, 2008, p. 362).

As the global security landscape is marked by multiplication of intra state conflicts, the rise of trans-national crime and the spread of terrorisn have become major sources of concern for Asia and the internationa community. The pandemic, which has engulfed the world since 2020, has slowed down economic growth. When funds are being diverted to contro the pandemic and its effects, there would be cost cutting on expenditure on welfare schemes, security mechanisms and counter-terrorism measures. Asian countries can embark on a path of economic progress and ensure that the human rights of the people are protected by co-ordinating their national efforts with the regional and global institutions to tackle the problem of terrorism. The objective of the global community should be to sustain a stable security environment where peaceful resolution of disputes is possible and respect for universal rights and freedom is ensured.

REFERENCES

Akmat, G.; Zaman, K.; Shukui, T. & Sajjad, F. (2013, November). Exploring the root cause of terrorism in South Asia: Everybody should be Concerned. *Quality and Quantity*, November, 2013. Retrieved from http://dx.doi.org/10.1007/s11135-013-9941-2

Alimov, R. (2017, November 16). The role of the Shanghai Cooperation Organization in counteracting threats to peace and security. *UN-iLibrary*, 54(3), 34-37. https://www.un-iLibrary.org/content/journals/15643913/54/3/19

Baylis, J.; Smith, S. & Owens, P. (2008). *The Globalization of World Politics*. New York : Oxford University Press.

Brown, V. F. (2018), Why Pakistan supports terrorist group, and why the US finds it so hard to induce change, *Order from Chaos*. Retrieved from https://www.brookings.edu>blog>2018/01/05

Burke, J. (2007). Al-Qaeda :*The True Story of Radical Islam*. Harmondsworth :Penguin

Burnel, P.; Randall, V. & Rakner, L. (2008). (3rd edn). *Politics in the Developing World*. New York : Oxford University Press.

Chakma, B. (2014), Global Flight Against Terrorism in Afghanistan: Impact on South Asian Security. In Chakma B. (ed.) (2014). *South Asia in Transition*. (pp. 155-173). Retrieved from https://www.link.springer.com

Challaney, B. (2001). Fighting Terrorism in Southern Asia : The Lessons of History. *International Security*, 26(3), 94-116. Retrieved from Google Scholar.

Chari, P. R.; Cheema, P. I. & Cohen, S. P. (2008). *Four Crisis and a peace process: American Engagement in South Asia*. Delhi: Harper Collins.

Chung, C. (2002, September 1). China's "War in Terror". *Foreign Affairs*. Retrieved from https://www.foreignaffairs.com/articles/asia/2002-07-01/chinas-war-terror-september-11-and-uighur-seperatism

Clarke, R. (2010). Laskhar-i-Taiba : Roots, Logistics partnership, and the fallacy of subservient proxies. *Terrorism Political Violence*, 22(3) : 395-418. Retrieved from Google Scholar.

Gaur, M. (ed.) (2003). *Terrorism and Human Rights*. New Delhi: *FPRC Journal*.

Ghosh, P. (2016). *International Relations*. New Delhi : PI Learning.

Heywood, A. (2014). *Global Politics*. New York : Palgrave MacMillan

Jamal, U. (2021), Treacherous Triangle: Afghanistan, India and Pakistan After US Withdrawal. Retrieved from https://www.thediplomat.com/2021/05treacherous-tringle-afganistan-india-and-pakistan

Johnson, C. G. (2016, November 1). The Rise and fall of Islamic State in Afghanistan. *USIP*. Retrieved from https://www.jstor.org

Khattake, A. (2021, April 29). US withdrawal from Afghanistan Means India, China and Russia Need to Cooperate. *South Asia*. Retrieved from https://thewire.in

Malone, D. M. (2019). *Does the Elephant Dance?* New Delhi : Oxford University Press.

Manoharan, N. (2009, November 14-20). Trojan Horses : Counter-terror Laws and Security in India. *Economic and Political Weekly*, 44(46), 22-24. Retrieved from https://www.jstor.org.stable

Mukhopadhyay, A. (ed.) (2012). *Social Movements in India*. New Delhi: Pearson–ICFAI.

Noor, S. (2007, April). Pakistan-India Relations and Terrorism. *Pakistan Horizon*, 60(2), 65-85.

Ogden, C. (ed.) (2016). *New South Asian Security*. New Delhi: Orient Blackswan.

Ollapally, D. M. (2009). *The Politics of Extremism in South Asia*. New Delhi : Cambridge University Press.

Patra, S. (2019, 13 May). Economic-Consequences of Terrorism in South Asia. In Das, R. C. (ed.) *The Impact of Global Terrorism on Economic and Political Development*. (pp. 179-190). Retrieved from https://books.emeraldinsight.com/resources/pdfs/chapters/9781787699205-TYPE23-NR2.pdf

Pokharana, B. (2017, February). Radical Islam and the Spread of Global Terrorism : An Analysis. *World Focus*, 38(2), 59-66.

Rosand, E.; Fink, N. C. & Ipe, J. (2009). *Countering Terrorism in South Asia :Strengthening Multilateral Engagement*. International Peace Institute. Doi: ipinst.org/wp-content/uploads/publications/ct-in-South Asia-epub.pdf.

Roy, C. (2011, November). Terrorism in India and Legislation for its Prevention. Retrieved from https://www.10.5958/j.0974-5041.5.2.020

Saigal, V. (2004). *Global Terrorism: The Way Forward*. New Delhi: New Dawn Press.

Sinai, J. (2015, Fall). The Terrorist Threats Against Russia and its Counterterrorism Response Measures. *Connection*. 14(4), 95-108. Retrieved from https://www.jstor.org/ stable/e26326412.

Tellis, A. J. (2019, March 14). A Smouldering Volcano: Pakistan and Terrorism after Balakot. Retrieved from https://carnegieendownment.org>2019/03/14>smoldering-volcanopakistan-and-terrorism-after-balakot-pub-78593.

The Economic Times (2019, October 19). Doi: economictimes.indiatimes.com/news/politics-and-nation/fatf-actions-pakistan-is-under-severe-international-pressure-that-india-has-helped-mount/article.

Tripathi, S. (2016, Spring). Understanding Terrorism and Geopolitics in West Asia. *World Affairs : The Journal of International Issues*, 20(1), 42-53. Retrieved from https://www.jstor.org

Tripathi, S. (2017, February). Radical Islam and Terrorism in West Asia, *World Focus*, 38(2), 39-45.

https://edition.cnn.com/

https://en.wikipedia.org/wiki/Global_Terrorism_Database

https://icct.nl>publication
https://ohchr.org
https://un.org
https://www.brookings.edu
https://www.em.wikipedia.org/wiki/terrorism-in-central-asia
https://www.ohchr.org/Documents/Issues/Rule of Law/Negative Effects of Terrorism NHRI-Afghanistan.pdf
https://www.thehindu.com

20

Cyber Security in Global Times: Overview, Issues and Challenges

Sumit Saurabh Srivastava

Introduction

> 'Securing cyber space will inevitably involve highly detailed engineering and computer science techniques. But those disciplines alone can only ever provide partial answers to what are inherently political questions' (Deibert, 2018).

We are living in an 'information age' centred around information and communication technology (ICT) denoted as a 'global village' by Marshall McLuhan which is characterized by increasingly (and frighteningly!) 'digitally wired' human existence. One can also invoke what Manuel Castells has termed as the 'network society' which now has metamorphosed into a hydra-headed, unfathomable and bottomless 'cyber space' which, sans geographical/territorial and legal boundaries is flagged by worldwide proliferation of information systems. Cyber space is thus fuelled by intensive and extensive globalization of Information and Communication Technologies (ICTs). As of now, cyber space, created and constructed through the World Wide Web Internet-based online activities gazes back at us as a hydra-headed entity. What frightens us today is its unfathomable vastness and bottomless expansion. Its uses (and abuses/misuses) affects today's geopolitics, economics, and social life. Globally, as we are increasingly being 'hooked up' to the Internet and making our presence 'online', it has seeped into our lives. It needs to be noted that the United Nations (UN) specialized agency for ICTs International Telecommunication Union (ITU) estimates that at the end of 2019, 53.6 per cent of the global population, or 4.1 billion people, are using the Internet.[1] Along with such massive 'digital footprints', we are also witnessing rapid Science and Technology (S&T) & ICT innovations like the Internet of Things (IoT), Big Data, Cloud Computing and, above all, artificial intelligence (AI) and their subsequent utility / use in our daily lives. Such a digitally connected scenario has led to the emergence of what has been coming to be known as cyber space / virtual world / cyber world / digital world among others. Today, on one hand, such digital footprints have made our lives much comfortable and advanced in terms of utilizing science and technology to suit our day-to-day mundane needs; on the other, it has also made us insecure to an extent hitherto unknown due to increase in cybercrimes and cyber attacks. Individual incidents related to phishing, computer virus and worm attacks, identity theft, and online bank / financial frauds have become a daily affair in today's times. Moreover, organized at the 'grand level', cyber space's fair share of disadvantages is also reflected in the alleged Russian interference in the United States presidential elections in the recent past (Fidler, 2017; Ohlin; 2017; CNN 2019)[2] among others. According to the World Economic Forum, 'Cyber criminals are using more advanced and scalable tools to breach user privacy, and they are getting results. Two billion data records were compromised in 2017 and more than 4.5 billion records were breached in the first half of 2018 alone.'[3] It further notes that 'economic loss due to cyber crime is predicted to reach $ 3 trillion by 2020, and 74 per cent of the world's businesses can expect to be hacked in the coming year.'[4] Most importantly, continuous and relentless attempts of cyber attack have become a regular common place feature of the international order in contemporary times wherein one nation-state / group / organization or the other is hacking (including ransomware, formjacking, and cloud security) its opponents' information network so as to further its (un)just cause. What we see here is that a nation-state's sovereignty, jurisdiction and control over itself becomes porous and superfluous in the wake of cyber activities and operations performed by the so-called 'hacktivists' or 'patriotic / nationalist hackers'. This paper stands at the intersection of such a scenario.

Cyber Space, Cyber Attack and Cyber Security: Terminology and Basic Concepts

Cyber space at the basic level is an abstract virtual 'space', which is underlined by the ICT-enabled computer networks wired across the globe. Through these 'networks' is the free flow of information at breakneck speed and ferocity. In his now classic text, *A Declaration of the Independence of Cyber Space* (1996), John P. Barlow stated that 'Cyber space consists of transactions, relationships, and thought itself, arrayed like a standing wave in the web of our communications. Ours is a world that is both everywhere and nowhere, but it is not where bodies live.'[5] For Schmitt, 'Since the digital revolution, the exponential growth of information and communication technology has created a complex web of networked systems. This is the new and vibrant environment that we know as cyber space' (Schmitt, 2015). Matania et. al. have outlined three fundamental characteristics of cyberspace which include, 'First, cyber space is a man-made domain of computerized systems, networks, and their interconnections—each of them ultimately owned and operated by a defined organization; Second, cyber threats all but ignore national borders as they take advantage of interconnectivity to target organizations directly; and Third, cyber security is inextricable from the organization's functioning' (Matania et. al., 2016). According to the National Cyber Security Policy 2013 of the Government of India, 'Cyber space is a complex environment consisting of interactions between people, software and services, supported by worldwide distribution of ICT devices and networks.' From these definitions, one can infer that cyber space is an abstract virtual entity, which is a by-product of the ever-increasing digitalization of our transactions and day-to-day activities through the World Wide Web, i.e., the Internet. In recent times, terms like cyber citizen and cyber sovereignty (Jensen, 2014) and cyber-diplomacy (Barrinha & Renard, 2017) have become prominent.

Cyber space is not free from its vices as it is marked by frequent incidents ranging from misdemeanour to criminal activities designated as cyber attacks, cyber crime, cyber espionage and cyber terrorism. It has consequently given rise to the urgent need for national/global laws pertaining to cyber security on the one hand and cyber ethics and cyber governance on the other. Way back in 1986, the Organisation for Economic Co-operation and Development (OECD) spoke of computer 'abuse', which was defined as 'any illegal, unethical or unauthorized behaviour relating to the automatic processing and transmission of data (OECD, 1986). In today's times, there are three ways by which cyber threats can manifest themselves; cyber crimes and cyber attacks, cyber security, and cyber warfare, which, according to Viano, have computer systems as their 'common denominator' (Viano, 2013). Brown and Tullos have outlined a 'Spectrum of Cyber Space Operations' wherein cyber operations are divided into broad categories named access, disruption and attack (Brown & Tullos, 2012). Highlighting the nefarious extent of info-terrorism and cyber warfare, Laqueur has noted the possibility of 'information warfare' (Laqueur, 2011; also see Jarvis & Macdonald, 2015).

Lin has used the term 'offensive cyber operations' (Lin, 2012) whereas, according to Jahankhani et. al., cyber crime categories include 'phishing, spam, hacking, cyber harassment or bullying, identity theft, plastic card fraud and Internet auction fraud' (Jahankhani, 2014). *The Global Risks Report 2019* by the World Economic Forum (2019) has flagged technological risks as one of the global risks (pp. 98).[6] Similarly, Lahmann has underlined a continuum of cyber crime, cyber espionage and cyber terrorism (Lahmann, 2020). Zouave et. al. have outlined various possibilities of artificial intelligence (AI) enabled cyber attack (Zouave, 2020). *The Global Cyber Security Index v3 (2018/2019)* speaks of cyber threats which are 'The potential of a malicious attempt to damage or disrupt a computer network or system with unauthorized access to a control system device using a data communications pathway' (*ibid.* 76).[7] Similarly, Choo and Grabosky have outlined three types of organized crime groups who exploit digital technology, which are traditional and organized crime groups along with organized groups of ideologically-motivated individuals (Choo & Grabosky, 2013). Cavelty has identified three threat representations within cyber space. These are 'the portrayal of malware by using a biological register (virus/worms); the description of disembodied miscreants (hackers); and complex interrelationships between critical infrastructures and the cyber-substructure, and a subsequent emphasis on vulnerability' (2013: 106). Some of the most common cyber-attacks include phishing, ransomware, DDoS (Distributed Denial-of-Service) and computer virus, among others. The types of malware include logic bomb, Trojan horse, key-logger, virus, root-kit and web-based malware. Another significant example is botnet which is a network of Internet-connected and malware-infected devices. It is used to distribute spam and malware, or launch distributed denial-of-service attacks. Rid and McBurney have discussed cyber weapons in detail (Rid & McBurney, 2012). More specialized and professional forms of cyber crime and cyber attack include 'cross-site scripting used to pilfer consumers' passwords, large-scale breaches of corporate customers' personal information, distributed denial-of-service attacks on websites, cyber espionage aimed at classified documents, and attacks on civil critical infrastructures' (Mulligan & Schneider, 2011). Many such cyber threats and attacks through Client-Server Platform Attacks and Security Platforms Manipulation among others have emerged in recent times causing severe strain in the relations between various countries.[8] The Global Programme on Cyber Crime of the United Nations Office on Drugs and Crime (UNODC) has outlined types of Internet-related crimes. They are i) offences against the confidentiality, integrity and availability of computer data and systems; ii) computer-related offences; iii) content-related offences; and iv) offences related to infringements of copyright and related rights.[9] Interpol has underlined "Pure cyber crime"[10] whereas, according to the National Cyber Security Policy 2013 of the Government of India, 'A cyber-related incident of national significance may take any form; an organized cyber-attack, an uncontrolled exploit such as computer virus or worms...'.[11]

As far as nation-states' cyber security against the use of cyber force and cyber armed attack is concerned, as 'cyber security goes beyond the boundaries of traditional information security' (Solms & Niekerk, 2013), Porche et. al. have rightly pointed out that 'From a defensive perspective, it is difficult to imagine how to defend a space that has no boundaries, changes constantly, lets anyone in, and exists virtually everywhere' (Porche et. al., 2011). In a comprehensive way, Cavelty has outlined three interlocking cyber-security discourses which are; first, viruses, worms and other bugs (technical discourse); second, cyber-crooks and digital spies (crime-espionage discourse); and third, conflicts and vital system security (military-civil defence discourse) (Cavelty, 2012; also see Stytz & Banks, 2014). O'Grady and Dwyer note that cyber security "involves and invokes socio-political complications around criminality, protection, inequalities, privacy, surveillance, private enterprise, and the role of the state in the life of citizens" (O'Grady & Dwyer, 2020). Table 1 details the variables of cyber-security.

Table 1: Mapping the Field of Cyber-Security

	I	II	III	IV
Main Actors	Hacking Subculture	Business Actors	Civil defence/ Homeland security	Military
	Computer (security) experts	Anti-virus industry		
		Law enforcement		
		Intelligence community		
Referent Object	Computers	Private sector (business networks)	Critical (information) infrastructures Society (particularly its 'functioning')	Networked armed forces (military networks)
	Computer networks	Classified information (government networks)		Nation/state
Threats	Malware	Advanced Persistent Threats (Malware)	Disruptions in critical infrastructures	(Catastrophic) attacks on critical infrastructures
	Network disruptions	Cyber-Criminals (Non-state)	Cascading effects	Cyber-terrorists (Non-state)
	Hackers (all kinds)	Cyber-Spies (State)	Cyber-terrorists (Non-state) Cyber-commands (State)	Cyber-spies (State) Cyber-commands (State)

Source: Cavelty (2013: 109).

Cyber Security and International Legal Framework: Framing the Issues

As already pointed out, the security concerns regarding cyber attacks, cyber crimes and cyber hazards easily transgress the geographical and territorial boundaries of the nation-states. Seen in this way, a global effort in this regard has been a welcome move. Michael N. Schmitt, the Project Director of the *Tallinn Manual on the International Law Applicable to Cyber Warfare* highlighted that 'Cyber espionage, theft of intellectual property, and a wide variety of criminal activities in cyber space pose real and serious threats to all states, as well as to corporations and private individuals. An adequate response to them requires national and international measures' (Schmitt, 2013). Commenting on how the emergence of cyber space has altered the basic tenets and vision of international relations, it has been noted that 'The deterrence theories and strategies created and employed during the Cold War are not easily portable to the cyber domain' (Choucri & Goldsmith, 2012) as the territorial boundaries of the nation-states in contemporary times have become vulnerable to the possibilities of cyber war and cyber warfare. Cyber attacks denote a global security threat which can be and needs to be effectively neutralized by cyber stability and cyber cooperation across nation-states, as a consequence of which global and/ or transnational cyber laws and legislations are needed to govern cyber space to counter not only cyber war, cyber-attack but also cyber terrorism (Tehrani et. al., 2013; also see Mulligan & Schneider, 2011; Lipton, 2015; Tsagourias, 2015).

Internationally, the World Summit on Information Society is a significant entity that has been working on devising mutually agreeable cyber policies and guidelines. Other similar global entities are the International Telecommunications Union (ITU) and the IGF (Internet Governance Forum), the Internet Corporation for Assigned Names and Numbers (ICANN) and the Internet Engineering Task Force (IETF); and the OECD Guidelines for the Security of Information Systems 1992, which subsequently have been replaced by the 2002 OECD Guidelines for the Security of Information Systems and Networks: Towards a Culture of Security.[12] Some of the steps taken at the global level which reflects upon the international community's concern regarding cyber space, cyber security and sovereignty of the nation-states are the Commonwealth of Independent States Agreement on Cooperation in Combating Offences related to Computer Information 2001; Council of Europe's Convention on Cyber Crime 23 November 2001 (entered into force 1 July 2004); Shanghai Cooperation Organisation, Agreement on Cooperation in the Field of International Information Security 16 June 2009; League of Arab States Convention on Combating Information Technology Offences 2010 and African Union Convention on Cyber Security (Draft) 2012, among others (see Nykodym & Taylor, 2004; Kettemann, 2017).

Notwithstanding the intricate, complex and multi-layered debates surrounding Article 2(4) of the UN Charter and the meaning of 'Force' inherent in it (Waxman, 2011; Kilovaty, 2015), it needs to be noted that some of the key resolutions of the United Nations (UN) like Resolution 55/63, January 2001 and Resolution 64/211, March 2010 among others are also related to the issue of cyber security.[13] In its Resolution 57/239, January 2003 (Creation of a global culture of cyber security), the UN underlined nine complementary elements of a global culture of cyber security which included awareness, responsibility response, ethics, democracy, security design and implementation, security management and reassessment.[14] The International Telecommunication Union (ITU) as the United Nations specialized agency for information and communication technologies and Global Cyber Security Agenda (GCA) initiated in 2007[15] also play important role in this regard. In spite of certain challenges in having global laws and policies for cyber safety and security (Chaturvedi, 2018); the Global Cyber Security Index v3 (2018/2019) states that by 2018, about 177 (91 per cent) countries have cyber crime legislation so as to counter the 'dangers of the Dark Web' in the information and digital age.[16]

State, Non-State Entities and Cyber Security Incidents

Cyber crimes more than often are considered as the handiwork of non-state actors, for example, the May 2017 WannaCry Ransomware attack. However, the recent past has witnessed an aggressive play enacted by various nation-states in the cyber world wherein they have been taking the lead in cyber attacks and cyber espionage; 'Of course, while no country takes responsibility for cyber-attacks, attribution is sometimes not too difficult to assign'.[17] It is in this context that Craig and Valeriano have aptly flagged that 'Cyber space is now considered the fifth domain of warfare after land, sea, air, and space' (Craig &Valeriano, 2016) and incidents of cyber attacks and cyber warfare are the fallout of the global cyber arms race. Some instances are discussed below in brief. Tikk et. al. (2010) have outlined 'cyber incidents that occurred in the world in 2007-2008 and were characterised by a strong political undertone' (Tikk et. al., 2010). The cyber incidents discussed by Tikk et. al. (2010) are cyber attacks against Estonia in April-May 2007; cyber attacks against Radio Free Europe/Radio Liberty, in particular its Belarus service, in April 2008; cyber attacks against Lithuanian websites in June-July 2008; and cyber attacks against Georgia in August 2008. Inkster has discussed cyber espionage linked with China (Inkster, 2015) and Segal has elaborated upon cyber espionage issues with reference to China and the USA (Segal, 2013; also see Gompert & Libicki, 2014). Some of the significant cyber attacks are discussed in brief. The Estonia and Russia standoff in 2007 is an incident of paramount significance in this regard.[18] It so appeared that Estonia suffered three waves of cyber attacks between April 26 and May 18, 2007 allegedly by Russia. Cyber weapons used in this cyber attack included Distributed Denial of Service (DDoS), website defacement and implanting malware among others which crashed Estonia's Internet system deeply affecting its political and financial institutions (Baezner, 2018). It appeared that Estonia's heavy dependence and reliance on IT infrastructure made it vulnerable to mass cyber-attack. What distinguishes this singular event from the earlier individualised cases of 'stray' events of cyber interferences was that cyber attacks on Estonia were seen as the first case of 'cyber war' (Mite, 2007; Ball, 2007) and in a way heralding 'Web War I' (Blank, 2008). In August 2008, Georgia was the victim of so-called 'Hybrid warfare'; it was 'Hybrid warfare' as the cyber attack was carried out during the Russo-Georgian war wherein the Russian military forces along with their army of hackers attacked Georgia. Cyber weapons used in this cyber attack were similar to those employed during the Estonian cyber attacks, i.e., Distributed Denial of Service (DDoS), website defacement and implanting malware. Along with these, the hackers/attackers used the SQL INJECTION method to hack 100 Georgian websites along with Border Gateway Protocol (BGP hijacking) to reroute Internet traffic (Napetvaridze & Chochia, 2019). Along with the government-owned websites, the Bank of Georgia had to suspend all electronic services from August 8 to 19, 2008. To counter such frequent cyber attacks, Georgia enacted the 'Law on Information Security', which entered into force on 1 July 2012. The cyber-attack infused incidents related to Estonia (2007), Georgia (2008), and Ukraine (2013-present) attests to the fact that 'Offensive cyber through hacktivists and cyber-criminal syndicates is playing a greater role in conventional Russian military operations and may potentially play a role in the future in Russia's strategic deterrence framework' (Connell & Vogler, 2017). In sync with the aims of the operation called 'Olympic Games' (Kaminski, 2020), the Stuxnet computer worm which reportedly destroyed numerous centrifuges in Iran's Natanz uranium enrichment facility in June 2010 'appeared to have been created by the U.S. National Security Agency, the CIA, and Israeli Intelligence'.[19] It significantly crippled Iran's uranium enrichment program allegedly aimed towards development of nuclear programmes by disrupting parts of the facility's control system. Since then, the 'invisible U.S.-Iran cyber war' has been escalating as is evident in the frequent incidents of cyber attacks by both the parties on each other (Hanna, 2019; O'Flaherty, 2020). The subsequent modified versions of the Stuxnet worm, which created cyber havoc across the world, include Duquin 2011, Flame 2012, Havexin 2013, Industroyer 2016, and Triton 2017. It also needs to be pointed out here that cyber attacks like Operation Aurora in the latter half of 2009 and Night Dragon in February 2011 both originated from China targeting Western countries.[20] The beginning of the year 2020 saw a border dispute between India and China which soon escalated to cyber attacks allegedly originating from China on India (CSIS, 2020). The same and other related cyber attack incidents were widely reported by media houses in India.[21] India practising its "Cyber Space Sovereignty' against China" (Jung, 2020), banned 59 Chinese mobile applications including Tik Tok, WeChat, and Weibo within its borders with immediate effect on 1 July 2020 (Press Information Bureau, GoI, 2020).

National Security and Cyber Security Policy: Some Cases

Cyber security, as a non-traditional security issue, is one of the most pressing issues on the national security agenda of respective nation-states in contemporary times aiming to 'establish their role in cyber space' (Malin et. al., 2017). Foreign policies are increasingly being reframed as 'digital' foreign and defence policy. As everything is globally connected, cyber security is a global challenge. Public policy initiatives taken by countries regarding national security engulfing cyber security focus on cyber criminal legislation and cyber security regulations along with cyber security research and development programs. Tikk et. al. (2010) have given an exhaustive list of requirements for an effective cyber policy and cyber law. One also finds the presence and significance of legal institutions and frameworks addressing cyber security and cyber crime mediated through digital governance so as to minimise the threat to data integrity and restrict data confidentiality breaches. Given the 'global/trans-regional/trans-national' nature of cyber space, it also includes elements of bilateral agreements and multilateral agreements along with participation of international associations. We also need to understand that cyber attacks and cyber wars have a significant impact on international ethics and politics.

It is also pertinent to note that the notions of security and national security have evolved over a period of time reflecting its changing nature and context (Sperling, 2014). Unprecedented technological developments have given rise to increasingly diverse new security threats to countries across the world. At the basic level, security may mean resilience to vulnerability or threat. Cha argues that globalization has transformed the meaning of security to non-physical security, i.e., 'protection of information and technology assets' (Cha, 2011). In International Relations in particular and Security Studies in general, the term 'security' is entangled with national security. According to Baldwin, 'National security has figured prominently in academic and political discussions of foreign policy and international politics since the end of World War II' (Baldwin, 1997). Pointing out the ambiguity in the concept of the security (national) and conflating it with national interest, Wolfers flags that "national interest" subordinates other interests to those of the nation' (Wolfers, 1952). For Tapia-Valdes, national security policies can be Outward Oriented, National Securitism and Inward Oriented (Tapia-Valdes, 1982). In recent decades, with the explosion of ICTs-enabled Internet and networks and increasing incidents of cyber attacks, cyber security has become an integral part of the national and international security policies and strategies, debates and concerns (Cavelty & Wenger, 2020). It has also been argued that cyber threats and cyber espionage should be addressed through international laws pertaining to them (Buchan, 2015). Matania et. al. have proposed a three-layered approach towards a comprehensive national cyber security strategy which entails 'robustness, resilience and defence' (Matania, 2016).

It is in this context that many countries at present have made cyber security the core of their national security policies and agenda. One can discuss a few instances of the same. The National Cyber Strategy of the USA, (September 2018) highlights how it aims to 'defend the homeland by protecting networks, systems, functions, and data.'[22] Subsequently, the Cyber Security and Infrastructure Security Agency (CISA) was established.[23] The National Cyber Security Centre, UK, established in 2016 and headquartered at London defines cyber security 'to protect the devices we all use (smartphones, laptops, tablets and computers), and the services we access—both online and at work—from theft or damage.'[24] In the footsteps of The 2011 National Cyber Security Strategy, UK's policy paper on National Cyber Security Strategy 2016 to 2021 was formulated.[25] The Russian Federation has one of the extensive lists of Acts, Guidelines and Protocols related to its own information security and cyber security, i.e., Doctrine of Information Security, out of which two distinctively stand out; first, the Federal Law of 27 July 2006 No. 149-FZ on Information, Information Technologies and Protection of Information; and second, the Federal Law of 26 July 2017 No. 187-FZ on Security of Critical Information Infrastructure of the Russian Federation (Ostashenko & Anyukhina, 2020; also see UNIDIR). Federal Law No. 152-FZ on Personal Data dated 27

July 2006 (widely known as the Personal Data Law) which in 2014 was amended into Data Localisation Law is also important. According to Schia and Gjesvik, 'For China, cyber sovereignty is a part of the larger field of information security which is critical for maintaining its core values' (Schia & Gjesvik, 2017). In line with this, it has a very impressive and wide ranging list of cyber regulations (Sacks, 2020). The Counter-Terrorism Law 2015, National Security Law 2015 and Cyber Security Law 2017 are the major Acts/Policies addressing cyber threat and cyber sovereignty in China (for details see Creemers et. al., 2018).

Coming to India, according to the Global Cyber Security Index 2018 in the global ranking GCI 2018, India is at the 47th position.[26] The development of cyber policies can be seen as an offshoot of recent incidents of cyber crime reported in India.[27] The Economic Survey 2017-18 (Volume 1) under its Chapter on 'Transforming Science and Technology in India' has given due importance to cyber warfare.[28] There is a plethora of policies and guidelines formulated and implemented to realise the aim of cyber security in India.[29] Some of the entities/bodies established for this purpose are the National Cyber Security Coordinator (NCSC) under the National Security Council Secretariat (NSCS); Indian Computer Emergency Response Team (CERT-In);[30] National Critical Information Infrastructure Protection Centre (NCIIPC); Chief Information Security Officers (CISOs); Cyber Swachhta Kendra (Botnet Cleaning and Malware Analysis Centre); and Cyber Crime Prevention for Women and Children (CCPWC), among others. The Cyber Swachhta Kendra (Botnet Cleaning and Malware Analysis Centre) is a part of the Government of India's Digital India initiative under the Ministry of Electronics and Information Technology (MeitY) to create a secure cyber space by detecting botnet infections in India and to notify, enable cleaning and securing systems of end users so as to prevent further infections.[31] In addition to these, a division has been established under the Ministry of Home Affairs to deal with Cyber and Information Security. The National Cyber Safety and Security Standards have been started with a great vision to safeguard the nation from the current threats in cyber space.[32] Along with these, the Data Security Council of India (DSCI), is a not-for-profit, industry body on data protection in India set up by NASSCOM®, committed to making cyber space safe, secure and trusted by establishing best practices, standards and initiatives in cyber security and privacy.[33] At the policy level in India, The Information

Technology Act, 2000 is an Act 'to provide legal recognition for transactions carried out by means of electronic data interchange and other means of electronic communication, commonly referred to as "electronic commerce"[34] and states that "cyber security means protecting information, equipment, devices, computer, computer resource, communication device and information stored therein from unauthorised access, use, disclosure, disruption, modification or destruction".[35] The vision of the National Cyber Security Policy 2013 is 'To build a secure and resilient cyberspace for citizens, businesses and Government' with a Mission to protect information and information infrastructure in cyber space, build capabilities to prevent and respond to cyber threats, reduce vulnerabilities and minimize damage from cyber incidents through a combination of institutional structures, people, processes, technology and cooperation.' It also aims to 'develop bilateral and multi-lateral relationships in the area of cyber security with other countries.' Such and similar steps taken by both state and non-state actors in the field of cyber security and cyber safety reflect the alert preparedness of India.

The national policies of the respective countries related to cyber security discussed above have one thing in common, that is, how to counter the real and/or perceived cyber threat and cyber attacks emanating from its opponent entity/entities and how to enhance its own cyber security measures so as to make it better and smart. All in all, they focus on certain basic tenets of cyber security which include proper maintenance of access control and identity management, to protect and secure critical information infrastructure (CII), enhancing encryption algorithms for digital security, patching digital vulnerability to check data breach, making their authentication fool-proof, employing the latest and updated malware scanners software to detect spam, malware and virus attacks, devising a ultra-stealth firewall program to protect its computer and Internet system, maintaining confidentiality, integrity, and availability of computer network security, cyber security early warning and detection systems along with installation of Intrusion Detection Systems (IDS) and use of Cryptography for information security, among others. Most importantly, they also 'pledge' themselves to global cyber norms, protocols and guidelines.

Conclusion

Humanity has come a long way from the primitive state of existence to the modern, post-modern and post-development cyber era. In between lies the exhaustive evidence-based extrapolation and interpolation of human history, polity, and society. Outlined as one of the earliest explanations of how humans 'triumphed' over the other species is Darwinism; both biological and social. At the end of the day, it all boils down to survival in the best possible way with minimum exposure to extinction. Such an individual act of 'staying alive' metamorphosed somewhere in the distant history the collective act of waging 'war' against the 'other' which can be best described as primitive unorthodox warfare. With the advancement of rudimentary techniques and technology of weapons and ammunition on one hand and the nascent idea of 'nationhood and state' on the other, there has been a 'quantum leap' in the ways nation-state/s used to engage in war with the 'other'. The brutal and brazen display of weaponry to strike terror at the hearts of opponents and enemies slowly and silently gave way to a more nuanced and subtle form of warfare which was more deadly than ever. We have also moved away from the earliest notions of traditional, industrial and modern (post) modern societies. Over a period of time, social scientists of various hues and colours have propounded industrial and post-industrial society; knowledge society and information society; risk society; Internet and network society, global society, knowledge economy, information society and digital society among others. The contemporary era can be suitably termed as the era of cyber society. The emergence of cyber space, cyber security and cyber war finally sealed the ways in which nation-states used to wage war against each other. The infinite, abstract, and virtual cyber space having its constituent elements as 0 and 1 engulfed the entire geographical/territorial boundaries and demarcations and blurred them. The 'conventional' understanding of how one state 'behaved/interacted' with its counterpart underwent a tectonic shift, i.e., international relations between countries were fundamentally transformed and the rules of engagement re-written not in the conventional language but in a language that is composed of' Zeroes' and 'Ones'. Subsequently, emerged the much-needed demand to maintain the geo-strategic and geo-political equilibrium in the larger interests of the 'survival' of the human 'race' as such. It led to the emergence of cyber security strategies being deployed by respective countries to protect their sovereignty. However, it had another fallout also as emerged from it was cyber crime, cyber espionage and cyber warfare so as to destabilise the 'other'. The 'super powers' like America, Russia, China, and the U.K., among others, have been engaging with each other through 'perceived/real threats' on the 'cyber front'. The invisibility and anonymity of the cyber crime perpetrator have been misused by both the sides thus leading to a 'trust-deficit' at a grand level in international relations. Such a 'bleak' scenario of state rivalries is an urgent need for transparency and confidence-building measures on the 'cyber front'.

The nature and content of the process of 'destabilising' the polity and economy of the opponent country/ies reflected a paradigmatic shift from a 'barbaric' war and invasion to a 'un/civilised' act of planting a virus/ worm in the computer network so as to infest it in totality. The paradox of such instances of cyber attacks is that it is very difficult to attribute such attacks to a definitive entity (be it a person, organization or a nation-state). At the same time, the global cyber arms race is increasingly becoming *detrimental* to both regional stability and global peace. As is evident in the spurt in incidents of cyber attacks worldwide engineered by both state and non-state parties on their opponents, one thing is very clear that the threats and dangers of cyber attacks are very real and states have to relentlessly 'upgrade' their cyber security mechanisms. Most importantly, national security and cyber security have to be merged together not only at the policy/strategy levels but also in action. In doing so, states need to also take into consideration the issues of data privacy and 'digital' autonomy of its citizens on a priority basis. It is so because, under the garb of protecting 'information and data flow' to safeguard itself and its citizens many a time the state transforms itself into a 'surveillance state'. Thus, the need of the hour is to come up with the idea, principle, and practice of cyber ethics, cyber peace, cyber democracy and cyber governance. It is high time that we understand that the conventional theory and practice of international relations have undergone a sea change as a result of advancements in science and technology with reference to ICT as embodied in cyber space. As of now, the international/global community has nothing to lose but to gain enormously by getting onboard on a priority basis with each other so as to deliberate and elaborate on the possibility of co-existence in cyber space already so marred by incidents of cyber crime and cyber warfare.

NOTES

1. Home > ITU-D > ITU-D ICT Statistics > Statistics. retrieved from https://www.itu.int/en/ITU-D/Statistics/ Pages/ stat/default.aspx (accessed 11 July 2020).
2. Russian Interference in 2016 U.S. Elections. Retrieved from https://www.fbi.gov/wanted/ cyber/ russian-interference-in-2016-u-s-elections (accessed 9 July 2019).
3. Here are the biggest cybercrime trends of 2019. Retrieved from https://www.weforum.org/agenda/2019/03/ here-are-the-biggest-cybercrime-trends-of-2019/ (accessed 9 July 2019).
4. Centre for Cybersecurity. Retrieved from https://www.weforum.org/centre-for-cybersecurity (accessed 22 July 2019).
5. *A Declaration of the Independence of Cyberspace* (1996). John P. Barlow. Retrieved from http://editions-hache.com/essais/pdf/barlow1.pdf. (accessed 26 July 2019).
6. The Global Risks Report 2019 (14th edition). Retrieved from http://www3.weforum.org/ docs/WEF_Global_ Risks _Report_2019.pdf. (accessed 17 July 2019).
7. Global Cyber Security Index v3 (2018/2019). Retrieved from https://www.itu.int/dms_pub/itu-d/opb/str/D-STR-GCI.01-2018-PDF-E.pdf. (accessed 16 July 2019).
8. Cyren Glossary of Cyber Threats. Retrieved from https://www.cyren.com/resources/cyber-threat-glossary. (accessed 5 July 2019).
9. Global Programme on Cybercrime. Retrieved from https://www.unodc.org/unodc/en/cybercrime/global-programme-cybercrime.html. (accessed 12 July 2019).
10. Cybercrime. Retrieved from https://www.interpol.int/en/Crimes/Cybercrime. (accessed 5 July 2019).
11. National Cyber Security Policy 2013. Retrieved from https://meity.gov.in/writereaddata/files/downloads/ National_cyber_security_policy-2013%281%29.pdf. (accessed 23 July 2019).
12. OECD Guidelines for the Security of Information Systems and Networks: Towards a Culture of Security. Retrieved from https://www.oecd.org/internet/ieconomy/oecd guidelines for the security of information systems and networks towards a culture of security.htm. (accessed 10 July 2020).
13. UN Resolutions Related to Cybersecurity. Retrieved from https://www.itu.int/en/action/cybersecurity/Pages /un-resolutions.aspx. (accessed 18 July 2019).
14. Robinson et. al. are of the view that the UN Peacekeeping mechanisms can be 'modified/altered' in a way so as to ensure a scenario of cyber peacekeeping. (2018: 70-80).
15. About GCA. Retrieved from https://www.itu.int/en/action/cybersecurity/Pages/gca.aspx. (accessed 27 July 2019).
16. In recent times cryptocurrency hacking and Bitcoin scams have also emerged as serious cyber crime and threat to privacy of the people concerned. Twitter Hack: Breach Compromises Many Public Figures Including Musk, Obama; Twitter Investigating Incident. Retrieved from https://www.news18.com/news/tech/twitter-hack-breach-compromises-many-public-figures-including-musk-obama-twitter-investigating-incident-2717995.html. (accessed 16 July 2020). Twitter blames 'coordinated' attack on its systems for hack of Joe Biden, Barack Obama, Bill Gates and others. By Rishi Iyengar, *CNN Business* [Updated 0325 GMT (1125 HKT) July 16, 2020]. Retrieved from https://edition.cnn.com/2020/07/15/tech/twitter-hack-elon-musk-bill-gates/index.html (accessed 16 July 2020).
17. Cyber Attack Trends Analysis: Key Insights to Gear Up for in 2019. (2019). Security Report Volume 1; Israel & San Carlos, U.S.: Check Point Research, p. 16. Retrieved from http://snt.hr/boxcontent/ CheckPointSecurityReport2019_vol01.pdf (accessed 10 July 2020).

18. Significant Cyber Incidents. Retrieved from https://www.csis.org/ programs/ technology-policy-program/ significant-cyber-incidents (accessed 29 July 2019).
19. McAfee. 2020. What Is Stuxnet? Retrieved from https://www.mcafee.com/ enterprise/ en-in/ security-awareness/ ransomware/what-is-stuxnet.html (accessed 13 July 2020).
20. Chinese hackers infiltrated five energy firms: McAfee. Diane Bartz. February 10, 2011 / 10:45 AM. Retrieved from https://www.reuters.com/ article/ us-energy-cyber-china/ chinese-hackers-infiltrated-five-energy-firms-mcafee-idUSTRE7190XP20110210 (accessed 13 July 2020). Hacker group in China linked to big cyber attacks: Symantec. Jim Finkle. September 17, 2013/6:42 PM. Retrieved from https://www.reuters.com/ article/us-cyberattacks-china/hacker-group-in-china-linked-to-big-cyber-attacks-symantec-idUSBRE98G0M720130917 (accessed 13 July 2020).
21. In five days, over 40,000 Chinese searches for vulnerabilities in Indian cyberspace: cops. Mohamed Thaver | Mumbai | Updated: June 24, 2020, 7:28:19 am. Retrieved from https://indianexpress.com/article/india/in-5-days-over-40000-chinese-searches-for-vulnerabilities-in-indian-cyberspace-cops-6473138/ (accessed 10 July 2020).
Rise In Cyber Attacks From China, Over 40,000 Cases In 5 Days: Official. Retrieved from https://www.ndtv.com/india-news/rise-in-cyber-attacks-from-china-over-40-000-cases-in-5-days-official-2251111 (accessed 10 July 2020). North Korea's Lazarus hackers plan 'phishing' attack in India to steal COVID aid. Arun Kumar Chaubey. June 18, 2020, 19:10 PM IST. Retrieved from https://zeenews.india.com/india/north-koreas-lazarus-hackers-plan-phishing-attack-in-india-to-steal-covid-aid-2290701.html (accessed 10 July 2020).
22. National Cyber Strategy of the United States of America (U.S.A.) (September 2018) Retrieved from https:// www. whitehouse.gov/wp-content/uploads/2018/09/ National-Cyber-Strategy.pdf (accessed 22 July 2019).
23. Homeland Security: Cybersecurity. Retrieved from https://www.dhs.gov/topic/ cybersecurity (accessed 22 July 2019).
24. What is cyber security? Retrieved from https://www.ncsc.gov.uk/ section/about-ncsc/ what-is-cyber-security (accessed 19 July 2019).
25. National Cyber Security Strategy 2016 to 2021. Retrieved from https:// assets.publishing.service.gov.uk/ government/uploads/system/uploads/ attachment_data/file/567242/national_cyber_security_strategy_2016.pdf (accessed 22 July 2019).
26. Global Cyber Security Index 2018. Retrieved from https://www.itu.int/en/ITU-D/ Cybersecurity/ Documents/ draft-18-00706_Global-Cyber security-Index-EV5_print_2.pdf (accessed 23 July 2019).
27. Cyber Security by Dr. V. K. Saraswat (NITI Aayog). Retrieved from https://niti.gov.in/ writereaddata/ files/document_publication/Cyber SecurityConclaveAtVigyanBhavanDelhi_1.pdf (accessed 23 July 2019).
28. Retrieved from http://mofapp.nic.in:8080/economicsurvey/pdf/119-130_Chapter_ 08_ ENGLISH_Vol _01_ 2017-18.pdf (accessed 5 July 2019).
29. For details see Cyber Laws & E-Security, Ministry of Electronics & Information Technology, Government of India (Retrieved from https://meity.gov.in/cyber-security). Also see (Kethineni, 2019: 305-326).
30. Indian Computer Emergency Response Team (CERT-In). Retrieved from https:// www.cert-in.org.in/(accessed 26 July 2019).
31. Cyber Swachhta Kendra (Botnet Cleaning and Malware Analysis Centre). Retrieved from https://www.cyberswachhtakendra.gov.in/ (accessed 26 July 2019).
32. National Cyber Safety and Security Standards. Retrieved from https://ncdrc.res.in/ organization-profile.php (accessed 25 July 2019).

33. Data Security Council of India (DSCI). Retrieved from https://www.dsci.in/ (accessed 25 July 2019).
34. The Information Technology Act, 2000. Retrieved from https://meity.gov.in/writereaddata/ files The %20Information %20Technology%20Act %2C%202000%283%29.pdf (accessed 24 July 2019).
35. The Information Technology Act, 2000. Retrieved from https://meity.gov.in/writereaddata/ files/The%20 Information%20Technology%20Act%2C%202000%283%29.pdf (accessed 28 July 2019).

REFERENCES

Baezner, Marie. 2018. *Cyber and Information warfare in the Ukrainian conflict*. Version 2, October, Centre for Security Studies (CSS), ETH Zürich. Retrieved from https://css.ethz.ch/content/dam/ ethz/special-interest/gess/cis/center-for-securities-studies/pdfs/20181003_MB_HS_RUS-UKR%20 V2_rev.pdf.

Baldwin, David A. 1997. 'The concept of security', *Review of International Studies*, 23, pp. 5-26.

Ball, Philip. 2007. Does this mean war? 23 May, *Nature*. doi:10.1038/news070521-8. Retrieved from https://www.nature.com/news/2007/070521/full/070521-8.html (accessed 12 July 2020).

Barrinha, André & Thomas Renard. 2017.'Cyber-diplomacy: the making of an international society in the digital age', *Global Affairs*, 3:4-5, 353-364, DOI:10.1080/23340460.2017.1414924 (https://doi.org/10.1080/23340460.2017.1414924).

Blank, Stephen. 2008. 'Web War I: Is Europe's first information war a new kind of war?', *Comparative Strategy*, 27:3, 227-247, DOI: 10.1080/01495930802185312.

Brown, Gary & Tullos, Owen. 2012. *On the spectrum of cyberspace operations*, December 11, Available at SSRN: Retrieved from https://ssrn.com/abstract=2400536 or http://dx.doi.org/ 10.2139/ ssrn.2400536 (accessed 10 July 2020).

Buchan, Russell. 2015. 'Cyber espionage and international law', in Nicholas Tsagourias & Russell Buchan. (eds.). *Research Handbook on International Law and Cyberspace*. UK: Edward Elgar Publishing Ltd., pp. 168-189.

Cavelty, Myriam Dunn. 2012. 'Cyber-security' in Allan Collins (ed.). *Contemporary Security Studies*. Oxford: Oxford University Press, pp. 362-378.

Cavelty, Myriam Dunn. 2013. 'From cyber-bombs to political fallout: threat representations with an impact in the cyber-security discourse', *International Studies Review*, vol. 15, no. 1, Special Issue (March), pp. 105-122.

Cavelty, Myriam Dunn & Andreas Wenger. 2020.'Cyber security meets security politics: Complex technology, fragmented politics, and networked science', *Contemporary Security Policy*, 41:1, 5-32, DOI: 10.1080/13523260.2019.1678855.

Centre for Strategic & International Studies (CSIS), 2020. *Significant cyber incidents*. Retrieved from https://www.csis.org/ programs/technology-policy-program/significant-cyber-incidents (accessed 13 July 2020).

Cha, Victor D. 2011. 'Globalization and security', in Christopher W. Hughes & Lai Yew Meng (eds.). *Security Studies: A Reader*. Oxon and New York: Routledge, pp. 406-416.

Chaturvedi, Subi. 2018. 'Cyberwarfare will threaten two things we hold dear—freedom and the Internet', *Economic and Political Weekly*, vol. 53, no. 19, 12 May. Retrieved from https://www.epw.in/ engage/ article/cyberattacks-threaten-freedom-internet (accessed 12 January 2020).

Choucri, Nazli & Daniel Goldsmith. 2012. 'Lost in cyberspace: Harnessing the Internet, international relations, and global security', *Bulletin of the Atomic Scientists*, 68:2, 70-77, DOI: 10.1177/ 0096340212438696 (https://doi.org/10.1177/0096340212438696).

Choo, Kim-Kwang Raymond & Peter Grabosky. 2013. 'Cyber crime', in Letizia Paoli (ed.). *The Oxford Handbook of Organized Crime*. New York: Oxford University Press.

CNN. 2019. '2016 Presidential campaign hacking fast facts'. Retrieved from https:// edition.cnn.com/ 2016/12/26/us/2016-presidential-campaign-hacking-fast-facts/ index.html (accessed 25 July 2019).

Connell, Michael & Sarah Vogler. 2017. *Russia's approach to cyber warfare*. CNA Occasional Paper March. Retrieved from https://www.cna.org/ CNA_files/PDF/DOP-2016-U-014231-1Rev.pdf (accessed 12 July 2020).

Craig, Anthony & Brandon Valeriano. 2016. *Conceptualising cyber arms races*. 8th International Conference on Cyber Conflict: Cyber Power. NATO CCD COE Publications, Tallinn. Retrieved from https://orca.cf.ac.uk/91754/1/Conceptualising%20Cyber%20 Arms%20Races.pdf (accessed 10 July 2020).

Creemers, Rogier; Paul Triolo & Graham Webster. 2018. *Translation: cyber security law of the People's Republic of China* (Effective June 1, 2017) [Blog post]. June 29. Retrieved from https://www.newamerica.org/cybersecurity-initiative/digichina/blog/translation-cybersecurity-law-peoples-republic-china/ (accessed 13 July 2020).

Deibert, Ronald. 2018. 'Trajectories for future cybersecurity research', in Alexandra Gheciu & William C. Wohlforth (eds.). *The Oxford Handbook of International Security*. United Kingdom: Oxford University Press, pp. 531-546.

Fidler, David P. 2017. 'The U.S. election hacks, cybersecurity, and international law', Retrieved from https://www.cambridge.org/core/services/aop-cambridge-core/content/view/ 187809808A346A 9346D 4719A20437ABD/ S2398772317000058a.pdf/ us_election_hacks_cyber security_and_ international_law.pdf.

Gompert, David C. & Martin Libicki. 2014. 'Cyber warfare and Sino-American crisis instability', *Survival*, 56:4, 7-22, DOI: 10.1080/00396338.2014.941543.

Hanna, Andrew. 2019. *The invisible U.S.-Iran cyber war*. Updated June 4, 2020, Original: October 25, 2019. Retrieved from https://iranprimer.usip.org/blog/2019/oct/25/invisible-us-iran-cyber-war (accessed 13 July 2020).

Inkster, Nigel. 2015. 'Cyber espionage', *Adelphi Series*, 55:456, 51-82, DOI:10.1080/ 19445571.2015.1181443. (https://doi.org/10.1080/19445571.2015.1181443).

Jahankhani, Hamid; Ameer Al-Nemrat & Amin Hosseinian-Far. 2014. 'Cyber crime classification and characteristics', in Babak Akhgar, Andrew Staniforth and Francesca Bosco (eds.). *Cyber crime and cyber terrorism: investigator's handbook*. Elsevier Inc., pp. 149-164.

Jarvis, Lee & Stuart Macdonald. 2015.'What is cyber terrorism? Findings from a survey of researchers', *Terrorism and Political Violence*, 27:4, 657-678, DOI:10.1080/ 09546553.2013.847827 (https://doi.org/10.1080/09546553.2013.847827).

Jensen, Eric Talbot. 'Cyber sovereignty: the way ahead', *Texas International Law Journal*, vol. 50, no. 2, pp. 275-304.

Jung, Chauncey. 2020. *India shows the world how to use 'cyberspace sovereignty' against China*, 2 July. Retrieved from https://thediplomat.com/2020/07/india-shows-the-world-how-to-use-cyberspace-sovereignty-against-china/ (accessed 13 July 2020).

Kamiñski, Mariusz Antoni. 2020. 'Operation "Olympic Games." Cyber-sabotage as a tool of American intelligence aimed at counteracting the development of Iran's nuclear programme', *Security & Defence Quarterly*, no. 2, vol. 29, DOI: 10.35467/sdq/121974.

Kettemann, Matthias C. 2017. 'Ensuring Cyber security through International Law', *Revista Española de Derecho Internacional*, vol. 69, no. 2 (Julio-Diciembre), pp. 281-290.

Kethineni, Sesha. 2020. 'Cyber crime in India: laws, regulations, and enforcement mechanisms', in Holt T. & A. Bossler (eds.). *The Palgrave Handbook of International Cybercrime and Cyberdeviance*. Cham: Palgrave Macmillan, pp. 305-326.

Kilovaty, Ido. 2015. "Rethinking the prohibition on the use of force in the light of economic cyber warfare: Towards a Broader Scope of Article 2(4) of the UN Charter', *Journal of Law & Cyber Warfare*, vol. 4, no. 3 (Winter), pp. 210-244.

Lahmann, Henning. 2020. *Unilateral remedies to cyber operations: self-defence, countermeasures, necessity, and the question of attribution*. UK: Cambridge University Press.

Laqueur, Walter. 2011. 'Terrorism', in Christopher W. Hughes & Lai Yew Meng (eds.). *Security Studies: A Reader*. Oxon and New York: Routledge, pp. 417-421.

Lin, Herbert. 2012. Escalation dynamics and conflict termination in cyberspace', *Strategic Studies Quarterly*, Fall, 6 (3): 46-70. Retrieved from https://www.hsdl.org/?view&did=722316.

Lipton, Jacqueline. 2015. *Rethinking cyber law: a new vision for internet law*. UK: Edward Elgar Publishing Ltd.

Malin, Cameron H.; Terry Gudaitis; Thomas J. Holt & Max Kilger. 2017. 'Asymmetric warfare and psyops: nation state-sponsored cyber attacks', in Cameron H. Malin; Terry Gudaitis, Thomas J. Holt & Max Kilger (eds.). *Deception in the digital age: exploiting and defending human targets through computer-mediated communications*. United States: Academic Press, Inc., pp. 207-226.

Matania, Eviatar; Lior Yoffe & Michael Mashkautsan. 2016. 'A three-layer framework for a comprehensive national cyber-security strategy', *Georgetown Journal of International Affairs*, vol. 17, no. 3, International Engagement on Cyber VI (Fall/Winter), pp. 77-84.

Mite, Valentinas. 2007. *Estonia: attacks seen as first case of 'cyber war'*. Radio Free Europe/Radio Liberty RFE/RL, Inc. 30 May, 13:10 GMT. Retrieved from https://www.rferl.org/a/1076805.html (accessed 13 July 2020).

Mulligan, Deirdre K. & Fred B. Schneider. 2011. 'Doctrine for cyber security', *Daedalus*, vol. 140, no. 4, Protecting the Internet as a Public Commons (Fall), pp. 70-92.

Napetvaridze, Vladimeri & Archil Chochia. 2019. 'Cyber security in the making—policy and law: a case study of Georgia', *International and Comparative Law Review*, 2019, vol. 19, no. 2, pp. 155-180. DOI: 10.2478/iclr-2019-0019.

Nykodym, Nick & Robert Taylor. 2004. 'The world's current legislative efforts against cyber crime', *Computer Law & Security Review*, volume 20, issue 5, September-October, pp. 390-395.

OECD. 1986. 'Computer crime', *The OECD Observer*, September, no. 142, pp. 19-21. Retrieved from https://www.oecd-ilibrary.org/docserver/observer-v1986-5-en.pdf?expires=1594483140&id=id & accname=guest&checksum=E42916CE3AB362EFE1D0B451A2D69C73 (accessed 12 July 2020).

O'Flaherty, Kate. 2020. Stuxnet 2? Iran hints nuclear site explosion could be a cyber attack. July 4, 07:03 a.m. EDT. Retrieved from https://www.forbes.com/sites/kateoflahertyuk/2020/07/04/stuxnet-2-iran-hints-nuclear-site-explosion-could-be-a-cyberattack/#6b67fa825ad2 (accessed 12 July 2020).

O'Grady, Nathaniel & Andrew C. Dwyer. 2020. Cyber security. *International Encyclopaedia of Human Geography* (second edition). pp. 135-141.

Ohlin, Jens David. 2017. 'Did Russian cyber interference in the 2016 election violate international law?',*Texas Law Review*, vol. 95, issue 7, Retrieved from https://texaslawreview.org/russian-cyber-interference-2016-election-violate-international-law/(accessed 13 July 2020).

Ostashenko, Maria & Irina Anyukhina. 2020. *Russia - data protection overview*. June. Retrieved from https://www.dataguidance.com/notes/russia-data-protection-overview.

Porche, Isaac R.; Jerry M. Sollinger & Shawn McKay. 2011. *A cyber worm that knows no boundaries*. CA: RAND Corporation. Retrieved from https://www.rand.org/ pubs/occasional_papers/OP342.html. (accessed 13 July 2020).

Press Information Bureau. 2020. *Government bans 59 mobile apps which are prejudicial to sovereignty and integrity of India, defence of India, security of state and public order*. Posted on: 29 June 2020 8:47 P.M. by PIB Delhi. Government of India. Retrieved from https:// pib.gov.in/ PressReleseDetailm.aspx?PRID=1635206 (accessed 13 July 2020).

Rid, Thomas & Peter McBurney. 2012. 'Cyber-weapons', *The RUSI Journal*, 157(1): 6-13, DOI: 10.1080/03071847.2012.664354.

Robinson, Michael; Kevin Jones, Helge Janicke & Leandros Maglaras. 2018. 'An introduction to cyber peacekeeping', *Journal of Network and Computer Applications*, volume 114, 15 July, pp. 70-87.

Sacks, Sam. 2020. *China's emerging cyber governance system*. Retrieved from https:// www.csis.org/chinas-emerging-cyber-governance-system (accessed 10 July 2020).

Schia, Niels Nagelhus & Lars Gjesvik. 2017. *China's cyber sovereignty*. NUPI Policy Brief: 2017-02 Norwegian Institute for International Affairs (NUPI). Retrieved from https:// nupi.brage.unit.no/ nupi-xmlui/handle/11250/2434904 (accessed 10 July 2020).

Schmitt, Michael N. 2013. 'Introduction', in Michael N. Schmitt (ed.). *Tallinn Manual on the International Law Applicable to Cyber Warfare* (prepared by the International Group of Experts at the invitation of the NATO Cooperative Cyber Defence Centre of Excellence). UK: Cambridge University Press, pp. 1-11.

Schmitt, Michael N. 2015. 'Introduction', in Nicholas Tsagourias & Russell Buchan. (eds.).*Research handbook on international law and cyberspace*. UK: Edward Elgar Publishing Ltd., pp. 1-10.

Segal, Adam. 2013. 'The code not taken: China, the United States, and the future of cyber espionage', *Bulletin of the Atomic Scientists*, 69:5, 38-45, DOI:10.1177/0096340213501344.

Solms, Rossouwvon & Johanvan Niekerk. 2013. 'From information security to cyber security', *Computers & Security*, volume 38, October, pp. 97-102.

Sperling, James. 2014. 'Governance and security in the twenty-first century', in James Sperling (ed.). *Handbook of Governance and Security*. UK: Edward Elgar Publishing Ltd., pp. 3-13.

Stytz, Martin R. & Sheila B. Banks. 2014. 'Toward attaining cyber dominance', *Strategic Studies Quarterly*, vol. 8, no. 1 (Spring), pp. 55-87.

Tapia-Valdes, J. A. 1982. 'A typology of national security policies', *Yale Journal of International Law*, vol. 9, issue 1, pp. 10-39. Retrieved from http://digitalcommons.law.yale.edu/ yjil/vol9/iss1/3.

Tehrani, Pardis Moslemzadeh; Nazura Abdul Manap & Hossein Taji. 2013. 'Cyber terrorism challenges: The need for a global response to a multi-jurisdictional crime, *Computer Law & Security Review*, volume 29, issue 3, June, pp. 207-215.

Tikk, Eneken; Kadri Kaska & Liis Vihul. 2010. *International cyber incidents: legal considerations*. Estonia: Cooperative Cyber Defence Centre of Excellence (CCD COE). Retrieved from http://www.digar.ee/id/nlib-digar:208175 (accessed 16 July 2020).

Tsagourias, Nicholas. 2105. 'The legal status of cyberspace', in Nicholas Tsagourias & Russell Buchan. (eds.).*Research Handbook on International Law and Cyberspace*. UK: Edward Elgar Publishing Ltd., pp. 13-29.

UNIDIR (United Nations Institute for Disarmament Research). (Pub. year not given). *UNIDIR cyber policy portal: Russian Federation*. Retrieved from https://cyberpolicyportal.org/ en/states/Russian federation (accessed 15 July 2020).

Viano, Emilio C. 2013. 'The information society and cyber crime: criminologists facing this growing challenge', Information Society and Cybercrime: Challenges for Criminology and Criminal Justice. The Asian Regional Conference. *World Crime Forum 2013*. Research Report Series 13-B-01. Korean Institute of Criminology & International Society for Criminology, pp. 11-18.

Waxman, Matthew C. 2011. 'Cyber attacks as "force" under UN Charter Article 2(4)', 87

International Law Studies. Retrieved from https://scholarship.law.columbia.edu/faculty_scholarship/ 847 (accessed 15 July 2020).

Wolfers, Arnold. 1952. '"National security" as an ambiguous symbol', *Political Science Quarterly*, vol. 67, no. 4 (December), pp. 481-502.

Zouave, Erik; Marc Bruce, Kajsa Colde, Margarita Jaitner, Ioana Rodhe & Tommy Gustafsson 2020. *Artificially intelligent cyberattacks*. FOI-R--4947—SE, March. FOI: Swedish Defence Research Agency. Stockholm. Retrieved from https://www.foi.se/rapportsammanfattning?reportNo=FOI-R--4947--SE (accessed 10 July 2020).

21

Analysing Water Security in Asia: Problems and Prospects

Sandhya Pathaniya

Introduction

Sustainable development will not be achieved without a water secure world. Water security is the key to global pliancy for human society to bloom in the face of universal change. Water security has been defined as "the reliable availability of an acceptable quantity and quality of water for health, livelihood, and production, coupled with an acceptable level of water-related risks (Grey & Sadoff, 2007). Asia is currently home to 4.5 billion people, who use around 65 per cent of the world's water supply. Around 30 per cent of the Asian population is already facing water scarcity (Satoh, 2018).

Water security has emerged as an important issue for Asia. With rapid growth in population, the need for water is growing to a great extent without increase in water resources. Many Asian countries are beginning to experience different levels of water shortages because of industrialization, agricultural growth, and urbanization and erratic weather phenomena, most notably the El Nino and La Nino. Sharing of water resources intra-state and interstate is another matter of concern. Singapore, for example, is highly dependent on (and vulnerable to) Malaysia for its water supplies. Many nations, such as those in the Mekong Delta region, share water resources and depend on mutual cooperation.

In South Asia, conflict over freshwater has strained relations between India and Bangladesh, as well as India and Pakistan. In the future, diminishing and degraded freshwater resources could lead to internal instability in many nations, and possibly even spark interstate conflict (Smith & Gross, 1999). The need for water security in Asia is likely to increase over the coming decades, and new research from the IIASA Water Program has shown that increased water demand due to socio-economic development is likely to be the main cause in large parts of the continent.

Water Security

Three things are critical for water security: good quality, well-managed water resources; well-managed water supply services; and management of disaster risk related to water. Water resources can be easily accessed by skilled people, with pumps, pipes, tanks, and taps. Similarly, water supply services alone are of little use without water resources (https://washmatters.wateraid.org). Water resources and water supply services will not be adversely affected if disaster risk is well managed, then people will be water secure.

Water Security Background: Access vs. Availability

Freshwater available in the world in all the forms is limited. Approximately 97.5 per cent of the world's water exists as salt water in the seas and oceans; out of the remaining 2.5 per cent freshwater, roughly 99 per cent is either in the form of ice caps and glaciers, held as soil moisture or as underground water too deep to access. Thus, only about one per cent of the world's total freshwater is easily accessible for utilization by fauna and flora. In the present scenario more than 31 countries around the world, having about 8 per cent of the world's population are in great need of water security. This number is increasing and is likely to touch the figure of 45 countries by the year 2025.

When analysing water security, it is useful to delineate two concepts: availability vs. access.

Freshwater Availability in Asia

In Asia, water security is the need of the hour because of water shortages that are emerging as a major social and economic threat. Map 2 throws light on the present position of Asia in relation to water security. The higher the water risk level in a country, the more is the need for water security.

Map 1: Political Map of Asia

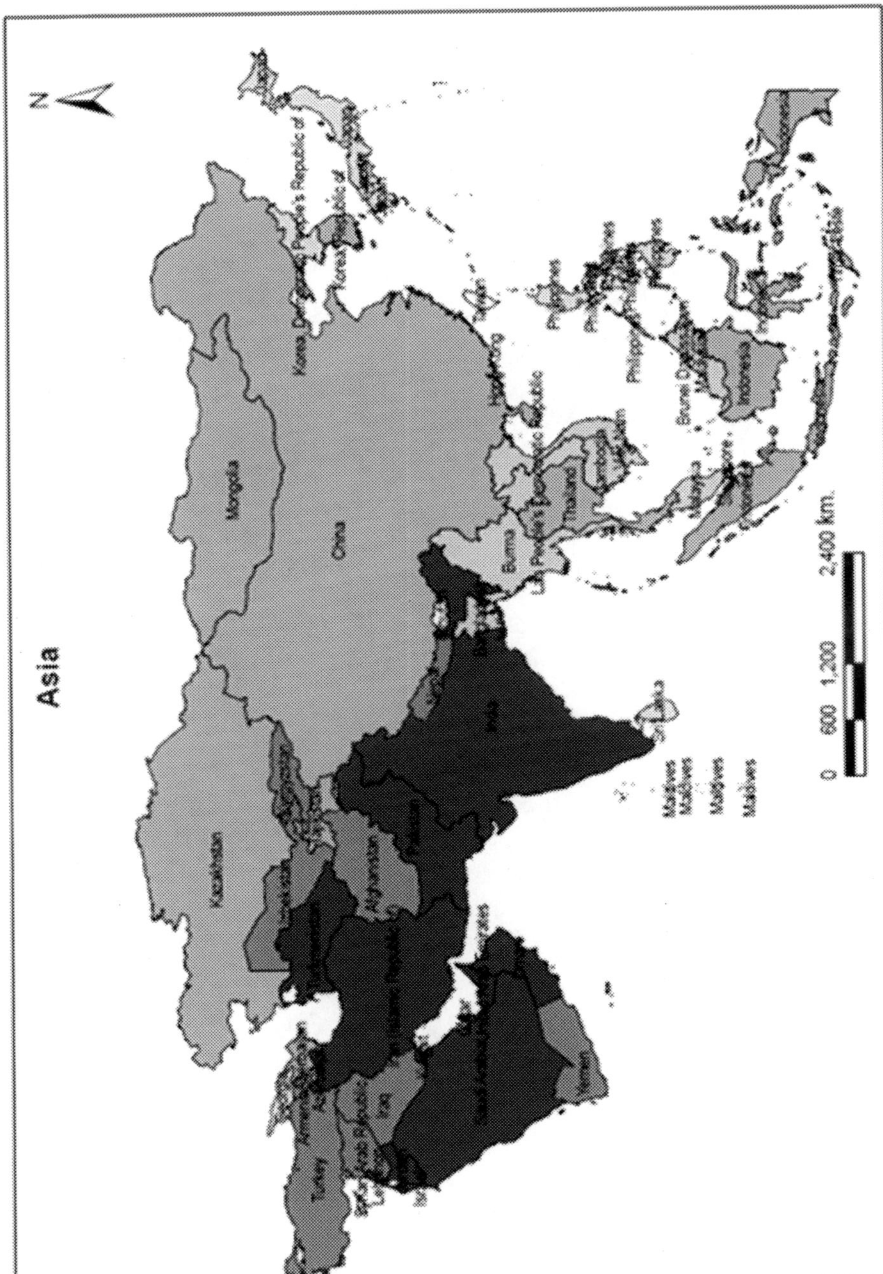

Map 2

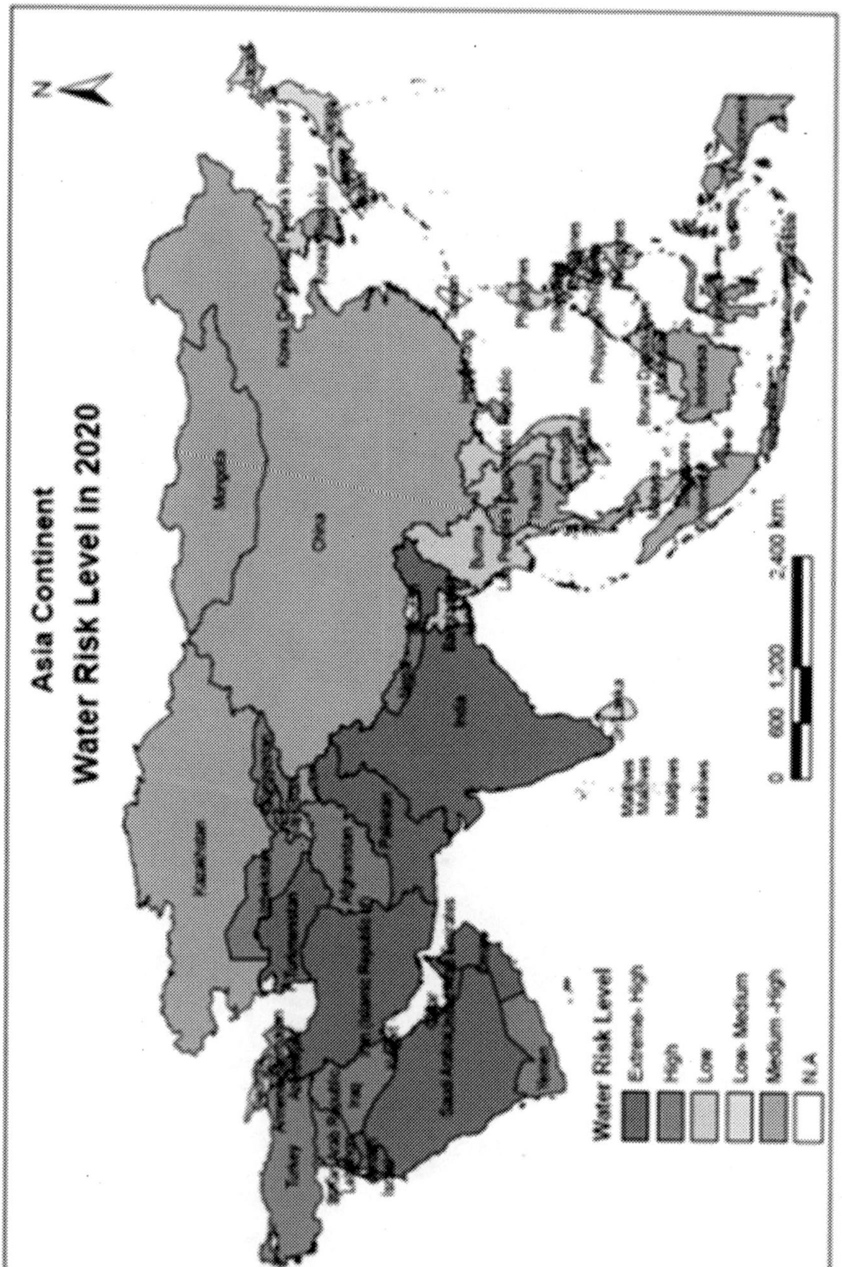
Asia Continent
Water Risk Level in 2020
N
Water Risk Level
Extreme- High
High
Low
Low- Medium
Medium- High
N/A
0 600 1,200 2,400 km

In Asia, the largest continent with varied topography and climatic conditions, the availability of freshwater resources both on the surface and underground are in abundance but they are distributed unevenly. Even precipitation all over Asia is erratic. The amount of rainfall in China ranges from 200 mm in inland desert areas up to 2,000 mm along the southern tropical coast (Kramer, 1999). Water shortage in China's urban areas is a matter of concern as more than 300 of China's major cities face water shortages. Every year in China, thousands of tons of pollutants from agricultural, industrial, and municipal sources are dumped into the nation's rivers, lakes, and reservoirs, a trend that is common throughout the region. The economic consequences of water shortages in China are significant. Water shortages in cities cause a loss of an estimated 120 billion Yuan (US$ 11.2 billion) in industrial output each year. The cost to human health of water pollution has been estimated to be as high as 41.73 billion Yuan (US$ 3.9 billion) per year (World Resources 1998-1999).

India is going through similar shortages. The per capita availability of freshwater is declining due to rapid population growth and industrialization. The per capita availability of freshwater in 2025 is expected to be 1,500 cubic metres per year, as compared to 2,200 cubic metres in 1997 and 5,300 cubic metres in 1955 (Deutsche Press -Agentur, 1998).

Water security is needed as Asian agriculture is highly reliant on irrigation and the anticipated increase in food production is likely to be dependent on even higher levels of irrigation and irrigation efficiency. Global freshwater use since 1900 is disaggregated by broad regional groupings like BRICS countries, which include Brazil, Russia, India, China, and South Africa. BRICS countries use the largest share of approximately 45 per cent of absolute freshwater (Ritchie, Roser, 2018).

Freshwater availability also depends on the technological advancement in a country and its development as it helps in making freshwater available through water withdrawal from surface water and underground water sources to meet the demand for agricultural, industrial, or municipal (domestic) uses. Freshwater withdrawal in Asia is depicted in Figure 1. It clearly shows that maximum withdrawal is in the field of agriculture followed by industrial and then municipal water withdrawal.

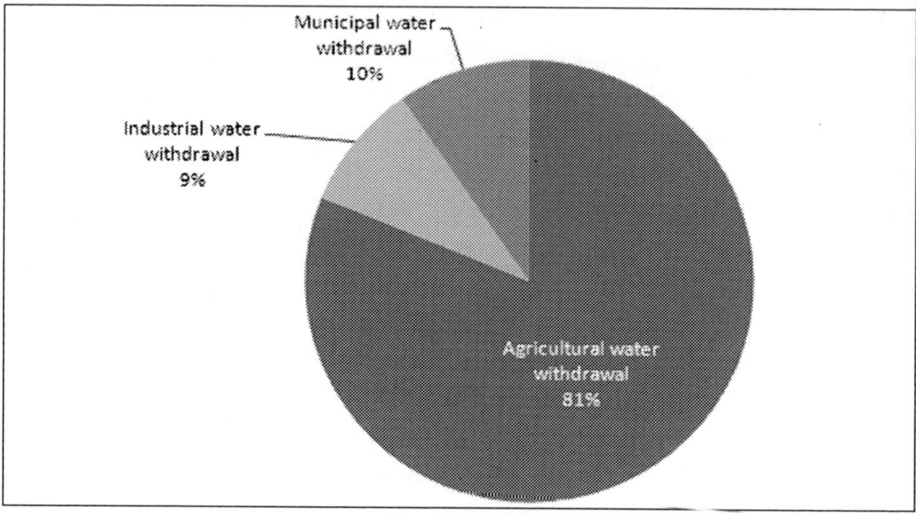

The ground water abstraction is unstable and unsustainable, and sustainable groundwater supplies are constrained by extensive contamination and depletion. In the Indo-Gangetic basin, groundwater abstraction is nearly 25 per cent. Asia is the biggest abstractor of groundwater. Pakistan, India, Nepal, and Bangladesh are the major dependents and use about 23 million pumps. Groundwater in 70 per cent of aquifers along the Brahmaputra and Ganga rivers are at a depth of 200 metres. However, groundwater levels are falling in the remaining 30 per cent, with a net annual depletion of 8.0 ± 3.0 km^3. While the demand is projected to grow by 30-40 per cent, in general, existing water resources in many areas in the region can be considered already fully utilised due to rapid groundwater depletion (Verma, 2016).

Need for Water Security

Lack of availability of water leads to water shortages, but the fact that people do not have safe drinking water is often an issue of access. As Sandra Postel has said, "It's a problem of inadequate government investment, of political will, of making it a priority to meet the basic water needs of the poor. It's a solvable problem, if we decide to do it" (Postel, 1998).

Water is an essential human rights issue. Assurance of adequate water supplies is implied in international human rights law. In developed countries, access to water is considered an entitlement; whereas in developing countries safe drinking water is often a luxury, sometimes available only to the affluent. The level of development of a country decides to a great extent the access of its population to safe drinking water. Industrialized countries like Japan, Singapore, and Taiwan have fewer freshwater availability problems whereas countries like China and India, face greater challenges. The problem in most of the developing countries is that water systems are often created because of local political considerations.

A growing global population and economic shift towards more resource-intensive consumption patterns means global freshwater use, that is, freshwater withdrawals for agriculture, industry, and municipal uses. The use of fresh water has increased nearly six-fold since 1900. The rates of global freshwater use increased sharply from the 1950s onwards, but since 2000 appears to be plateauing, or at least slowing. (Ritchie, Roser, 2018).

The need for water security is likely to increase over the coming decades in Asia. Climate change has long been accepted as the major cause of water scarcity. Agriculture remains the largest user of water. Demand change can be more significant in many parts of Asia especially due to socioeconomic development in large parts of the continent. Seasonal variations, such as extra irrigation in the dry season, further exacerbate the problem of water scarcity in Asia.

The water demand for industry, households, and agriculture will increase by 30-40 per cent by 2050 compared to 2010. By the 2050s, the water demand in Asia is projected to be larger than for all the other continents of the world put together. As a result of socioeconomic development in Asia, industrial water demand will rise by at least 136 per cent depending on the scenario, while municipal water demands will rise by a minimum of 176 per cent and up to 245 per cent (Satoh, 2018). The issue of water scarcity will increase in 74-86 per cent of regions in Asia depending on the scenario, with some 40 per cent of the continent's population facing severe water scarcity in the 2050s. Under the middle of-the-road scenario, by 2050, 20 per cent of the land area of Asia, with a population of 1.6–2 billion people, is expected to be facing severe water scarcity (Satoh, 2018).

Factors that Influence Water Security

Development and water security go hand in hand. A developed country looks forward to a water secure future. Various factors influencing water security are discussed below:

Agriculture

Water is an essential input to global agriculture, whether in the form of rain-fed sources or pumped irrigation. With the increase in population, food demand is increasing resulting in more food production by agriculture, mostly through irrigation. Irrigation is mostly dependent on adequate freshwater supply. The Green Revolution resulted in increased crop yields, but achieved these yields largely through extensive irrigation and with increased reliance on freshwater. In fact, almost 70 per cent of the world's freshwater supply is devoted to agriculture, and thus is unavailable for other uses (Kramer, 1999).

North China chronically is subject to frequent droughts and shortages of water. It uses underground water resources for irrigation. Roughly, half of China's cultivated land is irrigated; as demand for water rises, the country will need to deploy water-saving and waste-treatment technology.

About 70 per cent of the additional food supply in China during the next 25-30 years is expected to come from irrigated lands. Because irrigation is expensive, it will be very difficult to maintain adequate water supplies in the future. About half of the water that is used for irrigation is lost to seepage and evaporation. Irrigation is also a major concern for many Asian countries; six Asian countries (China, India, Indonesia, Korea, Pakistan, and Sri Lanka) have more than 30 per cent of their total cropland under irrigation (Abedin, Habiba & Shaw, 2013).

In 2010, India was the world's largest agricultural water consumer at nearly 700 billion m^3 per year. China is the world's second largest user at approximately 385 billion m^3 in 2015, although its agricultural freshwater use has approximately plateaued in the recent past. Globally, we use approximately 70 per cent of freshwater withdrawals for agriculture. However, this share varies significantly from one country to another because of variations geographically and by income levels. The average agricultural water use for low-income countries is 90 per cent; 79 per cent for middle income and only 41 percent for high incomes (Ritchie, Roser, 2018).

Industrialisation

The degree of industrialization adds to the need for water security. Water is used for various industrial activities like dilution, steam generation, washing, and cooling of manufacturing equipment, cleaning, air conditioning, processing, transportation, and energy production. Industrial water consumption tends to dominate in high-income countries, with an average of 17 per cent and is small in low-income countries on an average of two per cent.

Globally, approximately 19 per cent of total water withdrawals are used for industrial purposes (Ritchie & Roser, 2018). In developing countries, the percentage tends to hover around 10-30 per cent (Abedin, Habiba & Shaw, 2013). As developing countries industrialize, they will be using water in greater quantities. Most countries across East Asia regions use more than one billion m^3 for industrial uses per year. Rates are typically much lower across some parts of South Asia where most use less than 500 million m^3. China uses 130.8 billion cubic metres of water for industrial use (Xu, 2019); 500 billion cubic metres in India (Our World in Data).

The positive side of this factor is that water used for industrial processes can be recycled, since unlike in agriculture, very little of it is actually consumed. In developed industrial countries, the primary impetus for water recycling is compliance with pollution laws. Since it is often more economical to comply with pollution laws by recycling water, little is wasted (Lorey, 2003). Unfortunately, such trends are not as apparent in poorer developing countries where few governments provide industry with incentives to adopt more efficient water-use practices. Consequently, although the amount of water being used for industrial purposes is decreasing in the developed world, it is actually increasing in developing countries. This is a further strain on freshwater resources in countries already facing rapid urbanization.

Environmental Factors

Climate change, pollution, land degradation, rapid population growth, frequency of natural disasters, chaotic process of urbanisation and other environmental factors influence water security in Asia. Many countries throughout the world routinely dump human and industrial waste into their rivers and lakes. In developing countries, roughly 90-95 per cent of all domestic sewage and 75 per cent of all industrial waste are discharged into surface waters without any treatment (Population Reports, 1998).

Asia is the centre for human activities that cause global warming; home to three of the world's top five polluters, China, Japan, and India. In 2017, China, India, and Japan were ranked first, third and fifth among the world's worst polluting countries, according to the global Carbon Project (https://www.scmp.com, 2019). In many parts of Asia, pollution is a major culprit behind the dwindling availability of freshwater. In China, nearly three-fourths of the nation's rivers do not support fish as they are badly polluted (Population Report, 1998). Meanwhile, all of India's 14 major rivers are polluted, primarily because they transport 50 million cubic metres of untreated sewage into India's coastal waters every year. In South Korea, more than 300 factories along the Naktong River illegally discharged toxic wastes directly into the river (Postel, 1997). The same trend can be seen in many Southeast Asian countries. In Malaysia and Thailand, pollutants in those nations' rivers such as pathogens, heavy metals, and various poisons from industry and agriculture regularly exceed government standards by 30 to 100 times.

In 1997, the El Nino weather phenomenon left Thailand, the Philippines, Indonesia and many Southeast Asian countries with little rainfall. In Beijing, water tables beneath the city are dropping by a rate of roughly 1-2 metres a year, and a third of the city's wells have reportedly dried up. Moreover, in recent years, more than 100 Chinese cities in northern and coastal regions have experienced severe water shortages (Satoh, 2018). Another challenge to water security in Asia is deforestation. Asia's forest cover is reducing by 1 per cent per year for a variety of reasons, including illegal logging and conversion of forests to large-scale commercial agriculture and timber plantations. In Cambodia, forests covered over 70 per cent of the country in the late 1960s; now only about half are still in existence. Similar trends can be seen in Thailand where between 1961 and 1988, the forest cover shrank from 55 per cent of the country's land area to 28 per cent. In 2012, Indonesia became the fastest forest-clearing nation in the world (Deforestation in Indonesia is double the government's official rate, in *Scientific American*, 30 June 2014).

Figure 2 gives us a clear picture related to the forest area of different regions of Asia in relation to the total land area. It does not show the seriousness of the problem at the macro level but at the micro level it is a matter of concern related to some countries of Asia where water security is very much needed for which forests play a vital role.

Figure 2: Forest area as a proportion of total land area in 1990, 2010 and 2015

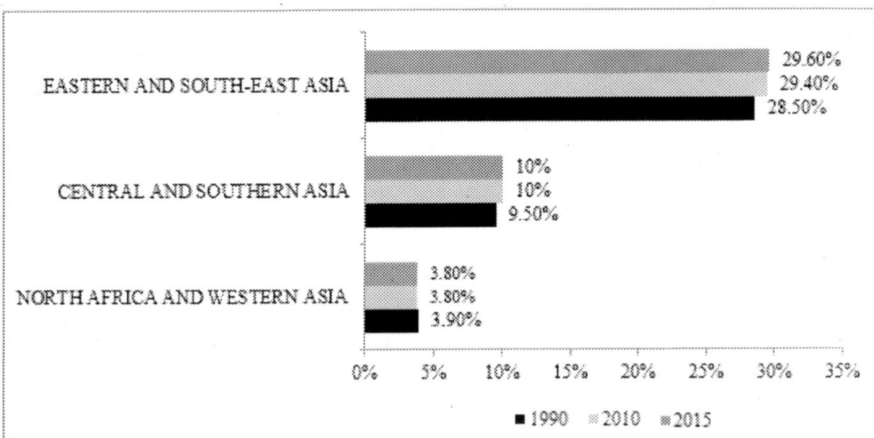

Source: Based on UN, 2017.

Demographic Factors

When looking at future scenarios involving water, it is important to consider the growth of the human population. The world's population was roughly 1.6 billion people at the beginning of the 20th century, but by 1990 it had increased to around 5.3 billion, an increase of 330 per cent (Sergiusz, 2015). Currently, world's population is around 7.8 billion as of January 2020 and is expected to reach 8.5 billion by the year 2025 (World Meter). Roughly half of this population will live in Asia—although Asian countries only occupy about 16 per cent of the world's total land surface. Population growth in Asia is seen as a major challenge for water security in the region (Abedin, Habiba & Shaw, 2013).

In Beijing, the requirement for water security is because of socioeconomic conditions. Beijing's population has surpassed 20 million. Each inhabitant consumes around 200 L of drinking water a day. Beijing is larger in terms of population size and more water-scarce. Urban water functions are fulfilled better because of good water governance in Beijing. (Varis et. al., 2006)

Table 1 shows the population, density, migration of all the countries of Asia, as per 2020 data. Related to population growth is the growing trend of urbanization, a phenomenon that is especially apparent in Asia. As per the above table, extreme high-risk levels of water security are found in countries where the urban population is more than 70 per cent with the exception of a few, namely, Turkmenistan, Pakistan, Indonesia and India. Thus, urbanization is expected to shift water out of agriculture to supply drinking water for growing cities.

Table 1

	Country (or dependency)	*Population, 2020*	*Density (Km²)*	*Migrants (net)*	*Urban Pop (%)*	*World Share (%)*	*Water Risk Level*
1	China	1,439,323,776	153	-348,399	61	18.47	Medium-High
2	India	1,380,004,385	464	-532,687	35	17.70	Extreme-High
3	Indonesia	273,523,615	151	-98,955	56	3.51	Medium-High
4	Pakistan	220,892,340	287	-233,379	35	2.83	Extreme-High
5	Bangladesh	164,689,383	1,265	-369,501	39	2.11	Low
6	Japan	126,476,461	347	71,560	92	1.62	Low-Medium
7	Philippines	109,581,078	368	-67,152	47	1.41	Low-Medium
8	Vietnam	97,338,579	314	-80,000	38	1.25	Low
9	Turkey	84,339,067	110	283,922	76	1.08	High
10	Iran	83,992,949	52	-55,000	76	1.08	Extreme-High
11	Thailand	69,799,978	137	19,444	51	0.90	Medium-High
12	Myanmar	54,409,800	83	-163,313	31	0.70	Low
13	South Korea	51,269,185	527	11,731	82	0.66	Medium-High
14	Iraq	40,222,493	93	7,834	73	0.52	High
15	Afghanistan	38,928,346	60	-62,920	25	0.50	High
16	Saudi Arabia	34,813,871	16	134,979	84	0.45	Extreme-High
17	Uzbekistan	33,469,203	79	-8,863	50	0.43	High
18	Malaysia	32,365,999	99	50,000	78	0.42	Low
19	Yemen	29,825,964	56	-30,000	38	0.38	High
20	Nepal	29,136,808	203	41,710	21	0.37	High
21	North Korea	25,778,816	214	-5,403	63	0.33	Low-Medium
22	Taiwan	23,816,775	673	30,001	79	0.31	N.A.
23	Sri Lanka	21,413,249	341	-97,986	18	0.27	Low-Medium
24	Kazakhstan	18,776,707	7	-18,000	58	0.24	Medium-High
25	Syria	17,500,658	95	-427,391	60	0.22	High
26	Cambodia	16,718,965	95	-30,000	24	0.21	Low
27	Jordan	10,203,134	115	10,220	91	0.13	Extreme-High
28	Azerbaijan	10,139,177	123	1,200	56	0.13	Medium-High
29	United Arab Emirates	9,890,402	118	40,000	86	0.13	Extreme-High
30	Tajikistan	9,537,645	68	-20,000	27	0.12	Medium-High
31	Israel	8,655,535	400	10,000	93	0.11	Extreme-High
32	Hong Kong	7,496,981	7,140	29,308	N.A.	0.10	N.A.

33	Laos	7,275,560	32	-14,704	36	0.09	Low
34	Lebanon	6,825,445	667	-30,012	78	0.09	Extreme-High
35	Kyrgyzstan	6,524,195	34	-4,000	36	0.08	High
36	Turkmenistan	6,031,200	13	-5,000	53	0.08	Extreme-High
37	Singapore	5,850,342	8,358	27,028	N.A.	0.08	N.A.
38	State of Palestine	5,101,414	847	-10,563	80	0.07	N.A.
39	Oman	5,106,626	16	87,400	87	0.07	Extreme-High
40	Kuwait	4,270,571	240	39,520	N.A.	0.05	Extreme-High
41	Georgia	3,989,167	57	-10,000	58	0.05	Low-Medium
42	Mongolia	3,278,290	2	-852	67	0.04	Medium-High
43	Armenia	2,963,243	104	-4,998	63	0.04	High
44	Qatar	2,881,053	248	40,000	96	0.04	Extreme-High
45	Bahrain	1,701,575	2,239	47,800	89	0.02	Extreme-High
46	Timor-Leste	1,318,445	89	-5,385	33	0.02	N.A.
47	Cyprus	1,207,359	131	5,000	67	0.02	N.A.
48	Bhutan	771,608	20	320	46	0.01	N.A.
49	Macao	649,335	21,645	5,000	N.A.	0.01	N.A.
50	Maldives	540,544	1,802	11,370	35	0.01	N.A.
51	Brunei	437,479	83	0	80	0.01	N.A.

Source: World Meters (www.Worldometers.info).

Conservation Factors

The degree of wastage is a key factor for water security. More efficient use of water in agricultural, industrial, and municipal settings can help ensure water security. In many irrigation systems, as little as 37 per cent of the water used is actually absorbed by crops; the rest is lost by either evaporation, seepage or runoff (Butts, 1997). According to the Food and Agriculture Organization of the United Nations (FAO), more than 10 to 20 per cent of the water used for agricultural purposes could be saved if more efficient irrigation methods are utilized.

In cities facing water scarcity pressures (Beijing), municipal water suppliers over-exploit local water resources. Cities use two strategies to guarantee water supply when local sources are depleted. First, they "build their way out of scarcity" (McDonald & Shemie, 2014) by inter-basin transfers from other catchments (Beijing). Alternatively, they turn to unconventional water sources (Dubai). The first strategy comes at a cost for water users elsewhere; the second strategy is highly energy-consuming (Wen et. al., 2017). Inter-basin water transfers are usually preferred by policy makers, since they are the cheapest and easiest option

Singapore and Hong Kong, host the busiest ports in the world. Both cities receive a high annual rainfall, 200 to 300 cm per year and 120 to 300 cm per year, respectively, which does favour water availability but has deteriorated the water quality due to marine and residential emissions as supply from local groundwater, reservoirs and lakes is limited. This makes Singapore and Hong Kong dependent on water resources beyond their jurisdictions. To rely less on water imports, Singapore and Hong Kong have turned to extensive desalination, rainwater harvesting and water reuse technology and increased attention to reduction of domestic water use.

Water wastage also occurs because of leakage in pipelines. In developed countries, experts calculate that about 10 per cent of water is lost due to leaks in municipal water networks; in developing countries this number could be as high as 60 per cent. In India, the city of Shimla faced this problem due to the old pipeline network set for 30,000 people in the year 1875; the leakage in old pipelines resulted in great unrest among its residents.

Water-use efficiency can be achieved by privatizing urban water supply and waste management, increasing service fees, transferring government responsibilities to beneficiaries or customers, and removing all subsidies from all water-related services (Lorey, 2003).

Cities that are water-scarce, over-exploit naturally available water resources before turning to unconventional sources or reducing water use. In Jakarta many residents (illegally) withdraw water from local aquifers because the municipal water supply system is unreliable. This causes large land subsidence, which in turn aggravates flood hazards, lowers water tables, increases pumping costs, causes saline intrusion, and other problems.

As new technological innovations continue to reduce the capital cost of desalination, more countries are building desalination plants in addressing their water crises. The world's largest desalination plant is the Jebel Ali Desalination Plant (Phase 2) in the United Arab Emirates. Over 60 per cent of Israel's territory is arid and another 20 per cent semi-arid. It has developed a variety of solutions for water security with desert technologies.

It desalinates about 80 per cent of its drinking water and in future it will go up to 100 per cent. Roughly 90 per cent of its sewage is being treated, recycled and reused for farming and gardening (Kolyohin, 2019). Singapore desalinizes water at 49 cents per cubic metre and also treats sewage with reverse osmosis for industrial and potable use. ("Black and Veatch-Designed Desalination Plant wins Global Water Distinction", Edie.net.2006-05-04). China and India, the world's two most populous countries, are also turning to desalination to provide a small part of their water needs ("Tamil Nadu/Chennai two sites of desalinization Plant Identified" (*The Hindu*, 17 January 2007-).

Water Security: A Concern

The availability of water for human use is being characterized as a security issue. Water is taken as a strategic resource. It needs to be protected and valued, from the quality and quantity point of view along with its inter-state and intra-state availability to meet the ever-growing demand. Consequently, when one or more countries share water resources, the potential for disputes or conflicts is always present. By now, no nation has gone to fight over water though this potential scenario could unfold given the right conditions. A set of factors including demographics, rising demand resulting from improved living standards, the predominance of upstream over downstream—the first-served control the flow of rivers, may stoke smouldering conflicts.

As one Chinese expression puts it: "upstream doesn't suffer". However, more equitable approaches to water rights are encapsulated in principles such as riparian rights and equitable utilization. Equitable utilization tends to benefit both upstream and downstream states and is especially beneficial to a weaker country that happens to be a downstream one. Even strong upstream countries have, in practice, tended to compromise with weaker downstream neighbours in order to promote some degree of equitable utilization of water resources (Nickum, 1999). Freshwater scarcity related to surface and underground water poses a very serious, complex and potentially wide-ranging threat to regional stability. The complexity of the water security issue has to be viewed on three basic levels:

Human Security

If security is defined by the number of deaths, then clearly water is a security issue. Experts estimate that about 60 per cent of all infant mortality throughout the world is tied to infectious and parasitic diseases, most of them related to water (Lorey, 2003). Diarrheal diseases, cholera, dysentery, typhoid, hepatitis A, trachoma, intestinal worms, and schistosomiasis moreover are prevalent in countries with inadequate sewage treatment. One in three persons does not have access to safe drinking water in the world (UNICEF, WHO, 2019). In Bangladesh, it is estimated that three-quarters of all diseases are linked to unsafe water and inadequate sanitation facilities.

Besides health, conflicts among states and individuals for water results in human casualties. Freshwater as a security issue results in thousands of deaths every day as water being the basic necessity for life, for economic growth, for environment and for climate, which directly and indirectly have an impact on the quality and quantity of humans. Water affects the population in terms of health, regional development, employment generation and gender-related matters.

Internal Security

Water security in a country adds to its economic development and contributes to healthy social behaviour that can, in turn, produce progress within societies. Freshwater scarcity is often related to poverty, population growth, infrastructure problems, environmental degradation, large-scale migration, and ethnic conflicts that can turn the "human security" problem into a national security issue. It can result in a decline in effective governance, potentially leading to a "failed state".

Few examples of different countries of Asia with internal water security issues; Yemen has little freshwater to use and relies on other sources to meet its needs which they are prevented to use because of political strife in the region; Jordan has to completely rely on the Dead Sea and the Jordan River to meet the demand of water in relation to its population and desertification; India is 13th among the world's worst-affected water stress countries (Khadka, 2019). Thousands of protesters take to the streets in Qidong, Jiangsu Province, to challenge a pipeline from a Japanese-owned paper factory that would discharge contaminated wastewater into the sea, potentially pollute a nearby fishery, and contaminate drinking water.

International Security

Nations have never entered into disputes solely over freshwater resources.

There is an understanding that water security issues can have an unrest effect on regional and international security. Ethnic unrest, mass migration, and declining economic conditions, fanned by freshwater scarcity, are likely to be confined within international borders. This can have an adverse effect on negotiation and implementation of international agreements related to water security.

India and Bangladesh see the dispute related to the water of the Ganga River from different perspectives. The two countries were able to reach an agreement in 1996 when the "Treaty on the Sharing of the Waters of the Ganga" was signed. Although some political parties on both sides were dissatisfied with the treaty, it was generally accepted by most political leaders (although in India, several states, including Bihar and Uttar Pradesh, were not happy with it). Since the treaty was signed, India has been relatively satisfied with the outcome; Bangladesh, however, continues to have a number of problems with it.

The Mekong Delta Region is an example of the real politic dimension of water conflict. Thailand and Laos are interested in the river's potential in producing hydro-electricity. Laos sees the river for its agricultural interests. Cambodia and Vietnam rely on the Mekong for agriculture. Cambodia is particularly dependent on the river for its fishing industry. The Mekong also provides critical transportation corridors.

In 2012, tensions escalated over two proposed dams in central Asia: Kambaratain Kyrgyzstan and the Rogun Dam in Tajikistan. These dams could affect water supplies in the downstream nations of Uzbekistan, Turkmenistan, and Kazakhstan.

In 2015, a dispute over the allocation and rights to water from the Hari Rud River between Afghanistan and Iran led to at least 10 deaths when Iranian border guards allegedly opened fire on Afghan villagers trying to collect river water. The river provides water for agricultural production in Herat province, Afghanistan, and to the downstream Iranian city of Mashhad, Iran's second largest city.

Thus, the above examples in various regions of Asia clarifies that natural climate variability, human-induced climate change, population increase and migration, settlement of hazard-prone land, poor service provision, uncontrolled discharge of pollutants into water, exclusion because of caste, race, social status or political affiliation combine to threaten water security. Many of these threats can be managed to ensure that their impact is minimal, but often the political will and institutional capacity does not exist to do so. As a result, hundreds of millions of people remain without access to this basic human right, i.e., water.

Conclusion

In Asia in order to achieve water security and avert the situation of a water crisis, the following key findings have been made:

- The global availability of freshwater is diminishing. Only about 1 per cent of the world's freshwater is readily available for human consumption...Furthermore, the distribution of water throughout the world is not fair for a variety of economic and geographic reasons.
- Environmental change could threaten water supplies in the succeeding years: climate change is the major unknown variable in discussions of water security. If prognosis regarding sea-level rise is correct, this could lead to flooding of underwater aquifers and river deltas with salt water. Climate change could also lead to several more droughts, which are accountable to the 'El Nino' weather phenomenon.
- "Access to Water" is essential to human health and it cannot be separated from notions of human rights.
- Water, a source of inter-state conflict: Water may spark conflict between states.
- Agricultural water demand has a major impact on water security: population growth is directly proportional to more food, which will lead to greater demands on the world's water supply.
- Water security and internal politics are often connected: water can often emerge as an issue in the relations between nation-states. The politics of water is not limited to the international sphere but often plays a major role in domestic politics also.
- No single strategy is sufficient for water security. Instead, multifaceted approaches will be needed.
- The need for water security can be classified in three categories: lower water quality, raised water demand, and increased flood events.
- Water security is also a function of a community's governance

capacity and resilience in the face of natural hazards.

- Data limitations continue to exist in describing water security. Water security is sometimes sought by implementing water desalination.

The good news is that the AWDO (Asian Water Development Outlook) 2016 report notes a positive trend in the number of countries attaining water security, with the number of water insecure countries dropping from 38 out of 49 in 2013, to 29 out of 48 in 2016 (Asian Water Development Report water centre. org case studies).

The bad news is that 29 countries are already water insecure, and that growing water demand from the region's domestic and industrial sectors is projected to increase by 55 per cent by 2050 (Four Steps Toward Improving Regional Water Security Development Asia http://development.asia.Summary).

Thus, freshwater being the basis for all life is the most important resource for mankind, touching all social, environmental and economic activities. The following suggestions related to future prospects for water security of Asia are:

- Policies and interventions need to improve targeting of actions for inclusive development and to achieve sustainable development as there is a widening gap between the haves and the have-nots with respect to access to water supply.
- Constant efforts are essential to strengthen water security through investments in institutions, infrastructure, and information.
- Other technologies that advance water security, such as improved methods to low-cost drip irrigation, and new crop varieties that can tolerate low water levels and drought, should be used.
- In the face of competing demands and climate variability, water is an economic good. Its productive use requires an enabling policy framework and accounting for water, knowing how much is available, who is using how much, and setting targets for resource utilization.
- Groundwater is a hidden resource; its extraction must be monitored and managed sustainably.
- Development interventions need to consider impacts on the overall water resource base. Agriculture consumes the major part

of water with little remaining for domestic use, industry, and the environment.

- Policy makers at every level, non-governmental organizations, civil society groups, and private enterprises, must be stakeholders in the responsible management of water resources.
- Data sets require expansion and rigorous collection.
- For river health, a more comprehensive and measurable set of indicators that can be applied across the Asia region is needed.
- The issue of water security should be included in the political and developmental agendas of national governments in Asia.
- Modern technologies both for agriculture and for domestic purposes should be encouraged like sea water, greenhouses that use solar energy to desalinate sea water, etc.
- Developing new water sources cannot meet the increasing water demand. It looks forward to better water management and more productive use of existing resources in agriculture and water services.
- Resolution mechanisms related to intra- and trans-boundary water issues should be developed.
- Disaster-warning systems and international coordination in response to water-related disasters should be intensified.
- Need to increase forest cover at a mass level.
- More emphasis should be on rainwater harvesting in drought-prone regions of Asia.
- Media engagement in spreading awareness related to water security amongst the common people needs to be encouraged.
- Best practices worked out from local leaders across sectors and societal spheres that are advancing sustainable water management practices and models of mediation and conflict resolution to address water-related disputes should be collected and circulated.
- Measurable and testable objectives to curtail greenhouse gas emissions should be adopted by all countries because it is necessary to lessen the impact on water resources resulting from global warming.

These suggestions are not meant to be exhaustive, but are indicative of the extent and preciseness of the efforts required to try to take care of the water challenges faced by Asia in order to make it water secure. With better planning and leadership, this resource crisis can be transformed into a spark for lasting cooperation between countries and across communities at micro, meso, and macro levels in Asia.

REFERENCES

Abedin, M.A.; Habiba, Umma & Shaw, Rajib. 2013 Water Insecurity: A Social Dilemma. *Nature.*

Archived from the original on December 16, 2008. retrieved November 21, 2012.

Asthana, Vandana & Shukla, A. C., "Water Security in India: Hope, Despair and the Challenges of Human Development", 2014.

"Black and Veatch-Designed Desalination Plant wins Global Water Distinction", Edie.net.2006-05-04. retrieved 2010-08-13.

Barber, Charles Victor. "Forest Resource Scarcity and Social Conflict in Indonesia," *Environment*, May 1998.

Bequette, France. "Water: Will There be Enough? Fresh or Drinking Water," *UNESCO Courier*, June 1998, p. 42.

Bender, William & Smith, Margaret, "Population, Food, and Nutrition," *Population Bulletin*, vol. 51, no. 4 (Washington, DC: Population Reference Bureau, 1997).

Butts, Kent H., "The Strategic Importance of Water," *Parameters*, Spring 1997.

"Cambodia Trade: Disappearing Trees," *EIU ViewsWire* (Economist Intelligence Unit), February 24, 1997.

cf. Varis et.al., 2006.

Chennai, India: *The Hindu*. 17 January 2007. retrieved 13 August 2010.

Cook, Frederick. "Grain Galore: China's Focus on Grain Production," *The China Business Review*, vol. 24, no. 5 (September 19, 1997), p. 8.

Dahal, Rajendra. "Development-Nepal: South Asian Mega-Projects Spark Water Quarrels," *Inter Press Service*, June 16, 1998.

Deforestation in Indonesia is double the government's official rate, in *Scientific American*, 30 June 2014.

Desalination is the solution to water shortages, red orbit, May 2, 2008.

Dupont, Alan. The Environment and Security in Pacific Asia (London: International Institute for Strategic Studies, 1998:46).

Dupont, Alan, *The Environment and Security in Pacific Asia* (Adelphi Paper, 1998), Chapter 5 on "Water Scarcity", p. 62.

Emerging Asia: Changes and Challenges (Manila: Asian Development Bank, 1997).

Explained: how climate change will affect Asia/ *South China Morning Post*, 11 March 2019, https://www.scmp.com.

"Freshwater Availability Going Down in India", Deutsche Press-Agentur, July 22, 1998.

Four Steps Toward Improving Regional Water Security Development Asia http://development.asia.Summary.

Fungladda, Doungsuda. "Water Shortage in Thailand Threatens Stability in Farm Sector," *The Nikkei Weekly* February 15, 1999, p. 20.

Grey, David & Sadoff, Claudia W. (1 September 2007). "Sink or Swim? Water security for Growth and Development", Water Policy. Iwapoline.com.9 (6): 545-571. retrieved 16 August 2014.

Homer, Thomas F.-Dixon. "Environment, Scarcity, and Violence", Princeton University Press, 1999, p. 69.

Hughes, Kent. "The Strategic Importance of Water," *Parameters*, Spring 1997.

Iyer, Ramaswamy R. "Ganga Waters: Dispute and Resolution," paper prepared for the "Water and Conflict in Asia Seminar," held at the Asia-Pacific Centre for Security Studies, Honolulu, Hawaii (17 September 1999).

Khadka, Navin Singh. "Indian Water Crisis flagged up in global report", 6 August 2019.

Kolyohin, Nick, "Israel aims to secure all of its water supply through desalination", 22 November 2019.

Kramer, Bert L., "Factors that Influence Water Security," paper prepared for the "Water and Conflict Seminar" held at the Asia-Pacific Centre for Security Studies, Honolulu, Hawaii, 17 September 1999.

Lorey, David E. "Global Environmental Challenges Of the Twenty-first Century", Water and conflict in Asia? 2003.

Mead, Gary, "Drought Hits Rice Crop in Indonesia," *Financial Times*, August 20, 1998, p. 26.

Motavalli, Jim & Robbins, Elaine, "The Coming Age of Water Scarcity," *E* Sep./Oct. 1998.

Nickum, James E. "Some Factors that Influence Water Security, and Some that Don't," paper prepared for the "Water and Conflict Seminar," held at the Asia-Pacific Centre for Security Studies, Honolulu, Hawaii, 17 September 1999.

"One in Four Hit by Drought," *BBC Summary of World Broadcasts*, January 8, 1998.

"Pakistan embarks on nuclear desalination". Archived from the original on December 16, 2008. retrieved November 21, 2012.

Postel, Sandra L. "Water for Food Production: Will there be enough in 2025?" *Bioscience*, August 1998.

Satoh, Yusuke, 18 June 2018, International Institute for Applied Systems Analysis: Is Asia facing a coming water crisis?.

Sergiusz, Prokurat. (2015) Drought and water shortages in Asia: threat and economic problem (PDF), Jozefow. *Journal of Modern Science*, 26 March 2015, pp. 235-250, retrieved 13 August 2016.

Solutions for a Water-Short World, *Population Reports* (vol. 26, no. 1), September 1, 1998.

The Hindu. 17 January 2007. retrieved 13 August 2010.

"Thailand: Demographic and Social Trends," *EIU Country Forecasts* (Economist Intelligence Unit), March 7, 1997.

Verma, Rashmi. "The reality of water security in Asia and Pacific regions", 1 September 2016.

Wen et.al., 2017.

Water and Conflict in Asia? Asia-Pacific Centre for Security Studies, September17, 1999, Honolulu, Hawaii, https://apcss.org>Publications.

Water Shortages in China: Facts and Details, Jaffery Hays 2008; updated 2014.

Water Use and Stress—Our World in Data by Hannah Ritchie & Max Roser, 2018.

World Resources 1998-99: A Guide to the Global Environment (New York: Oxford University Press, 1998).

Xinjiangin. 2013. In Eastern Asia (Source: Water Conflict Chronology).

Index

*